LEARNING DISABILITIES

Systemizing Teaching and Service Delivery

David A. Sabatino
Southern Illinois University at Carbondale

Ted L. Miller
University of Tennessee at Chattanooga

Carl R. Schmidt
Southern Illinois University at Carbondale

AN ASPEN PUBLICATION®
Aspen Systems Corporation
Rockville, Maryland
London
1981

Library of Congress Cataloging in Publication Data

Sabatino, David A.
Learning disabilities, systemizing teaching and service delivery.

Includes bibliographies.
1. Learning disabilities.   2. Ability—Testing.
3. Educational tests and measurements.
I. Schmidt, Carl,
1951-   II. Miller, Ted L.   III. Title.
LC4704.S227   371.9   81-7886
ISBN: 0-89443-361-X   AACR2

LC 4704

S 227

Copyright © 1981 by Aspen Systems Corporation

Library of Congress Catalog Card Number: 81-7886
ISBN: 0-89443-361-X

Printed in the United States of America

1 2 3 4 5

It provides us, the authors, with a great deal of satisfaction
to make the following very special dedication:
We respectfully dedicate our work

to Mr. Curtis Whitesel.

Without his help, this text never would have existed.

Table of Contents

Preface

This book attempts to identify a number of practical issues that confront the learning disability specialist. The effort is to offer a state-of-the-art review from an organized vantage point. Specific questions concerning the construct, theory, or problem in question, assessment strategies, and instructional strategies related to specific age/type of program delivery formats are analyzed.

The primary audience is the practitioner. The focus is on special education considerations from the point of view of multidisciplinary diagnostic and treatment team members. Therefore, the book is prepared for inservice audiences, but as such is equally well suited to serve as an introductory text for preservice audiences. It may also supplement other texts for students in advanced problem, methods, and assessment courses at the graduate level as well.

The effort is to organize a perspective and offer a coverage of topics somewhat different from, if not more comprehensive than, most current texts. This does not mean providing ready-made solutions to the problems that do indeed exist. It merely means that we hope to encourage the practitioner to seek answers beyond those found in these pages. Therefore, as noted, this is written for those who it is hoped will examine the information critically, extract personal meaning, or disagree with its content, and emerge from this experience strong and informed advocates, capable of developing, implementing, and staffing programs for learning disabled children.

As a point of reference, we consider a learning disability to be an information processing disability (our view) requiring a mosaic of services composed of most of the helping (human resource) disciplines in a team relationship. This position discourages the adoption of a learning disability specialist as a "one-person band" capable of finding solutions to all of the problems these children and youths may present.

The contents are presented in a logical sequence (we hope). Beginning in Chapter 1, we review selected current issues. Chapters 2 and 3 examine formal and informal assessment procedures in some detail. Chapter 4 analyzes instructional materials from an evaluation or systems standpoint. The approach reflects our view that because only limited evaluation data are available on specific materials it is impossible to recommend one over another. The problem faced by the special educator with a limited budget is: What should be purchased? In the absence of firm recommendations, we can be definitive only on how to examine materials, how to identify the persons who evaluate them, and where to find lists, reviews, and descriptive information on instructional materials. To many inservice practitioners, our response in Chapter 4 is "nice to know" information and something they will need in the future. The here and now problem is how to purchase materials most wisely with a $100 budget.

In Chapter 5, we review usable teaching materials. The counterpart of Chapter 5 appears as Chapter 6. This chapter examines in considerable detail potential learning objectives under five headings, with intervention strategies for each: (1) motor, (2) perceptual, (3) language, (4) academic, and (5) vocational.

Chapters 7, 8, and 9 discuss at length program development and implementation techniques at the preschool, elementary, and secondary school age levels, respectively. Chapter 10 provides strategies for social-personal objectives. It also examines the construct of achievement motivation and the ultimate phenomenon that entraps the student—learner helplessness.

In short, we attempt to review the constructs of program delivery under a best-practice rubric, that is age sensitive. The reason is that we believe that the child's age may be a determinant of the type of program to be delivered.

The very theme of, and indeed the driving force for, our efforts is quite simply to open Pandora's box and to raise the critical question: If learning disability is a diagnostic entity, what are the associated categories, subcategories, and substructures it presents? It makes sense to describe this population as complex and thus requiring multifaceted interventions and program delivery strategies.

We now invite readers to explore with us the frontiers facing the field of learning disabilities described in the pages that follow.

In preparing this text, we have elicited the expert help of Dr. Pat Schloss, Mrs. Pam Miller, and Dr. Leon Silber. We extend our appreciation to them and to you, the practitioner, for the help you have provided children who far too frequently are restricted into a diagnostic ledger where they simply don't fit. To their growth, development, happiness, and quality of life, we dedicate this effort.

David A. Sabatino
Southern Illinois University at Carbondale
Ted L. Miller
The University of Tennessee at Chattanooga
Carl R. Schmidt
Southern Illinois University at Carbondale

Acknowledgments

The authors wish to acknowledge the typists, Mrs. Sue Izett, Mrs. Cindy Marini, Ms. Sherry Watson, and Ms. Donna Wulff for their present and persistent help. We also would like to include a special note of appreciation to Mrs. Pam Miller, contributor and coordinator of the writing project, as well as Ms. Donna Filips and Ms. Connie Sullivan for their endless search for references and assistance to the authors in completing this work.

Chapter 1

Overview for the Practitioner in Learning Disabilities

David A. Sabatino

ORIENTATION

Learning disability as a professional element of special education has been a service, as opposed to a research field of study. In fact, it may well be described as a service-motivated field in a hurry, or at least hurried by the times. This includes the litigation and legislation that prompted its development and culminated in its inclusion in Public Law 94-142, the Education for All Handicapped Children Act, which was passed by Congress in 1975. The learning disabled now must face a host of problems associated with the fact that the service motivation has far outrun the science motivation (Hewitt & Forness, 1974).

The absence of data to define learning disabilities, to validate assessment and instructional procedures, and to establish a meaningful baseline by which program effectiveness may be judged impairs the field's ability to provide facts, leading to a best-practice procedure in identification of these students, placement decisions, and instructional or social development. In some areas, however, i.e., elementary and middle school programs, there is a vast reservoir of data. In other areas, such as secondary and postsecondary school programming, the information on identification and attempts to develop learning disabilities programs in military, college, or vocational settings is, at best, very slim. One phenomenon does appear consistently: controversy surrounds both the research and the interpretation of its results. This is a most healthy sign for a field still in its infancy. Readers have an obligation to draw their own conclusions from statements by authorities that, in 1981, rarely are based on data.

THE PROBLEM OF DEFINITION

The historic antecedents of the term *learning disabilities* explain much of the confusion surrounding the modern problem of definition. Learning disability as a diagnostic entity, if it in fact is an entity, has grown from the historic search to explain mental processes.

The history accompanying that search is as old as any attempt to explain education or how the mind learns. A current text on the subject by Mann (1980) describes how mental traits evolved through the generations into the 1968 definition of learning disabilities, which is dependent upon "basic psychological processes" as the critical factor.*

The idea that the mind was subdivided into traits or mental processes (psychological processes being the same thing) occurred slowly. Essentially, it was to explain the various brain functions now associated with cognition, i.e., perception, memory, language, etc. For several centuries argument flourished among scholars on localization of brain function. The British empiricists-associationists began to introduce information processing theory as a counter-attack on the Descartes doctrine of innate learning. The German psychologist Christian Wolff (1679–1754) reintroduced faculty psychology and ushered in the psychoneurological study of cerebral lesions to localized areas of the central nervous system. The person responsible for expanding this thesis was a Viennese physician, Franz Joseph Gall (1758–1828), who contended that damage to certain areas of the brain would result in loss of a specific function. Gall's belief in localization was so strong he postulated that intelligence could be determined by measuring the protrusions of the skull, hence the birth of phrenology. Mann and Goodman (1973) consider Gall the father of modern-day learning disability studies.

Gall's beliefs in mental processes (faculties) and phrenology soon were struck down by one of Germany's leading psychologists, an associationist (one who thinks the brain works as a unit), George Frederick Herbart (1774–1841). Herbart was so persuasive that Wundt (1832–1920), the father of experimental psychology, disregarded cognition as having any structured aspect relating to isolated mental processes. Thus, cognition was abandoned by the mainstream of psychology.

Many early special educators were influenced, in part, by a dependence on psychometric tests to classify and place children and in part by the belief that disabilities were related specifically to brain area function; they thus adhered to a strong belief in basic mental processes. Pestalozzi (1747–1827), Bastian (1887), and Jackson (1915), using speech, epilepsy, and sensory functions as examples, devised maps of localized brain function. Itard, Seguin, Montessori, Fernald, and Descoendres continued the practice of modality training with handicapped children. The work of Goldstein, Strauss, and Werner in

---

*Students and practitioners interested in the history of cognitive development may wish to review Dr. Mann's excellent reference on this topic, *Perceptual Training: A Critical Retrospect.*

the 1940s and 50s drew a parallel between brain damage and perceptual-motor disturbances.

The 1960s might well be referred to as the perceptual-motor era. Contemporary notables such as Kephart, Barsh, Getman, Frostig, and Cruickshank all contributed teaching methods for children assumed to be brain damaged who performed poorly on perceptual-motor tests. For 25 years, authority figures such as Strauss, Monroe, Lehtinen, Gillingham, and Kirk were teaching, researching, and preparing others to teach, using mental process training techniques (motor, perceptual, and language). Thus, an information-processing approach became the order of the day in defining the handicapping conditions by which primary identification procedures were dependent on perceptual-motor tests.

Until 1963, children who performed poorly or inconsistently in school and on perceptual-motor tests were diagnosed as brain damaged. In fact, as monographs published by the National Institute of Neurological Diseases and Blindness (NINDB) attested, the correct diagnostic terminology was *minimal brain damage* (Chalfant & Scheffelin, 1969). The word minimal suggests an absence of neurological indicators upon physical examination and the presence of information processing errors ascertained by psychological instruments.

THE LANDMARK KIRK ADDRESS

A historic moment came on April 6, 1963, when Kirk addressed the parent group responsible for the Fund for Perceptually Handicapped Children, Inc. (the predecessor to the Association for Children with Learning Disabilities). Kirk provided a critical examination of the diagnostic irrelevance of a search for neurological signs when in fact the diagnosis of minimal brain injury resulted from an absence of such findings. (Minimal brain damage is diagnosed upon completion of a neurological examination that reveals negative findings—normal function—but where perceptual-cognitive tests display positive findings—information processing deficits.) More critical was the instructional and behavioral management built on a diagnostically useless nomenclature—minimal brain damage.

The result of Kirk's speech was the creation of the Association for Children with Learning Disabilities (ACLD) and the widespread replacement of terminology on brain damage with the words learning disabilities. In 1968, the National Advisory Committee on Handicapped Children developed the most widely used definition. It became widespread because of its use in P.L. 91-230, a 1969 amendment to the Elementary and Secondary Education Act (ESEA, Title VI, of the Education of the Handicapped Act of 1967), which included children with specific learning disabilities. To qualify for federal funds under this act, most states adapted the so-called federal definition, which reads:

> Children with special learning disabilities exhibit a disorder in one or more of the basic psychological processes involved in understanding or using spoken or written language. These may be manifested in disorders of listening, talking, reading, writing, spelling, or arithmetic. They include conditions which have been referred to as perceptual handicaps, brain injury, minimal brain dysfunction, dyslexia, developmental aphasia, etc. They do not include learning problems which are due primarily to visual, hearing or motor handicaps, to mental retardation, emotional disturbance, or to environmental disadvantage. (National Advisory Committee on Handicapped Children, 1968)

LEARNING DISABILITIES DEFINED

Who, then, is learning disabled? It would appear that a nebulous definition was coined to describe, not define, a learning disability. The definition excludes several other handicapping conditions and therefore is regarded as more of a description of a nonhorse than it is of the horse it was designed to identify (McCarthy, 1971). Hammill (1972) reported that as many as 60 definitions were available, although the majority would require the interpretation of a Philadelphia lawyer. The crux of the problem with the 1968 definition is its breadth, in that it attempts to include children with every imaginable type of information processing deficit. The result is a "fuzzy definition" that in turn has resulted in fuzzy diagnostic practices (Cohen, 1976).

ARCHAIC ASSESSMENT PRACTICES

What, then, is the problem associated with measuring "basic psychological processes?" Mann and Goodman (1973) repeatedly have challenged perceptual test developers and users to define the mental process (trait) they are attempting to measure. Traits primarily are names given to tests, and Mann and Goodman question whether the mind can be partitioned into the specific functions so ascribed. Mann and Goodman could be right; at least, research on perceptual tests might well indicate they are right. But this approach would give credence to calling all children or youths with central (brain) information processing problems merely an undifferentiated mass of academic underachievers. Even if that were bearable, the fact remains that children with perceptual-cognitive deficits do not respond well to academic remediation (Birch & Belmont, 1964), and Chalfant & Scheffelin (1969) clearly document that children with perceptual problems do respond to perceptual training.

That is the point at which Hammill (1972) enters into the fray by claiming that perceptual skills are not transferable. Hammill's review of 25 cognitive interventions indicated that 13 studies used the Frostig and Horne (1964) visual perceptual training program, five the Kephart (1960) Purdue Motor Training Program, and one the Winter Haven Program (McQuarrie, 1967). Results indicated that 21 of the 25 studies did not result in improved reading. Bortner (1974) reviewed 22 additional studies, 14 of which reported primary reading achievement and eight of which did not. Bortner concluded (Bortner & Birch, 1960, 1962) that perception is not an either/or unitary phenomenon (Hallahan, 1975) but rather consists of levels or stages of development.

To say the least, the current diagnostic state of the art in learning disabilities reflects too many previously developed tests (Bender, 1938; Terman & Merrill, 1937; Wechsler, 1955) designed to ascertain developmental lag, intelligence, or the lack of it. There also exists an inability to agree upon a procedure, or for that matter what constitutes a perceptual-cognitive deficit (in amount). Put another way, several authorities (Doehring, 1968; Lezar, 1976) simply do not believe there are perceptual-language-neuropsychological procedures currently available to diagnose known minimal brain damage.

These criticisms, unfortunately, although related to the problems of diagnosing learning disabilities, are in fact associated with assessment practices. In the past, learning disabilities have been associated with deficit scores from specific measures of assumed traits (e.g., information processing behaviors) or aptitude measures (Chalfant & Scheffelin, 1969). Yet most of the procedures developed to ascertain deficits in aptitudes lack statistical stability (Salvia & Clark, 1973) and therefore many test manuals' "rules of thumb" for determining "clinical difference" are inaccurate (Salvia & Ysseldyke, 1978; Ysseldyke, Sabatino, & LaManna, 1973). Then, too, there is always the question of the nature of the trait being measured, i.e., the issue of construct validity. It is evident by now that the constructs ostensibly measured by many tests common to learning disabilities (e.g., *Developmental Test of Visual Motor Perception, Illinois Test of Psycholinguistic Ability, Wechsler Intelligence Scale for Children—Revised*) are less clearly defined and measurable than once was assumed (see Coles, 1978). Thus, even if these constructs eventually prove to be of importance in service, the reliability and validity concerns of contemporary instrumentation will continue to plague the measurement of learning disabilities when they are used in the definition. New, more precise instrumentation is vital if current constructs are to be retained in actual practice.

In sum, it might appear that the failure of the concept of learning disabilities in service and in science can be linked to definitional problems. These problems can be seen in several events: (a) the continued use of "fuzzy" instrumentation measuring "fuzzy" definitions, (b) the pressure of service overcoming the cautions (and capacity) of science, (c) the unsuitability of many research designs, and (d) a failure to redefine learning disabilities by the incorporation of improved theory. At the very least these problems have resulted in (a) faulty stereotypes of learning disabilities (Bryan, 1974), (b) grossly vague service definitions (Gillespie, Miller, & Fielder, 1975), (c) a slowed entrance of new theory, (d) perhaps an inclination toward intrafield professional schisms, and (e) some not so subtle criticisms of the field. Doubtless other pejorative activities and perceptions have appeared. Yet while these failures eventually must become historical if the field is to survive, the reality remains that the diagnostician first must know what the quest is all about before service or research can begin.

LEARNING DISABLED YOUTH OF SECONDARY AGE

The very language of P.L. 94-142 places the focal point of specialized educational services on the child of elementary school age. The National Center for Educational Statistics (1978) reported that 95 percent of the handicapped students at the elementary level were receiving special education services, while only 78 percent of those in middle schools were being served.

There is growing evidence to suggest that as early as the beginning of the middle school, handicapped children encounter attitudes prejudicial to their attendance (Lilly, 1970). There seems to be an attitude that "cute little handicapped children who can be controlled" should be provided an appropriate educational opportunity in compliance with the law (P.L. 94-142). But among educators there is a resistance to the education of larger, more difficult to control, and frequently aggressive and/or abusive, if not chronic disruptive, norm violating adolescents (Keogh & Levitt, 1976).

Contributing to this resistance is the attitude of many secondary school leaders that the education of troublesome adolescents is the responsibility of the juvenile institutions, courts, drug centers, or other private and public agencies (Morgan, 1979). Many secondary level educators also view school as a privilege, not a right. As such, if a youth fails to learn it is because that individual is lazy or indifferent. Awareness of such subtle handicapping conditions as learning disabilities is limited and only the deprived are considered handicapped (Iano, Ayers, Heller, McGettigan, & Walker, 1974).

Another prevailing attitude in the secondary schools is self-determination, which is translated as the capability to learn with good instruction and without specialized intervention (Shotel, Iano, & McGettigan, 1972). Short-term remediation is somewhat acceptable, but long-term special education is not considered a part of the regular curriculum flow (Rucker & Vincenzo, 1970). What results is that 44 percent of the adjudicated youth in correctional facilities are learning disabled (Morgan, 1979).

HIGH RISK PRESCHOOL CHILDREN

The plight of preschool handicapped children is somewhat similar. P.L. 94-142 is less of a mandate for these children than most special educators would have hoped. Federal legislation for the preschool handicapped population is little more than a decade old. P.L. 90-538—the Handicapped Children's Early Education Assistance Act—was passed by the Congress in 1968. Most states still do not provide mandatory special education for children 3 to 5 years old. In fact, only 13 states have responded to P.L. 94-142 with 3-to-5 legislation that names or includes learning disabilities. Eight states have mandatory legislation for 4-to-5-year-olds and only one state provides for 2-year-olds. Only eight states include learning disabilities in the 3-to-5 legislation.

Less than 4 percent of the students entering public school special education programs have had a preschool program. In contrast, Head Start is serving 13 percent of the handicapped population. Head Start is a natural setting for learning disabled (high risk) preschoolers, and four states have earmarked it clearly as the primary service provider. Technical assistance and flow-through funding is available from 14 resource access projects funded by the Administration for Children, Youth, and Family. Funds for outreach activities are provided by the Handicapped Children's Early Education Program. One difficulty is that families must qualify for Head Start income standards before service is available.

In short, P.L. 94-142 does not provide for preschool children, but the program will offer funding if a state has a mandate to serve preschool handicapped children 3 to 5 years of age. Learning disability does not fare well as a handicapping category for preschool children even when states have mandates, because it is held to be difficult to be learning disabled before formal instruction begins. This "Catch-22" entrapment is created by the very definition of the category that might be the best one to prevent through adequate preschool programming.

SEVERITY

Learning disability has fallen into an elementary-remedial bog from which it must become unstuck if it is to achieve the rich range of programmatic objectives so badly needed in the lives of these children. If this field, as a discipline, had the capability to assess the type and amount of learning disability, then research to identify the "rules" for the most appropriate placement and instructional and behavioral management could result.

Rarely does a practitioner see a prognostic statement on a learning disabled child suggesting that, with or without particular intervention, certain results would or would not occur. Since it is assumed that the handicapping condition called learning disability reflects observable and measurable deficits, a prognostic index ranking the child's program needs against a mild, moderate, or severe (or some statement of intervention application) disposition should be developed and followed by an assessment of an appropriate level of reimbursement for excess financial costs. The gain in focusing on severity to reflect a ratio of dollars spent (i.e., mild, least amount of funding; severe, highest level of funding) would be an attempt to obligate learning disability programs to differentiate their services.

The question must be asked: Why has such variable ratio funding among special education programs not been instituted? There are several reasons:

1. There has been no reason for administrators to program for it, or diagnosticians to search for it, since ". . . categorically differentiated instruction is largely nonexistent" (Hallahan & Kauffman, 1976).
2. The entire order of the identification and placement process involves social organizational phenomena. The referred student's social class, appearance, parents' economic status and prestige, and parental involvement in the schools, not learner characteristics, are the factors that differentiate pupil placement. Diagnosticians, however, still toy with the "kinds of educational decisions" (Salvia & Ysseldyke, 1978), considering screening, classification, identification/eligibility/placement, instructional planning, pupil evaluation, and program evaluation as the process entities. The upheaval that results is that gross processes generate gross classification. Most special educators confuse *seriously* handicapped, an intercategorical descriptor, with intracategorical severity terminology. A case in point is Anderson and Greer (1976), who note that severely handicapped students have made more notable gains than mildly handicapped. Given the confusion in the use of the terms, a statement such as that is most difficult to interpret.
3. A most convincing argument can be made for including behavioral severity in any index in identifying learning disability. If a behavioral disorder is so intense that it masks a disability, the learning handicap

will not be the primary concern for the intervention. On the other hand, mild to moderate behavioral disorders may reflect a reaction to school failure and social rejection.

4. Beneath all this is the inescapable quest for instructional sensitive classification. The importance in sensitizing the curriculum to the child is twofold: (a) learning disabled children still are being bent to meet inflexible programs, and (b) few learning disability teachers offer a full continuum of instructional programs, ranging from developmental to remediation to functional approaches.

LACK OF PROGRAM VALIDATION

Public education requires the expenditure of tax dollars and therefore to some degree is accountable to the people who fund it. That accountability has required some data on learning disability programs as a whole (school systemwide). Data on the capability of an objective, a teacher, a resource room program, the efficiency of the multidisciplinary team, the dollar amount spent vs. academic gain made, are indeed rarities. The absence of such data suggests that the source of the elements necessary to implement a planning effort are scarce. Johnson (1979) makes the following cogent points.

- Referral to special education frequently is based on teacher (or system) needs, not on the instructional or behavioral requirements of the students.

- It is impossible for an instructional (special education) effort using 5 percent of the total resources made available to the school system to correct the wrongs for the "regular" program that has 85 percent of the resources.

- It is an erroneous assumption that learning disability programs are built on an operational system, a major theory, or are constructed by design to mask either the special or regular education program already in existence.

- Special education is a "paternalistic, jargon-saturated, and sometimes overbearing way of dealing with parents of handicapped children and with students themselves" (Johnson, 1979, p. 47).

- There is no recognized principal programmatic factor (instructional method or service delivery), more efficient or less efficient, known to an organization in constructing a learning disability program.

- There is an absence of either a linear or a centralized decision model for allocating resources to meet individual student needs.

- Learning disabilities remain overdependent on norm assessment procedures in determining the instructional objectives of the children they
  serve.

- Many of the instructional objectives reflect a canned curriculum and are
  derived from it rather than from the ascertained educational, vocational,
  social, or personal growth factors relating to the child.

- Learning disability programs rarely are planned over the next five-year
  period, nor do they reflect the maximum use of resources.

Few directors of special education take the time to chart for other
administrators (principals or superintendent), boards of education, teachers,
and community any program growth except the number of students served.

Public education is nearly a century removed from the one-room school-
house, yet most administrative decisions are made from the seat of someone's
chair on the basis of little information, frequently far from the action related
to that ruling. In fact, most decision makers in the public schools are those
least familiar with the critical aspects (task areas) of a learning disabilities
program. The results of such seat-of-the-pants decision making are programs
that reflect a lack of preplanning and that frequently are inefficient in the use
of financial or personnel resources. It is recommended that a school system
not enter into a learning disabilities program with less than one year of
preplanning time in which the goals and objectives are stated clearly.

However, administrators have not found research data to assist them in
responding to the questions facing them in the preplanning process. It is not
that data are not available nor that meaningful interpretations have not been
made from those data; rather, the fact is that confidence in, and respect for,
much of the data available has fallen into a low level of trust (Erickson,
1979).

Good and Scates (1954) document a persistent pessimistic attitude toward
research maintained by many educators dating back to 1935. Gallagher
(1975) and Krathwohl (1977) have described the negative attitude teachers
continue to maintain for research. Yet DeVault (1978) indicates clearly that
teachers are key to the implementation of applied research in their schools.
Why does this discrepancy exist? Marks (1972) notes that few teachers
receive either the preservice or inservice preparation necessary to understand
or appreciate laboratory research.

Kerlinger (1977) has identified two common misconceptions educators
hold with regard to research:

1. *Pragmatic-Practical Misconception.* Research cannot solve educational
   problems or improve schooling practices. Traditional research can

identify a solution only on the basis of "if one practice is better than another for a group," which is at best implied, not inherent. It is inconceivable that scientific research will provide a decision that can improve education in general. The quality of instruction may be improved by basing it on reliable data rather than on an overdependence on subjective teacher or administrator opinion.

2. *Demand for Relevance.* Research may supply understanding and explanation but not relevance to a situation. For example, teacher A, using the same program as teacher B, with a matched group of children, gets better results year after year. Research may provide understanding. Teacher A is a joy to be around, a charming, stimulating person; teacher B has an affectless personality. *Relevance,* in this case, is to fire teacher B, and that usually is not possible if the person is tenured. The relevance of the research depends upon the use to which the data are put. The purpose of educational research is to understand the instructional process. That does not mean research data will change the instructional process but may supply the reason for someone to make that highly relevant decision. In other words, what if the school district had a policy saying that no persons with affectless personalities were to be employed because it was *speculated* that they were less effective in the classroom, although data on a population of teachers, ranked on that factor, refuted that speculation?

Program validation will result only when professional practitioners and teachers see their role in the applied research process.

Given that program validation is predicated upon (1) commonly recognized, operational definitions of learning disabilities; (2) controlled studies looking at carefully defined variables; (3) replicability; (4) cost-effectiveness data, the following blank space represents all the available program validation studies in the 20-year history of learning disabilities:

MEDICALLY RELATED PRACTICES: FAD OR FRONTIER

The attentional difficulties of many learning disabled students have been attributed to diet-related factors. Although popular opinion holds that a well-balanced diet is a prerequisite to adequate and appropriate school performance, in recent years there has been a growing awareness that some foods commonly provided to students as part of a nutritious diet or as "reinforcers" may contribute to learning and behavior problems (Reuban, 1978; Rinkel, Randolph, & Zeller, 1951; Speer, 1954; Rowe, 1959; Randolph, 1945).

Allergies contributing to learning disorders in school-age children may be classified into two groups: (1) those occurring as a reaction to food substances, and (2) those due to food additives. Adler (1978) has found that very common foods, e.g., milk, sugar, and cocoa, can cause allergic reactions.

Common food additives (colors, flavors, fillers, preservatives, residue from insecticide and herbicides, and many others) may trigger reactions in the form of inappropriate behavior, including hyperactivity (Adler, 1978; Dally, 1967; Goyette, 1978; Millman, Campbell, Wright, & Johnston, 1976; Bell, 1975; Hall, 1976). Feingold's (1975) diet, which omits artificial food coloring and flavoring as well as natural salicylates, has been suggested as a means of relieving hyperactivity in children. Some studies that attempted to replicate Feingold's work have reported positive results from an "elimination" diet treatment* (Connors, Goyette, Southwick, Lees, & Andrulonis, 1976; Harley, Ray, Tomasi, Eichman, Matthews, Chun, Cleeland, & Traisman, 1978). Three consecutive challenge studies (Connors, 1980), each employing a similar design, have been conducted to validate a version of the Feingold diet without the reduction of salicylate, with inconsistent results. The amount of improvement subjects exhibited as a result of diet in Study 3 was significantly less than in Studies 1 and 2. There also was significantly more improvement in student performance during the placebo stages of Study 2 than in Studies 1 and 3. Although several explanations for this discrepancy can be given, such as lack of experimental control, Feingold's diet remains unsubstantiated.

Two other diet-related conditions are vitamin/mineral deficiencies and hypoglycemia. Vitamin/mineral deficiencies may arise from problems in metabolism as the result of any medication the student may be taking, as well as the variability of individual requirements for vitamins and minerals. Even the types of food an individual consumes can increase the need for certain vitamins and minerals. Vitamin therapy typically consists of giving the student large doses of specific vitamins and supplements as well as a high protein diet.

Hypoglycemia is a metabolic condition characterized by abnormally low blood-sugar levels. This condition can cause radical swings in mood or behavior level. For example, a hypoglycemic individual may appear "hyped up" for a while after eating a candy bar, then suddenly slow down almost to the point of falling asleep.

---

*A diet from which sugars and most nonorganic chemicals are removed.

Each year physicians write countless prescriptions to control hyperactivity and convulsive disorders and to increase attention span. There is little question that antiepileptic drugs usage has and continues to be a major breakthrough in the medical management of brain-damaged children. It probably is safe to conclude that the pioneer work by Dr. Samuel Livingston, founding director of the Samuel Livingston Epilepsy Diagnostic and Treatment Center in Baltimore, established the basis for the medical treatment of convulsive disorders. The phenomenal success, beginning in 1853 with bromides, phenobarbital in 1912, and Dilantin in 1937, have demonstrated the capability of making 85 percent of epileptic children either completely seizure free (about 50 percent) or with reduced seizure patterns (35 percent).

One of the spinoffs of such an effective approach to medical management for brain-injured children has been the search for medication to control hyperactivity. Evidence of this lies in the report by Krager and Safer (1975) in which the prevalence of drug treatment in Baltimore County, Maryland, was found to be 1.7 percent in 1973. Four years later this figure had risen to 2 percent (Krager, Safer, & Earhardt, 1977). Ritalin was by far the most frequently prescribed drug for hyperactivity (82 percent), while 9 percent received Dexedrine, 6 percent Cyleit (pemoline), and 3 percent nonstimulant drugs.

Gadow (1979) examined drug usage against five behavioral areas of study: (1) activity level, (2) motor performance, (3) learning and cognitive performance, (4) conduct problems, and (5) school achievement. Stimulant drugs do appear to help children sit still and pay attention (Sprague & Sleator, 1973). However, the behavioral modifications are more qualitative than quantitative (Gadow, 1979). Knights and Hinton (1969) have introduced evidence suggesting that Ritalin successfully alters motor skill acquisition (i.e., handwriting). To date, work on drug usage and cognitive performance is exceedingly limited. The data on conduct problems suggest that a full quarter of the drug-taking population does not show improvement.

The ultimate interest has been the relationship of medication and school achievement. Gittelman-Klein (1978) reports that Ritalin, without specialized remediation in reading, did not improve reading—used alone, it simply did not help.

While most clinicians feel strongly that when a calming effect on hyperactivity is reached, school performance increases, but there is an absence of data to demonstrate that fact.

MOSAIC OF SERVICES

When special educators were isolated in self-contained classes to serve most areas of exceptionality, both they and regular educators needed only to acknowledge one another's existence. The serious problems in implementing mainstreaming strategies certainly are a case in point. The articulation of common goals, regardless of variance in historic philosophies about children (particularly the handicapped), has revealed more differences between regular (basic) and special education than some would have thought existed.

A learning disabilities program is identifiable by the sum of its parts. Its character is its contributing aspects, the personalities and skills of its members, and the view maintained by those who use its services in an attempt to satisfy its reasons for existence (credibility). The roles of resource instructors must be delineated clearly by all the teaching members of a school system or confusion will result. The role differences between learning disabilities resource room teachers and psychologists or speech therapists must be specified clearly. Crucial to the effectiveness of a learning disabilities program is the role of parents as members of the treatment team.

A NEW ROLE FOR PARENTS

Karnes and Zehrbach (1972) outline three points that influence the establishment of the team relationship:

1. The attitude of the professional—there must be a positive attitude that connotes that parents have a contribution to make to the growth of their child.
2. The recognition that there is more than one way to involve parents—they have individual needs that must be recognized to help them select the best way to involve themselves in the educational program of their child at a given time.
3. The belief that each parent is capable of growth—the amount of growth will vary; the extent of progress is dependent upon the degree to which the teacher changes, expands, and increases the breadth and depth of activities in the parent involvement program. (pp. 8–9)

When parents are actively involved with professionals, three processes occur: (1) the parents and professionals exchange information, (2) the parents are encouraged to grow in their role, and (3) a trusting, productive relationship between parents and teachers is built (Northcott & Fowler, 1976). Professionals and parents recognize their relationship if it is based on respect and cooperation. A partnership in assessing and remediating the child's learning disability has begun (McLoughlin, Edge, & Strenecky, 1978).

Parents' views of their role in the education of handicapped children have been altered significantly in just the last 25 years. The best single description is that parents have changed from being passive consumers to active participants. They have abandoned their role of simply receiving information and responding to the professional and have become team members in sharing ideas and materials for the development of a *mutually* sponsored child management plan.

P.L. 94-142 has made that mandatory. There is, however, no role change in the feelings associated with the responsibility inherent in rearing handicapped children. It has been said that learning disability is the easiest exceptionality to face. Certainly, it would appear that parents may be more willing to receive information that associates their child's behavior with learning disabilities than with mental retardation. And yet the day-to-day management in the home, preparation for school, and expectation for class performance may be even more difficult for the child who is hyperactive but looks so very "normal" in every physical way. The variations in hour-to-hour and day-to-day performances of learning disabled children can place tremendous strains on the family, since parents observe partial successes that elevate their hopes for a major breakthrough, only to find performance plateaus or inconsistencies in response patterns, as occur so very, very frequently.

The professional must not forget that parenting a handicapped child brings strong emotions to the surface. The literature supports the fact that many parents reject their handicapped children. Hurley (1967) notes that the love-hate or acceptance-rejection dimension apparently is the most prominent parental behavior variable relevant to the parent-child relationship. McCarthy (1954) indicates that children with functional language disorders have disturbed family relationships, which cause the youths to experience emotional insecurity. Berry and Eisenson note that "rejection on a level which is conscious or close to conscious is not infrequently found in cases where children have physical abnormalities" (Blair, 1956, p. 108). The literature also supports Blair's statement that children who are "organically" handicapped have problems of adjustment that are more complicated than those of the average child.

Strickler states that:

> The accumulated evidence about family interactional patterns suggests that communication barriers and inappropriate role behaviors in the home may contribute to serious difficulties in the child's efforts to adapt to the social milieu of the school classroom. The consequences of such poor social adjustment may be an inhibition of normal learning. (1969, p. 31)

If improved parent-child relationships can be achieved early, the result will be better emotional adjustment for both and maximal success for the intervention program. The author believes this is the most exciting challenge in developing the potential of the handicapped child for if it is handled well, therapy stands a better chance of providing "real" help.

Brown and Moersch (1978) delineate the rights of parents in their advocacy role for their child:

- Parents have the right to be respected as competent members of the treatment team.

- Parents have the right to knowledge over time.

- Parents have the right to know all the options.

- Parents have the right to help set programming priorities for their child.

- Parents have the right to advocate without fear of ostracism.

- Parents have the right to withdraw their efforts.

- Parents have the right to legal recourse when due process has been violated.

PRESERVICE PROFESSIONAL PREPARATION

Thirty-five states require a special teaching certificate for those who either teach or receive state reimbursement for instructing learning disabled children. Eleven states have a specific certificate but group it with either the mildly handicapped or generically with most of the teaching (as opposed to speech therapy, audiology, school psychology) certificates. It is difficult to cite a clear trend toward noncategorical teaching certificates in special education. A number of the larger, more heavily populated states were making some movement toward generic certificates but that seems to have stopped. Many state certification boards, certification offices, and universities (colleges) are examining the success of such ventures.

The major improvement tends to be an increased ease in finding special educators, since the certificate area specialty has been removed and an individual may be qualified to teach a greater range of handicapped children. There are, however, several opponents who feel the educational needs of learning disabled children are being less well met by the generic approach. The issue of generic vs. categorical specific training is a state certification issue, a professional conflict, and a disciplinary note of considerable importance in the 1980s.

The remaining question, central to the categorical/noncategorical issue and to assurance of a quality program for all learning disabled children under the law, is of course the identification, learning, and demonstration of competencies needed to instruct learning disabled children. Little is known about what those competencies should be (or are). Herr, Algozzine, and Heuchert (1976) conclude that the literature on teacher competencies in learning disabilities is scanty, with only scattered studies, whose results rarely are integrated.

One conclusion is that most learning disability programs in colleges and universities follow a similar course structure based on characteristic, diagnostic, and instructional courses. Some universities require a practicum experience and some do not. While the format itself should be challenged, it must be concluded that no matter what courses constitute the student's preservice professional exposure, the critical difference is the training and experience of the professor. It is possible a student (if one can cross geographic lines) should "shop" for the best training program.

The question then becomes what to look for, and the answer in the absence of professional or disciplinary program approval standards is a professor with a solid reputation as a classroom teacher. It is sad to conclude that little is known about this most important area of special education—preservice professional preparation.

INSERVICE STAFF DEVELOPMENT

Schools have the awesome job, in the end, both of employing people who should be versed in learning disabilities and of advancing their competencies during their employment. The purpose of inservice training is to provide teachers with current information, updating their skills on techniques and procedures previously unavailable to them.

The goals of any inservice program therefore must be set at the local level. Generally, one of the first tasks in developing an inservice program is to conduct a needs assessment survey. The program's effectiveness and successfulness is directly related to the accuracy with which the recipient's training needs were established (Hohenshil, 1977). A national survey of training priorities ranked instructional procedures and classroom management first (Rude, 1978). The second most frequently ranked item was curriculum, programming, and materials (resources), and the third was individualized educational programming.

The U.S. Bureau for Education of the Handicapped (now the Office of Special Education) spent $9.6 million, or 21.3 percent of its entire 1979 training budget, on advancing the skill development of regular educators. Some 260,000 special educators and more than 2 million regular teachers received inservice training in 1979 on the law (P.L. 94-142) alone. It is obvious that inservice education has reached staggering proportions, with many school systems developing a coordinator or identifying a responsible person to administer it as a separate department that requires massive coordination with other school departments. To date, the question of the effectiveness of such training remains a matter for speculation.

TOWARD 1990

What is the field of learning disabilities today?

It suffers from an absence of theoretically based information derived from systematic data collection procedures, beginning with identification and terminating in program validation. Therefore, it is defined operationally by local education agencies (LEAs) to the extent that even state education agencies' (SEAs) standards must be interpreted by the LEA. For all intents and purposes, a learning disabled child could be diagnosed and programmed in one district or state and denied service in another district or state.

Given the definition dilemma and the limitations imposed by current diagnostic instruments, programs for learning disabled children still are what LEA directors of special education or regular teachers make them. The amazing aspect of these programs is that they generate very little usable data on what does or does not work, and for whom. The result is that teachers use what they are comfortable using.

Mandates for the field the author would like to see achieved during the 1980s include:

- Certification for teachers of learning disabled students that is age sensitive, specifies minimum entry behaviors into the profession, requires a supervised internship, and is based on coursework in formalized assessment, developmental reading, and instructional and behavioral management.

- The Individualized Education Program (IEP) viewed as a legal document and reduced in length, reflecting all aspects of the student's educational program.

- Programs for students who are mild, moderate, and severely learning disabled.

- Support services provided in sufficient quantity to allow teachers to act as "brokers" rather than as direct providers of instruction.

- Study of the critical interaction between student and instructional process to determine the type and amount of program, prognosis, and specific instructional behavioral management needed.

- Development of management information systems to determine whether learning disabilities programs are proceeding in the direction and at the pace planned.

- Development of college or university programs to provide supportive services to learning disabled students.

- Encouragement of secondary programs for learning disabled youth including: consumer education, distributive education, work/study evaluation, work/study cooperative placement, and prevocational as well as specific vocational technical training.

- The establishment of services for 3-to-5-year olds, including adaptive developmental curricula, language stimulation, and other continuous special therapy to increase the growth rate of the mental process.

In conclusion, the purpose here is to provide the preservice teacher planning on entering the field with a review of the state of the art and a guide to more successful practice. For the more seasoned professional working in this area, it is an attempt to update the current state of the art and provide information on programming strategies, techniques, and service delivery models that should be most helpful in keeping vital or revitalizing an instructional and behavioral management effort for children or youth.

The point of departure here is that the field has grown rapidly, responding to many external organizational pressures (e.g., the schools, other disciplines teaching exceptional children, professional organizations, etc.) but now needs to provide self-direction, which it will continue to develop, with an even greater emphasis on quality. There are three conceptual themes in the chapters to follow:

1. Learning disabilities programs require a continuum of services much too broad for any one teacher to deliver appropriately.
2. The remedial model as an intervention strategy in the resource room setting has developed as the program currently in vogue.
3. Remediation should be supported with equal efforts in cognitive training, particularly where language learning and behavioral management are indicated.

REFERENCES

Adler, S. Behavior management: A nutritional approach to the behaviorally disordered and learning disabled child. *Journal of Learning Disabilities,* 1978, *11* (10), 651–656.

Anderson, R., & Greer, J. (Eds.). *Educating the severely and profoundly retarded*. Baltimore: University Park Press, 1976.

Bell, I. A kinin model of medication for food and chemical sensitivities: Biobehavioral implications. *Annals of Allergy*, 1975, *35* (4), 206–215.

Bender, L. A visual motor Gestalt test and its clinical use. *American Orthopsychiatrist*, 1938, *3*.

Berry, M.F., & Eisenson, J. *Speech disorders: Principles and practices of therapy*. New York: Appleton-Century-Crofts, Inc., 1956.

Birch, H.G., & Belmont, L. Auditory-visual integration in normal retarded readers. *American Journal of Orthopsychiatry*, 1964, *34*, 852–861.

Blair, G.M. *Diagnostic and remedial teaching: A guide to practice in elementary and secondary schools*. New York: MacMillan Publishing Co., Inc., 1956.

Bortner, M. Perceptual skills and early reading disability. In L. Mann & D.A. Sabatino (Eds.), *The second review of special education*. Philadelphia: JSE Press, 1974.

Bortner, M., & Birch, H.G. Perceptual and perceptual-motor dissociation in brain-damaged patients. *Journal of Nervous and Mental Disease*, 1960, *134*, 103–108.

Brown, S., & Moersch, M. (Eds.). *Parents on the team*. Ann Arbor: University of Michigan Press, 1978.

Bryan, T.H. Learning disabilities: A new stereotype. *Journal of Learning Disabilities*, 1974, *7*(5), 304–309.

Chalfant, J.C., & Scheffelin, M.A. *Central processing dysfunction in children* (National Institute of Neurological Diseases and Strokes Monograph No. 9, U.S. Public Health Service Publication). Washington, D.C.: U.S. Government Printing Office, 1969.

Cohen, A.S. Fuzziness and the flab: Some solutions to research problems in learning disabilities. *The Journal of Special Education*, 1976, *10*(2), 129–136.

Coles, C.S. Learning-disabilities test battery: Empirical and social issues. *Harvard Educational Review*, 1978, *48*, 313–340.

Connors, C.K. *Artificial colors in the diet and disruptive behavior: Current status of research*. Washington, D.C.: National Institute of Education and National Institutes of Health, 1980.

Connors, C.K., Goyette, C.H., Southwick, D.A., Lees, J.M., & Andrulonis, P.A. Food additives and hyperkinesis: A controlled double-blind experiment. *Pediatrics*, 1976, *58*(2), 154–166.

Dally, P. *Chemotherapy of psychiatric disorders*. New York: Plenum Press, 1967.

DeVault, M.U. Research and the classroom teachers. *Columbia University Teachers College Record*, 1978, *11*, 10–23.

Doehring, D.G. *Patterns in impairment in special learning disability*. Bloomington, Ind.: Indiana University Press, 1968.

Erickson, D. Research on educational administration: The state of the art. *Educational Researcher*, 1979, *8*(3), 9–14.

Feingold, B. Hyperkinesis and learning disabilities linked to artificial food flavors and colors. *American Journal of Nursing*, 1975, *75*, 797–803.

Frostig, M., & Horne, D. *The Frostig program for the development of visual perception*. Chicago: Follett Publishing Co., 1964.

Gadow, K.D. *Children on medication: A primer for school personnel*. Reston, Va.: The Council for Exceptional Children, 1979.

Gallagher, J. The prospects for governmental support of educational research. *Educational Researcher*, 1975, *4*(7), 13–14.

Gillespie, P.H., Miller, T.L., & Fielder, V.D. Legislative definitions of learning disabilities: Roadblocks to effective service. *Journal of Learning Disabilities,* 1975, *8*(10), 660–666.

Gittleman-Klein, R. Psychopharmacology in children. *Drug Therapy,* January 1978, pp. 18–24.

Good, C.V., & Scates, D.E. *Methods of research.* New York: Appleton-Century-Crofts, Inc., 1954.

Goyette, C. Effects of artificial colors on hyperactive children: A double-blind challenge study. *Psychopharmacology Bulletin,* 1978, *14.*

Hall, K. Allergy of the nervous system: A review. *Annals of Allergy,* 1976, *36*(1), 49–64.

Hallahan, D.P. Comparative research studies on the psychological characteristics of learning disabled children. In W. Cruickshank & D.P. Hallahan (Eds.), *Perceptual and learning disabilities in children* (Vol. 1). New York: Syracuse University Press, 1975.

Hallahan, D.P., & Kauffman, J.M. *Introduction to learning disabilities: A psycho-behavioral approach.* Englewood Cliffs, N.J.: Prentice-Hall, Inc., 1976.

Hammill, D. Training visual perceptual processes. *Journal of Learning Disabilities,* 1972, *5*(9), 552–559.

Harley, J.P., Ray, R.S., Tomasi, L., Eichman, P.L., Matthews, C.G., Chun, R., Cleeland, C.S., & Traisman, E. Hyperkinesis and food additives: Testing the Feingold hypothesis. *Pediatrics,* 1978, *61,* 818–828.

Herr, D.E., Algozzine, R.F., & Heuchert, C.M. Competencies of teachers of the mildly handicapped. *The Journal of Special Education,* 1976, *10*(1), 97–106.

Hewitt, F.M., & Forness, S.R. *Education of exceptional learners.* Boston: Allyn & Bacon, Inc., 1974.

Hohenshil, T.H. How to plan and direct short-term professional developmental activities. *American Vocational Journal,* 1977, *52*(5), 28–30.

Hurley, J.L. Parental malevolence and children's intelligence. *Consulting Psychology,* 1967, *31*(1), 199–204.

Iano, R.P., Ayers, D., Heller, H.B., McGettigan, J.F., & Walker, V.S. Sociometric status of retarded children in an integrative program. *Exceptional Children,* 1974, *40*(4), 267–271.

Johnson, M.C. Communication skills inservice for paraprofessionals. *International Journal of Instructional Media,* 1979, *6*(3), 291–295.

Karnes, M.B., & Zehrbach, R.R. Flexibility in getting parents involved in the school. *Teaching Exceptional Children,* Fall 1972, pp. 6–19.

Keogh, B.K., & Levitt, M.L. Special education in the mainstream: A confrontation of limitations. *Focus on Exceptional Children,* 1976, *8,* 1–11.

Kephart, N.C. *The slow learner in the classroom.* Columbus, Ohio: The Charles E. Merrill Publishing Co., Inc., 1960.

Kerlinger, F. Influence of research on education. *Educational Researcher,* 1977, *6*(8), 5–12.

Knights, R.M., & Hinton, G.G. The effects of methylphenidate (Ritalin) on the motor skills and behavior of children with learning problems. *Journal of Nervous and Mental Diseases,* 1969, *148,* 643–653.

Krager, J., & Safer, D. Type and prevalence of medication used in treating hyperactive children. *New England Journal of Medicine,* 1975, *291,* 1118–1120.

Krathwohl, D.R. Improving educational research and development. *Educational Researcher,* 1977, *6*(4), 8–14.

Lezar, M.D. *Neuropsychological assessment.* New York: Oxford University Press, 1976.

Lilly, S. Special education: A teapot in a tempest. *Exceptional Children,* 1970, *37*(1), 43–49.

Mann, L. *On the trail of mental processes.* New York: Grune & Stratton, Inc., 1980.

Mann, L., & Goodman, L. *Perceptual training: A critical retrospect.* Paper presented at the First International Leo Kanner Colloquium on Child Development, Deviations and Treatment, Chapel Hill, N.C., November 1973.

Marks, M.B. Research: The preservice missing link. *Journal of Teacher Education,* 1972, *23,* 453–456.

McCarthy, D. Language disorders and parent-child relationships. *Journal of Speech and Hearing Disorders,* December 1954, 514–523.

McCarthy, J. Learning disabilities: Where have we been? Where are we going? In D. Hammill & N. Bartel (Eds.), *Educational perspectives in learning disabilities.* New York: John Wiley & Sons, Inc., 1971.

McLoughlin, J., Edge, D., & Strenecky, B. Perspective on parental involvement in the diagnosis and treatment of learning disabled children. *Journal of Learning Disabilities,* 1978, *11*(5), 32–37.

McQuarrie, C.W. *A perceptual testing and training guide for kindergarten teachers.* Winter Haven, Fla.: Lions Research Foundation, 1967.

Millman, M.M., Campbell, M.B., Wright, K., & Johnston, A. Allergy and learning disability in children. *Annals of Allergy,* 1976, *36*(3), 149–160.

Morgan, D.I. Prevalence and types of handicapping conditions found in juvenile correctional institutions: A national survey. *The Journal of Special Education,* 1979, *13*(3), 283–295.

National Advisory Committee on Handicapped Children. *First annual report.* Washington, D.C.: U.S. Office of Education, 1968.

National Center for Educational Statistics (NCES). *Digest of education statistics.* Washington, D.C.: U.S. Government Printing Office, 1978.

Northcott, W.H., & Fowler, S.A. Developing parent participation. In D. Lillie & P. Trohanis (Eds.), *Teaching parents to teach.* New York: Walker and Company, 1976.

Randolph, T.G. Fatigue and weakness of allergic origin (allergic toxemia) to be differentiated from nervous fatigue and neurasthenia. *Annals of Allergy,* 1945, *3*(6), 418.

Reuban, D. *Everything you always wanted to know about nutrition.* New York: Simon and Schuster, 1978.

Rinkel, H.J., Randolph, T.G., & Zeller, M. *Food allergy.* Springfield, Ill.: Charles C. Thomas, Publisher, 1951.

Rowe, A.H. Allergic toxemia and fatigue. *Annals of Allergy,* 1959, *17*(1), 70–79.

Rucker, C.N., & Vincenzo, F.M. Maintaining social acceptance gains made by mentally retarded children. *Exceptional Children,* 1970, *36*(9), 679–680.

Rude, C.R. Trends and priorities in inservice training. *Exceptional Children,* 1978, *45*(3), 172–179.

Salvia, J., & Clark, J. The use of deficient scores in identifying learning disabled children. *Exceptional Children,* 1973, *39,* 305–308.

Salvia, J., & Ysseldyke, J.E. *Assessment in special and remedial education.* Boston: Houghton Mifflin Company, 1978.

Shotel, J.R., Iano, R.P., & McGettigan, J.F. Teacher attitudes associated with the integration of handicapped children. *Exceptional Children,* 1972, *38,* 677–683.

Speer, F. The allergic-tension-fatigue syndrome. *Pediatric Clinics of North America,* 1954, *1,* 1029–1037.

Sprague, R.L., & Sleator, E.E. Effect of psychopharmacological agents on learning disabilities. *Pediatric Clinics of North America,* 1973, *20,* 719–735.

Strickler, E. Family interaction, factors in psychogenic learning disturbance. *Journal of Learning Disabilities,* 1969, *2*(3), 147–154.

Terman, L.M., & Merrill, M.A. *Measuring intelligence: A guide to the administration of the new revised Stanford-Binet tests of intelligence.* Boston, New York: Houghton Mifflin Company, 1937.

Wechsler, D. *The Wechsler intelligence scale for children.* New York: The Psychological Corporation, 1955.

Ysseldyke, J.E., Sabatino, D.A., & LaManna, J.A. Convergent and discriminant validity of the Peabody individual achievement test with educable mentally retarded children. *Psychology in the Schools,* 1973, *10,* 200–204.

Chapter 2

Formal Assessment of Learning Disabled Children and Youth

Ted L. Miller
and Brenda B. Miller

INTRODUCTION

The measurement of students' psychoeducational abilities and skills has been, historically, a major theme in the development of special education programs and services. The fact that assessment is and long has been a central theme is evident by its inclusion in virtually all aspects of the services and programs now provided by special educators, e.g., identification of the handicapped student, selection of the program, provision for instructional and behavioral management, and evaluation of the pupil's progress.

Probably no other activity is more inclusive of special education than is assessment, and with good cause: assessment is the first step in the process of teaching—the collection of relevant information—and it is a supporting practice to all subsequent instructional activities. Individuals who reject assessment by downplaying its importance and carrying it through in nonsystematic fashion should be aware that to do so ultimately places teaching in the category of a minimally guided activity.

The teacher and the pupil can little afford the severing of conceptual models that are reflected in nonsystematic evaluation, for information important to teaching and learning certainly will be lost or delayed in realization. The loss of learning time that would result because of erroneous or absent assessment practices is a problem that should be avoided. Few professionals challenge this belief and as this chapter and Chapter 3 will reflect, more statements critical of assessment are directed at "How should assessment be conducted properly?" than "Why should assessment be conducted?"

Specific, comprehensive, systematic assessment is a considerable undertaking, one that requires a degree of instruction (and, eventually, experience) that is beyond the scope of this book. Indeed, these two full chapters are needed to convey even an overview of the procedures used with learning disabled students. An elaboration of these approaches or an expansion of procedures used with other handicapping conditions could dictate many additional topics. Therefore, the overall purpose of these two chapters is to provide sufficient orientation and structure to allow the opportunity to develop skills and opinions essential for the measurement of learning disabled students. More specifically, this chapter concerns what are collectively termed *formal measures*. The main element of formal measures is the standardized test. The theme here is that formal measures (largely tests) are neither panacea nor anathema but instead are only one approach to the goal of understanding educational problems. Wisely used, tests are beneficial tools; foolishly used, they can be detrimental. Ultimately, outcomes are derived from the skill *and* attitudes of the test user—elements that lead to test "wisdom." This chapter analyzes the elements that can lead teachers to "wisdom" in the selection and use of formal measures.

THE FORMAL ASSESSMENT APPROACH

Historically, the beginnings of formal assessment probably are lost to antiquity. It is known that the Chinese utilized tests up to 3,000 years ago (DuBois, 1970). But in the more contemporary vein of this book, the elements discussed in this chapter may be traced to the awakening of interest in individual differences that characterized experimental psychology of the late 19th century. Pioneering work by Sir Francis Galton, among others, led to James Cattel's development of the first mental test by about 1890. In turn, these developments led to the direct antecedents of modern assessment practices, particularly the intelligence tests developed by Alfred Binet and his coworkers. By 1916, these scales had been translated by Louis Terman at Stanford University and put into use throughout the United States. One of the initial uses of the *Stanford-Binet Scales* was the identification of individuals who would require the special education services then evolving in public schools in the United States.

World War I brought about a further incentive to refine measures for the evaluation of individual differences. One of the major outcomes of the selection activities associated with the war was the development of group tests, which remain in widespread use today. The second outcome was the development of aptitude tests, designed to measure rather specific skills. The technical data acquired from these efforts soon were applied to the refinement of standardized achievement tests. Thus by 1923, when the first edition of the *Stanford Achievement Test* appeared, a minimum of three major factors were contributing to the proliferation and use of formal tests: (1) the increased technical capacity of test construction just described, (2) the growing interest in individual differences and, more particularly, individual educational differences, and (3) the recognition that teacher-made (informal) tests could not accomplish some tasks accurately and readily.

Since 1923 testing procedures and materials have been refined significantly. In addition, many more specialized areas now are measured routinely with tests and some once popular types of measures are beginning to dwindle in use. Although tests have increased greatly in number and quality, there now is a widespread awareness that they are but one of the major data collection areas for understanding the characteristics of children and youth. A more encompassing and, the authors think, preferred term is assessment.

Assessment in special education can involve many theoretical and pragmatic outcomes so it is impossible to discuss the concept as if it were an entirely known commodity. Instead, it is a rather broad term that relates many practices, approaches, and procedures for a common problem, viz., obtaining accurate information for the educational management plan (or the Individualized Education Program—IEP—as it is now termed). However, assessment can be divided along fairly well-recognized though never quite formalized lines. The distinctions of formal assessment are emphasized in this chapter and informal assessment in Chapter 3. Both of these assessment practices are essential and complementary in the provision of services to the learning disabled student. It is important that teachers recognize the relative merits and best practice procedures in each approach.

General Characteristics

Paradoxically, the much-discussed concept of formal assessment does not stipulate a precisely identifiable set of practices. However, it does tend to have some rather consistently accepted characteristics. A summary of the more common of these might yield the following definition:

> Formal assessment can be considered to be the use of norm referenced, standardized tests to accomplish the purpose of identification, the analysis of learning abilities; or the global analysis of learned academic skills.

The various components of this definition are quite straightforward. In its simplest sense, *norm referenced* refers to measures that attain meaning and interpretability by the comparison of one child's score to a representative sample of other learners. Thus, the results obtained for a particular pupil are examined to determine where a child falls in the array of scores that characterize others of that age and, it is to be hoped, similar background. *Standardized* refers to the fact that the conditions of formal assessment are as similar for each individual as is feasible. For example, if ten children take a test under standardized conditions, each will receive the same instructions, time limits, encouragements, and so on. The outcomes of formal assessment usually are either to determine the unique ways in which a child learns or to gather a general, global impression of what the individual has learned. As is demonstrated in Chapter 3, informal assessment is complementary to these initial steps and links formal assessment to instruction in a systematic way.

The outcome of norm referenced standardized tests can be expressed in a raw score, that is, the number of points earned or the total number of correctly solved problems, but that has little meaning for several reasons. First, if a person were to receive a mark of 93 on an examination, the individual might tend to be very happy with that score until discovering that the test totaled 200 points. So, given that total test points vary, raw scores do not yield a ready index to the child's performance. This phenomenon is complicated further by a second factor: most formal tests are designed to be used across several age ranges. Obviously, a child of age 6 cannot be expected to earn as many points as one of 9 because the former probably has had neither the developmental time nor learning experience of the 9-year-old.

Clearly such a comparison would be unfair, so outcome scores usually are translated into special scores that relate a child's performance to others of similar age and background. For example, two children ages 8 and 12 may have measured intelligence quotients (IQs) of 100. However, the raw score (the number of correctly answered questions) certainly will be lower for the younger child. The mechanics of this process are somewhat complicated and readers are referred to other sources for a thorough discussion (Anastasi, 1976; Sabatino & Miller, 1979). However, that need not be a factor here since the more common scores can be mentioned briefly and described without a complex explanation.

Scoring Systems

Developmental scores are common in special education, particularly in the form of age equivalent and grade equivalent ratings. An age equivalent score means that a raw score is the average attained for children of the particular age. If Todd, age 8, receives a raw score of 57, that is transformed (converted) to an age equivalent of 6.5; this means that 57 is the raw score attained by the average student of age 6.5. Similarly, if Todd's raw score is transformed to a grade equivalent of .5, this means that raw score 57 is attained, on the average, by children in the middle of the first year of school.

It must be noted that both grade equivalent and age equivalent figures are average scores and do not necessarily mean that the child is prepared to work with others of that grade placement or age. It must be remembered that the raw score is only the average attained by students of the same age or grade. The fact that a pupil can perform in one dimension that characterizes a given age or grade (e.g., "academics") does not suggest that the child can perform equally well in some other capacity (e.g., age appropriate verbal expression). This brief example should help clarify one of the ways in which simple testing can lead to conclusions that comprehensive assessment will discount.

The figures used most commonly on formal tests, and the ones most likely to be seen on year-end comprehensive test reports or on psychological reports, are those referred to as scores of relative standing. The percentile is the most commonly used of several possibilities. Percentiles represent a numerical band extending from .1 to 99.9. The 50th percentile is the average and as a score becomes higher numerically (e.g., 75th percentile) the performance is considered to be better. More specifically, percentiles are interpreted in the following way: if a child were to have a raw score of 65 that equated to a percentile rank of 85, the pupil could be considered as having a score equal to or better than 85 percent of the others in the class. Because percentiles are easy to interpret and easy to report, they probably are the best scores for the teacher to work with.

Standard scores are those that are established in such a manner that raw scores always will have the same mean and standard deviation (SD). The mean is simply the average score, just as the average price of gasoline is found by totaling prices at various pumps, then dividing that total by the number of stations sampled. The standard deviation is technically more difficult but it essentially describes the size of units of divergence—the movement (price differences) away from the mean.

For example, test scores vary from administration to administration and both above and below the average. This difference from high to low around the mean is known as dispersion and a measure of it is essential; the standard deviation is a handy statistic because it describes the amount of this dispersion. Further, the proportion of scores that fall within certain standard deviations on the normal curve—the pattern that characterizes most measures of human ability—is well known. For example, about 68 percent of all test scores will fall within one standard deviation below to one standard deviation above the mean, about 96 percent will fall within two standard deviations below and above the mean. Significantly for testing, this information can be used to estimate how many persons will fall above or below any particular child's score.

Scores can exist with many different means and standard deviations but convention has established a mean = 100 and a SD = 15 for many tests common to special education (as is shown later). Frequently, so-called Z scores (mean = 0, standard deviation = 1) are used. In either case, (100/15 or 0/1) or in other less typical cases of standard scores, the key to interpretation is to find the mean and determine in which standard deviation the child's score stands (Figure 2-1).

Outcomes of Formal Tests

In returning to the definition of formal tests, it can be seen that the essential measures, however reported and however well reported, usually fall

---

Figure 2-1 Idealized Normal Distribution with Illustrative Scores

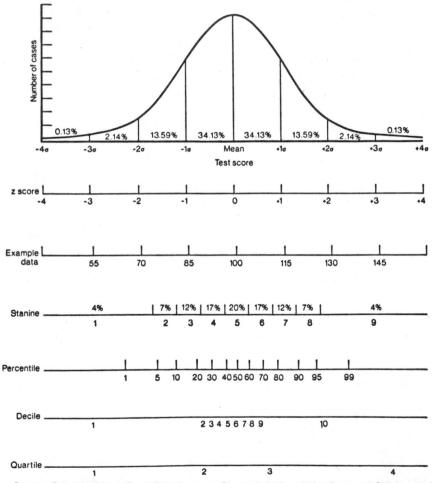

Source: Reprinted from *Describing Learner Characteristics of Handicapped Children and Youth* by Ted L. Miller by permission of Grune & Stratton, Inc., ©1979.

into one of two types of outcomes: (1) the analysis of learner abilities, and (2) the global analysis of learned academic skills. The first of these approaches the question of *how* (or sometimes why) a child learns best, the second is directed at *what* the child currently knows. The first measure is an analysis of learner abilities and sometimes is referred to as trait measures or learning style. Either way, these scores may be thought of as the personal characteristics that in some way affect the course of instruction or the interactional patterns of the child in school.

These abilities usually are regarded as relatively well established in the child and as only partially modifiable, although there is much debate over the concept of whether they are largely innate or largely learned. Whatever the case, the teacher will need to respond to these characteristics in the course of instruction since most special students are so identified because of their variance on these dimensions. How that response should proceed is discussed later.

Ability Scores

Conceptually, abilities usually are considered to be within the cognitive affective or perceptual motor domains. In the case of the learning disabled child, measurement in all three domains is important and warranted. The cognitive domain is the thinking domain. In practice, it often is referred to, at least operationally, as intelligence, although this is certainly a drastic simplification. The affective domain is the realm of emotion and feeling and sometimes is equated with personality, although that, too, is an obvious oversimplification. Finally, the perceptual motor domain refers to the manner in which information is acquired and acted on by the fine and gross musculature of the body. Further, perception often is subcategorized by the responsible sensory systems—sight, sound, and touch.

Analyses of the content of the cognitive, affective, and perceptual motor domains may be found in many sources; among the more thorough are Bloom (1956), Krathwohl (1964), and Harrow (1972). The immense value of these taxonomies (as they are termed) for assessment may become even more apparent when informal assessment procedures are examined in Chapter 3. Still, the difficulty of establishing any rigid taxonomy is apparent when it is considered that one important topic, language, actually overlaps and makes use of elements of each domain.

Ability measures invariably concentrate on one of these domains in attempts to identify the essential variance within the domain of an individual, for this variance is viewed as influential for all subsequent learning. These domains are seen as largely intrinsic to learners and sometimes are referred to as basic psychological processes. Most theorists, and the most accepted definitions, maintain that the causes of learning disabilities are locked up inside disorders of some of these basic psychological processes. In fact, the most widely held definition, that issued by the National Advisory Committee on Handicapped Children (NACHC, 1968) specifically relates the learning disability concept to psychological processes.

Precisely how such deficits occur developmentally and create learning problems is a matter of speculation requiring more detail than space permits. However, a particularly lucid theoretical overview of the development of basic psychological processes, and the relationship of faulty development to learning disabilities, may be found in the analysis of exceptionalities related by Wyne and O'Connor (1979).

Skill Scores

The measurement of gross skills also is an essential task for formal assessment, although a note on what constitutes gross skills is in order. Essentially what is meant here is an approximation of what has been learned; little effort is made to determine precisely what is to be learned. Gross skill assessment provides an approximation of grade equivalent or age equivalent performance, for example, but does not state directly the origin of the faulty learning that produced the score the student achieved. The key here is the word *learned* for, unlike abilities, skills are assumed to be fully acquired capacities, i.e., learned. Formal assessment of gross skills is a type of evaluation termed summative because, as that term implies, it summarizes what is now available information to the child. Normally, it is a fairly infrequent event, showing up annually or less and very often associated with the process of identification.

In the past, gross skill assessment in learning disabled students has been thought of as traditional academic scores, particularly reading but also arithmetic, spelling, and writing. At least one new emphasis is appearing that is expanding that view: the measurement and training of vocational and occupational skills. Unfortunately, this emphasis is relatively recent and there is a paucity of formal test batteries. Because of this, most existing tests and measures are adaptations of procedures developed for other populations.

Uses of Formal Assessment

There are several reasons why formal evaluation is now important to the practitioner. First, there are the matters of identification, screening, and child-find, all somewhat different but all interrelated. Pragmatically, it is a simple fact that children cannot receive special services until a handicapping condition is identified. These conditions are in and of themselves normative distinctions: if no one could read, then an individual's failure to read would not be considered a handicap. So, within current definitions of learning disabilities and legal requirements for services, norm referenced measures of abilities are demanded in determining whether a child is learning disabled.

Contrary to the damage that sometimes is ascribed to this practice, it should be noted that most social and political gains for exceptional children through special education, for example Public Law 94-142, rest very heavily on the use of norm referenced measures (Mercer, 1979; Wyne & O'Connor, 1979).

Stripped of jargon, *identification* in special education is precisely the dictionary meaning of the term. Although controversy exists as to effectiveness (the manner in which identification is done, and some of its outcomes— see Hobbs, Egerton, & Mathery, 1975), current options are few or nonexistent.

Screening is a collective term that refers to any simplified and rapid assessment procedure that will identify students potentially at risk of one or more types of failure. Since many children are screened, the approach always is quick, sometimes inaccurate, and dependent upon further comprehensive assessment to pinpoint specific skill or ability deficiencies in those students who are suspected of being handicapped.

Child-find is a very special task that sometimes represents a special use of screening. A component of P.L. 94-142, child-find is a requirement that all public schools actively seek to identify all handicapped children and youth. Under this law, all children who normally are served by public schools must receive special education if a handicapping condition exists. Obviously, one major time for identification is when children enter public schools. However, child-find now is charged with screening for the identification of handicapped children down to age 3, which was to be lowered to birth. Mercer (1979) provides an excellent and thorough discussion of general screening and child-find procedures.

Confirmation of Severity

Another particularly useful approach lies in the fact that formal assessments provide some insight into the confirmation of the problem, its severity, and its differential aspects. Collectively, these tasks might be termed diagnosis. Diagnosis provides the practitioner with information on the idiosyncratic nuances of the problem; it is not, as some authors state erroneously, a preoccupation with etiology. Further, good diagnosis does not constitute an unrealistic elevation of the construct of learning disabilities.

As an illustration, consider the difference between a learning disability and a learning disabled child. They are not the same. The former is a case of assigning reality to a hypothetical construct, something that should never occur, particularly if it is poorly defined and poorly understood, as is the case with "learning disabilities" (see Chapter 1). Should the diagnostician blunder into this position, the learning disability becomes an entity, something educators are obliged to find, to verify, or to identify as to its source. In short, the diagnostic approach, for programming at least, is greatly weakened before it starts.

For the second phase, the learning disabled child, the goal is to evaluate the sources of problems that may be thwarting learning. The task of diagnosis is clear: specify and quantify the source(s) of the learning problem and search for ways to facilitate the process. Obviously, this is the approach of choice in all cases (except possibly basic research). So it should be kept in mind that a learning disability should (and truly can) exist only when a particular child exhibits some deficiency attributable to disorders of basic psychological processes. The difference between a learning disability and a learning disabled student denote a subtle but very important distinction in the diagnostician's orientation.

The attempt to determine the severity of these basic learning problems and to differentiate the aspects most affected is largely a task of formal assessment because only formal procedures contrast the individual child with others. The practitioner who accepts the notion that peoply vary in the manner in which they learn and that learning can be improved by capitalizing on cognitive strengths and weaknesses has little option but to use formal assessment procedures. No other procedure seems so uniquely devised and technically developed for the eventual measurement of styles of learning. That is to say that norm-referenced measures are but one of several avenues of individual assessment that lead to diagnosis but technically are very well-developed and important ones. A review of the formal assessment approach makes clear that this technology is put to manifold uses: screening, identification, and diagnosis. Properly conducted, all of these tasks are very important to the provision of services to learning disabled students.

Specific Controversies in Formal Testing

Controversy over formal tests is evident as to their technical capacity, whether or not they measure what is intended (and advertised), and if so, how well. This controversy is not limited to special education; in fact, some of the more recent criticisms have occurred in nonspecial education assessment practices. Excellent discussions of this controversy exist for both special and nonspecial education, and readers should have no trouble locating voluminous reviews. Criticisms are multifaceted, however. Theoretical, practical, ethical, and legal are but a few of the adjectives that have been used to precede the phrase "issues of testing." Several of the more critical points in these arguments are highlighted here.

The Privacy Problem

One issue, perhaps *the* issue, in testing is protection of privacy. It has been argued that because of the influential value of test outcomes, the power of performance is considerable. Tests thus represent a particularly worrisome source of invasion of privacy, not only as an immediate harrassment but also as a long-term effect that may be very pejorative in outcome. For example, a considerable body of literature speaks of the expectancy phenomenon. Applied to this example, this would imply that tests to some extent influence and hence create, rather than solely measure, performance. While this criticism has some basis in fact, pending legislation tends to diminish if not fully remove the threat by strict enforcement of permission prior to testing, strict control of access to test data, and assurance of guaranteed access to records by the individual being tested (or the parent or guardian).

The Bias Factor

A second controversy involves so-called test bias. The arguments on the topic are complex. In simplified form, bias may exist when the performance of one subgroup of persons is systematically overestimated or underestimated. This bias can occur through background characteristics, faulty test construction, examiner-induced variation, unknown influences, or more likely, some complex arrangement of most or all factors. Yet part of the problem certainly must lie in society's greater failure to define the criterion sought; for example, what is "academic success?" The fact that a test cannot measure what society and schools have only vaguely defined should not be an indictment of tests. Unfortunately, much energy has been wasted describing test bias while steadfastly failing to acknowledge this fact.

The Educational Value

A third controversy involves the educational value of tests. The reasons for this are numerous, but it would be fair to say that virtually all aspects of the formal assessment model have been criticized. Some authors (Howell, Kaplan, & O'Connell, 1979; Lovitt, 1977) argue that formal global achievement measures may not be very useful, while others (Salvia & Ysseldyke, 1978) demonstrate that many achievement tests have limited use. Controversy in the assessment of abilities is even more acrimonious. Many authors (Arter & Jenkins, 1977; Coles, 1978; Hammill & Larsen, 1974; Larsen & Hammill, 1975; Mann, 1971) suggest that the measurement of abilities is difficult and that the current pedogogical implications are too weak to justify the cost and time devoted to this process.

This may be so with today's measures, yet there is no reason to believe that assessment practices and tools must remain static at their current level of development. Indeed, there is a resurgent interest in the "process issue," the way educators look at and use information. These data, as they emerge, should help educators to better understand and therefore measure the abilities of learning disabled children. This is important conceptually because, as Mann (in press) points out, the measurement of processes is the basis of the learning disabilities movement, so it is important for educators to recognize that the possible commissions of the past are not before the fact harbingers or the state of the future.

The Federal Requirements

A final reason that formal testing remains important is that it is an integral part of the procedures in federal laws on the handicapped. These laws, particularly P.L. 94-142, demand that students be screened for handicapping conditions, certified prior to the provision of services, and regularly evaluated for changes in status and performance. Moreover, the law recommends that standardized tests should be used for some purposes. Lest the reader believe this may smack of high-handed bureaucracy, recall the opening statement that assessment parallels all instruction.

Since the law also provides for, and even encourages, alternative strategies, what really emerges is a reasonable legislative mandate to provide comprehensive assessment through all known avenues. This is a worthy goal and simultaneously a complex and often misinterpreted task. For example, through the polemics of the last decade or more, many professionals have been lured into an either/or decision between formal assessment techniques and other approaches. This situation should not exist, for both professional prudence and legal requirements clearly mandate that data from all available sources are to be collected and studied.

An objective examination of the criticisms presented here, and in many other sources, leaves little doubt that formal assessment is not without flaws. While many of these criticisms have a basis in fact, it is far too harsh, and equally foolish, to suggest that formal tests be rejected. Recent efforts have reduced greatly the possibility of invasion of privacy and the likelihood of bias, hence educational placement decisions concerning the child also have improved by these legal mandates. To be sure, much of this desirable state is the result of legally mandated administrative procedures (Bersoff & Miller, 1979) but the outcome remains the same: the capacity of formal measures to injure has been reduced.

Similarly, those who might advocate a return solely to teacher-made tests might be well advised to investigate the historical factors that precipitated the creation of standardized tests. The rapid expansion of psychometrics (the study of test theory) was related closely to the recognition that informal tests often were inferior, inaccurate, unfair, and generally unable to accomplish some tasks. While it is true that current achievement tests are useful under some conditions and that the measurement of abilities is controversial yet seemingly related to learning (see, for example, Messick & Associates, 1976), it seems prudent to retain these measures for assessing the capacity of learning disabled children and youth. Certainly today's formal measures are not as effective as might be desired, yet options to formal tests do not meet all of the requirements of assessment.

What safeguards can be applied readily for the protection of both examiner and child? What should every teacher do?

1. The examiner should be well informed concerning the technical merits of any test. Review of a basic text on testing (e.g., Sabatino & Miller, 1979; Salvia & Ysseldyke, 1978) and the *Standards for Educational and Psychological Tests* (1974) or a summarized discussion of it (Miller, 1979, pp. 90–93) are advised.
2. The teacher should recognize that every test score is an approximation, subject to change in interpretation for a number of reasons, and never should assume that a particular score represents the child's exact performance.
3. The teacher should select and accept only the best possible tests, since there is no guarantee they all are equally well designed; in fact, some current and widely used measures are quite shabby indeed.
4. The educator never should rely totally on formal test data, which by themselves are little more, or no more, illustrative than other (especially informal) data sources. Formal scores are useful, even quite valuable, but they are not inviolate measures of children's performance.

Who Conducts Formal Assessment?

Almost everyone who has taught in the public schools for any length of time has participated in formal assessment, at least within the definition offered here. For example, the screening of young children with readiness measures or the year-end administration of comprehensive academic evaluations constitute examples of formal assessment. In special education, much formal assessment is conducted by a complement of professionals: a resource teacher, a special educational diagnostician, a speech-language clinician, a school psychologist, or other supportive personnel. Teachers sometimes are unhappy with this arrangement, but it should be pointed out that the tests that are described in this chapter (and others) tend to be very specialized and require considerable training and experience to be beneficial. This conception is not based on the capacity to administer and score the tests, although this is a common erroneous argument. Instead, it is because adequate interpretation of the tests requires knowledge far beyond the mechanics of administration: the appropriate use of tests requires much more than mechanical knowledge.

Classroom or special education teachers may have had occasion to examine formal tests and perhaps have administered some of them. Quite possibly they have received a summary report of one sort or another, perhaps without adequate explanation of what the information meant. Therefore, the rest of this chapter focuses on tests commonly used in the formal assessment of the learning disabled child. A somewhat subjective but, the authors hope, fair appraisal to each test is presented.

SPECIFIC TESTS FOR THE LEARNING DISABLED

This section is organized under two main headings. The first part, ability assessment, concentrates on abilities commonly measured in the learning disabled child. It is further subdivided into tests associated with each of the domains—cognitive, affective, or perceptual motor. The second section focuses on tests used to measure gross academic skills, reading, spelling, and so on. Some of the tests included here may be considered by others to be more precise than global measures. However, these tests usually represent only beginning points and seldom are used for other than the most basic aspects of programming. Therefore, the authors consider them to be, at best, gross starting points.

In this chapter only the more common tests can be covered and, necessarily, very briefly. Readers therefore are advised of a few approaches that can be taken to expand on the information provided here. The test manual is an excellent source of information on the mechanics and technical adequacy of the test, but it seldom is judgmental. The manual can clarify the administration procedure of a test, how to score it and, in some cases, provide helpful clues toward interpretation, but it seldom will provide all of the desired data. Therefore it is good practice to examine critical review of tests. These reviews are detailed carefully in the *Mental Measurements Yearbook series* (e.g., Buros, 1972; 1978), a series widely available and invaluable for judging the quality of specific tests. Careful reading of the manual and a review of the particular test will go a long way toward assuring that both the child's and the teacher's time is not wasted with inadequate or inappropriate formal assessment procedures.

ABILITY ASSESSMENT

Cognitive Domain

The cognitive domain may constitute many theoretical positions but in practice it invariably refers to measurement of intelligence. Although the concept and measurement of intelligence is itself both controversial and difficult, the assessment of learning disabled children usually is accomplished with one of a very few measures. Although some studies reviewed (e.g., Hallahan & Kauffman, 1977) have found many of these students certified as having below normal intelligence, most definitions and practitioners assume normal or near normal levels as a major point of differentiation among learning disabilities and other handicaps, particularly mild mental retardation. This practice may be changing if the concept of the degree of learning disabilities becomes established (cf. Dunn, 1973) but for the immediate future a major aspect of formal assessment will be intelligence and the assumption will be largely held that this should be within the normal range.

Unfortunately, the normal range of intelligence is not precisely definable and varies depending upon the practitioner's (a) selection of a specific test, (b) guidelines provided by state and local agencies, and (c) the precision the user demands from the test. Most tests are transformed in such a way as to set a score of 100 as the average or mean score; for example, 100 is average whether the child is 6, 8, or 10 years of age. Beyond this, however, the tests' construction is an important factor because their standard deviations vary. The two most common intelligence tests have different standard deviations; the *Stanford-Binet Intelligence Scales* (Terman & Merrill, 1973) has a standard deviation of 16, and the *Wechsler Intelligence Scale for Children, Revised (WISC-R)* (Wechsler, 1974) of 15. Simply put, these tests are not numerically equatable. It also must be remembered that a given score may be considerably above or below 100 and remain within a normal range of intelligence as judged by these tests.

Both the Binet (as it is commonly termed) and the WISC or WISC-R, or "Wisker" (as it is called), should be considered global measures of intelligence. Precisely what they measure is a source of debate but they are highly related to and predictive of academic success, although somewhat less predictive of nonacademic behavior (McClelland, 1973). As an example of the factors that may be included in one common test, the *Stanford-Binet Test of Intelligence,* Sattler (1974) provides the following description:

> *Language.* This category includes tests related to maturity of vocabulary (in relation to the prekindergarten level), extent of vocabulary (referring to the number of words the child can define),

quality of vocabulary (measured by such tests as abstract words, rhymes, word naming, and definitions), and comprehension of verbal relations.

Memory. This category contains meaningful, nonmeaningful, and visual memory tests. The tests are considered to reflect rote auditory memory, ideational memory, and attention span.

Conceptual Thinking. This category, while closely associated with language ability, is primarily concerned with abstract thinking. Such functions as generalizations, assuming an "as if" attitude, conceptual thinking, and utilizing a categorical attitude are subsumed.

Reasoning. This category contains verbal and nonverbal reasoning tests. The verbal absurdity tests are the prototype for the verbal reasoning tests. The pictorial and orientation problems represent a model for the nonverbal reasoning tests. Reasoning includes the perception of logical relations, discrimination ability, and analysis and synthesis. Spatial reasoning may also be measured by the orientation tests.

Numerical Reasoning. This category includes tests involving arithmetic reasoning problems. The content is closely related to school learning. Numerical reasoning involves concentration and the ability to generalize from numerical data.

Visual-Motor. This category contains tests concerned with manual dexterity, eye-hand coordination, and perception of spatial relations. Constructive visual imagery may be involved in the paper folding test. Nonverbal reasoning ability may be involved in some of the visual-motor tests.

Social Intelligence. This category strongly overlaps with the reasoning category, so that consideration should be given to the tests classified in the latter as also reflecting social comprehension. Social intelligence includes social maturity and social judgment. The comprehension and finding reasons tests are seen to reflect social judgment, whereas obeying simple commands, response to pictures, and comparison tests likely reflect social maturity. (p. 135)

In Table 2-1, the information is organized by age and by category of information. Thus, for example, the Stanford-Binet test samples language behavior quite heavily at nearly all age levels and has relatively few items related to nonverbal reasoning. An examination of this chart for any particu-

Table 2-1 Binetgram Indicating Relative Number of Items by Each of Sattler's Categories from Stanford-Binet Test of Intelligence

BINETGRAM

Name _____ Date of testing _____ CA: _____ SD +1 ____ +2 ____ +3 ____

−1 ____ −2 ____ −3 ____

Date of birth _____ Grade _____ IQ _____ MA _____ MA: SD +1 ____ +2 ____ +3 ____

−1 ____ −2 ____ −3 ____

Instructions: 1. Circle basal year level and ceiling year level.   2. Circle all tests passed by examinee.

CATEGORIES	II	II-6	III	III-6	IV	IV-6	V	VI	VII	VIII	IX	X	XI	XII	XIII	XIV	AA	SA I	SA II	SA III	Total Tests Passed
Language	3(1) 5(2) 6(3) A	1(4) 2(5) 3(6) 4(7)	2(8)		1(9) 4(10)	A	3(11)	1(12)		1(13)	4(14) A	1(15) 3(16) 5(17)	3(18)	1(19) 5(20) 6(21)	2(22) 5(23)	1(24)	1(25) 3(26) 8(27)	1(28) 3(29) 5(30)	1(31)	1(32)	
Memory		5(1)	4(2) A		2(3)	5(4)			6(5) A	2(6)	3(7) 6(8)	6(9)	1(10) 4(11)	4(12) A	3(13) 6(14)			4(15)	6(16)	6(17)	
Conceptual Thinking					3(1)	2(2)		2(3) 5(4)	2(5) 5(6)	4(7)			6(8)			6(9)	5(10) 7(11)	6(12) A	3(13) 5(14)	2(15) 3(16) A	
Reasoning	2(1)			1(2) 2(3) 3(4) 5(5) A	5(6)	3(7)	5(8) 6(9)	3(10)		3(11)	2(12)	A	2(13)	2(14)	1(15) 4(16)	3(17) 5(18)	6(19)		2(20) A	4(21) 5(22)	
Numerical Reasoning								4(1)			5(2)	2(3)				2(4) 4(5) A	2(6) 4(7)	2(8)	4(9)		
Visual-Motor	1(1) 4(2)	A	1(3) 3(4) 5(5) 6(6)				1(7) 2(8) 4(9) A	6(10)	3(11)		1(12)		5(13) A	3(14)	A						
Social Intelligence	6(1)			4(2) 6(3)	6(4)	1(5) 4(6) 6(7)		A	1(8) 4(9)	5(10) 6(11) A				3(14)							

Source: Reprinted from *Assessment of Children's Intelligence* by J. M. Sattler by permission of W. B. Saunders Co., ©1974.

lar child should assist the teacher to recognize what was measured. But while some use may be made of this explanation, it should be noted that other, somewhat different, analyses have been offered (Meeker, 1969; Valett, 1964). Meeker's efforts are especially noteworthy and have resulted in a test, *The Structure of Intellect* (see also Chapter 8), that has promise of producing a greater knowledge of the entire cognitive domain.

Two Uses of Intelligence Measures

In practice, two uses are made of intelligence measures with the learning disabled child. The first relates to the clause of the definition of learning disabilities that the child's deficiency not be attributable to other handicapping conditions, notably mental retardation (see Chapter 1). Since an IQ that is two or more standard deviations below the mean is a necessity for the identification of mental retardation, the learning disabled child must possess an IQ greater than two or more standard deviations below the mean. On the WISC-R, this would be equal to an IQ of 70 or more and on the Binet an IQ of 68 or greater. As was mentioned, relatively few children with IQs in the bottom of this range are identified as learning disabled, but this practice is possible and surely has occurred. At any rate, the first major purpose of formal measurement of intelligence is to rule out other handicapping conditions and to establish at least near normal levels of intelligence.

The second use is far more controversial: this is to measure systematically the various abilities that may constitute intelligence and hence affect learning. There is little doubt that in the hands of a skilled clinician, perceptions concerning the manner in which a child approaches a task can be gathered during the administration of an intelligence test. Factors such as the ability to perceive tasks, to organize responses, to prefer one type of problem to another, to be cooperative and interested, to stick with a job, and to be able to cope with the pressure of timed tasks are readily observable events. But a major question here is: How accurate are these measures of the manner in which children process (act upon) information?

Rate of Development

Until quite recently a common assumption was that basic processes of learning (attention span, auditory perception, visual perception, etc.) developed very unevenly in learning disabled children. This view has been attenuated in recent years (see, for example, Ross, 1976); some learning disabled children may be very imbalanced in psychological processes while others may not. A number of authors (e.g., Bannatyne, 1968) have argued that some intelligence tests yield information on these imbalances of psychological processes and that programmatic decisions can be based on these data.

A second common function of formal assessment is to examine the strengths and weaknesses of basic psychological processes. Although this task is controversial, and may be difficult or even impossible (Ysseldyke, 1973), the WISC-R almost certainly is better suited for this purpose than any other test and therefore usually is the measure of choice for formal assessment. Accordingly, a broad discussion of this test as the primary formal cognitive measure of the learning disabled is in order.

The WISC-R

The WISC-R is one of three scales constructed by the psychologist David Wechsler. The *Wechsler Adult Intelligence Scale* (WAIS) (1955) is intended for adults while the *Wechsler Preschool or Primary Scale of Intelligence* (WPPSI) (1967) is a downward extension of the earlier (1949) WISC for very young children. The age ranges are WAIS, 16 years and up; WISC (and now WISC-R) 6 through 16, and the WPPSI, 4 to 6½. Of these tests the WISC (WISC-R) probably has been used most extensively because it spans the age range within which most learning disabled children are identified.

The WISC-R yields three intelligence quotient scores: the full scale, verbal scale, and performance scale. All three scores have a mean (average) of 100; those higher than 100 represent better than average performance and those lower than 100 indicate poorer than average. The full scale score is a composite or summary of both the verbal and performance scores, each of which is organized around six distinct subtests. The verbal scale contains subtests on information, comprehension, similarities, arithmetic, vocabulary, and digit span. The performance scale contains subtests on picture completion, picture arrangement, block designs, object assembly, codings, and mazes. Interpretation of these subtests varies, although an excellent and thorough analysis of the meaning of those of the WISC-R has been provided by Gustavson (1978).

Although many interpretive frameworks exist for the WISC-R, many authorities consider the verbal scale to be closely related to language behavior and highly influenced by the effects of past educational experience. The performance scale is seen as more heavily involved with perceptual and perceptual-motor tasks and to be more dependent on the formulation of problem solving strategies than upon formal academic training. Moreover, the performance tests rely quite heavily upon speed, the child attaining higher scores if the problem is solved correctly *and* quickly. Exhibit 2-1 provides an analysis of WISC-R IQ scores based upon Gustavson's (1978) analysis. It is important to point out that that analysis is clear and seems to have both accuracy and utility as guidelines. Therefore, the teacher may find this schema useful in the interpreting programs.

Exhibit 2-1 Analysis of IQ Scores Derived from the WISC-R

I. Verbal IQ significantly above Performance IQ (15–20 points or more)
  A. Verbal IQ high (130–140) and Performance IQ average suggests academic and intellectual orientation, not much motor or performance orientation; that is, not much of a doer.
  B. Verbal IQ average or above (although this varies greatly) and Performance IQ low (80s, although this, too, may vary) suggests:
    1. Depression or depressive conditions, particularly if the performance subtests are down owing to a general slowness of the subject and verbalizations allude to self-punishment.
    2. With particularly low (7 or under) scaled scores in block design, coding, object assembly, and picture arrangement—organic brain damage in the right hemisphere is suggested; physiological immaturity; and/or poor eye-hand coordination involving the visual-motor area of the brain.
    3. With particularly low scaled scores in digit span, coding, arithmetic, and block design—anxiety and tension states.
II. Performance IQ significantly above Verbal IQ
  A. Performance IQ average or above (although this varies greatly) and Verbal IQ slightly below average suggests:
    1. A performance-oriented doer with limited verbal ability.
    2. Acting out and/or delinquent tendencies, especially if accompanied by impulsive, aggressive, or destructive verbalizations.
    3. Marked verbal problems and motor performance strength.
    4. Organic brain damage in left cerebral hemisphere.
    5. Cultural deprivation or impoverishment.
III. Similarity between Verbal and Performance IQ
  A. Both Verbal and Performance IQ high (130+) suggests:
    1. A powerful problem solver with equal strength in most areas of problem solving.
    2. Tremendous intellectual ability and potential.
  B. Verbal and Performance IQ low (below 75) with all scale scores below 7 or 8 suggests mental retardation.
IV. Wide intersubtest variability or scatter
  A. Each scaled score differing 5 or more points from each other suggests:

Exhibit 2-1 continued

> 1. Specific learning disability.
> 2. Emotional disturbance or maladjustment.
> V. Certain measures may be derived by the combination and analysis of certain subtests:
>   A. Spatial—picture arrangement, block design, object assembly.
>   B. Conceptual—comprehension, similarities, vocabulary.
>   C. Sequencing—coding, digit span, picture arrangement.
>   D. Concentration—arithmetic, digit span.
>   E. Academic—information, arithmetic, vocabulary.
>
> *Source:* Reprinted from *A Brief Analysis of the Subtests of the Wechsler Scale for Children—Revised* by J. L. Gustavson by permission of the Department of Educational Psychology Semester Project, Brigham Young University, Provo, Utah, 1978, and of C. F. Ingram as the material appeared in *Fundamentals of Educational Assessment,* Van Nostrand Co., Inc., ©1980.

The Use of Variables

The extent of possible variables that can be investigated in the study of cognition and the ways that they can be interpreted are legion. As should be evident from earlier discussion and from Table 2-1 and Exhibit 2-1, interpretations of cognition may be considered to be quite different even when identical data are compared. Sabatino (in press) has examined this issue in detail and concludes that cognitive assessment is a difficult though feasible task that not only aids in the differentiation of handicaps but also yields instructional implications.

For the learning handicapped child, excessive scatter or unevenness among the various aspects of cognition often are seen as containing data for the existence of a disability and as information that may alter the course of instruction. In practice, this belief is tested by examination of variance within the subtests of the WISC-R. Excessive scatter (by no means an easy judgment, see Salvia and Ysseldyke, 1978, pp. 407–433) within a profile (graph) of cognitive abilities may be taken as evidence of information processing problems. In addition, some authors (e.g., Bannatyne, 1968; Keogh & Hall, 1973) have proposed that specific patterns of scatter may indicate certain types or origins of a learning disability, that is, specific learning strengths and weaknesses. A hypothetical plot of such scattered response of abilities in comparison to other responses is presented in Figure 2-2.

A skilled psychometrician might use these data to ascertain the nature of information processing (broadly, how the child's cognitive structure responds to presented information) and thereby assist in the development of an instructional program. The overall attempt would be to match a learning

Figure 2-2 Hypothetical Profiles of Test Score Scatter on WISC-R

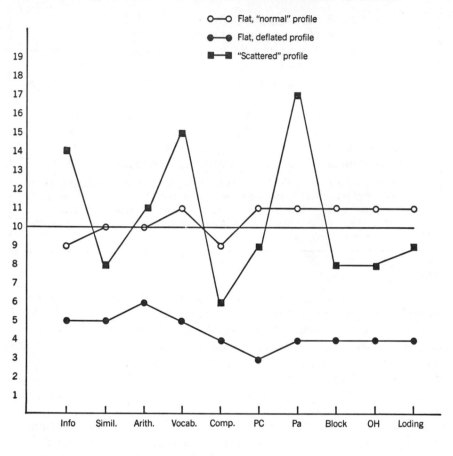

SUBTESTS OF WISC-R

Source: Reprinted from *Manual for the Wechsler Intelligence Scale for Children—Revised* by David Wechsler by permission of The Psychological Corporation, © 1974.

characteristic to a treatment approach. Such an effort is referred to as an aptitude (learner characteristics) by treatment (teaching approach) interaction (match). Some authors (e.g., Ysseldyke, 1973) have been critical of this approach for special education since aptitude by treatment interactions thus far has been difficult to isolate.

Nevertheless, profiling of abilities from the WISC-R continues for learning disabled children, although it now is conducted far more as a component of identification than for programming. The teacher is advised to listen to any recommendations that may emerge from such ability profiles, to consider and perhaps explore the possible ramifications, and to collect systematic data to verify the outcomes of modified instruction. However, the teacher is ill advised to adhere dogmatically to the outcomes of process measures taken from the profiling of ability scatter from formal measures of intelligence.

Affective Domain

Learning disabled children tend to experience considerable social-emotional disorders. They often find it difficult to be friendly, they may be unhappy, they may find it difficult to interact with others. As a group, these children do not respond well to stress or frustration and tend to be prone to temper outbursts that may be verbally or physically destructive. Some studies (e.g., Bryan, 1977; Bryan & Bryan, 1978) suggest that classmates, parents, and teachers tend to evaluate learning disabled children negatively and often wish to disassociate themselves from them. There also is evidence that these children are less task oriented and therefore prone to classroom disruptions.

The list of possible social-emotional problems is extensive but the mostly commonly cited are summarized by Wallace and McLoughlin (1975) as (a) extreme dependence on adults, (b) poor self-concept, (c) distractibility, (d) perseverant behavior, (e) disruptive behavior through physical acts, (f) emotional withdrawal, and (g) excessive activity (hyperactivity). It must be stressed, however, that virtually every social-emotional problem at some time has been suggested as a component of the handicap that is termed learning disability (Chapter 10).

Measurement for Identification

As is the case in cognitive assessment, measurement of the affective domain is used more often to provide identification than for programming information. Should the child be highly disorganized, similar characteristics may lead the practitioner to conclude that the particular individual is behaviorally disordered rather than learning disabled. Differentiation is one far more of degree than of specific behavior because the potential behaviors greatly overlap between these exceptionalities (Hallahan & Kauffman, 1977). The instrumentation associated with establishing distinctions in affective development also is far less completely developed and therefore more subjective.

The measurement of affective development in learning disabled children tends to fall in part to the teacher because of the characteristics of the procedures used. In the vast majority of cases, formal measures can be classified as either checklists or rating scales. Checklists simply are lists of behavior that an individual familiar with the child is asked to complete, usually simply by checking whether the conduct does or does not exist. Rating scales are similar but attempt to gather additional information by evaluating the behavior on a bipolar scale, such as from "sometimes" to "frequently," from "little trouble" to "major problems," and the like. Both approaches are summaries based on past experiences and are not tests in the sense of being a set of stimuli for response. Those who know the child best usually complete the forms; in practice, this often is the teacher.

The most common examples of checklists or rating scale approaches for ascertaining the social-emotional characteristics of learning disabled children include the *Burks Behavior Rating Scales* (Burks, 1969); *Devereux Adolescent Rating Scale* (Spivack & Spotts, 1966), *Quay-Peterson Checklist* (Quay & Peterson, 1967), *Vineland Social Maturity Scale* (Doll, 1965), and the *Walker Behavior Problem Checklist* (Walker, 1970).

All of these scales may be considered to be screening instruments; that is, these forms are useful for identifying potential problems and, in some cases, types of problems. Any of them will provide a broad appraisal of the social-emotional characteristics cited as potential problem areas for the learning disabled. But the scales are not intended for extensive diagnosis or treatment planning and should not be used for this.

Use of the Sociogram Technique

Since the learning disabled student often is isolated socially, the sociogram technique is used frequently to judge this characteristic. This approach attempts to look at the method of social interaction within a particular location—for example, a classroom. At least two variations are possible. In the first variation students are asked to indicate the child they would like to be with in a specified or unspecified activity. Peer nominations are counted and the resulting distributions can be used to identify the children who are isolated. Since such scales tend to be influenced by the social desirability of responses, a second variation simply counts the observable interaction of the group, and an equivalent but more readily verifiable pool of information is attained.

The final technique is the self-report measure. As the name implies, these are reports made by the individual concerning feelings or opinions about some set of questions. Although this technique can measure any number of characteristics, it probably is used most extensively with learning disabled children in evaluating self-concept. Self-concepts may be thought of as the impression one has of one's abilities and competence and is related to achievement, probably as both an effect and, subsequently, as a cause.

Given that learning disabled children experience excessive school failure, it is little wonder that low self-concept is a frequent affective component and often inhibits future academic performance. Although self-concept can be inferred directly, it often is measured through the self-report procedure. The *Piers-Harris Children's Self Concept Scale* (Piers & Harris, 1969) and the *Tennessee Self Concept Scale* (Fitts, 1965) are commonly used for this function. The teacher may expect to see results from both of these measures.

In sum, the assessment of affective disorders in learning disabled children is conducted largely to rule out some severe disturbances and, to a lesser extent, to identify some specific characteristics of a particular pupil for programming purposes. A variety of approaches can be used but the problems associated with the measurement of "personality" are so legion that schools may be reluctant to undertake the task through formal assessment. Instead, they often use specific target assessment. This approach can be considered informal assessment and is discussed in Chapter 3.

Perceptual Motor Domain

Perception and perceptual motor deficiences have long been associated with learning disabilities. Perception is a cognitive process that gives meaning to sensation; perceptual motor activities are those that link the perception of events with motor-based responses. The clinical study of perception invariably concentrates on visual, auditory, or haptic perception (sensation, touch). All three are essential for proper learning but visual perception is by far the most studied and evaluated, while haptic perception almost never is included in formal assessment and therefore is not discussed in this chapter.

A central issue dominates the study of perceptual deficiencies in the learning disabled child, that is, the pupil's use of a preferred perceptual modality: Does the child learn best through information presented visually? Auditorily? Does the child have the capacity for cross-modal perception (the simultaneous interpretation of information from two or more perceptual channels)?

Although current research data suggest limits to the extent that the phenomena can now be measured by formal tests, there is substantially less doubt that some children do in fact have perceptual deficiencies that force compensation through alternative modalities. Such children may not be able to comprehend information when it is presented too rapidly, through a single modality, or simultaneously through two or more modalities. Ascertaining the status of a child is important for identification and, in some cases, essential for programming.

As might be expected, the assessment of perceptual deficiencies is a difficult task. Among the more common tests for the measurement of visual perception are the *Bender Visual-Motor Gestalt Test* (Bender, 1938), the *Developmental Test of Visual Motor Integration* (Beery & Buktenica, 1967), the *Frostig Developmental Test of Visual Motor Integration* (Frostig, Maslow, Lefever, & Whittlesey, 1964), and subtests of the *Detroit Tests of Learning Aptitude* (Baker & Leland, 1959). Of these tests, the first three probably are the more common, perhaps because of their apparently simple administration (none of the three is truly simple to score *and* apply). The *Detroit* (as it often is termed) is difficult to administer and score, and interpretation may pose more problems than many other tests. Generally, formats for visual perceptual tests vary considerably, but most emphasize drawing experience and thereby actually are visual perceptual motor tasks.

Auditory perception usually is taken to consist of discrimination, association, memory, and blending. Discrimination is the ability to recognize similarities and differences in sounds and words. Auditory association refers to the capacity to associate sounds with references; for example, the child can associate a barking sound with a dog, a whistle with a train, and so. Auditory memory is the child's capability of recalling information that is presented through the auditory channel. Finally, auditory blending is the ability to blend disordered sounds into a word (duh-o-g—dog).

As in the case of visual perception, several tests predominate in the assessment of learning disabled students. The *Goldman-Fristoe-Woodcock Test of Auditory Discrimination* (Goldman, Fristoe, & Woodcock, 1970) has the unique feature of measuring auditory discrimination in quiet and noisy backgrounds through the use of taped records. The *Auditory Discrimination Test* (Wepman, 1958) is a simple and quick-to-administer measure of the auditory discrimination of sounds (phonemes) attached to sound-alike words (up—cup). The *Roswell-Chall Auditory Blending Test* (Roswell & Chall, 1963) is a measure of ability to blend phonic sounds into complete words. Selected subtests of the *Illinois Test of Psycholinguistic Abilities* (Kirk, McCarthy, & Kirk, 1965) measure auditory and sequential blending of sounds. These tests, components of intelligence and achievement tests, and some others (e.g., *Carrow Elicited Language Inventory,* Carrow, 1974; *Northwestern Syntax Screening Test,* Lee, 1969; *Peabody Picture Vocabulary Test,* Dunn, 1965) can provide the main elements of the formal educational assessment of language. Those interested in a comprehensive review of language disabilities should consult Wiig and Semel (1976).

Several common problems are revealed in the existing measures of both visual and auditory perception:

1. The number of tests is relatively limited, and they have received extensive, largely nonsupportive, analysis.
2. Most of the existing tests have narrow age ranges that leave them at best useful only for young children (generally below age 10).
3. Most "perceptual" tests, while easy to administer and score, require extensive training to interpret and, even then, are quite subjective.

Thus the formal assessment of visual and auditory perception is difficult and may not represent a substantial gain for the teacher from what can be conjectured through informal means, such as watching the child at work in the classroom.

As pointed out earlier, most visual perceptual tests are in fact visual perceptual motor tests. However, motor tasks may be considered either fine or gross motor and tests may be selected for measuring either fine or gross motor coordination. Perhaps the most comprehensive test is the *Purdue Perceptual Motor Survey* (Roach & Kephart, 1966), which assesses both fine and gross motor capacity. The *Lincoln-Osertsky Motor Development Scale* (Sloan, 1955) may be used in a similar capacity. Components of the *McCarthy Scales of Children's Abilities* (McCarthy, 1972) may be used for selected components of perceptual motor development.

Preschool Screening

Preschool screening actually is a synthesis of measures of many possible abilities and skills. It is placed in this section because it tends to synthesize data from all of the domains of ability; it also may measure additionally learned behaviors and achievement. The majority of these measures are easily and quickly administered and scored and none are intended to provide more than an indication of potential problem areas. When these tests are applied to older children in the general age range of preschool screening (about 5 in a range from near birth to about 6), the measures are called tests of readiness. At around 6 years of age, the tests tend to evidence more group-administered items and to reflect more learned than strictly developmental skills. It can be understood, then, why it is difficult to classify this group of tests as more "ability" or "skill" in nature or to conclude that they are predominantly individually or group administered.

Denver Developmental Screening Test

Typical of the tests administered to children from preschool screening is the *Denver Developmental Screening Test* (DDST) (Frankenburg, Dodds, & Fandel, 1970). This is norm referenced, multiple skill, and individually administered, usually in less than 20 minutes. The test is useful from birth to 6 years of age and measures performance in four areas: personal-social development, fine motor development, language development, and gross motor development.

The scores indicate delayed or abnormal development. All items are scored as passed, failed, passed by report, refused, or no opportunity. As might be expected, the examiner's judgment is critical. The norms for the DDST are at best fair. Evidence of reliability might be regarded as adequate, given the screening purpose of the test. Validity data would necessarily be inferred from the composite of the test, i.e., the fact that it was developed from well-known scales of development. Evidence for validity is not stated in the manual.

Preschool Inventory

The *Preschool Inventory* (PI) (Caldwell, 1970) is designed for children in the age range from 3 to 6 years. It can be administered in less than 15 minutes and provides measures on skills commonly developed or acquired in this age range. The test essentially is norm referenced, and interpretation is accomplished through the use of percentile scores. The sample of children was small and was drawn from Head Start classes. Given these facts and the relatively small behavioral sample, the test cannot be considered for use beyond a very superficial screening level.

Boehm Test of Basic Concepts

The *Boehm Test of Basic Concepts* (BTBC) (Boehm, 1971) is a norm referenced, group-administered device that measures abstract concepts, e.g., "next to," "above," "below," and so on. In the test, the child responds to a picture stimulus and the examiner's verbal direction. The student's response is indicated by marking the picture that best illustrated the examiner's statement. Two forms of the test are available, in each of which the child responds to 25 items, each a distinct concept. The test requires about 15 minutes to administer and is scored easily.

Although the BTBC contains norms and raw scores and may be converted to percentiles, the test is best considered a criterion referenced measure. Thus, its usefulness as a screening device will rest upon the assumption that virtually all questions should be answered correctly. That is, without norms, users must determine that all, or at least a specific number of, concepts must be understood prior to school entrance. The examiner or school system must study entrance requirements before the test can be useful as a screening instrument.

Tests of Basic Experience

The *Tests of Basic Experiences* (TBE) (Moss, 1972) are designed to measure the conceptual background of children from preschool through first grade. The tests are group administered and are intended to determine how well the child's background has prepared the pupil for scholastic activities. Four tests are included in the battery: language, mathematics, science, and social science. The four subtests are complemented by an overall score termed the General Concepts Test. Two age levels are available and either may be administered in about 25 minutes. The raw score outcome may be transformed to stanines, percentiles, and standard scores. The battery is designed to yield information about the child and about the characteristics of the class. The latter may be especially helpful to kindergarten and first grade teachers.

Unfortunately, the standardization procedure is not appropriate in some aspects and the teacher can attach only moderate faith to the norms provided. However, this in fact is the status of most screening instruments and, while it must be taken into account, many teachers will tend to use the test as a criterion reference measure. Therefore, the essential issue is validity and, to the extent that the items are judged to parallel the curriculum of the following year, the test may be useful. It would be well to remember, however, that extreme caution should be given to any conclusion reached concerning readiness or the prediction of future achievement. These comments are equally true of the other tests cited in this section and, in fact, point to the problems that emerge when screening is undertaken.

Summary: Ability Assessment

There is little doubt that ability assessment plays a unique role in the evaluation of the learning disabled. However, recent years have seen that role change from one largely of programmatic importance to one largely of identification. Controversy surrounds ability assessment, whether of cognitive, affective, or perceptual motor skills, and it is undetermined at this time whether existing scales are appropriate for this task. Along with this change in purpose came a shift in the measurement procedures most frequently used by teachers, for educators are involved with programming above all else.

At this point, although teachers are largely consumers of measures of ability, their use of these data is only intermittent. It is likely, however, that some useful programming information can be drawn from formal measures of ability, and certainly identification procedures are inextricably linked to them. The essential information emerges in the interpretation offered by the experienced clinician who presumably is well grounded in the theoretical aspects of the ability being measured. In the authors' estimation, all collected information, especially formal measures, should receive the teacher's attention and consideration. But such information—in fact, no single source—should be allowed to dictate the approaches chosen for instruction.

SKILL MEASURES

Formal Measures: Academic Skills

Although not free from concern, the global measurement of academic skills is perhaps theoretically sounder than that of the assessment of abilities. This is so because the subject of measurement is less a conceptual construct to explain behavior and more an outcome measure of where the child now stands in relation to necessary learned skills. As with ability measures, formal measures of general academic skills usually are norm referenced standardized tests.

However, there is one important difference: ability assessment almost always is conducted through individually administered tests, while general academic achievement could be evaluated through tests that are either group administered or individually administered (or, preferably, both). This potential option requires some attention to test characteristics, their purposes, and their capacities.

The Measurement Paradox

Unfortunately, a paradox exists in achievement assessment because several of the formal group batteries are of greater technical capacity than are individually administered tests. This presents a problem, for even though several group tests are virtual models of the formal approach to measurement, the characteristics of learning disabled children demand that individually administered measures be given as primary sources of information. Most persons and most texts, in fact, do not suggest the use of group tests with learning disabled students. However, the authors take exception because the technical inadequacy of individual assessment demands consideration of the use of group tests, at least to a limited complementary extent.

There are several reasons for advocating the use of both types of tests, at least contemporarily (although this situation could change quickly as new, well-developed, comprehensive, individual achievement tests emerge and are accepted in the battery for learning disabled students). One factor is the rationale given for the use of individually administered tests, namely, that the close proximity of an adult allows optimal performance and ensures that the student is attending to and perceiving the items on the test. Such topics as establishing rapport, external pacing, and direct person-to-person contact are often-discussed and often-researched topics. It often is suggested that an individually administered test provides an opportunity for obtaining a structured set of observations.

There is little doubt that, to at least some extent, the examiner can determine how the task is received, how it is approached, and how it is resolved or failed. Critical factors such as timing, number of required explanations, ability to remain at the task, general interest, and cooperation can be judged. This information allows the formation of instructional hypotheses and if they are carried through systematically in informal evaluation, then facts of some importance to instruction can emerge. Obviously, these points are well taken, and it remains true that most of them cannot be accomplished with group tests. But it also is true that individually administered tests are ill suited to probe the extent of knowledge. Group tests are better suited if the student can approach the tests. To see why, a brief technical excursion is necessary.

All norm referenced tests represent samples of potential items within a topic, e.g., general achievement. For this sample to be useful as a measure of performance, the outcome scores must be consistent and accurate. Those with prior knowledge of formal testing will see that this is leading to the psychometric ideas of reliability and validity.

Briefly, reliability is the consistency of test scores. Naturally this is important because the scores should be accurate across time so that any differences reflect true changes. No test is ever totally reliable but some are more so than others. But, even if a test is reliable, it may or may not be valid. Simply put, a valid test is one that measures whatever it claims it measures. Reliability can be estimated in several ways but the essential task is to demonstrate consistency. Validity, on the other hand, is not a singular notion; there are several types, or indicators, and each may be estimated in several ways. For achievement tests, content validity is of fundamental importance because it is a direct measure of the test's relationship to the content of the task being evaluated.

The Point of the Exercise

Now comes the point of the technical excursion. All things being equal, the longer the test (the more items), the greater is reliability. Similarly, the more items on a test, the better educators can study the knowledge (content) gaps that a student may possess: the more questions that are asked, the more certain teachers can be of their knowledge of the depth and spread of the student's achievement. Theoretically, this could be done with either group or individual achievement tests but, in practice, individual tests have been limited to few questions and short time limits while group tests tend to be longer and to request more information.

Therefore if adequate responses to the test can be received, the results are superior diagnostically; if not, the results are useful only for constructing hierarchies for informal tests. But that, too, is very important, as is shown in Chapter 3. Either way, whether used as formal tests or as guides to hierarchies in informal tests, the group instruments and their technical sophistication demand that they receive attention despite the current practice of overlooking their merits.

Some final distinctions must be made before formal measures of academic ability are examined. As noted, formal measures may be considered to be either group or individually administered, but achievement measures also may be regarded as (1) more or less useful as screening or diagnostic devices, as (2) predominantly norm referenced or criterion referenced, and as (3) single or multiple skill measures. Screening devices are very global instruments designed to sample (usually briefly) the many skills a pupil has acquired. This may be a single ability or a group of skills. Diagnostic devices are intended to identify specific strengths and weaknesses, again either singly or as a group of skills.

Criterion referenced testing (CRT) is an interpretive framework that draws meaning from comparing a child's performance to a hierarchy of skills. Thus, a performance is not specified compared to others (e.g., grade equivalence, percentiles) but to position in the instructional sequence (skill hierarchy). As might be expected, such an approach is quite useful for educational diagnosis, and indeed the CRT approach forms the backbone of informal assessment. In fact, it has proved so useful since its beginning in the early 1960s that it has since become a part of several important formal measures used with learning disabled children. But it, too, is not without flaws (lengthy administration, difficulties in establishing skill hierarchies, few direct ways to establish quality of the tests, and so on) and therefore should be considered as an inclusive but not exclusive practice in the assessment of the learning disabled child.

With these distinctions in mind, the rest of this chapter concentrates on examining achievement tests by their respective characteristics. Necessarily, only the more common tests are discussed. This review proceeds under headings that cluster tests along the dimensions of group vs. individually administered, and screening vs. diagnostics. Each test is classified as single or multiple skill and as norm referenced, criterion referenced or, in some cases, both.

Group Administered: Screening

A number of test batteries can be classified as group administered units for screening. None of the tests described here are useful for preschool screening because young children typically are measured more accurately by individually administered tests. Of the tests discussed here, all are multiple skill, although the skills that are measured vary somewhat; only one, *Stanford Achievement Test* (Madden, Gardner, Rodman, Karlson, & Merwin, 1973), contains a criterion referenced component. The *Iowa Test of Basic Skills* (Hieronymous & Lindquist, 1974) and the *Metropolitan Achievement Test* (Durost, Bixler, Wrightstone, Prescott, & Balow, 1971) and other common tests qualify for this category and are in wide use, but only two exemplary models are reviewed as illustrative of this category.

California Achievement Test (CAT)

The CAT (Tiegs & Clarke, 1970) measures achievement in three general skill areas: reading, mathematics, and language. Reading is divided further into vocabulary and comprehension; mathematics into computation, concepts, and problems; language ability into mechanics, spelling, usage, and structure. The test is useful for grades 1.5 to 12. Five distinct forms are employed, one for each of five specific grade ranges (level 1 for grades 1.5 to 2.0, level 2 for grades 2 to 4, etc.). The examiner must be careful to provide the correct level and to note which of the two available forms of the test are used.

The CAT is a timed test and can be relatively lengthy to administer; in the longest possible case it can require slightly more than two and a half hours plus administration time (totaling well over three hours). As might be expected, the number of items and the time allotted to solving them varies from level to level. The CAT is considered a good example of a test of its type. Within reason it conforms to the standards for such tests and the user can place considerable confidence in it as a screening device of academic difficulty. It offers scores of several different types (percentiles and grade equivalents are included), two of which are unique to the test and may be somewhat suspect, as they frequently are quite high, producing an inflated grade achievement score.

Stanford Achievement Test (SAT)

The SAT is perhaps even more comprehensive than the CAT. Eleven separate subtests are provided: vocabulary; reading comprehension; word study skills; mathematics concepts, computation, and application; spelling; language; social sciences; science; and listening comprehension. The test is useful for grades 1.5 to 9.5 and is organized on six levels and three alternate forms (A, B, C). The cautions concerning levels and forms for the CAT also apply for the SAT.

The price that must be paid for the comprehensive measures of the SAT is administration time. Even though each subtest is timed, the total battery can require as long as 320 minutes plus administration time. This certainly will necessitate several sessions in the case of many learning disabled children. However, a number of factors may make the "price" more palatable.

- The SAT is an excellent test, perhaps the very best in the group administered achievement field.

- The SAT is both norm referenced (with the usual scores presented) and criterion referenced in the sense that specific test items are related to specific instructional objectives provided for the teacher.

- The test is comprehensive and allows measurement of some topics (e.g., science) that often are overlooked.

- The SAT, as alluded to above, is one of those most useful to classroom teachers because of its emphasis on instructional implications. This results in no small part from its exceptionally complete manual, for this document that is specific by age level contains directions for administration, complete normative data, technical reports, and a teacher guide for interpretation. The last three items are unusual and desirable.

- The SAT, even beyond all this, offers special editions for the blind and deaf.

- The SAT makes practice tests available.

- The SAT publisher can provide machine scoring, an analysis of individual standards (or classes), local norms, and a variety of other unique diagnostic functions.

Given the superb technology of the test and the wide range of extras available from the publisher, the SAT is one group test that should be given very strong consideration by the teacher of learning disabled children.

Group Administered Diagnostic Tests

Surprisingly few tests exist under the general definition of this heading. Of those that do and that may prove useful to special education teachers, the *Stanford Diagnostic Reading Test* (SDRT) probably would be the most common. The test is similar to the SAT in that it consists of two forms in four levels (red, green, brown, blue) that are based on grade approximations. The test is different, however, in that it is intended to be a diagnostic device and therefore is limited to measurement of a single skill.

The four domains that are measured are decoding, vocabulary, comprehension, and rate (rate is included in only the higher—brown and blue—levels). Accordingly, since some domains are omitted within levels and some contain more than one test, levels vary from five to seven in the number of specific subtests available. Overall, the subtests include the following: auditory vocabulary, auditory discrimination, phonetic analysis, structural analysis, word reading, reading comprehension, and rate of reading.

The SDRT, like the SAT, is both norm referenced and criterion referenced. Six types of scores can be obtained and many of the special services offered for the SAT also can be obtained for the SDRT. Because great care was taken to sequence the skills within each test, the teacher can use it very effectively in planning instruction. Coupled with the fact that the test conforms to the highest standards of design, the teacher who is certain that the learning disabled child approached it appropriately will find it to be an especially useful assessment device.

Individually Administered Achievement Tests: Screening

Of the tests that could be included in this category, two are exceptionally prevalent, even predominant. The *Wide Range Achievement Test* (WRAT) (Jastak & Jastak, 1965) and the *Peabody Individual Achievement Test* (PIAT) (Dunn & Markwardt, 1970) are quick to administer and score and are quite global in nature. Because of their prevalence in use with learning disabled children, a brief discussion of each is in order.

Wide Range Achievement Test

The WRAT is a norm referenced, multiple skill, quick screening instrument. Reading, spelling, and arithmetic are assessed in one of two levels, the first for children under 12, the second for those over 12. To a considerable degree the screening nature of the test compromises the meaning of the traits or academic achievement skill areas that are sampled: reading equates to letter and word recognition; spelling to copying marks, writing one's name, and writing words that are dictated by the examiner; arithmetic to counting, reading numerals, answering oral problems, and performing written problems. As may be seen, the screening orientation of the test forces divergence away from some important aspects of academic assessment for each skill; for example, comprehension is not measured at all.

Three scores are available from the WRAT: grade equivalents, percentiles, and standard scores (mean = 100 and standard deviation = 15, analogous to the standard scores of the WISC-R). Technically, the WRAT can be faulted for two reasons: (1) its normative sample is quite small; (2) its behavioral sample of items is simply inadequate for many purposes and there are too few items for the test to be sensitive to faulty learning in children's abilities. In fairness, this is the price that screening extracts because few items equate to rapid administration. But when the WRAT or similar tests are used exclusively in place of comprehensive measures (paradoxically, comprehensive group measures such as obtained from the CAT) for placement or programming, a disservice to handicapped children results. Teachers would be well advised to request more achievement test data than are contained in the WRAT or, for that matter, other screening devices.

Peabody Individual Achievement Test (PIAT)

The PIAT is strictly a norm referenced, individually administered global measure of achievement. It sometimes is considered to be diagnostic, probably because it provides samples of behavior through five subtests: mathematics, reading recognition, reading comprehension, spelling, and general information (see Figure 2-3). The last subtest is unique and measures some aspects of social science, science, fine arts, and sports, i.e., very common experiences for most children. The test is normed for kindergarten through grade 12 and, since it is a screening device with few items, behavioral samples for most children are extremely limited. Thus the criticisms of the WRAT when used as more than a screening device also apply to the PIAT.

The PIAT provides four interpretive scores: age equivalence, grade equivalence, percentile ranks, and standard scores (mean = 100, standard deviation = 15). Overall, the technical adequacy of the PIAT is roughly equivalent to the WRAT, and both the norming population and the behavioral sample are relatively small. Technical indexes probably place the PIAT in an acceptable range for screening but, again like the WRAT, it probably should not be used for truly diagnostic purposes. Teachers should be cautious of the data obtained from it and should consider these data as only an approximation of behavior and as points for continued assessment.

Individual Administered Tests: Specific Diagnostic

Specific diagnostic tests are, virtually by definition, domain specific. Although other tests exist in this category, two instruments are especially illustrative and prevalent in the academic diagnostics applied to learning disabled children: the *Woodcock Reading Mastery Tests* (Woodcock, 1973) and the *Key Math Diagnostic Arithmetic Test* (Connolly, Nachtman, & Pritchett, 1971). Both tests provide exceptionally thorough screening for academic deficiency and are capable of the initial steps of diagnosis. Further,

Figure 2-3 Scoresheet for PIAT

PiƏt

by Lloyd M. Dunn, Ph.D. and Frederick C. Markwardt, Jr., Ph.D.

NAME_____ SEX: M F
(last)   (first)   (middle initial)   (circle)

SCHOOL_____
(or agency or address)

PROFILE

TEACHER_____
(or counselor or supervisor)

EXAMINER_____

TESTING TIME_____GRADE_____CODE_____
(min.)   (or phone) (or race or descent)

Profile columns: Adjusted M.A. | Chronological Age | Grade Placement | Mathematics | Reading Recognition | Reading Comprehension | Spelling | General Information | Total Test | Percentile Rank | I.Q. Score

AGE DATA

Date of testing_____ _____ _____
(year)   (month)   (day)

Date of birth _____ _____ _____
(year)   (month)   (day)

Age at testing _____ _____
(years)   (months)

TEST SCORES

NORMS RECORDED (Check one) ....▶ ☐ Age ☐ Grade

▼SUBTESTS	Raw Scores	Equivalents	Percentile Ranks	Standard Scores
Mathematics ▶				
Reading Recognition ▶				
Reading Comprehension ▶				
Spelling ▶				
General Information ▶				
Total Test ▶				

Circle the equivalent and/or percentile rank scores plotted on the profile.

INTELLIGENCE TEST DATA

▼NAME OF TEST	Date at testing	I.Q. Score	Adjusted M.A.

Note: See Part I of the Manual on calculating adjusted M.A.

Note: To assess the significance of difference between subtest scores consult the reliability section of Part IV of the Manual.

Published by
AMERICAN GUIDANCE SERVICE, INC. • Publishers' Building, Circle Pines, Minn. 55014

Source: Reprinted from *Peabody Individual Achievement Test* by Lloyd M. Dunn and Frederick C. Markwardt, Jr., by permission of American Guidance Service, Inc., ©1970.

because of their design, both provide an exceptionally good basis from which informal diagnosis (Chapter 3) can proceed.

Woodcock Reading Mastery Tests (WRMT)

The WRMT consists of five individually administered tests covering the public school years K–12. Two alternate forms (A and B) are available and the entire battery can be administered in about 45 minutes. The five specific tests are letter identification, word identification, word attack, word comprehension, and passage comprehension (Figure 2-4). The WRMT does not require extensive training to administer or score, although special attention should be given to the manual because scoring and plotting the test profile can be confusing at first. Four common scoring frameworks exist (grade scores, age scores, percentiles, and standard scores). A fifth, a mastery score, provides a measure of mastery (e.g., 75 percent) at various grades. The test is designed to allow the measurement of performance across subtests as well as a total index to reading and to report all scores in any of the available interpretive frameworks.

Technically, the WRMT is marginally adequate as a norm referenced instrument. The manual is at least adequate and certainly straightforward in drawing the examiner's attention to the test's areas of strength, but its appeal lies in its suitability for adaptation to instruction. For this purpose it is clearer than many tests and may form the basis both for further assessment and, in some cases, for direct programming.

Key Math Diagnostic Arithmetic Test (KM)

The KM is an individually administered diagnostic test of arithmetic. It is similar in format to the *Woodcock Reading Mastery Test,* although it is intended for use only for kindergarten through the eighth grade. Fourteen separate subtests are organized under three areas of academic achievement—content, operations, and applications. The test is relatively simple to administer (about half an hour) and score and provides useful information at four levels: total test, area (e.g., content) performance, subtest performance, and item performance. Although all levels are useful, fewer items (and hence less information) are provided as the teacher works down the levels (e.g., total test to item).

Total test performance is analyzed thoroughly by means of grade equivalent scores. The examiner may analyze any score further across areas or within areas or may look at individual scores and compare performance on them to the specific behavioral requirements stated in the manual. This latter procedure probably will be of most interest to the teacher but it actually is a criterion referenced procedure more akin to informal than formal assessment. In fact, it represents the initial styles of informal assessment of arithmetic described in Chapter 3.

Technically the development of the Key Math is only fair if the test is to be considered as a norm referenced instrument. The sample is small and the standardization procedure not optimal. However, the strength of the KM lies not in its norms but in its use as a criterion referenced test. It therefore is valuable for educational diagnosis—its intended purpose—but probably less useful as an identification procedure where, for example, the Stanford (SAT) would be more appropriate.

BEST USE OF FORMAL ASSESSMENT INFORMATION

There are several cautions and emphases that can help the teacher use formal measures to the greatest possible benefit without exceeding that undefined boundary where data are too speculative. Put another way, there are some approaches that can and should be applied to all formal measures that can help the teacher stretch the effectiveness of any test. This section explores some of those possibilities.

The Psychometric Approach

First, the teacher must recognize the strengths and weaknesses of the formal psychometric approach to the measurement of children's abilities and skills.

As has been pointed out, the formal approach has been both attacked and defended in recent years. An essential argument tends to get lost in the technical foray, namely, the purpose of the test. If a test serves a screening or identification function in either the realm of abilities or skills development, a norm referenced instrument is well suited to the task. If the interpretive framework is to be a single child's performance, a norm referenced test, particularly if it is a shortened screening version, cannot possibly be adequate to the task.

An analogy here might be the manner in which two tools, a saw and a screwdriver, are used. Either can be used to cut wood or to set a screw into wood, but neither accomplishes the task of the other very effectively.

So the first task of the teacher is to answer the question: Are the instructional questions concerning this child better answered by reference to a norm or by reference to a hierarchy of skills? The reply often will be a mixture of both approaches. The trick, then, is to select and use the most appropriate tool.

Figure 2-4 Scoresheet for Woodcock Reading Mastery Tests

INTERPRETATION OF TEST RESULTS / FORM A

SUMMARY OF SCORES

Subject's Grade Placement (G)

	RAW SCORES AND MASTERY SCORES		READING GRADE LEVELS AND RELATIVE MASTERY LEVELS									PERCENTILE RANKS
TEST	Raw Score	(MS) Mastery Score TABLE I	(E) Easy Reading Level TABLE I	Relative Mastery at E	(R) Reading Grade Score TABLE I	Relative Mastery at R	(F) Failure Reading Level TABLE I	Relative Mastery at F	(MS$_G$) Mastery Score at G TABLE II	(MS)–(MS$_G$) Achievement Index (Indicate + or –)	Relative Mastery at G TABLE III	Percentile Ranks TABLE III
Letter Identification .... (45)				96%		90%		75%		3	___ %	
Word Identification ....(150)				96%		90%		75%		3	___ %,	
Word Attack .... (50)				96%		90%		75%		3	___ %	
Word Comprehension ... (70)				96%		90%		75%		3	___ %	
Passage Comprehension ... (85)				96%		90%		75%		3	___ %	
(Total)												
TOTAL READING² ...... (Total ÷ 5)		___ ³		96%		90%		75%		3	___ %	

SPECIAL INSTRUCTIONS

1 Assume a mastery score of 173 for pupils reading at grade six or above who were not administered the Letter Identification Test.

2 Total reading score is based on the average mastery score for the five tests.

3 Double-check all arithmetic calculations.

4 Complete the Mastery Profile as follows:

a) place dots within each bar to represent points E, R, and F

b) draw a double-ended arrow (↔) between each pair of E and F points to represent the instructional range

c) record, above the bar, the percent of mastery for each E, R, and F point

d) using a different color, place an "X" within each bar to represent point G

e) record, below each bar, the percent of mastery at G.

MASTERY PROFILE[4]

Letter
Identification
1.0[01] 1.0[00] 2.0 3.0 4.0 5.0 6.0 7.0 8.0 9.0 10.0 11.0 12.0 12.9[90] 12.9[99]

Word
Identification
1.0[01] 1.0[00] 2.0 3.0 4.0 5.0 6.0 7.0 8.0 9.0 10.0 11.0 12.0 12.9[90] 12.9[99]

Word
Attack
1.0[01] 1.0[00] 2.0 3.0 4.0 5.0 6.0 7.0 8.0 9.0 10.0 11.0 12.0 12.9[90] 12.9[99]

Word
Comprehension
1.0[01] 1.0[00] 2.0 3.0 4.0 5.0 6.0 7.0 8.0 9.0 10.0 11.0 12.0 12.9[90] 12.9[99]

Passage
Comprehension
1.0[01] 1.0[00] 2.0 3.0 4.0 5.0 6.0 7.0 8.0 9.0 10.0 11.0 12.0 12.9[90] 12.9[99]

TOTAL
READING
1.0[01] 1.0[00] 2.0 3.0 4.0 5.0 6.0 7.0 8.0 9.0 10.0 11.0 12.0 12.9[90] 12.9[99]

1234-AC-75-3701

Printed in U.S.A.

See the manual for additional procedures including age scores, standard scores, separate percentile rank norms for boys and girls, SES-adjusted norms, and use of the Reference Scales in criterion-referenced interpretations.

Source: Reprinted from *Woodcock Reading Mastery Tests* by R. W. Woodcock by permission of American Guidance Service, Inc., © 1973.

The Quality of Tests

Second, formal assessment, under the definition used in this chapter, is composed of norm referenced instruments. Just as with other products, from household cleaners to automobiles, some tests are better made than others. The importance of determining the quality of any selected instrument, for any selected task, cannot be overstated.

A poorly built test can only yield poor information and, as in the product analogy, it invariably is no real bargain despite its lower price in dollars and cents, easier administration, or whatever. Sources were suggested earlier for examining and evaluating tests, but teachers who do not have access to these or do not feel confident to perform their own evaluations by all means should consult with someone in their school system. They usually will find school psychologists and educational diagnosticians both eager and anxious to assist. The teachers also may find them a bit surprised.

The Behavioral Samples

A third important consideration is to examine carefully the behaviors that are sampled on the test. There are several subfactors to be considered here. For example, does the test seem to measure what it proposes to measure—is it valid? Are indexes of validity clearly stated in the manual? If so, how were they developed? Teachers may be amazed at the relative inattentiveness given to validity in many test manuals.

What is the nature of the behavioral sample? How many (or how few) items exist on the test? Too few items seldom lead to an accurate judgment, so teachers must be aware that rapid administration time can be a very mixed blessing.

Finally, what is the nature of the behavioral requirements placed upon the child? What, exactly, does the child have to do? Is a listening task really a listening task? Actually, it cannot be because the child must make some sort of response to indicate an answer and probably must have processed information to formulate that reply. So a test of listening comprehension really is combined (confounded, for the technically oriented) with other tasks.

Teachers are advised to think in terms of a stimulus—response—consequence model when analyzing a test, for this is exactly the model experienced by the child.

Process and Product

A fourth important point is to separate process questions (or hypotheses) from product questions (or hypotheses). A process question is a how or why question and is characterized by the following: "I wonder *how* Jimmy solved that?" "Why *would* he do that?" "How *could* Sally's verbal responses be so poor when her written responses are so well done?"

How/why questions usually are oriented toward the assessment of abilities and seek to explain the motivations or limitations of behavior. Such questions tend to (1) be speculative, (2) be very theoretical, (3) make excessive use of psychoeducational constructs, (4) possess elusive answers, and (5) lead into the training of abilities, an avenue that, as noted, is contemporarily fruitless. On the other hand, questions that begin with *what* generally are more straightforward and simpler to answer. *What* is John's grade equivalent in reading comprehension? *What* arithmetic operations does Lisbeth know? Although not always simple, *what* questions tend to be less speculative, more pragmatic and objective, and to lead to outcomes directly related to future instruction.

All of this is not to suggest that educators should never ponder *why* or *how* a child performs some behavioral act. It is to point out that such questions usually cannot be answered with certainty and invariably require extensive measurement, as well as knowledge of the child and of children. Because of these prerequisites and limitations, it may be wise for the teacher to consciously formulate *what* questions as well as *how/why* questions when approaching the assessment of children.

Organization and Analysis

A fifth point is to systematically organize and analyze the collected data. Quite a few models have been organized for this purpose. Sabatino (1979) has reviewed many of the traditional models in special education, including the rather specific demands of the Individualized Education Program (IEP) as now required by P.L. 94-142. Readers also may find the detailed models provided in Howell, Kaplan, and O'Connell (1979) and the discussion offered by Lerner (1976) to be valuable. But whatever model is chosen, it is important that the teacher systematically collect information, organize it in some way that it is interpretable, then analyze it for its instructional implication.

Should the reader feel like the Lone Ranger sans Tonto at this point, it should be pointed out that this is, in reality, the function of the case conferencing committee (multidisciplinary team). Still, it must be remembered that the very best data are useless unless and until they are analyzed and brought together in some meaningful way. Comprehensive assessment simply cannot be achieved solely by the administration of multiple tests.

Fluidity of Data

A final clue to achieving maximum value from formal assessment results is to approach all data as if they were "fluid" rather than "static." Old Man

River has nothing on good assessment because both just keep on "rolling along." More technically, and perhaps more sanely, both are continuous events and only their form changes. While it is the height of naiveté to repeatedly administer the same achievement test, the same intelligence test, and so on, it is at the same time the height of foolishness to (a) fail to plan each step of assessment so that it leads into the next step or (b) cease to take performance measures on exceptional children.

In some ways the successful billiards player is not unlike the successful educational diagnostician: several shots always are planned in advance and continuous evaluation of position molds and modifies the game plan. So, far from the "static" property that assessment sometimes is accused of being, in actuality it is a "fluid" event, flowing with the needs of the child, the teacher, and the educational setting. Remembering this fact is a clear asset.

REFERENCES

Anastasi, A. *Psychological testing* (4th ed.). New York: The Macmillan Company, 1976.

Arter, J.A., & Jenkins, J.R. Examining the benefits and prevalence of modality considerations in special education. The *Journal of Special Education,* 1977, *11*(3), 281–287.

Baker, H.J., & Leland, B. *Detroit Tests of Learning Aptitude.* Indianapolis: Bobbs-Merrill, 1959.

Bannatyne, A. Diagnosing learning disabilities and writing remedial prescriptions. *Journal of Learning Disabilities,* 1968, *1*(4), 242–249.

Bender, L. *A visual motor Gestalt test and its clinical use.* New York: American Orthopsychiatric Association Research Monograph, 1938, No. 3.

Bersoff, D.N., & Miller, T.L. Ethical and legal issues of behavioral assessment. In D.A. Sabatino & T.L. Miller (Eds.), *Describing learning characteristics of handicapped children and youth.* New York: Grune & Stratton, Inc., 1979.

Beery, K.E., & Buktenica, N. *Developmental test of visual motor integration.* Chicago: Follett Publishing Co., 1967.

Bloom, B.S. (Ed.). *Taxonomy of educational objectives: Handbook I, cognitive domain.* New York: David McKay Company, Inc., 1956.

Boehm, A.E. *Boehm test of basic concepts manual.* New York: The Psychological Corporation, 1971.

Bryan, T. Learning disabled children's comprehension of nonverbal communication. *Journal of Learning Disabilities,* 1977, *10*(5), 510–516.

Bryan, T., & Bryan, J. *Understanding learning disabilities* (2nd ed.). Port Washington, N.Y.: Alfred Publishing Co., 1978.

Burks, H. *Burks' Behavior Rating Scales.* El Monte, Calif.: Arden Press, 1969.

Buros, O.K. (Ed.). *The seventh mental measurements yearbook.* Highland Park, N.J.: Gryphon Press, 1972.

——————. *The eighth mental measurements yearbook.* Highland Park, N.J.: Gryphon Press, 1978.

Caldwell, B. *Preschool inventory* (Rev. ed.). Princeton, N.J.: Educational Testing Service, 1970.

Carrow, E. *Carrow elicited language inventory.* Austin, Texas: Learning Concepts, 1974.

Coles, G.S. The learning disabilities test battery: Empirical and social issues. *Harvard Educational Review,* 1978, *48,* 313–340.

Connolly, A., Nachtman, W., & Pritchett, E. *Key math diagnostic arithmetic test* (Manual). Circle Pines, Minn.: American Guidance Service, Inc., 1971.

Doll, E. *Vineland social maturity scale.* Circle Pines, Minn.: American Guidance Service, Inc., 1965.

DuBois, P.H. *A history of psychological testing.* Boston: Allyn & Bacon, Inc., 1970.

Dunn, L.M. *Peabody picture vocabulary test.* Circle Pines, Minn.: American Guidance Service, Inc., 1965.

——————. (Ed.). *Exceptional children in the schools: Special education in transition* (2nd ed.). New York: Holt Rinehart Winston Inc., 1973.

Dunn, L.M., & Markwardt, F.C. *Peabody individual achievement test.* Circle Pines, Minn.: American Guidance Service, Inc., 1970.

Durost, W.M., Bixler, H.H., Wrightstone, J.W., Prescott, G.A., & Balow, I.H. *Metropolitan achievement test.* New York: Harcourt Brace Jovanovich, 1971.

Fitts, W. *Tennessee self concept inventory.* Nashville: Counselor Recordings and Tests, 1965.

Frankenburg, W.K., Dodds, J.B., & Fandel, A.W. *Denver developmental screening test.* Denver: Ladoca Project and Publishing Foundation, 1970.

Frostig, M., Maslow, P., Lefever, D.W., & Whittlesey, J.R. *The Marianne Frostig test of visual perception: 1963 standardization.* Palo Alto, Calif.: Consulting Psychologists Press, 1964.

Goldman, R., Fristoe, M., & Woodcock, R.W. *Goldman-Fristoe-Woodcock test of auditory discrimination.* Circle Pines, Minn.: American Guidance Service, Inc.. 1970.

Gustavson, J.L. *A brief analysis of the subtests of the Wechsler intelligence scale for children—Revised.* Unpublished manuscript, Brigham Young University, 1978. In C.F. Ingram. *Fundamentals of educational assessment.* New York: D. Van Nostrand Co., Inc., 1980.

Hallahan, D.P., & Kauffman, J.M. Labels, categories, behaviors: ED, LD, EMR reconsidered. The *Journal of Special Education,* 1977, *11*(2), 139–149.

Hammill, D., & Larsen, S. The relationship of selected auditory perceptual skills and reading abilities. *Journal of Learning Disabilities,* 1974, *7*(7), 429–434.

Harrow, A.J. *A taxonomy of the psychomotor domain.* New York: David McKav Company, Inc., 1972.

Hieronymous, A.N., & Lindquist, E.F. *Iowa test of basic skills: Manual for administrators, supervisors and counselors.* Boston: Houghton Mifflin Company, 1974.

Hobbs, N., Egerton, J., & Mathery, M. Classifying children. *Children Today,* 1975, *4*(4), 21–25.

Howell, K.W., Kaplan, J.S., & O'Connell, C.Y. *Evaluating exceptional children: A task analysis approach.* Columbus, Ohio: The Charles E. Merrill Publishing Co., Inc., 1979.

Jastak, J.F., & Jastak, S.R. *The wide range achievement test* (Manual). Wilmington, Del.: Guidance Associates, 1965.

Keogh, B.K., & Hall, R.J. *Functional analysis of WISC performance of children classified EH and EMR.* Report SERP 1973–79, Graduate School of Education, University of California, Los Angeles, 1973.

Kirk, S., McCarthy, J., & Kirk, W. *Illinois test of psycholinguistic abilities.* Urbana, Ill.: University of Illinois, 1965.

Krathwohl, D.R. (Ed.). *Taxonomy of educational objectives: Handbook II—affective domain.* New York: David McKay Company, Inc., 1964.

Larsen, S., & Hammill, D. The relationship of selected visual perceptual abilities to school learning. The *Journal of Special Education,* 1975, *9*(3), 281–292.

Lee, L. *Northwestern syntax screening test.* Evanston, Ill.: Northwestern University Press, 1969.

Lerner, J.W. *Children with learning disabilities* (2nd ed.). Boston: Houghton Mifflin Company, 1976.

Lovitt, T.C. *In spite of my resistance I've learned from children.* Columbus, Ohio: The Charles E. Merrill Publishing Co., Inc., 1977.

Madden, R., Gardner, E.R., Rodman, H.C., Karlson, B., & Merwin, J.C. *Stanford achievement test.* New York: Harcourt Brace Jovanovich, 1973.

Mann, L. Why hello process! *The Journal of Special Education,* in press.

——————. Psychometric phrenology. *The Journal of Special Education,* 1971, *5*(1), 3–14.

McCarthy, D. *Manual for the McCarthy scales of children's abilities.* New York: The Psychological Corporation, 1972.

McClelland, D.C. Testing for competence rather than for "intelligence." *American Psychologist,* 1973, *28,* 1–14.

Meeker, M.N. *The structure of the intellect: Its interpretation and uses.* Columbus, Ohio: The Charles E. Merrill Publishing Co., Inc., 1969.

Mercer, C.C. *Children and adolescents with learning disabilities.* Columbus, Ohio: The Charles E. Merrill Publishing Co., Inc., 1979.

Messick, S., & Associates (Eds.). *Individuality in learning.* San Francisco: Jossey-Bass, Inc., 1976.

Miller, S.R. Career education: Lifelong planning for the handicapped. In D.A. Sabatino & T.L. Miller (Eds.), *Describing learner characteristics of handicapped children and youth.* New York: Grune & Stratton, Inc., 1979.

Miller, T.L. A review of the psychometric approach to measurement. In D.A. Sabatino & T.L. Miller (Eds.), *Describing learner characteristics of handicapped children and youth.* New York: Grune & Stratton, Inc., 1979.

Moss, M.H. *Tests of basic experiences.* Monterey, Calif.: CTB/McGraw-Hill, Inc., 1972.

Piers, E., & Harris, D. *The Piers-Harris children's self concept scale.* Nashville: Counselor Recordings and Tests, 1969.

Public Law 94-142 (Education for All Handicapped Children Act of 1975).

Quay, H.C., & Peterson, D.R. *Manual for the behavior problem checklist.* Unpublished manuscript, University of Illinois, 1967.

Roach, E.F., & Kephart, N.C. *The Purdue perceptual motor survey.* Columbus, Ohio: The Charles E. Merrill Publishing Co., Inc., 1966.

Ross, A.O. *Psychological aspects of learning disabilities and reading disorders.* New York: McGraw-Hill Book Company, 1976.

Roswell, R., & Chall, J. *Roswell–Chall auditory blending test.* New York: Essay Press, 1963.

Sabatino, D.A. Systematic procedure for ascertaining learner characteristics. In D.A. Sabatino & T.L. Miller (Eds.), *Describing learner characteristics of handicapped children and youth.* New York: Grune & Stratton, Inc., 1979.

——————. Cognitive development of mildly handicapped children and youth. In T.L. Miller & E. David (Eds.), *The mildly handicapped child.* New York: Grune & Stratton, Inc., in press.

Sabatino, D.A., & Miller, T.L. (Eds.). *Describing learner characteristics of handicapped children and youth.* New York: Grune & Stratton, Inc., 1979.

Salvia, J., & Ysseldyke, J.E. *Assessment in special and remedial education.* Boston: Houghton Mifflin Company, 1978.

Sattler, J.M. *Assessment of children's intelligence.* Philadelphia: W.B. Saunders Co., 1974.

Sloan, W. *Lincoln-Osertsky Motor Development Scale.* Genetic Psychology Monographs, 1955, *51,* 183–252.

Spivack, G., & Spotts, J. *Devereux child behavior rating scale.* Devon, Pa: Devereux Foundation Press, 1966.

Standards for educational and psychological tests. Washington, D.C.: American Psychological Association, 1974.

Terman, L., & Merrill, M. *Stanford-Binet intelligence scales, 1972 norms ed.* Boston: Houghton Mifflin Company, 1973.

Tiegs, E.W., & Clarke, W.W. *California achievement test.* Monterey, Calif.: CTB/McGraw-Hill, Inc., 1970.

U.S. Office of Education. *First annual report of National Advisory Committee on Handicapped Children.* Washington, D.C.: U.S. Department of Health, Education, & Welfare, 1968.

Valett, R. A clinical profile for the Stanford-Binet L-M. *Journal of School Psychology,* 1964, 49–54.

Walker, H. *Walker problem behavior checklist.* Los Angeles: Western Psychological Services, 1970.

Wallace, G., & McLoughlin, J.A. *Learning disabilities: Concepts and characteristics.* Columbus, Ohio: The Charles E. Merrill Publishing Co., Inc., 1975.

Wechsler, D. *Wechsler adult intelligence scale* (Manual). New York: The Psychological Corporation, 1955.

——————. *Wechsler intelligence scale for children, revised* (Manual). New York: The Psychological Corporation, 1974.

——————. *Wechsler preschool and primary scale of intelligence* (Manual). New York: The Psychological Corporation, 1967.

Wepman, J.M. *Auditory discrimination test.* Chicago: Language Research Associates, 1958.

Wiig, E.H., & Semel, E.M. *Language disabilities in children and adolescents.* Columbus, Ohio: The Charles E. Merrill Publishing Co., Inc., 1976.

Woodcock, R.W. *Woodcock reading mastery tests.* Circle Pines, Minn.: American Guidance Service, 1973.

Wyne, M.D., & O'Connor, P.D. *Exceptional children: A developmental view.* Lexington, Mass.: D.C. Heath and Co., 1979.

Ysseldyke, J.E. Diagnostic prescription teaching: The search for aptitude treatment interaction. In L. Mann & D. Sabatino (Eds.), *The first review of special education* (Vol. 1). Philadelphia, JSE Press, 1973.

Chapter 3

Informal Assessment of Learning Disabled Children and Youth

Ted L. Miller
and Brenda B. Miller

INTRODUCTION

In many ways the phrase *informal assessment* can be considered a semantic misnomer. Although practices vary widely, the phrase should not convey a less capable, less complete, less useful, or less important aspect of measurement even though this sometimes is the case. In fact, informal assessment is an extension of formal procedures that form an essential complementary link with programming. Like formal assessment, few if any definitions of informal assessment are fully agreed upon or commonly accepted, although several factors appear to dominate the distinction.

Perhaps the first and foremost attribute of informal assessment is that it serves a singular purpose, namely, the collection of personal data that are directly useful in initiating educational programming. Whereas formal assessment may serve a diagnostic classification function, the linkage between diagnosis and actual programming is notably frail because the abilities and skills measured are not directly applicable to a classroom learning task. Therefore, while formal procedures may specify the general parameters of programming, informal procedures attempt to elaborate the specific skills that are to be taught, and how, and to serve in evaluating the quantity and quality of academic achievement growth demonstrated by the student.

Second, informal assessment is virtually the opposite of formal assessment in that it seldom if ever uses norm referenced tests as standardized measures. In informal assessment, norms thus usually are not the yardstick of interpretation, as is demonstrated later.

Third, there is a very strong tendency for informal procedures to focus on the learning process, on the environment in which it occurs, and on directly observable behaviors in response to that task. This rarely is the case with formal assessment, where constructs (abilities, psychological processes) such

73

as intelligence are routinely measured and operationally defined, e.g., the presence or absence of learning disabilities. While this tendency probably is not absolute in informal measures, it is predominant.

Fourth, informal measures sometimes do not employ (deliberate) stimulus—response techniques or standardized administration criteria. In fact, the observation of behaviors normally conducted during regular classroom assignments, or an analysis of these activities, may shape the data collection format.

Fifth, where a formal assessment procedure may tend to be of a single setting that extends over a broad time span, an informal procedure is nearly continuous but in a short single setting, i.e., a few minutes each day. Accordingly, such measures form the heart of continuous monitoring procedures.

Sixth, informal measures usually are tailored to the child's needs, i.e., procedures often are built to answer specific questions concerning a specific child. There is little likelihood that the same informal analytical procedure will be used for more than one child.

Seventh, informal measures nearly always occur in the classroom or at least in the instructional environment in which the behavior under consideration is thought to be important.

Therefore, as an eighth and final point, the teacher usually is the primary data collector and the direct consumer of informal information. Invariably, then, the results of informal measures find their way into the instruction.

BENEFITS OF INFORMAL ASSESSMENT

These characteristics of informal assessment suggest certain benefits for the instructional process. Heilman (1972) has indicated that informal procedures may be used in the classroom for nearly any purpose, can be constructed from widely available materials, and have many advantages for children with learning problems because their untimed, natural, familiar properties reduce the students' tensions and perhaps are more motivating.

Furthermore, such tests generally are inexpensive to construct. Indeed, the emphasis on learned behaviors and on the precise skills that an individual must acquire, as well as the fact that data are collected within the learner's "natural environment," suggest certain strengths for educators, chiefly that they need spend little time on collecting other than the most pragmatic and essential data. Since special children invariably are behind in their learning progress and ability to learn comparable to others of their age, it is imperative that time not be lost to efforts that are less than essential.

Informal techniques often have the capacity to collect accurate data without requiring an undue amount of the learner's time; similarly, because the teacher is the primary collector of information, less time is lost in putting the information into practice. There need be little concern about generalization of behavior. What is measured in the classroom is likely to reflect classroom behavior more adequately than data taken outside class. Finally, informal measures blend naturally into the Individualized Education Program (IEP). In fact, much of the technology that characterizes the IEP was developed mutually with many types of informal assessment, so the blending of the two is not coincidence. It is, however, a distinct cue that informal procedures should be used.

LIMITATIONS OF INFORMAL ASSESSMENT

Beyond these largely beneficial aspects, informal assessment has limitations. The first of these is that while time may not be a great burden on the student, it can be on the teacher. The teacher may have to build or modify the test procedure and, in the case of observation, devote considerable time to continuous monitoring. These may not be difficult tasks but the need to construct the procedures can produce some limitations under the restricted personnel budgets of today's schools.

A second major limitation is that the construction of some informal tests may require extensive command of the subject, or at least access to considerable technical literature. It can be argued that this should be a prerequisite for all testing; however, experienced teachers can verify that it is one thing to be responsible for interpretation of a test and quite another to be responsible for both development and interpretation.

A third hazard lies in the fact that the technical aspects of informal, criterion referenced tests are not well understood. For example, procedures for determining the validity and reliability of such instruments are not well formulated. The tests then can become slipshod, and hence inaccurate, since the teacher does not have the tools to judge reliability or validity.

Finally, as with formal tests, informal ones are useful only for some purposes and cannot be a panacea for all the flaws inherent in measurement practice. Given this view and criticism, the teacher must be as cautious in the use of informal tests as with formal ones. Yet there is considerable value in utilizing the informal assessment approach with learning disabled students.

TYPES OF INFORMAL ASSESSMENT

The informal assessment techniques touched on in Chapter 2 may be conceptualized as consisting of two basic formats: (1) those that utilize a response to verbal or graphic stimulus and (2) those that obtain data through observational procedures. A third approach is structured interviews, but the rather specialized techniques for interviewing are beyond the scope of this book. Verbal-graphic stimuli informal tests may be further conceptualized along several dimensions:

- These tests may be commercially prepared or teacher prepared.

- Each of these types may vary considerably by the precise tasks the student is asked to do and how the work is initiated. In some cases the student will be asked only to respond to printed matter by verbal indication or by pointing; in other cases, the child will be asked to respond in writing, whether checking off an item, circling a correct answer, or providing a composition.

- These tests may vary substantially as to the scope of their information, i.e., a given test may be more or less comprehensive and may sample either a quite finite set of skills (informal skill tests) or a more global set of information (informal survey tests) (Wallace & Larsen, 1978).

It is important to consider each of these variations because no informal verbal-graphic stimuli tests can be suited for all tasks even though, regardless of format, they generally are involved with the measurement of academic skills.

Observational procedures, on the other hand, are very much as their name implies. Although observation sometimes is used to mean the completion of checklists and the like (Cartwright & Cartwright, 1974) the word as invoked here indicates the use of specific observation to measure and record target behaviors. In this sense, observation refers to the careful selection, definition, and recording of observable behavior accompanied by the charting and monitoring of progress. Such techniques are applied to social-personal behaviors although they also can be used with measures of academic success.

While these comments may denote one way to conceptualize the various approaches to informal assessment, it should be reemphasized that these distinctions are in fact arbitrary. Without doubt, other conceptual lines could be drawn, and procedures do exist that are blends of the two methods. Still, this schema represents an organizational framework that may help clarify the various approaches in the commonly used phrase *informal assessment*.

TECHNICAL ANTECEDENTS

Before commercially prepared or teacher-prepared informal tests (and possibly observational techniques) can be discussed, it is essential to review their technical roots. Several important terms must be understood: criterion referenced, task hierarchy, task analysis, and behavioral objectives.

Criterion referenced testing has its roots in behavioral psychology and the programmed learning movement. The criterion referenced method is traced to Glaser (1963), who questioned certain fundamental approaches to the measurement of subjects, i.e., whether student performance on academic matters should be evaluated in relationship to the standards set for that subject. Such an approach assumed a certain number of identifiable skills that would indicate proficiency toward a criterion and that would signify and direct the course of educational instruction. A main element here is the theme that the individual's relationship to the acquisition of a known set of skills is the essential thrust of instruction and assessment. Glaser clearly saw this approach as one alternative to the traditional psychometric approach, in which a student's score is derived from a comparison with other pupils, and as particularly well suited to the teaching of academics.

Several factors coincided with the appearance of Glaser's paper. One theme was the initial use of the behavioral approach in education. Mager (1962) popularized the use of behavioral objectives as testable statements of what is to be taught, i.e., behavioral objectives become the operative criteria for tests. Simultaneously, the principles of learning theory were applied to classroom settings with special children, and the application of behavioral objectives to criterion referenced tests became widely accepted. Offshoots of these elements, e.g., programmed learning and precision teaching (see Kunzelman et al., 1970) firmly established the concept of criterion referenced procedures in educational measurement.

The Task Hierarchy Concept

One inextricable component of criterion referenced testing is the concept of a task hierarchy. A task hierarchy is a sequentially ordered list of the elements necessary to reach some identifiable criterion. Such a skill hierarchy would be invariant and would list early skills necessary for the completion of the general tasks. Carrying the method a step further, each subskill in the task hierarchy would be written as a behavioral objective and would be tested using a criterion referenced procedure. Mastery (reaching an acceptable criterion) would be necessary before instruction in future skills.

The task hierarchy can be refined and detailed through a procedure known as task analysis. Task analysis is the systematic breaking apart of some complex function into a series of smaller, sequenced, teachable, and measurable steps. (See Howell, Kaplan, & O'Connell (1979) for a practical overview of task analysis.) No attempt is made to teach the skills at once but instead to instruct only in the steps, then chain them together in a hierarchical arrangement.

These concepts in combination underlie most informal assessment procedures. And therein lies the unique value of informal tests: by definition these procedures were developed to better measure instructional progress—the most essential aspect of service delivery to students with learning problems. Accordingly, the advantages of criterion referenced tests (hence, informal tests) are summarized by Proger and Mann (1973) as: (a) adaptability to the requirements of a specific situation, (b) continuous monitoring of behavior, and (c) allowing judgment of students in relation to past performance or necessary (criteria) performance. When balanced against the disadvantages cited earlier, informal procedures may be seen to possess considerable appeal for the special education teacher.

Given this orientation, the remainder of this chapter is organized under three main headings: observation techniques, essentials of constructing teacher-made tests, and commercially available procedures. The first two are procedural in nature, that is, (1) general techniques for conducting either one are reported in some detail and (2) references are provided for continued study. Neither section is content specific and their procedures could be applied to ascertaining the learner characteristics of virtually any student in many areas. (3) The third segment describes many of the more common commercially available informal procedures for measuring student skills in three vital areas.

The Importance of Techniques

Observation and teacher-constructed test procedures are extremely important for measuring student progress. Poor techniques in either inevitably lead to erroneous conclusions and, in part, have been responsible for the sometimes unflattering comments directed at informal assessment.

The use of poor techniques is not justified because teachers, by following even the relatively few guidelines provided here, can contribute greatly to the adequacy and accuracy of these measures. Moreover, the application of these procedural standards to the commercial materials discussed later greatly increases the probability that they are adequate and are used wisely. Thus, in a sense, this chapter is an overview of both the technology of informal assessment and of some of the commercially prepared procedures available.

APPROACHES TO OBSERVATION TECHNIQUES

Observation plays a critical role in informal assessment, although this term does not mean simply the casual watching of students. Instead, systematic observation carries with it specific characteristics that are well recognized and documented (see Kazdin, 1980; Sulzer-Azaroff & Mayer, 1977). While it is true that these techniques often are associated with applied learning theory—behavioral analysis—it is in fact more accurate to consider them as integral parts of many positions concerning the study and alteration of behavior (e.g., see Barker, 1968; Rogers-Warren & Warren, 1977; Weinberg & Woods, 1975).

There are several fundamental reasons for the use of systematic observation. First, carefully identified observable behaviors are among the most objective measures available to the teacher. Opinions may differ over the point that James was angry and therefore that is *why* he threw the toy, but there is little argument concerning the observable event of toy throwing. Second, there is a growing recognition that students respond differently in various environments (Bersoff, 1973; Wallace & Larsen, 1978). Traditional formal tests cannot readily ascertain these effects since those techniques are limited to a testing booth situation, yet this information is important in educational programming, as has been noted by Wallace and Larsen (1978):

> An individual does not usually act independently of outside forces in any given situation, but is continually responding to a series of situational factors that may or may not be apparent to the casual observer. Such variables as peer pressure, teacher and parent demands, school climate and the child's own self concept all have the potential to either "positively" or "negatively" influence a child's academic and social behavior. (p. 99)

A third point is that observational techniques may be conceptually bound to theories of behavior or they may be pragmatically directed toward documenting a specific behavior. Thus, observational techniques are quite flexible in actual practice.

Systematic observation can be conducted in several ways within the limited framework provided here. Of the general approaches that can be identified, two of the more important are the ecological and the applied behavioral analysis. Although these emphases share many commonalities (see Rogers-Warren & Warren, 1977, for a review) some conceptual distinctions and therefore pragmatic differences do emerge.

Because the ecological approach so heavily emphasizes the production of behavior in response to its setting (or ecology), observational approaches developed in this method strongly emphasize person-environment interactions. Therefore, one effective observational procedure is the analysis of teacher-pupil interaction. This approach often is complemented by an analysis of behavior in relationship to task demands, curriculum topic, student interaction, and so on, the latter being accomplished by checklists. Observational procedures derived from applied behavioral analysis may note these factors, too, but will be far more inclined to examine a particular behavior's relationship to its ensuing consequences. In practice, teachers can use the techniques that flow from both of these approaches, so the purpose here is to discuss the most useful practices and exemplary techniques of both.

Elements of Observation

The first task of any observation is to define or accept a definition of behavior. The concept of accepting a definition of behavior is included here because, in some cases, existing observational systems are used. In fact, catalogs of observational behaviors exist. Such observational systems usually are based upon some theoretical model and contain already constructed definitions that the observer must follow. In other instances, however, the teacher will wish to define a behavior that is of interest but not a part of an existing observational procedure. In such instances the conduct must be defined carefully; once this is accomplished, it is referred to as the target behavior.

Producing an acceptable definition in order to construct a target behavior is not necessarily difficult but it does require careful attention. Hawkins and Dobes (1975) assert that the target behavior must be objective, clear and complete. Repp (1979) suggests that a behavioral definition should:

> (1) describe the behavior in objective terms; (2) include the conditions under which it will be recorded; (3) be complete, providing appropriate information on what should and should not be included; and (4) describe the behavior so that it can be measured. (p. 98)

Taking the time required to produce such a definition is quite worthwhile as it facilitates objectivity and lends credence to the eventual data. Mager (1962) and Mager and Pipe (1970) provide greater detail and practice on this topic.

The second task is to select or develop an appropriate observation system. In either case, specification of the behavior must follow next. Specification of the behavior means determining how it can best be quantified. Although many variations exist, the options essentially involve counting behaviors or measuring their duration or intensity. Typically, behaviors are counted when they are sufficiently prevalent and fast paced to allow enumerating their occurrence within some reasonable recording period. Duration or intensity usually is noted when the conduct is better recorded by its length of time or strength. Such behaviors may not occur frequently but are likely to be lengthy and/or particularly abrasive. In either case, Sulzer-Azaroff and Mayer (1977) caution that in the selection-development of observational procedures, strict attention must be given to the behavioral dimensions or topography of the events to be recorded: "... we must be very precise about the nature of the response desired and the situations in which it is to occur. Only then will behavioral procedures be effective" (p. 52).

Once the teacher is satisfied that these conditions can be met, the third task is to select the observation recording procedure. If the behavior of interest is noninteractional, i.e., if data are being collected solely about the student, the record is likely to be one of four types: frequency record, interval record, duration record, and time sample record. Other variations and nomenclature are possible. The discussion here parallels the description by Repp (1979). If the behavior of interest is interactional, an interval record usually is selected. A brief review of these four types is in order.

Frequency records, in essence, simply are counts of the target behavior's occurrence that then are compared across the various sessions in which events are recorded.

Sessions, the times of observation, should be of equal length, about the same time daily, and unless contrasts across locations are desired, should take place in the same place (as, indeed, all types of observation recording should). Care also should be taken that the behaviors remain roughly equivalent, i.e., that there are few changes in the quality of the conduct, the only changes occurring in the frequency.

Interval records are designed so that the session is divided first into a number of intervals of equal length. The observer's task is simply to note the number of intervals (usually very brief time periods of 5 to 10 seconds) in which the behavior occurred. Performance is quantified by comparing the number of intervals containing the target behavior to the total number of intervals. In this manner a percentage of cases per time is established for informal analyses. If the selected observation system is interactional (e.g., teacher-pupil response interactions) a single interval will record both teacher and pupil response. Subsequent data analyses attempt to determine the interactional relationship of teacher upon student (or, perhaps, the converse).

At least two variations are used with interval records. First, interactional data are taken, e.g., teacher-pupil behavioral relationships. Thus a single interval will record the responses of both persons. Second, the data that are taken in this record often are characterized by alternative target behaviors. That is, instead of merely noting the occurrence or absence of a single behavior, the observer often selects the action that was occurring because of several possibilities. These may be combined in such a manner that the observer judges the behavior of both persons involved in an interaction. In this way the data become reasonably complex and can benefit from computer analysis. Valuable as this information is, it has not attained widespread use in areas other than research because of the complexity of its interpretation.

Duration records denote the total time of a behavior compared to some unit of time (session). Generally, the observer notes the start-stop times of an action, calculates the time spent for each one, then summarizes the behavior over the session. A percentage then is calculated in a manner basically analogous to the interval record procedure.

Time sampling procedures are those in which the observer ignores the behavior during most of the session and samples it only occasionally. For example, during a 60-minute session the observer might make a check every 15 minutes, noting the behavior's presence or absence. The record is the number of occasions the behavior was present compared to the number of occasions of the session sampled.

After having completed these steps, the observer would possess (1) a carefully defined behavior and (2) a carefully selected recording procedure. It then would be necessary to (1) develop observation record forms, (2) take steps to ensure the adequacy of the data, and (3) use the information through plotting and charting. Each of these topics is analyzed briefly.

Observational record forms are merely organizational tools that allow the observer to collect information easily. However, these forms will vary somewhat according to the type of observation record made and/or the number of behaviors measured (cf. Cartwright & Cartwright, 1974; Repp, 1979; Sulzer-Azaroff & Mayer, 1977; Walker & Shea, 1980).

The Reliability Requirement

But whatever format is adopted, it must contain sufficient data to allow the teacher to readily list the behaviors, the observer's identity, when and where the actions occurred, what observational system was used, and any other pertinent information. The effort always should be to create a record that is accurate and that can serve as a permanent document should a return to the data be required.

With the behaviors carefully defined, the record sheets prepared, and the time and location of the observation decided upon, steps are taken to ensure the reliability of the data. Individuals concerned with behavioral observations have invested much time in discussing procedures for assessing their reliability (Johnson & Bolstad, 1973) and events that may undermine that validity (Kent, Kanowitz, O'Leary, & Cheikem, 1977; Repp, Deitz, Boles, Deitz & Repp, 1976; Repp, Roberts, Slack, Repp, & Berkler, 1976). Reliability as the term is used here means that the records of behavior are consistent across time and that observers see and record the same conduct. As Sulzer-Azaroff and Mayer (1977) have reported:

> Before formal data can be collected, it is necessary to ensure that observations can be reliably recorded. This goal is best accomplished through operationalizing target behavior precisely and training and supervising those who record the behaviors. (p. 52)

Three Sources of Misinformation

Precisely what adverse properties are careful observers trying to overcome? While there may well be others, the essential sources of misinformation through inaccurate data are (1) reactivity, (2) bias, and (3) nonsystematic error.

Reactivity refers to atypical effects produced by the observer's presence. Usually, reactivity is controlled by the observer's making certain that the procedures do not directly alter behavior and by recording data for some time prior to intervention, i.e., a baseline. If the baseline is stable (behavior neither accelerates/rises nor decelerates/sinks excessively), then the teacher may assume that reactivity is not a major problem.

Bias actually is error that is systematic in direction, i.e., the constant overestimation or underestimation of the quantity of some behavior. Perhaps the best single control against bias is the use of naive observers who do not possess a rationale to find (or ignore) a particular behavior. After all, it may be difficult for the teacher to remain objective about Billy's hair-pulling behavior! But, given that the presence of naive observers is not possible (particularly in classrooms), perhaps the best safeguards are thoroughly objective definitions and carefully defined recording procedures.

Nonsystematic error involves mistakes attributable to an infinite array of sources such as observer drift (falling asleep at the task), recording errors, vague definitions, recording in different time periods and considering them to be the same, and so on. Any of these are potential causes of nonsystematic error. Nonsystematic error is a clear and significant danger to observational data because it leads to records that are not accurate and in fact may well be so inaccurate as to be useless. Inaccuracy in this case is a product of inconsistency. Perhaps the most effective, certainly the most common, manner in which nonsystematic error is estimated is by calculating interobserver agreement. Therefore, the teacher who is likely to use observational data for collecting an important set of information or wishes this record to constitute an enduring document of behavior is well advised to calculate interobserver agreement.

Interobserver agreement often is termed reliability. But since reliability implies consistency from Time 1 to Time 2, agreement seems to be the preferred term. Presumably, two observers who can agree at one time can agree at another time; however, the two can have lessened agreement over time (hence the need for spot checking) and it is possible for them to have very high agreement yet be recording the "wrong" behavior (Johnson & Bolstad, 1973).

Following Sulzer-Azaroff and Mayer (1977), seven formulas are relevant (see Johnson & Bolstad (1973) and Repp (1979) for a complete discussion).

The general formula for estimating agreement between two observers taking a frequency record is:

$$\frac{\text{smaller total}}{\text{larger total}} \times 100 = \text{percentage of agreement}$$

Agreement may be calculated for the whole session or for several partial sessions. The latter may be preferable since observers can have high agreement without marking behavior at the same time. Therefore, it may be preferable to use the partial session technique (Repp, 1979) in which the whole period (perhaps 50 minutes) is divided into a number of smaller segments (of 5 to 10 minutes each) and the five fractions are summarized.

The formula for duration records and the rationale for it are entirely analogous to frequency records:

$$\frac{\text{smaller duration}}{\text{larger duration}} \times 100 = \text{percentage of agreement}$$

The calculation of agreement between observers collecting an interval record is a bit more complicated, though it, too, is quite straightforward:

$$\frac{\text{agreements}}{\text{agreements \& disagreements}} \times 100 = \text{percentage of agreements}$$

In this formula, each interval is examined to determine whether both observers noted the same behavior (i.e., an agreement) or did not (a disagreement). These respective numbers are then entered into the formula. In a system in which two behaviors are recorded (e.g. teacher-pupil interaction) both must be identical for both observations in order that agreement can be assumed. Generally, this formula also is applied to time-sample procedures.

Reliability always should be calculated at least at the outset of observation and probably several times during the construction of the record. Outcomes should remain in the high 80s or 90s. There are at least two reasons for this bold statement:

1. As discussed, the record possessing high reliability is almost certain to be better accepted as evidence and to adequately project a basis for programming.
2. In the event of the first observer's absence, the systematic data (accurate, consistently collected information) need not be undermined or lost, for the second observer is equally capable of standing in on that date.

For at least these two reasons, the cautious teacher is urged to conduct interobserver checks as the data are taken.

Using Observational Data

One of the clearest advantages of observational data is the ease with which they may be interpreted and utilized. Behaviors are recorded in a straightforward manner and therefore require little interpretation beyond increasing, decreasing, and maintaining the conduct, although another point, termination of measurement of a particular activity, should always be considered. As indicated in Chapter 2, many of the behaviors that are measured will involve social-personal characteristics and therefore cannot be assessed easily by other means. Directly observable behaviors can be related directly to the goals and objectives provided in the Individualized Education Program, so observation becomes a focal point of program evaluation.

So, in essence, observation allows the teacher to measure the student's current levels of specified behaviors, relate them to an instructional-behavioral management plan, and finally evaluate and draw conclusions concerning the efficiency of specific treatment procedures. Accordingly, two topics are germane here for the advanced practitioner but must necessarily be eliminated because of the scope of the chapter:

1. The topic of behavioral change strategies is very important. Techniques such as use of positive reinforcement, negative reinforcement, modeling, self-control techniques, and many others are directly applicable to observational measures. These procedures are widely recognized but, for a review, the reader is advised to consult Blackham and Silberman (1980), Kazdin (1980), Meichenbaum (1977), Thoresen and Mahoney (1974), Morris (1976), Stephens (1975), Sulzer-Azaroff and Mayer (1977), Tharp and Wetzel (1969), or Walker and Shea (1980).
2. The task of thoroughly documenting behavioral change, and especially without disrupting any progress that is achieved, may well require data analysis designs that are beyond the scope of this discussion.

Frequently, these single subject, N = 1, or behavioral designs (terms often used interchangeably) are erroneously considered to be strictly applicable to research. In fact several of the designs (for example, the changing criterion design) are well suited to instructional practice, particularly the monitoring of academic or social progress. Initial and possibly ample discussion may be located in Kazdin (1980), Kratochwill (1977), and Sulzer-Azaroff and Mayer (1977), and a complete discussion is in Hersen and Barlow (1976). Readers should select at least one reading from each of these topics in order to maximize the efficacy of observational techniques as a component of informal assessment, instructional programming, and behavioral management.

It is well to recognize that the purpose of any plot or chart derived from an observation record is to make data interpretable and consumable. The importance of examining behavioral change techniques and of assuring that the data are accurate is reflected in the fact that the information consumer can be the teacher, the parent, or the student. In fact, feedback of observable data to students has been shown to be a powerful behavioral change strategy (Kazdin, 1974) and certainly readily usable information is a distinct plus for the teacher who needs to share it with parents.

Therefore a few cautions are in order. First, casually drawn charts may be subject to distortion, as inspection of those that do not have equivalent axes may lead users to conclude falsely that behaviors are different. A second problem may emerge if the teacher bases a conclusion on insufficient data. Generally, trends (acceleration or deceleration of behaviors) cannot be determined adequately on less than four or five points. Similarly the difference between points should be substantial and relatively constant. Otherwise the observer may simply be examining random error within the records.

Finally, there is the problem of recordkeeping. The teacher must know whom is being recorded, what exactly was written, who was recording, where the data were listed, etc. Such housekeeping information generally is found on record sheets but unless the data in some way are referenced to the figure, confusion can occur. Therefore, it is advisable to label all information on the graphs by coding them to the original data sheets or otherwise noting permanent information, perhaps upon the back of the chart.

Summary

The use of observational information no longer is in its infancy; it is a full-fledged approach to informal assessment that is tied directly to instructional-behavioral management.

Observation need not be linked solely to behavioral approaches for, as has been seen, it is a component of many views of conduct. As a tool, it is useful for confirming the results of other indexes to behavior and for monitoring actions that are speculated to exist but have not yet been measured. It is relatively inexpensive in all senses except time, and it is relatively simple to accomplish and therefore can be conducted by a variety of auxiliary personnel.

As for objectivity, observation need not take second place to any measurement technique. Adherence to the procedures cited in this chapter will help make this data format among the more useful of all informal approaches. Systematic observation should always be considered an essential component of informal assessment.

TEACHER-MADE INFORMAL TESTS

The preponderance of measures of the academic progress of students can be considered teacher-made informal tests. Using the nomenclature provided earlier in this chapter, educators can consider the majority of these measures as verbal-graphic stimuli, i.e., they use verbal or written stimuli and, frequently, students' written responses. These tests are common to virtually all academic measures and may be used to evaluate performance in most aspects of reading, arithmetic, spelling, and so on. Such informal verbal-graphic stimuli tests are developed by the teacher, tend to parallel specific subsets of instruction, are of short duration, are administered frequently, and are criterion referenced. Clearly, this approach is of exceptional value to the teacher engaged in everyday instruction.

Smith (1969) has outlined some of the purposes and advantages of informal teacher-made tests. Perhaps foremost among these is the fact that teachers cannot wait for the results of formal tests when they attempt to plan their class programs:

> The infrequent formal testing schedules of most school systems are inadequate to aid in planning daily lessons for the teacher who knows that a child's educational performance varies from one day to another and from one subject area to another. An alert and dedicated teacher wants to know today how she must approach a student tomorrow—how she can help him get the most from his school years. (p. *v*)

Smith asserts the characteristics that underlie formal procedures, culminating in the suggestion that

> Frequent, informal, and specific educational assessment is feasible and can assist the educator in practice, rather than wishing for or

paying lip service to, the principle of individualization of instruction. (p. 2)

It can be seen, then, that informal assessment is essential in the instruction of students with learning problems. However, without proper assurance that the tests are in fact appropriate and suitable, it is unsatisfactory to use the technique in a systematic approach to instruction. Therefore, this section provides an overview of the approaches and techniques used with informal teacher-made tests and suggests guidelines for development that will make their use an effective aid in instruction.

Using Teacher-Made Informal Tests

A number of factors must be weighed as the instructor approaches the construction of an informal teacher-made test. Exhibit 3-1 provides a checklist of items to consider. While this checklist may not be comprehensive, consideration of its items can greatly improve the quality of tests developed in the classroom without undue efforts on the part of the teacher. Careful referral to Exhibit 3-1 as the chapter progresses and as tests are developed should be advantageous.

Is the Topic to Be Measured Defined Adequately?

It is patently impossible to begin the construction of any test without a thorough understanding of precisely what is to be measured. Generalities such as arithmetic achievement, oral reading skills, and so on simply are not adequate to the task. Gronlund (1973) suggests that a major part of the solution to this problem is to divide classroom instruction carefully into smaller, easily manageable units that can be tested frequently. While this is sound advice, it also is wise to (a) avoid measuring outcomes in more than one domain per test and (b) avoid mixing the elements of the test even from within a domain. For example, both reading *and* arithmetic questions (mixed domains) or both addition *and* multiplication facts (mixed elements) should not be asked on the same test. It should be remembered that each test is (or should be) designed to reveal information about some specific facet of behavior. Adequate definitions can emerge only from instructional objectives.

Is the Test Related to Instructional Objectives?

Instructional objectives are clear statements of learning outcomes provided in behavioral terms. Outcome refers to the fact that the test constructor knows exactly what constitutes a learned behavior. Gronlund (1978) provides

Exhibit 3-1 Improving the Construction of Teacher-Made Tests

CHECKLIST OF KEY FACTORS

1. Is the topic to be measured defined adequately?
2. Is the test related to instructional objectives?
3. Has the proper level of generality been determined?
4. Has the appropriate level of the domain been considered?
5. Have questions been constructed in the correct format and are their formats constructed properly?
6. Has the domain been sampled adequately?
7. Is there an objective way to score and interpret the test and to judge mastery?
8. Are there safeguards?
   a. Have questions been sampled more than once?
   b. Are there alternative methods?
   c. Have questions been measured in alternative locations?

---

a clear guideline for the advantages to be gained from instructional objectives written as a learning outcome:

1. It provides direction for the instructor, and it clearly conveys his instructional intent to others.
2. It provides a guide for selecting the subject matter, the teaching methods, and the materials to be used during instruction.
3. It provides a guide for constructing tests and instruments for evaluating student achievement. (p. 4)

Instructional objectives generally are written as declarative sentences that state the learning outcome precisely. The following examples of instructional objectives declare that the student will be able to:

1. describe the important persons, places, and events in a story
2. list the steps of a subtraction problem in proper order
3. choose the correct answer for multiplication problems from among four alternatives

The following examples of statements that are not so acceptable as instructional objectives state that the student should be able to:

1. comprehend the importance of the story
2. realize the sequence of steps in a subtraction problem
3. know the correct answer for a multiplication problem

Inspection of these objectives indicates that the first set is measured more easily because a learning *outcome* is stated. *Comprehend, realize,* and *know* are vague terms that are not measured easily and in fact are nonbehavioral in the sense that verbs of that type do not reflect observable actions. Does this mean that the teacher cannot get to such important ideas as "know"? Actually, it doesn't, for one of the more essential reasons for careful verb selection is that the choice will signify the level of generality of the instructional objective.

Has the Proper Level of Generality Been Determined?

Generality refers to the scope of the question, i.e., its specificity. In Gronlund's (1978) view this can be accomplished by detailing general instructional objectives through lists of the specific behaviors that will give evidence of knowledge of the general objective. Readers should note the parallel here between general and specific instructional objectives and the concept of long-term and short-term goals demanded by IEPs. The following is an example of instructional objectives for a test:

The student:
1. Comprehends the meaning of addition
   1.1 States whether problems do or do not involve addition.
   1.2 Identifies accurate and inaccurate answers to problems.
   1.3 Provides correct answers to problems.

The general instructional objective is somewhat more vague, beginning with a verb (comprehends) that is difficult to verify directly; in fact, this verb was used earlier to demonstrate its relatively nonbehavioral qualities. However, by its inclusion and verification through more specific objectives, the teacher can reasonably assume that the student does in fact comprehend the meaning of addition and subtraction. Additional specific objectives or a third level of objectives (1.21, 1.22, etc.) could further increase teacher confidence.

In general, teacher-made tests must operate at the level of these specific objectives since they are in fact the outcomes that are directly measurable. It should be noted that the teacher's ability to measure student progress actually is expanded and made more accurate. For while it is not possible to measure "appreciates," "comprehends," "understands," and similar general objectives directly, it is reasonably straightforward to determine progress through the use of quite specific statements. The major advantage is, of course, that the teacher can be quite certain of what has been achieved. The key to writing general and specific objectives lies in the selection of the verb initiating the sentence. An excellent list of appropriate verbs may be found in Gronlund (1978).

Has the Appropriate Level of the Domain Been Investigated?

In Chapter 2, the concept of a taxonomy of the cognitive (affective and perceptual motor) domain was mentioned. Consideration of the nature of these domains must be granted, for how a question is asked has great bearing on the teacher's ability to recognize a student's level of knowledge. For example, it is possible to "know" the formula for water, H_2O, as many young children do, without the vaguest comprehension of what it reflects. The following examples are questions to students:

1. What was the year that Columbus landed in America?
2. What are five outcomes of the arrival of Columbus in America?
3. What are five events that might not have happened between 1500 and 1600 if Columbus did not arrive in America until 1592?

These objectives require a growing command of information if they are to be answered appropriately, i.e., the student's knowledge is increasingly examined and probed. The type or level of knowledge also is altered drastically. Should the teacher be satisfied with only the initial level of response, it is obvious that a significant amount of important assessment information will never be collected.

For the teacher, the implication is straightforward: the manner in which a question is asked greatly dictates the level that learners will be measured on and probably, over time, will learn to study toward. That is, *how* the question is stated certainly reflects the level of cognition necessary to respond and therefore provides insight into the level of knowledge at the student's command.

Insight into the cognitive domain as it relates to an ordering of educational objectives (sometimes called a taxonomy) has been provided by several authors. (The cognitive domain is alluded to only briefly here; a full discussion appears in Chapter 8.) However, in Gronlund's (1978) view some learning outcomes may be characterized as minimum essentials and others as developmental learning. The former are somewhat low level, achieved rather easily, and can be considered as prerequisites to future learning. This last represents levels that probably will never be mastered fully. As a general rule, the farther one proceeds up the cognitive domain the more likely the learning outcome (cognitive process) is developmental.

Developmental learning is important and should be sought through properly developed tests. However, most special education instruction in fact is concerned with minimum essentials, i.e., the mastery of basic facts. Therefore it is quite probable that teachers will invest the majority of their efforts in constructing items that reflect mastery rather than developmental learning. It is very important, however, to verify mastery (not simply knowing) and to move up the taxonomy as conditions permit.

Have Questions Been Constructed in the Correct Format and Are They Drawn Properly?

The format of questions plays a significant part in determining their level. While it may be possible to use a simple format (true-false) to reflect lower levels of the domain, it is unlikely that this can sample developmental levels. If questions must reflect the behavior that is specified and dictated by the instructional objectives, then it is easy to see how the format of test questions is essential.

In all likelihood, though, one or more of the following four types of questions probably will be selected: (a) matching, (b) short answer, (c) true-false, (d) multiple choice. Of these, short answer is the least objective and multiple choice the most common and best suited for the majority of uses. Readers interested in a complete review of procedures for writing these items should refer to Gronlund (1976); however, a summary based on Gronlund's analysis is provided in Exhibit 3-2.

Has the Domain Been Adequately Sampled?

Obtaining a proper sample of the domain is not easy but is important. The essential points to be raised are (a) were sufficient questions asked to allow judgment concerning the student's concept of the subject matter? and (b) were the questions equally distributed over all aspects of the domain? While there is no certain way to judge these events, the use of a table of specifications clearly can be of value to the test developer.

A table of specifications is no more than a matrix, with one element being content and the other instructional objectives. Earlier, a brief example of instructional objectives was provided covering a child's understanding of addition. Exhibit 3-3 is an example of a table of specifications developed from this procedure. The table interacts upon two dimensions, objectives and

Exhibit 3-2 Alternative Test Question Formats

MATCHING QUESTIONS

Purpose: Measure factual information.

Advantages: Compact, easy to construct.

Disadvantages: Limited to measurement of memorized answers, subject to guessing through subtle undetected cues.

Hints:
1. Use only homogeneous materials in a single exercise.
2. Include an equal number of items in each column to be matched.
3. Keep the list of items to be matched brief and place the shorter responses on the right.
4. Arrange the list of responses in a logical order.
5. Give proper directions.
6. Place all items on a single page.

SHORT ANSWER QUESTIONS

Purpose: Measure a wide variety of simple learning outcomes.

Advantages: Easy to construct, require student to recall rather than simply recognize answer, reduce guessing.

Disadvantages: Cannot readily measure complex learning, can be difficult to score.

Hints:
1. Response should be both brief and definite.
2. Don't use statements directly lifted from textbook material.
3. Use direct statements rather than incomplete statements.
4. Blanks for answers should be equivalent and placed into a column to the immediate right of the question.
5. Be careful to avoid excessive blanks, i.e., the statement must be intelligible by itself.

Exhibit 3-2   continued

TRUE-FALSE QUESTIONS

Purpose:	Identification of facts, definitions of terms, accuracy of statements.
Advantages:	Perhaps easy to construct, can be used to sample many types of information.
Disadvantages:	Limited to very elementary learning, susceptible to guessing.
Hints:	1. Avoid broad statements.

1. Avoid broad statements.
2. Avoid statements that are trivial in nature.
3. Avoid negative statements and long complex statements.
4. Avoid two ideas contained in one question.
5. Cite sources for any opinions that are used to form basis of question.
6. Make all statements of about equal length.
7. Split the number of true and false statements about evenly.

MULTIPLE-CHOICE QUESTIONS

Purpose:	Most widely recognized objective measure of mastery and developmental learning; can be used to measure terminology, facts, procedures, general understanding, application, and other outcomes.
Advantages:	Widely applicable, somewhat resilient to ambiguity, greater reliability per item, freedom from response sets (i.e., patterns of scoring such as all true in true-false questions).
Disadvantages:	None that are not characteristic of other paper and pencil tests, i.e., student may know answer but not demonstrate it in practice, cannot measure ability to organize and present ideas, and so on.

Exhibit 3-2 continued

Hints:	1. The stem of the question should be meaningful by itself.
	2. The stem should contain as much of the entire item as is possible, and should be free of irrelevant information.
	3. Avoid, as much as possible, the case of a negatively stated stem.
	4. All alternatives must be grammatically consistent.
	5. Provide only one correct answer.
	6. All distractors should be plausible.
	7. Avoid any verbal cues that give away the correct response.
	8. Alternatives should be of approximately equal length.
	9. Vary the position of the correct answer across test items.
	10. Use special approaches like "all of the above" sparingly.

Source: Adapted from *Measurement and Evaluation in Teaching* (3rd ed.) by N. E. Gronlund by permission of Macmillan Publishing Co., Inc., © 1976, pp. 164–209.

content; the resulting figure indicates the number of questions that will be asked. The authors also have found it useful to code cells (A, B, C, etc.) with the types of items used. Using this procedure the teacher can be relatively certain that (a) all instructional objectives are measured, (b) all are measured at several levels of the cognitive domain hierarchy, (c) all relevant content is sampled, and (d) no cell is systematically overestimated or underestimated without the teacher's awareness. A table of specifications also allows a critique of the student's response and the opportunity to pinpoint errors.

Exhibit 3-4 presents a summary of a student's hypothetical errors, i.e., the pattern of errors that appear across the cells. The results indicate that oral problems are more difficult for the student than are written problems and that problems that require the pupil to provide information seldom are solved. The overall mastery level (26 of 48, or 54 percent) suggests that the student does not yet comprehend addition and that more work will be necessary. Careful examination of the profile of errors (fractions in the margins) should help the teacher to pinpoint where that instructional work should begin.

Exhibit 3-3 Example of a Table of Specifications

General level: Comprehends meaning of addition

Instructional Objectives / Content Areas	States . . .	Identifies . . .	Provides . . .	Total	Score
Written Problems	A 4	B 4	C 4	12	
Written Story Problems	D 4	E 4	F 4	12	
Oral Problems	G 4	H 4	I 4	12	
Oral Story Problems	J 4	K 4	L 4	12	
Total	16	16	16	48	
Score					

Exhibit 3-4 Hypothetical Error Pattern Using Table of Specifications

General level: Comprehends meaning of addition

Instructional Objectives / Content Areas	States . . .	Identifies . . .	Provides . . .	Total	Score
Written Problems	A 4 / 4	B 4 / 4	C 1 / 4	12	9/12
Written Story Problems	D 3 / 4	E 2 / 4	F 0 / 4	12	5/12
Oral Problems	G 4 / 4	H 2 / 4	I 1 / 4	12	7/12
Oral Story Problems	J 3 / 4	K 2 / 4	L 0 / 4	12	5/12
Total	16	16	16	48	26/48
Score	14/16	10/16	2/16	26/48	

Is There an Objective Way to Score and Interpret the
Test and to Judge Mastery?

Actually, little explanation for the first concern is necessary. However, objectivity implies a clear decisional basis for determining the correctness or incorrectness of a response and a decision that is free from last-minute (perhaps arbitrary) conclusions. In practice, this equates to decisional criteria being established before the test is administered.

The second concern is a problem generic to all criterion referenced procedures: what level of performance constitutes mastery, i.e., an acceptable performance level? The clearest guideline is that the earlier a measured set of behaviors falls into the skill hierarchy, the higher the student's competency must be. In fact, many early skills must virtually be free from error—it is not possible to proceed very quickly in arithmetic if $+$, $-$, $\times$, and $\div$ constantly are used interchangeably. So, criteria are related to the position of the items in the skill hierarchy, although ultimately the decision as to mastery level must be the instructor's. Seldom, however, is a criterion of less than 85 percent to 90 percent justifiable for academic instruction at the basic skills (mastery) level.

Safeguards: Sampled More Than Once? Alternative Methods?
Measured in Alternative Locations?

Several safeguards must be applied to teacher-made informal tests. The following three are among the more critical.

First, how often has the student had the opportunity to display a behavior? The answer should be "several," for the teacher never should estimate a behavior based upon a single record. This is true whether the answer was correct or incorrect. Multiple administration of a test or, preferably, the development of parallel tests should always be undertaken. Special students simply are too capricious in their behavior to be able to judge performance from a single or even few measures.

Second, has the student had an opportunity to demonstrate the behavior in more than one way? For reasons that probably are quite idiosyncratic, students sometimes find a particular test constructed in a specific format to be especially difficult. Since informal procedures are not bound by norms to a specific administrative approach, the teacher has the option of several different methods, e.g., written or observation or specific question formats. The point here is that the teacher wants to measure student knowledge, not student knowledge encumbered by test formats.

Finally, the teacher probably will want to measure performance across a variety of similar tasks in dissimilar situations. For example, the teacher may wish to determine whether the student can add $00 + 00$, $2 + 2$, $+\underline{2}^{2}$, $00 + 2$, and so on; this can be accomplished wherever the student may be at any given moment. While stimulus properties can be incorporated into the test simply by indicating the question format in the table of specifications (A, B, etc.), this often is forgotten and a single written format is administered. Allowing the table of specifications to plan the form and content of the test, rather than the reverse, is by far the choice for the teacher of special students.

Summary

Informal teacher-made verbal-graphic stimulus procedures have many positive attributes that may be capitalized on in the assessment of students with learning problems. Such tests are inexpensive, can be administered quickly and beneficially, and are particularly valuable for further investigating responses to norm referenced tests, for elaborating on errors made in specific lessons, for monitoring progress toward specific goals in the IEP, and countless other measurement tasks. Yet the history of the teacher-made informal measure is, understandably, an admixture of promises and failures, perplexities, advocates and detractors. But with the advent of the criterion referenced movement, the demand for individualized instruction, accountability with individual children, and the recognition that formal procedures are neither so proficient nor adaptable as once was thought, the trend toward teacher-made tests has revived. For this to reach fruition, however, attention to the technical considerations just cited in this chapter—and more—must occur.

COMMERCIALLY PREPARED INFORMAL TESTS

Commercially prepared informal tests occupy an important niche in the systematic delivery of service to special students. These tests usually parallel the majority of guidelines cited earlier and are designed for rapid administration and for collecting data referenced to a criterion rather than to a norm. Occasionally, tests will provide cursory norms, but this seems more of an afterthought, and a review of most instruments suggests that the norms should not in fact be used extensively. As a result, the strength of the tests invariably lies in the teacher's skill and most particularly in the ability to relate the prepared tests to the academic concerns of a particular student.

This section notes some of the more common tests for teaching learning disabled students. This does not exhaust the list of procedures available, because dozens of informal tests exist. Only tests judged to have received extensive use in the field are discussed. Readers are cautioned not to infer that these tests are, as a group, easy to administer *and* score. On the contrary, some informal procedures require considerable practice and experience before their best results can be attained. Careful preparation and study always should precede the use of these tests, for ultimately their data are only as valuable as the care taken in their use will allow.

Reading

The Individual Reading Inventory (sometimes Informal Reading Inventory, or IRI) may be the most common approach to the informal diagnosis of reading. Usually it consists of a series of graded (grade level) passages that the student reads out loud to the teacher. The passages then are scored, as they are read, for the types of decoding errors made by the student. Errors are scored for two purposes: (1) to determine reading level and (2) to determine an error pattern. Reading level is termed *easy reading level, instructional level,* and *frustration level.* Precisely what constitutes these levels varies from test to test and should be noted by the teacher on that basis.

Error patterns refer to mistakes made in decoding the printed materials, it being assumed that the student will be prone to committing the same type of errors repeatedly. As in the case of the determination of levels of reading performance, various test procedures employ different decoding errors. Exhibit 3-5 provides a generalized list of potential errors and the standardized marking system that the teacher may use.

Finally, the teacher may assess the student's comprehension of the material that has been read. This procedure also varies from test to test but generally is accomplished by orally asking the student questions about the passage that has been read. Not all IRIs use this feature, however, and only some make a distinction between literal and inferred comprehension, literal comprehension being the recall of fact, inferred comprehension requiring the student to analyze and conclude a correct answer when one was not directly provided.

A second type of IRI is a graded word list that the student is required to decode and pronounce and sometimes to define. When these steps are combined, the test exceeds simple decoding accuracy and is, in a manner, a partial measure of comprehension. Word list IRIs have proved quite popular (Lerner, 1976) with learning disabled students and should receive consideration.

Although it is quite possible to develop IRIs from graded work materials, many teachers find it convenient to use commercially prepared informal tests. The following two are among those used most often and are illustrative of this group of measurement instruments.

The Ekwall Reading Inventory

This self-contained reading inventory (Ekwall, 1979) is useful for students preprimer to ninth grade. Four reading passages are provided at each level

Exhibit 3-5 Marking System for Errors in an IRI

Type of Error	Description	Marking
Assistance	Teacher had to supply word after 5 seconds	<u>Underline words</u> aided.
Hesitations	Learner hesitated at word but teach did not have to supply assistance	✓ check above hesitated word.
Insertions	Learner inserts word not on page	Put in word or word parts with caret (∧).
Mispronunciation	Learner does not accurately pronounce word	Write in learner's "pro-noun-shun" (pronunciation) above the missed word.
Omissions	Learner leaves out a word or words and reads on	Circle the ⟨omitted⟩ word(s) or punctuation.
Order reversals	Learner inverts word order	Mark reversals with this symbol: ⌐‿⌐
Regressions	Learner reads word(s) and then rereads them	Put a wavy line under word(s) repeated.
Self corrections	Learner makes a mistake but corrects it spon-taneously	When the learner sc errors <u>errs</u> note the mistake and write sc above it.
Substitutions	Learner reads one word as another	Then <u>When</u> the learner sub-stitutes a word underline the omitted word and write in the given one.

Passage example:

The person had been waiting all afternoon for a call. She was anxious to know whether her poem would win the contest and the fifty dollars prize. If it did then she could take her friend, Jack, out to a fine dinner. But little did she know that the phone.

Source: Reprinted from "Ascertaining the Reading Skills of Atypical Learners" by J. Lloyd, in D. A. Sabatino & T. L. Miller (Eds.), *Describing Learner Characteristics of Handicapped Children and Youth* by permission of Grune & Stratton, Inc., © 1979.

and the test is designed to measure a student's oral and silent independent, instructional, and frustration grade levels. The test also is useful for measuring the student's listening comprehension. Of the reading passages, two are to be read orally and two silently; each student reads one oral and one silent passage, with the others reserved for later use. The *Ekwall* also contains a graded word list termed the *San Diego Quick Assessment*. This list contains ten words at each of the levels and is used as a quick judge of where to begin the oral and silent reading passages. The teacher manual provides information on scoring and interpreting the test results and on behavioral characteristics of the reading levels. The test is relatively easy to administer and score, particularly since only a few types of decoding errors are measured.

References to standardization procedures are largely absent. Grade level passages were developed by use of a readability formula and 50 students were tested. After adjustments were made, 60 students were given the test. Apparently, however, no further validity or reliability studies were conducted, so as in the case with other IRIs, teacher judgment is vital.

The Classroom Reading Inventory

This test by Silvaroli (1976) was designed for teachers with little previous experience with individualized reading programs. It attempts to provide diagnostic information concerning a child's specific problems. The test is exceptionally quick to administer, requiring 12 minutes or less, and is intended for use from preprimer to grade 8. Both decoding and comprehension skills are measured (the usual levels are included) and a word per minute (WPM) formula is included so the rate can be calculated. A listening comprehension measure also can be taken. Graded word lists, typical graded paragraphs, and sheets for summarizing types of errors are provided. Abbreviated case studies are offered but data concerning validity and reliability are absent, so again the teacher's judgment of the value of the test is the main criterion.

IRIs are perhaps the most common informal approach to the measurement of reading. Two forms predominate—graded word lists and graded passages. Both forms are available commercially, although the latter can be constructed by the teacher from materials available in the classroom. Readers interested in word lists should consult LaPray and Ross (1969), and for graded passages, the tests cited in this section and Zintz (1975). In either case, the strengths of IRIs are evident in their ability to pinpoint specific errors. However, the contrary evidence is that IRIs are very subject to measurement error and highly dependent upon the relationship of curriculum exposure by specific tests. That is, students can be grossly overestimated or underestimated simply by the random arrangement of curriculum by test (see

Jenkins & Pany, 1978). This supports the use of teacher-made rather than commercially available IRIs, even though the former are somewhat more tedious to develop.

Mathematics

The informal assessment of mathematics is similar to that of reading in at least two ways: (1) it often is based upon the evaluation of classroom activities, (2) it is a complex learned behavior that is related intimately to cognitive development. Therefore, developmental, motivational, and affective factors should be studied before assessment of skills can begin. A review of some of the factors to be considered can be found in Wiederholt, Hammill, and Brown (1978).

A number of tests predominate in the informal assessment of mathematics, although many are available.

Basic Education Skills Inventory (BESI)

This criterion referenced device (Adamson, Shrage, & Van Etten, 1972) measures skills in a broad band of areas, with prescriptive materials keyed to the outcome. The test covers grades K-6.

Fountain Valley Teacher Support System in Mathematics

This approach to informal assessment (1976) integrates both testing and instructional activities. Useful for the diagnosis of student deficiencies in mathematics K-8, the procedure is criterion referenced and contains 785 behavioral objectives sequenced to various elements of arithmetic instruction. The test is one of the more well known and widely used in the field.

Project Math: Mathematics Concept Inventory

This method (Cawley, Fitzmaurice, Goodstein, Lepore, Sedlak, & Althaus, 1976) was designed specifically for use with handicapped students. The content reflects about the first six years of school but is structured so that other factors common to handicapped children (such as social skills) are served concomitantly. Probes are provided and a profile of pupil performance can be achieved.

Sequential Testing and Educational Programming

This device (Greenburger & Thum, 1975) is a testing and resource guide that provides assessment related to specific objectives in 24 developmental areas. It is based on Osgood's (1957) model and therefore is organized on channels and levels, although all assessment is criterion referenced. Commercially available instructional materials and further diagnostic procedures are referenced to each objective.

Analysis of Computational Errors

A number of other programs contain similar procedures. However, the emphasis in the informal assessment of mathematics is closely tied to curricula; perhaps nowhere else have informal assessment and instruction been linked so systematically. On the other hand, the informal assessment of a student's mathematics skills without extensive, comprehensive tests often is based on the informal analysis of classroom production. This task can be accomplished by careful analysis of computational errors.

Ashlock (1976) provides an excellent introduction to this topic that should be essential in the assessment of students who consistently demonstrate errors in computation. This semiprogrammed method provides a unique diagnostic tool that can be applied to the results of standardized tests, classroom tests, or classroom exercises. Ashlock provides convincing evidence that students' errors often are learned patterns that are not detected before the response becomes habitual. The error patterns are further supported by the fact that many are begun as students' guesses as to what is demanded, i.e., a rule is created that seemingly provides an appropriate solution. On other occasions, students combine partially learned rules to produce sometimes humorous (to the knowledgeable teacher at least) procedures. For example:

$$
\begin{array}{r} 74 \\ +80 \\ \hline 154 \end{array} \qquad
\begin{array}{r} 18 \\ +13 \\ \hline 211 \end{array} \qquad
\begin{array}{r} 22 \\ +29 \\ \hline 411 \end{array} \qquad
\begin{array}{r} 14 \\ +188 \\ \hline 912 \end{array}
$$

$$
\begin{array}{r} 150 \\ -13 \\ \hline 140 \end{array} \qquad
\begin{array}{r} 148 \\ -90 \\ \hline 50 \end{array} \qquad
\begin{array}{r} 163 \\ -122 \\ \hline 41 \end{array} \qquad
\begin{array}{r} 109 \\ -13 \\ \hline 106 \end{array}
$$

What are the errors?* In reality, this is an exceptionally effective way to attack computational errors. When placed in the diagnostic context with any of the more comprehensive measures, it makes available a rigorous procedure for establishing the nature of mathematics problems that learning disabled students encounter.

---

*The errors: in the first set, tens are not carried; in the second set, any subtraction including zero results in zero. In both cases, the student has applied a rule erroneously.

Spelling

According to Hammill and Noone (1975) there are few diagnostic spelling tests available. Most spelling tests are a part of formal assessment or are strictly classroom exercises accompanying instruction. In part, this is a result of theoreticians' difficulty in determining the nature of spelling (Wallace & Larsen, 1978). Therefore, aside from the procedures discussed in Chapter 6, the teacher is left with only a few guidelines. However, in a manner analogous to the error patterns in reading and arithmetic, spelling, too, has persistent gremlins that are likely to show up in any assessment. Edgington (1967) provides a sample of frequent student spelling errors (Exhibit 3-6) that could form the basis for teacher-made diagnoses.

In approaching diagnosis it is useful to recognize that (a) a relatively few words account for most adult written expression and (b) a few words are most commonly misspelled. Exhibit 3-7 presents Horn's (1926) list of 100 words that account for some 65 percent of all words written by adults. An astounding 10 words (I, the, and, to, a, you, of, in, we, for) account for 25 percent of all words written. Therefore, study of Horn's list seems advisable. What are the more commonly misspelled words? Kuska, Webster, and Elford

---

Exhibit 3-6 Common Misspelling Patterns

Addition of unneeded letters
Omission of needed letters
Reflections of child's mispronunciation
Reflections of dialect
Reversal of whole words
Reversal of consonant order
Reversal of consonant or vowel directionality
Reversal of syllables
Phonetic spelling of nonphonetic words or parts thereof
Wrong associations of a sound with a given set of letters, such as *u* has been learned for *ou* in *you*
"Neographisms," or letters put in a word that bear no discernible relationship to the word dictated
Varying degrees and combinations of these or other patterns

Source: Adapted from "But He Spelled Them Right This Morning" by R. Edgington, *Academic Therapy,* 1967, *3,* 58–59, in *The Resource Teacher: A Guide to Effective Practice* by J. L. Wiederholt, D. D. Hammill, & V. Brown, by permission of Allyn & Bacon, Inc., © 1978.

Exhibit 3-7 The 100 Most Commonly Written Words

1. I	21. at	41. do	61. up	81. think
2. the	22. this	42. been	62. day	82. say
3. and	23. with	43. letter	63. much	83. please
4. to	24. but	44. can	64. out	84. him
5. a	25. on	45. would	65. her	85. his
6. you	26. if	46. she	66. order	86. got
7. of	27. all	47. when	67. yours	87. over
8. in	28. so	48. about	68. now	88. make
9. we	29. me	49. they	69. well	89. may
10. for	30. was	50. any	70. an	90. received
11. it	31. very	51. which	71. here	91. before
12. that	32. my	52. some	72. them	92. two
13. is	33. had	53. has	73. see	93. send
14. your	34. our	54. or	74. go	94. after
15. have	35. from	55. there	75. what	95. work
16. will	36. am	56. us	76. come	96. could
17. be	37. one	57. good	77. were	97. dear
18. are	38. time	58. know	78. no	98. made
19. not	39. he	59. just	79. how	99. glad
20. as	40. get	60. by	80. did	100. like

Source: Adapted from *A Basic Writing Vocabulary of 10,000 Most Commonly Used Words in Writing* by Ernest A. Horn, Universityof Iowa Monograph in Education, First Series, No. 4, by permission of the University of Iowa, © 1926.

(1964) provide a list of 100 of them (Exhibit 3-8). The words are largely irregular but also are remarkably common. In fact, for a fun exercise ask a friend to spell the words—assuming you are willing to risk the friendship, of course!

The fact remains that spelling assessment is difficult to conduct. The few procedures offered here represent what is known and has been done to date. It should be emphasized that the teacher's creative work in this area is essential.

MAKING THE MOST OF INFORMAL ASSESSMENT

As the reader probably has discerned, one of the major advantages and attractions of informal assessment is the freedom it gives the practitioner to develop, revise, adapt, and adopt procedures to specific situations. While it is

Exhibit 3-8 The 100 Most Commonly Misspelled Words

ache	families	neither	sandwich
afraid	fasten	nickel	scratch
against	fault	niece	sense
all right	February	ninety	separate
although	forgotten	ninth	shining
angry	friendly	onion	silence
answered	good-bye	passed	since
asks	guessed	peaceful	soldier
beautiful	happened	perfectly	speech
because	happily	piano	squirrel
beginning	here's	picnic	stepped
boy's	holiday	picture	straight
buried	hungry	piece	studying
busily	husband	pitcher	success
carrying	its	pleasant	taught
certain	it's	potato	their
choose	kitchen	practice	there's
Christmas	knives	prettiest	through
clothes	language	pumpkin	valentine
climbed	lettuce	purpose	whose
course	listening	quietly	worst
double	lose	rapidly	writing
easier	marriage	receive	yours
eighth	meant	rotten	
either	minute	safety	
enemy	neighbor	said	

Source: Adapted from *Spelling in Language Arts 6* by A. Kuska, E. J. D. Webster, & G. Elford by permission of Thomas Nelson & Sons (Canada) Ltd., © 1964.

true that a price must be paid for this opportunity, a priceless advantage is gained, namely, the opportunity to explore a student's behavior from as many angles as time and circumstances permit. While the teacher must be careful of the procedure (some informal tests do specify administration techniques), that is a major factor on relatively few occasions. Getting the most from informal procedures begins initially with encouragement to approach measurement problems with an open and creative mind. Beyond that, a few hints to the teacher of the learning disabled:

First, determine precisely what is to be measured and be certain that the yardstick is student (i.e., criterion) referenced. It cannot be stressed too strongly that good measurement flows from knowing what is sought. No assessment tool can overcome the deficit of ambiguity in the analysis of behavior.

Second, select the best possible procedures and be certain to carry them through accordingly. It is hoped that the guidelines in this chapter will be valuable in that effort. But it must be remembered that it is relatively easy to induce bias, to measure the wrong conduct, to miscalculate in an approximation of behavior. Care must be taken, and since there are no norms to follow, the teacher's careful judgment again is paramount.

Third, examine the stimulus-response properties of the test to be certain that (a) the student can approach them and (b) that they are a part of what is sought to be measured. Competency skills may involve cutting an angle of 60°, but should they involve a written request that the student cut such an angle? From this context, it is not possible to say, but it is known that if the student fails to read *and* understand the request to cut the angle, the failure may be attributable to more than one source.

Fourth, take into consideration the taxonomy of educational objectives; vary levels of questions to fit the desired learning outcome. How a question is asked in terms of format greatly affects the interpretation and meaning of the answer. Practice in constructing teacher-made tests is essential.

Finally, do not hesitate to analyze the nature of responses. As has been seen, many teacher-made tests can be evaluated from the table of specifications, while IRIs and Ashlock's (1976) procedures represent, in truth, analytical techniques. In fact, it is the analysis of the test that is the most valuable aspect of informal procedures. Examination of the data is intriguing and challenging and can be one of the more revealing aspects of the measurement of learning disabled students. The quality of the questions the teacher prepares and the way they are followed up will be the major determinants of the answers.

REFERENCES

Adamson, G., Shrage, M., & Van Etten, G. *Basic education skills inventory.* Santa Monica, Calif.: Winch and Associates, 1972.

Ashlock, R.B. *Error patterns in computation: A semi-programmed approach* (2nd ed.). Columbus, Ohio: The Charles E. Merrill Publishing Co., Inc., 1976.

Barker, R. *Ecological psychology.* Stanford, Calif.: Stanford University Press, 1968.

Bersoff, N. Silk purses into sow's ears: The decline of psychological testing and a suggestion for its redemption. *American Psychologist,* 1973, *28,* 892–899.

Blackham, G.J., & Silberman, A. *Modification of child and adolescent behavior* (3rd ed.). Belmont, Calif.: Wadsworth Publishing Co., Inc., 1980.

Cartwright, C.A., & Cartwright, G.P. *Developing observation skills.* New York: McGraw-Hill Book Company, 1974.

Cawley, J., Fitzmaurice, A., Goodstein, H., Lepore, A., Sedlak, R., & Althaus, V. *Project math: Mathematics concept inventory.* Educational Development Corporation, Tulsa, Okla., 1976.

Edgington, R. But he spelled them right this morning. *Academic Therapy,* 1967, *3,* 58–59.

Ekwall, E.E. *Ekwall reading inventory.* Boston: Allyn & Bacon, Inc., 1979.

Fountain Valley teacher support system in mathematics. Huntington Beach, Calif.: Richard L. Zweig Associates, Inc., 1976.

Glaser, R. Instructional technology and the measurement of learning outcomes: Some questions. *American Psychologist,* 1963, *18,* 519–521.

Greenburger, S.M., & Thum, S.R. *Sequential testing and educational programming.* San Rafael, Calif.: Academic Therapy Publications, 1975.

Gronlund, N.E. *Preparing criterion-referenced tests for classroom instruction.* New York: Macmillan Publishing Co., Inc., 1973.

————. *Measurement and evaluation in teaching* (3rd ed.). New York: Macmillan Publishing Co., Inc., 1976.

————. *Stating objectives for classroom instruction* (2nd ed.). New York: Macmillan Publishing Co., Inc., 1978.

Hammill, D.D., & Noone, J. Improving spelling skills. In D.D. Hammill & N.R. Bartel (Eds.), *Teaching children with learning and behavior problems.* Boston: Allyn & Bacon, Inc., 1975.

Hawkins, R.P., & Dobes, R.W. Behavioral definitions in applied behavior analysis: Explicit to implicit. In B.C. Etzel, J.M. LeBlanc, & D.M. Baer (Eds.), *New developments in behavioral research: Theory, methods, and applications.* Hillsdale, N.J.: Lawrence Erlbaum Associates, 1975.

Heilman, A.W. *Principles and practices of teaching reading* (3rd ed.). Columbus, Ohio: The Charles E. Merrill Publishing Co., Inc., 1972.

Hersen, M., & Barlow, D.H. *Single case experimental designs: Strategies for studying behavior change.* Elmsford, N.Y.: Pergamon Press, 1976.

Horn, E.A. *A basic writing vocabulary of 10,000 words most commonly used in writing.* Iowa City, Iowa: University of Iowa Monographs in Education, First Series, No. 4, 1926.

Howell, K.W., Kaplan, J.S., & O'Connell, C.V. *Evaluating exceptional children: A task analysis approach.* Columbus, Ohio: The Charles E. Merrill Publishing Co., Inc., 1979.

Jenkins, J., & Pany, D. Standardized achievement tests: How useful for special education? *Exceptional Children,* 1978, *44,* 448–453.

Johnson, S.M., & Bolstad, O.D. Methodological issues in naturalistic observation: Some problems and solutions for field research. In L.A. Hamerlynck, L.C. Handy, & E.J. Mash (Eds.), *Behavior change: Methodology, concepts, and practice.* Champaign, Ill.: Research Press Co., 1973.

Kazdin, A.E. Self-monitoring and behavior change. In M.J. Mahoney & C.E. Thoresen (Eds.), *Self-control: Power to the person.* Monterey, Calif.: Brooks/Colé Publishing Co., Inc., 1974.

————. *Behavior modification in applied settings* (Rev. ed.). Homewood, Ill.: The Dorsey Press, 1980.

Kent, R.N., Kanowitz, J., O'Leary, K.D., & Cheikem, M. Observer reliability as a function of circumstances of assessment. *Journal of Applied Behavior Analysis,* 1977, *10,* 317–324.

Kratochwill, T.R. N = 1: An alternative strategy for school psychologists. *Journal of School Psychology,* 1977, *15,* 239–249.

Kunzelman, H., Cohen, M., Hulten, W., Martin, G., & Mingo, A. *Precision teaching: An initial training sequence.* Seattle: Special Child Publications, 1970.

Kuska, A., Webster, E.J.D., & Elford, G. *Spelling in language arts 6.* Ontario, Canada: Thomas Nelson & Sons (Canada) Ltd., 1964.

LaPray, M., & Ross, R. The graded word list: A quick list of reading ability. *Journal of Reading,* 1969, *12,* 305–307.

Lerner, J.W. *Children with learning disabilities* (2nd ed.). Boston: Houghton Mifflin Company, 1976.

Mager, R.F. *Preparing instructional objectives.* Belmont, Calif.: Fearon Publishers, 1962.

Mager, R.F., & Pipe, P. *Analyzing performance problems or "You really oughta wanna."* Belmont, Calif.: Fearon Publishers, 1970.

Meichenbaum, D. *Cognitive behavior modification: An integrative approach.* New York: Plenum Publishing Co., 1977.

Morris, R.J. *Behavior modification with children: A systematic guide.* Cambridge, Mass.: Winthrop Publications, Inc., 1976.

Osgood, C.E. A behavioristic analysis of perception and language as cognitive phenomena. In *Contemporary approaches to cognition.* Cambridge, Mass.: Harvard University Press, 1957, 75–118.

Proger, B.B., & Mann, L. Criterion referenced measurement: The world of gray versus black and white. *Journal of Learning Disabilities,* 1973, *6,* 72–84.

Repp, A. Describing and monitoring behavior. In D.A. Sabatino & T.L. Miller (Eds.), *Describing learner characteristics of handicapped children and youth.* New York: Grune & Stratton, Inc., 1979.

Repp, A.C., Deitz, D.E.D., Boles, S.M., Deitz, S.M., & Repp, C.F. Differences among common methods for calculating interobserver agreement. *Journal of Applied Behavior Analysis,* 1976, *9,* 109–113.

Repp, A.C., Roberts, D.M., Slack, D.J., Repp, C.E., & Berkler, M.S. A comparison of frequency, interval, and time sampling methods of data collection. *Journal of Applied Behavior Analysis,* 1976, *9,* 501–508.

Rogers-Warren, A., & Warren, S.F. (Eds.). *Ecological perspectives in behavior analysis.* Baltimore: University Park Press, 1977.

Silvaroli, N.J. *Classroom reading inventory* (3rd ed.). Dubuque, Iowa: William C. Brown Co., 1976.

Smith, R.M. (Ed.). *Teacher diagnosis of educational problems.* Columbus, Ohio: The Charles E. Merrill Publishing Co., Inc., 1969.

Stephens, T. *Implementing behavioral approaches in elementary and secondary schools.* Columbus, Ohio: The Charles E. Merrill Publishing Co., Inc., 1975.

Sulzer-Azaroff, B., & Mayer, G.R. *Applying behavior analysis procedures with children and youth.* New York: Holt, Rinehart & Winston, Inc., 1977.

Tharp, R.G., & Wetzel, R.J. *Behavior modification in the natural environment.* New York: Academic Press, 1969.

Thoresen, C.E., & Mahoney, M.J. *Behavioral self-control.* New York: Holt, 1974.

Walker, J.E., & Shea, T.M. *Behavior modification: A practical approach for educators* (2nd ed.) St. Louis: The C.V. Mosby Company, 1980.

Wallace, G., & Larsen, S.C. *Educational assessment of learning problems: Testing for teaching.* Boston: Allyn & Bacon, Inc., 1978.

Weinberg, R.A., & Woods, F.H. (Eds.). *Observation of pupils and teachers in mainstream and special education settings: Alternative strategies.* Minneapolis: University of Minnesota Leadership Training Institute in Special Education, 1975.

Wiederholt, J.L., Hammill, D.D., & Brown, V. *The resource teacher: A guide to effective practice* . Boston: Allyn & Bacon, Inc., 1978.

Zintz, M.V. *The reading process, the teacher and the learner* (2nd ed.). Dubuque, Iowa: William C. Brown, 1975.

Chapter 4

Curriculum Planning and the IEP Process

Carl R. Schmidt

INTRODUCTION

Alicia is 14. She is interested in horses, rock-and-roll, and oceanic life. She has certain perceptual deficits, a reading level of 2.5, and is attending a learning disability resource class. If Alicia were alone in that class, her learning disability teacher could, as special educators have over the ages, identify commercially developed materials, or develop teacher-made items, appropriate to Alicia's interests, learning style, and ability level. Alas! Alicia is not alone. Her teacher sees 30 other students weekly in a school system serving more than 2,000 handicapped children. To compound the problem, her teacher must keep abreast of new materials as they are generated at an alarming rate by numerous publishers. Further, Alicia, with her 30 compatriots, deserves and needs an Individualized Education Program (IEP), a written list of instructional objectives, and steps to accomplish them.

Dr. Tayle is a special education administrator in Alicia's school system. He has just been notified that an IEP monitoring team from the state education office is visiting next week to review pupil performance records and has requested the IEP accounting reports on incidence of handicapped served, nature of services, efficacy data on program success, and testing schedules.

Twenty-five years ago, Alicia's teacher would have had no ethical alternative but to spend laborious hours writing objectives and making use of materials closest to hand. Dr. Tayle probably would not have had his answers in less than six months, if at all. In the last ten years or so, however, many information retrieval systems, most of them computerized, have been developed to provide a rapid and efficient match between learner needs, written objectives, and teaching resources. Information management systems have become commonplace at local or institutional levels (Bower & Ritchardson, 1975) as well as at state, national, and even international levels (Laska, Logemann, Honigfeld, Weinstein, & Bank, 1972). There are two distinct

111

purposes to this chapter: (1) to discuss several materials retrieval systems, and (2) to describe IEPs and their implementation.

DEFINITIONS

An IEP is a plan written for a handicapped child by that child's teacher, parent, and/or other school personnel. All handicapped children in the United States must have IEPs written each year to guide their educational development. A materials retrieval system is a procedure for selecting and/or accessing a given piece or set of educational materials according to specified criteria, usually learner needs or characteristics.

It might be useful to draw a distinction between media and materials. Media means the hardware, the machines or devices for presenting materials. Media alone are without curriculum content. Included under media are filmstrip projectors, movie projectors, Language Masters, tape recorders, television sets, videotape players, microcomputers, etc. Materials are the software or content that may or may not be presented through a media format. Basal readers, filmstrips, videotape programs, microdisc programs, and this text all would be considered materials.

Educational technology is a phrase that encompasses both media and materials as well as all other systematic approaches to presenting curricular information. Included in systematic instructional approaches are structured environments such as the engineered classroom (Hewitt & Forness, 1974), and the formatted use of principles by which instruction is applied, such as applied behavior analysis (Commission on Instructional Technology, 1970).

A BRIEF HISTORY

As Aserlind (1970) states, even as empirical evidence grew throughout the history of special education, indicating that exceptional children were different from their "normal" peers in important learner characteristics (i.e., need for repetition of materials, optimal mode, or style of materials presentations),

> teachers of the handicapped, with the exception of the deaf and blind, most often had to use instructional materials developed for the normal learner or in many instances had to develop materials for their own classroom usage, and most frequently they had no immediate resource from which to seek help. (p. 33)

The federal government, in an attempt to help remedy the situation, funded two Special Education Instructional Materials Centers (SEIMCs), which were operational by 1964 at the University of Washington and the University of Southern California. The goals of the SEIMCs were to:

1. Collect, catalog, and lend special education instructional materials
2. Consult with teachers on the utility of specific materials
3. Offer workshops on media and material usage
4. Publish a media and materials newsletter
5. Develop and implement a materials search and retrieval system
6. Develop the capability to design and produce educational materials (McCarthy, 1966, pp. 27–28)

In 1967, the U.S. Office of Education made provisions to expand the original two regional SEIMCs to 14, to make the effort truly nationwide, and to make the centers more responsive regionally (Olshin, 1967).

At about the same time, Regional Media Centers for the Deaf (RMCs) were established at the University of Massachusetts, the University of Tennessee, the University of Nebraska, and New Mexico State University. Their mandate was similar to that of the SEIMCs, except that their emphasis was to be directed toward educators of hearing impaired and deaf individuals.

These two types of agencies were merged in 1968 into the Special Education IMC/RMC Network, housed in Arlington, Virginia. Since then, several IMC/RMCs have become either state or university supported, and other independent agencies and companies have established their own media/materials retrieval systems.

The importance of making careful, educated decisions on curricular materials is made clear in view of research investigating their actual use in the classroom. Komoski (1978) reports that 90 to 95 percent of all classroom instruction time (K–12) is spent in teacher or student use of instructional materials.

The rest of this chapter discusses specific approaches and programs for matching learner characteristics and needs with instructional programs and materials, as well as one of the planning tools that employs these materials— the IEP.

MATERIALS RETRIEVAL SYSTEMS

What follows is a description of devices and systems designed to achieve, quickly and efficiently, a match between learner characteristics and materials. It is suggested that the reader look at the utility of the information produced by the various systems, the simplicity with which each (from the teacher's point of view) can be operated, and the ease with which updated information can be entered. These factors (especially the first) determine whether a system becomes a working part of a teacher's daily instructional activities, or an expensive paperweight.

The systems in this chapter were chosen as a group to reflect the range of options available in materials retrieval methods. Their inclusion is not meant as an endorsement but rather that the system is representative of a particular portion of the spectrum.

Rationale for Systematic Material Description

As a school psychologist, the reader has conducted a formal evaluation and determined that Maxine is learning disabled. As a resource teacher, the reader has informally determined Maxine's baseline on the skills of concern. Now what? Goals have been established but now, how to achieve them? Reese (1976) refers to an instructional system as "the interrelated and interacting teaching components organized to attain satisfactory learning progress" (p. 211). He identifies the components of that system as assessment, establishment of goals and objectives, selection of instructional strategies and materials, and progress evaluation. This chapter now turns to that selection of strategies and materials.

If educators accept the premise that the population of learning disabled children is composed of individuals with strengths and weaknesses that are unique, it follows that strategies and materials for these persons must be custom tailored. The entire diagnostic-prescriptive instructional paradigm is established on this premise (Peter, 1965; Johnson & Myklebust, 1967; Prillaman, 1968; Popham & Baker, 1970; Gerlach & Ely, 1971; Lerner, 1971; Reese, 1976; Hewett & Forness, 1974; Hallahan & Kauffman, 1976).

A critical question arises at this point: What dimensions are used to evaluate learner differences? How do educators differentiate dimensions of strength and weakness from those that simply involve preference? Is chronological age a dimension? Probably. Is sex a factor? Possibly, in terms of level of interest for various materials. Is mode of input important? Yes, if the child has a sensory or perceptual deficit in hearing or vision. And so on.

The universe of objectives to be learned or salient characteristics of instructional materials to be used are segmented in different ways depending on the learning model. These differences in philosophy are reflected in the different taxonomies' breakdown of the universe of "things-to-be-learned" upon which the various materials retrieval systems operate.

For reasons of practicality, materials retrieval systems must rest upon an underlying organizational structure. Whether consciously or not, each structure also reflects philosophical biases. These structures are sets of dimensions through which a given piece of material is reviewed, then matched to a similar learner characteristic or stored for retrieval, to be called upon in response to a particular need. The presence or absence of a given dimension is a direct index of its relative importance in the cataloger's organizational structure. If, under the dimension of academics, reading existed as a single, catchall category, it would be assumed that this cataloger didn't feel reading was as important as one who divided reading into form recognition, letter recognition, phoneme-grapheme relationships, phonetic blending/decoding, reading comprehension, etc.

Structure

Most of the cataloging systems that follow are hidden beneath their computer printouts, but since it is important to be familiar with such a structure, a sample is included. Sabatino (1968) has generated an information processing model that stands as such a sample. The model identifies four major areas:

> Visual perception, auditory perception, perceptual integration, and receptive-expressive language. Since these four information processing behavioral complexities can only be studied through selective stimulus input and while the exact nature of the component traits of each complex behavior is not clear, a stimulus response descriptor system has been developed to assist the diagnostician classify learner characteristics. The system has four major classifications:

1. Sensorimotor
2. Perceptual-motor
3. Language-cognitive
4. Academic.

The taxonomy in Exhibit 4-1 further subdivides these areas. Since this descriptor system was used for primary level materials, the age dimension was not deemed as critical. In larger systems, the descriptors would include other cross-referencing dimensions such as age, interest level, or format and would expand the academic dimension to include vocational education materials. Other material descriptor systems merit examination.

Exhibit 4-1 Information Processing Model

DESCRIPTOR SYSTEM

1.0	MOTOR
1.1	GROSS
1.11	Coordination-Balance
1.12	Strength-Endurance
1.2	PERCEPTUAL-MOTOR
1.21	Eye-Hand Coordination
1.22	Directionality
1.3	BODY AWARENESS
2.0	PERCEPTION
2.1	VISUAL
2.11	Discrimination
2.12	Memory
2.13	Figure-Ground
2.14	Closure
2.2	AUDITORY
2.21	Discrimination
2.22	Memory
2.23	Figure-Ground
2.3	TACTILE
3.0	LANGUAGE
3.1	CONCEPTUAL
3.11	Concrete
3.12	Functional
3.13	Abstract
3.2	EXPRESSIVE
3.21	Vocabulary
3.22	Syntax
3.3	RECEPTIVE
4.0	ACADEMICS
4.1	READING
4.11	Letter Recognition
4.12	Word Attack
4.121	Phonics
4.122	Structural Analysis
4.13	Word Recognition
4.14	Vocabulary

4.15	Comprehension
4.2	SPELLING
4.3	WRITING
4.31	Manuscript
4.32	Cursive
4.4	ARITHMETIC
4.41	Numeration
4.42	Computation
4.43	Measurement

Source: Reprinted from "The Information Processing Behaviors Associated With Learning Disabilities" D. A. Sabatino by permission of *Journal of Learning Disabilities,* 1969, *1,* 177–178, © 1969.

MATERIAL DESCRIPTOR SYSTEMS

SEIMC

Perhaps the most direct approach to materials retrieval is a basic library code system. The *Southwest and West Central Educational Cooperative Service Unit, Special Education Services* (SEIMC) network (1980) operating out of Montevideo, Minnesota, is such a system. It catalogs more than 9,000 pieces of material in a linear fashion under 29 topic categories with six format descriptors (Exhibit 4-2).

A teacher needing a piece of material would scan the listings under the desired category until an item of interest was found. This piece then could be ordered directly from SEIMC. SEIMC is developing an annotated listing of its holdings, but so far titles, publishers, and their letter-descriptors are the only guides available.

Select Ed

The Select Ed Prescriptive Materials Retrieval System (PMR) (1972) is an early, noncomputerized approach to matching student needs to available teaching resources. The system is based on more than 400 specific descriptors organized under seven generic descriptor dimensions and two indexes:

1. Specific Content, including English composition, handwriting, linguistics, literature, mathematics, perceptual motor development, and phonics
2. Format and Special Characteristics, including workbook, tape, filmstrip, large print, or color-cued print

Exhibit 4-2 Materials Retrieval Coding System

SEIMC CATEGORIES

CR	Classroom Resources
EGC	English Grammar and Composition
GU	Guidance
HA	Handwriting
HE	Health
HI	Hearing Impaired
HV	High Interest, Low Vocabulary
LAC	Language Arts, Correlated Reading
LI	Literature
MA	Mathematics
MI	Miscellaneous
ML	Minilessons
MU	Music
PE	Physical Education
PM	Programmed Mathematics
PMD	Perceptual Motor Development
PR	Programmed Reading
PS	Preschool
RB	Reading, Basal
RL	Reading, Linguistics
RP	Reading, Phonics
RR	Reading, Readiness
SC	Science
SLD	Speech and Language Development
SP	Spelling
SS	Study Skills
SST	Social Studies
TM	Teaching Machines
VDW	Vocabulary Development and Word Analysis

SEIMC MATERIAL FORMAT DESCRIPTORS

K	Kits: materials that are assembled so that everything necessary for teaching is packaged in one unit.
FS	Filmstrips: materials using a filmstrip with or without audio

Exhibit 4-2 continued

R	Records: instructional materials prepared in disc form
SP	Study Prints: materials consisting of pictures and/or prints that may have questions to stimulate discussion or study on the reverse side
T	Tapes: materials prepared for use on tape requiring a reel or cassette player or recorder
F	Films: materials prepared for use with a 16 mm film projector

Books carry no prefix except for category

EXAMPLES

SS 180—a book in the study skills area
K-RP 27—a kit in the phonics area
FS-RR 1—a filmstrip in the readiness area
R-PE 23—a record in the physical education area
SP-SLD 5—a study print in the speech and language area
T-MA 4—a tape in the mathematics area
F-CR 3—a film in the classroom resources area

3. Grade Level
4. Reading Level
5. Mental Age
6. Input-Output, including auditory, visual, and tactile input and oral and written output
7. Process, based on the information processing model upon which the *Illinois Test of Psycholinguistic Ability* (Kirk, McCarthy, & Kirk, 1968) is built
8. Major Area, all materials listed within a given subject or content area
9. Alphabetical Arrangement of Specific Content Descriptors by Major Areas, an alphabetical arrangement of all specific content descriptors listed in Item 1 above; this section is to be used as a reference to locate appropriate descriptors

The multistage retrieval process operates as follows:

1. The teacher selects the appropriate descriptors relating to particular child's needs from the *Select Ed* thesaurus.
2. The descriptors are keyed numerically to large file cards with holes or slots indicating materials appropriate to that descriptor.
3. The file cards are stacked on a light box. The light shines through only those holes that are common to the descriptor cards chosen; the holes are keyed numerically to specific materials listed in the three-volume set of *Select Ed Descriptive Analysis Sheets,* which include entries from 155 publishers

Select Ed also has developed the *Basic Educational Skills Inventory* (BESI) covering reading and mathematics. The BESI is a set of criterion referenced inventories linked to the specific educational descriptors in the PMR thesaurus.

The primary advantage of the *Select Ed* system is its technological simplicity. However, it has two primary disadvantages: (1) to update the system, new cards and Descriptor Analysis Sheets must be developed and (2) the more pieces there are to handle, the more pieces there are to get lost and the longer it takes to use this method.

Behavior Resource Guide

The *Behavior Resource Guide* (Cawley, 1973), issued by Educational Sciences, Inc., is a cross-referencing system in a three-ring notebook. The guide lists 266 Desired Learner Outcomes (DLOs) ranging from "identifies object that produces nonlanguage sound" to "demonstrates body symmetry." The DLOs are grouped under 22 separate subheadings organized under three major topic areas: developmental aural skills, developmental visual skills, and social/emotional development.

Cross-referencing indexes include the following:

- DLO to test correlations—given any of the 266 DLOs, which items on which tests measure that DLO accurately?

- Test to DLO correlations: given any of more than 500 items from 43 widely used psychological tests and test batteries, which DLOs follow from that test item?

- DLO to media correlations: given any DLO, what materials are available to aid in acquisition of that DLO?

- Media to DLO correlations: given any of more than 1,000 instructional items from 63 publishers, which DLOs are addressed by each item?

As with *Select Ed,* the system's primary appeal is its simplicity, but its primary weakness is its rigidity. What if a school doesn't have the 1,000 pieces of material from 63 publishers? What happens when the guide is three years out of date? While a useful concept, the *Behavior Resource Guide* could well have awaited the computer revolution for its inception, thereby increasing its flexibility and utility.

Computer Based Resource Units (CBRU)

The *Computer Based Resource Units* (CBRU) system (Cross, 1974) was originated at the State University College at Buffalo, New York (SUC Buffalo), as part of the nationwide SEIMC network. The system uses teacher-consultants to write units of instruction for specific children they have taught. The units include instructional objectives, materials lists, activities, and evaluative criteria. These units then are made available via learner variable codes.

Gearheart (1973) describes the retrieval process:

> To obtain . . . information, the teacher must first indicate the unit in which she is interested. The center (at SUC Buffalo) mails back a list of 100 to 200 objectives for that unit. The teacher then selects a limited number of objectives in which she is primarily interested *for the class as a whole* and a smaller number *for each child* in the class. (p. 139)

The objectives are computer selected, based on the cross-referencing of unit subobjectives, student interest lists, developmental task areas, reading level, mental age, chronological age, and physical handicaps. While a great deal of overlap exists from unit to unit on the selector variables (i.e., many units may have "13-language" as a student interest category) each set of variables is custom tailored to each unit.

Far from being a carefully sequenced program unit, however, the CBRU printout received by the teacher is more a set of handy-dandy teaching suggestions. For example, if a teacher were to submit a request under the unit "Management of Social Behavior, Subobjective #12—To avoid self-inflicting physical punishment," the educator would receive more than 20 small group activity suggestions such as:

#310   I love _____
        I love you
        I wish I could call you and tell you a secret
        That I love you _____

Have students fill in the blanks and discuss. This is followed by:

#316   Tape or film a child who is physically hurting himself (i.e., banging head, biting nails, poking self with sharp object, etc.)
Show and discuss film—elicit possible antecedents and alternative behaviors.

#317   Write a story about getting your own way. What do you do to get your own way? How can you get your own way? Should you always get your own way?

This section is followed by large group activity suggestions, a list of 22 activities that duplicate 22 of the 23 small group items to the letter. Only objective #3, "Students make posters showing behavior that is appropriate or inappropriate in a given situation," is unique to the small group suggestions.

The CBRU system has unlimited potential for program expansion and continued development. So far, however, it does little more than expand the box of 3" × 5" cards found on the desk of most competent teachers. This may be a worthwhile service in itself, but given the potential of computerized retrieval it is rather like using a food processor for a doorstop. It does the job, but there are so many more complex functions it can perform.

The Improved Individual Instruction Program

Project REACH, the Western Pennsylvania Special Education Resource Center, has developed an integrated system in response to the federal mandates regarding Individualized Education Programs (IEPs) (Minick, 1980). As this chapter notes later, IEPs are written plans requiring (among other things) compilation of evaluation information, establishment of appropriate learner goals and objectives, and specification of services that will meet the needs of each handicapped child. Especially in large school districts, the volume of paperwork involved in the process is practically unmanageable. In virtually all school districts, the specification of materials and media is not considered part of detailing the services and is limited by building resources and teacher resourcefulness. Project REACH has developed and implemented the *Improved Individual Instruction Program* (IIIP) in response to these problems.

The IIIP "is a computerized recordkeeping and resource listing system designed to assist teachers with tracking student performance and suggesting possible teaching materials and techniques" (Minick, 1980). The system operates as follows:

1. Initial testing is conducted on each child. The IIIP system includes its own student checklist/progress forms. These forms are detailed skill checklists in mathematics and reading. In reading, for example, the checklist specifies mastery of each phonic element, as well as students' structural analysis skills, word recognition, oral reading, oral and silent reading comprehension, and vocabulary expansion.
2. The evaluation information is recorded on OPSCAN (optical scanning) sheets that can be "read" directly by a computer.
3. The computer analyzes the data, generates a portion of the IEP, and suggests appropriate teaching materials from a bank of more than 5,000 pieces applicable to K–12 students.
4. The teacher receives the IEP and the suggested materials lists, makes necessary editorial changes, selects materials and/or requests additional items.
5. The IIIP center also acts as a library and sends requested materials to the teacher.
6 The teacher periodically updates each student's evaluation and the computer in turn updates the teacher with information on materials.

The IIIP system represents a laudable integration of professional judgment and computer efficiency. Its computer base allows for continual update. The IEPs produced are among the most detailed anywhere in the nation, and the materials listings dramatically increase the facilitation of the objectives.

Project HELPS

Ohio has developed the *Handicapped Education Learners Planning System* (HELPS), a computer-based instructional management system "that has the capability of interrelating student based psychoeducational data with educational objectives, instructional activities, curriculum materials, and supportive information for teaching handicapped learners" (Lehrer & Daiker, 1978, p. 580).

HELPS can be accessed either via completion of a learning resources list questionnaire, mailed to a central location, or via an interactive terminal. Cooperating districts offer two-hour training courses designed to teach educators how to operate the telephone-linked terminals. Student reading level, educational objectives, learner interests, and type of learning situation are numerically coded into HELPS. The computer feeds back short-term instructional objectives with associated resource lists. In the interactive mode, teachers can delimit parameters further to obtain materials and resource suggestions for each child. A typical search generates 25 to 75 resources. The resources fall under one of three categories: materials, activities, and performance measures (objectives). More than 32,000 such resources are accessible via HELPS. The cost per search is about $6, or an average of $90 for 15 pupils on an annual basis.

The HELPS system was designed originally as an aid in developing IEPs. Lehrer and Daiker (1978) report that the system has proved most helpful in this regard. However, the prime drawback in systems of this type is that, especially in a numerically coded set of objectives, the teacher can be in the position of bending the child to fit the objectives. The ultimate success of such programs will depend on the system's capacity for continual expansion and update in terms both of generating new and more useful objectives and of matching new materials and resources to existing objectives.

National Instructional Materials Information System (NIMIS)

NIMIS is a computer-based information retrieval system designed to locate information on instructional materials for use in the education of handicapped children (National Center on Educational Media and Materials for the Handicapped, 1976). Originally developed at Ohio State University under contract with the Bureau for Education of the Handicapped, NIMIS is one of the largest projects of its kind in the world with more than 20,000 nonprint instructional materials on file. Beginning in 1966, NIMIS operated under the auspices of the SEIMC/RMC network mentioned earlier. NIMIS is housed now at the University of Southern California and is accessed via the Lockheed computer system.

NIMIS utilizes a thesaurus including 868 descriptors and 175 user references to access 20,000 pieces of instructional materials. These descriptors are retrieved via five dimension specifications:

Content Areas:	language arts, mathematics, social studies, reading
Skill/Concept Area:	social skills, locomotor skills, shapes, reversals
Grade, Instructional/Interest Levels Format:	kits, games, filmstrips
Instructional Approaches:	color keyed materials or linguistic approach
Exceptionalities:	learning disabled input/output modes

Reporting on the National Information Center for Educational Media (NICEM), a related catalog/retrieval system dealing with a broader spectrum of materials (more than 400,000 pieces), Woodbury (1976) complains

"Despite their ambitious scope this . . . is difficult to use, bibliographically inadequate and short on needed information" (p. 189). Unfortunately, as the data base increases, there seems to be an upper limit of accessibility. It is possible that NIMIS and NICEM, both of which must be accessed either through a large centralized computer terminal or through a set of complex reference texts, may have reached that limit.

Midcoast Teacher Center

On a smaller scale, regional efforts are proving quite successful. Vogel (1980) describes a materials retrieval system that is targeted toward 650 teachers in 42 schools in rural Maine. The *Midcoast Teacher Center* maintains its own data base with Bibliographic Retrieval Systems (BRS), an organization based in Scotia, N.Y. This data base includes commercial as well as teacher-developed materials. Storage/retrieval is effected through the following descriptors:

Format Presentation:	preferred input/output modality such as visual-pictorial, auditory, demonstration, written, Braille, large type
Presentation Descriptors:	size of group
Student Material Descriptors:	immediate vs. delayed feedback, concept vs. fact oriented

Curriculum Area Descriptors
Grade Level (interest, content)
Readability level
Format (book, kit, film)

Two important features of this system make it noteworthy:

1. The system is interactive, thereby allowing teachers to enter their own materials.
2. The system includes an evaluative component. After using a piece of material, teachers are asked to enter their impressions as to the quality or special quirks of the material for subsequent users. Few systems include such a feedback component.

Educational Products Information Exchange Institute (EPIE)

EPIE was established in 1967 to act as a national consumer product evaluation service. As such it is not, strictly speaking, a materials retrieval system but its service in the area of materials selection/utilization is so unique and vital that it warrants mention. Operating out of New York City, EPIE publishes six in-depth reports and 18 biweekly newsletters a year, providing general advice on media/materials selection as well as evaluations of specific materials by teacher-users (Woodbury, 1976).

OTHER SELECTED INFORMATION SOURCES

Educational information and instructional materials abound in an almost endless stream, the new combining with the old to create a plethora of good, usable, poor, or even unusable materials. As has been noted, the dilemma for practicing special educators is to make wise selections in the purchase and use of particular instructional props while overcoming their dependence on a few items that they have become comfortable using.

This brief discussion of materials systems concludes with a description of an array of information retrieval or descriptor systems available to educators. The list is by no means exhaustive. It should be stressed that information on a product should not make the decision for the potential user. The materials ordered and used remain in the sphere of the educator's professional judgment. The purpose here in recommending information libraries and retrieval structures is to provide the best available information upon which to base decisions. The abbreviated list includes vocational, reading, behavioral, and other subject-centered resource pools from which educators can draw. These items are abstracted or indexed or provide awareness of printed and nonprinted materials. For additional information, educators are strongly urged to consult an excellent source on these and other elements: Woodbury's *A Guide to Sources of Educational Information,* Information Resources Press, Washington, D.C. (1976). Some of the systems she references are listed in Exhibit 4-3.

Exhibit 4-3 Educational Information Systems

Abstracts of Instructional and Research Materials in Vocational and Technical Education (AIM/ARM). Columbus, Ohio: Center for Vocational and Technical Education, established 1967.

Abstracts, instructional and research materials dealing with vocational and technical education.

[It] covers a wide variety of fields, including agricultural education, business education, career education, health occupations, consumer and home economics, various aspects of trade and industrial education, and related fields such as occupational guidance and rehabilitation. A "Projects

Exhibit 4-3 continued

in Progress" section announces curriculum and research projects funded through the Office [Department] of Education's Bureau of Occupational and Adult Education. (p. 88)

Education Abstracts. Washington, D.C.: American College Public Relations Association, established 1963.

More a new digest than an abstract journal; summarizes articles and book notices on higher education topics from newspapers, periodicals, and education journals. (p. 91)

Education Index. Bronx, N.Y.: H. W. Wilson, established 1932.

[Reviews] 250 of the more valuable and accessible English language education periodicals, which are selected by subscriber and user vote on criteria of subject balance and reference value. It also indexes proceedings, yearbooks, monographs, bulletins, and some U.S. government publications. Subjects include education and curriculum in all subjects (preschool to adult), plus school administration and finance, counseling, and guidance. (p. 91)

Exceptional Child Education Abstracts (ECEA). Reston, Va.: The Council for Exceptional Children, established 1969.

Coverage includes research reports, journal articles, curriculum guides, teachers' activity manuals, administrative surveys and guidelines, texts for both professionals and beginning students, plus current nonprint media (tape cassettes). (pp. 92–93)

Mental Retardation and Developmental Disabilities Abstracts.

Cover all aspects of mental retardation. The abstracts on developmental aspects and on treatment and training are perhaps the most valuable available for educators concerned with the mental retardate. (p. 94)

Research Relating to Children. ERIC Clearinghouse on Early Childhood Education. Washington, D.C.: U.S. Government Printing Office, established 1954.

Materials, arranged by subject, include long-term research, growth and development, special groups of children, the child in the family, socioeconomic and cultural factors, educational factors and services, social services, and health services. Information on the projects reported includes investigators, purpose, subjects, methods, findings, directions, cooperating groups, and publications. Indexes are arranged by institution, investigator, and subject. (p. 96)

Resources in Education (RIE).

It includes resumes of hard-to-find or limited-distribution documents selected by ERIC clearinghouses located throughout the country, technical

Exhibit 4-3 continued

and research reports, conference papers, documents from school districts, etc. Reports are arranged by clearinghouse and then assigned ED (educational document) numbers in the ERIC system (so the output of any clearinghouse can be read each month); they are indexed by author and institution, and by subject descriptors selected from the *Thesaurus of ERIC Descriptors.* (p. 97)

Books and Non-Book Media: Annotated Guide to Selection Aids for Educational Materials, by Flossie L. Perkins. Urbana, Ill.: National Council of Teachers of English, established 1972.

A comprehensive listing of more than 250 guides and selection aids for all kinds of educational materials: books, pamphlets, films, records, and some government sources. Arranged alphabetically by title, with price and bibliographic information. Annotations are thorough, if unevaluative, and include purpose, scope, subjects, special features, usefulness, and comparative tools. (p. 134)

Catalog of Free Teaching Materials, 1973–1976 (8th Ed.), by Gordon Salisbury. Riverside, Calif.: Rubidoux Printing, 1973. $3. From: P.O. Box 175, Ventura, Calif. 93001.

A well-indexed guide to available free materials (booklets, charts, posters, maps, etc.) related to the curriculum, "evaluated by accredited teachers." Contains approximately 8,000 items. Annotations, including grade level, type of item, and number of copies that may be acquired free, are listed in the first section; the second section lists the names and addresses of approximately 1,000 organizations. (pp. 134–135)

CEDaR Catalog of Selected Educational Research and Development Programs and Products (4th Ed). Denver: CEDaR Information Office, 1974. 2 Vols. $14.50. From: P.O. Box 3711, Portland, Ore. 97208.

Information on completed projects includes target audiences and teachers' materials, as well as overall philosophy and development procedures. The program sheets discuss ongoing programs and provide expected completion dates. Subject areas include school organization and administration, early childhood education, elementary and secondary school education, higher education, teacher education, basic research, urban education, and vocational education. Reader service cards are included to assist users in requesting publication lists and further information on individual products. Subsequent annual editions are planned. (p. 135)

Educator's Purchasing Guide (5th Ed.). Philadelphia: North American Publishing, 1973. $29.50 / single copy.

A comprehensive guide, based on producers' catalogs, that indexes sources of instructional materials, equipment, and supplies, including text-

Exhibit 4-3 continued

books and other printed materials, audiovisual materials, atlases, globes, maps, tests, teaching aids, and services. Equipment and supplies cover art education, athletic and physical education equipment, graphic arts equipment, and science laboratory equipment for use in libraries, learning centers, music instruction, and vocational education. Materials and equipment are indexed by grade, subject, and trade name. Producers are listed alphabetically, dealers and distributors geographically. (p. 135)

Evaluating Educational Programs and Products, Gary D. Borich (Ed.). Englewood Cliffs, N.J.: Educational Technology, 1974. $12.95.

Incorporates the works of many prominent evaluators in one handbook. Its three sections cover roles and contexts, models and strategies, and methods and techniques. Includes an interesting directory chart that relates chapter contents to readers' occupational roles. (p. 136)

Free and Inexpensive Educational Aids (4th Ed.), by Thomas J. Pepe. New York: Dover Publications, 1970. $2.

Uses the following criteria for selection: objectivity; educational soundness; whether the aid was simple to incorporate in the classroom, research project, or individual study; whether the presentation was without company sales influence or political bias; and whether the cost was 25¢ or less (82 percent of the items are free; 9 percent are under 25¢). Materials are arranged by broad subject areas, beginning with a list of other teaching aid catalogs. Subjects include agriculture; arts, crafts, and hobbies; business, management, and labor; communications; conservation, energy, and fuels; government; guidance and careers; health and hygiene; homes and homemaking; language arts; manufacturing; music; nutrition and diet; pets; safety; science, weather, and climate; social studies; and transportation. (p. 136)

Guide to Reference Books for School Media Centers: Sources for Print and Non-Print Media, by Christine L. Wynar. Littleton, Colo.: Libraries Unlimited, 1973. $17.50

A guide to reference materials, designed to fit the needs of elementary and secondary media centers. Evaluates and annotates 2,500 titles, with complete bibliographical data, price, and references to original reviews. Includes evaluations of specialized selection tools for print and nonprint media in all subjects. Arranged by subject, with an author-title-subject analytic index. (p. 137)

Improving Materials Selection Procedures: A Basic "How To" Handbook New York: Educational Products Information Exchange Institute, 1973. (EPIE Educational Product "In Depth" Report No. 54.) Members, $5; nonmembers, $10; quantity discount.

A brief, comprehensive summary of recommendations for rationalizing and systematizing selection procedures. Covers the roles and requirements of

Exhibit 4-3 continued

both schools and producers as well as methods for developing, applying, and following through on appropriate criteria, with a useful criterion checklist. (p. 137)

New Educational Materials, 1970 (4th Ed.), compiled by Lois Markham. New York: Citation Press, 1970. $3.75.

The latest edition of this classified guide to elementary and secondary curriculum-related materials, which annotated approximately 500 new items a year. Arranged by grade level, it includes resource articles as well as annotations of selected films, recordings, multimedia kits, filmstrips, transparencies, teaching/learning games, professional guides, posters, study prints, tapes, laboratory kits, charts, and maps. All four volumes still are usable and still in print. (p. 137)

Selecting Instructional Materials for Purchase: Procedural Guidelines, by Joint Committee of the National Educational Association and Association of American Publishers. Washington, D.C.: National Education Association, 1972. $2 (paperback)

A simple but comprehensive and thorough handbook that considers legal and administrative factors (laws, school boards, administrators), means of organizing and selecting materials, guidelines for expenditures, and changing conditions affecting procedures. (p. 138)

Selecting New Aids to Teaching, by Richard I. Miller. Washington, D.C.: Association for Supervision and Curriculum Development, 1971. $1. From: National Education Association, 1201 16th Street, N.W., Washington, D.C. 20036.

Thoroughly but concisely outlines the steps that should be taken and the criteria that should be followed in selecting instructional units. (p. 138)

Sources of Teaching Materials, by Catherine M. Wilson. Columbus, Ohio: Ohio State University. 1971. $3 (paperback).

The first part of this guide—on developing a strategy for locating information—is a narrative description of 190 basic reference and research sources, with complete entries at the end of the section. Other parts cover media, broad curricular areas, publishers, and distributors, as well as references to materials and methods of instruction. Provides many other references (some obsolete) and a detailed table of contents, but no index. (p. 139)

Active Learning: Games to Enhance Academic Abilities, by Bryant J. Cratty. Englewood Cliffs, N.J.: Prentice-Hall, Inc., 1971. $7.95; paperback, $4.50.

Exhibit 4-3 continued

Written by an expert in movement education, this book describes more than 100 active learning games designed to improve coordination while teaching geometry, numbers, letters and letter sounds, language arts, skills, memory, and concentration. Includes clear instructions and helpful suggestions for dealing with clumsy children. (p. 141)

Analyses of Basic and Supplementary Reading Materials. New York: Educational Products Information Exchange Institute, 1974.

This report uses an "Instructional Design Analysis" system to analyze and evaluate 76 commercially marketed reading series. Materials are arranged alphabetically by category (general audiences, grade levels, supplementary materials). (p. 144)

Career Education Resource Guide, James E. Bottoms et al. (Eds.). Morristown, N.J.: General Learning Corp., 1972. $5.70.

Provides overviews, lesson plans, and classroom activities for career education at three levels: kindergarten/elementary, middle/junior high, and high school/adult. (p. 147)

Curriculum Guides: A Selective Bibliography. Reston, Va.: Council for Exceptional Children, established 1972. Microfiche, 75¢; hard copy, $1.85 (plus postage). ERIC Document Reproduction Service, No. ED 065 959. P.O. Box 190, Arlington, Va. 22210.

A bibliography of 100 abstracts dealing with curricula for gifted and handicapped children, from the files of the ERIC Clearinghouse on Handicapped and Gifted. Items included were selected on the basis of currency, author's reputation, information value, contents, and availability of documents. Includes subject and author indexes as well as forms for ordering documents. (p. 150)

Curriculum Materials, 1974, compiled by Richard D. Kimpston and Joan Black. Washington, D.C.: Association for Supervision and Curriculum Development, established 1974. Annual. $2.

Although descriptions are not included, this catalog is an annual review providing access to a large number of current noncommercial curricula displayed at the annual ASCD (spring) conference. The latest issue lists approximately 800 resources in 15 curriculum areas, mostly by state and local school districts. The subject arrangement is subdivided by grade level and subject; subsequent arrangement is by state and issuing agency (whether district, state, or other agency). (p. 151)

Exhibit 4-3 continued

A Directory of Selected Resources in Special Education, compiled by Merrimack Education Center, Chelmsford, Mass., 1975. 75¢. From 101 Mill Road, Chelmsford, Mass. 01824.

An excellent, compact, annotated guide to hard-to-locate but valuable products designed to meet the needs of children with different learning styles through diverse programs and materials. Provides a partial guide to agencies, as well as a directory of resources covering home-school communications, classroom techniques, testing and assessment, media and materials, teacher training materials, and other bibliographies. (p. 152)

Early Childhood Information Unit, by Far West Laboratory for Educational Research and Development. San Francisco, 1973.

A comprehensive, decision-making information unit to assist teachers, parents, administrators, and community groups in evaluating 15 early childhood programs. Includes an introductory filmstrip and audiocassette presentation of major trends in early childhood education, detailed descriptions of eight early childhood programs (written form, filmstrip, and audio), summary descriptions of seven other early childhood programs, EPIE guidelines for evaluative techniques, and an extensive bibliography. (p. 153)

Good Reading for Poor Readers. (Rev. Ed.), by George D. Spache. Champaign, Ill.: Garrard Publishing, 1974. $5.75 (paperback).

The first four chapters discuss choosing books to match children's abilities and needs, and present a survey of readability formulas. The next eight chapters list 1,800 titles for remedial reading, arranged under broad categories, with brief annotations and bibliographic descriptions, omitting prices but including reading and interest levels. Materials consist of trade books, simplified books, textbooks, magazines, series, programmed materials, games, and visual aids. Appendixes include Spache's Readability Formula, author and title indexes, and a directory of publishers. (p. 157)

Instructional Aids, Materials and Supplies, by Educational Development Center Follow-Through Program. Newton, Mass.: Educational Development Center, Inc., 1970. $1.

A list of possible materials for an open classroom. (p. 159)

Audio-Visual Equipment Directory, 1975–1976, Sally Herickes (Ed.). Fairfax, Va.: National Audio-Visual Association, Inc., established 1975. Annual. $11.25, prepaid; $12.50, if billed. From: 3150 Spring Street, Fairfax, Va. 22030.

This attractive guide, issued around May of each year, is now in its 21st edition. It is based on information supplied by manufacturers rather than on independent ratings. More than 2,000 models of audiovisual equipment are listed by type of equipment (74 categories), then alphabetically by company name, and finally numerically or alphabetically by model. There is a picture of each piece of equipment, along with price, operation, dimensions, weight,

Exhibit 4-3 continued

and electrical requirements. Includes a list of manufacturers with addresses and phone numbers and a geographical listing of dealers. (p. 177)

Learning with Games: An Analysis of Social Studies Educational Games and Simulations, Cheryl L. Charles and Ronald Stadsklev (Eds.). Boulder, Colo.. Social Science Education Consortium, 1973. $4.95.

Emphasis is on 70 social studies games K–12, using SSEC's parallel analysis technique. Also includes annotated bibliographies on simulation design and games, directories of games and simulations, descriptions of game developers, listings of newsletters and journals dealing with games, and a guide to 80 producers of social studies educational games and simulations—altogether a good guide for its field. (p. 187)

Research and Information Services for Education (RISE), 198 Allendale Road, King of Prussia, Pa. 19406. (215) 265-6056

Sponsored by the Montgomery County (Pennsylvania) Intermediate Unit, RISE provides information services to educators and education students in that county, to the Bureau of Planning in the Pennsylvania State Department of Education, and to the general public. Resources, dealing primarily with administration, curriculum, and supportive services for education, include 3,000 books, 18,000 documents, 328 periodical subscriptions, some standard education indexing and abstracting services, a file of 1,040 literature searchers, and complete microfiche collections of ERIC, the Curriculum Materials Clearinghouse, and UNIPAC's (I106). It can perform online interactive computer searches of ERIC, *Psychological Abstracts, Social Sciences Citation Index,* National Technical Information Service, *Exceptional Child Education Abstracts, AIM/ARM,* and many scientific and commercial files. (p. 308)

This section has provided a brief annotation on selected information sources that may be useful in selecting materials or teaching procedures. At this juncture, the material from Chapter 3 (Informal Assessment) and this chapter are brought into a meaningful response to the mandatory Individualized Education Program (IEP) required under Public Law 94–142.

INDIVIDUALIZED EDUCATION PROGRAMS

In the not too distant past the fate of a handicapped child's educational planning rested almost solely on the skills and integrity of the particular teacher and the degree of support that instructor received from the school district. Radical differences existed in the quality of service from state to state, district to district, and even school to school within a district. In an attempt to ensure appropriate services that reflect a coordination of planned educational goals and activities agreed upon by the child's parents as well as by school personnel, Individualized Education Programs (IEPs) were included as a critical element of P.L. 94-142, the Education For All Handicapped Children Act of 1975.

When President Gerald Ford signed P.L. 94-142, he did so reluctantly, cautioning that while the spirit of the law was most admirable, its actual implementation might prove impractical. In short, the federal government might be making promises it would be unable to keep. The law took effect in the 1976–77 school year, with a phase-in period lasting until October 1980. To this point, it appears to be working.

The Concept and the Law

Before discussing IEPs, it would be helpful to see how the concept fits in the context of P.L. 94-142. The purpose of the law is to ensure the rights of handicapped individuals to a free and appropriate education and to assist state and local agencies in providing that schooling. The act has several subcomponents, of which IEPs are one. Other provisions include a team decision-making process, periodic nondiscriminatory testing, parent access to student records, education in the least restrictive environment, recourse to due process procedures, child-find inservice training, and barrier free schools.

Team decision making is a theme central to P.L. 94-142 and is built into the IEP process described later. In brief, the law recognizes the need for including the child's parent, the child (when appropriate), and pertinent support personnel (such as school psychologists or speech therapists) as well as the special teacher in arriving at critical decisions regarding the handicapped pupil's education. In this manner all of the persons most closely attuned to the child's needs and abilities will have a say in determining the pupil's educational future, producing a plan that is more thorough than any one individual might develop. It also produces a plan that is deemed reasonable by all concerned before implementation, thereby avoiding charges later that it was ill-conceived from the outset.

Periodic nondiscriminatory testing is a safeguard against evaluation practices that produce results that don't reflect the child's actual current level of performance. Considerations include making sure that children are tested in their native language, using tests normed on populations similar to the pupil, and verifying that a handicap is not interfering with performance on an instrument evaluating something other than the known disability.

This latter point needs elaboration. For example, if a child is known to have dysgraphia (an inability to write) it would be appropriate to administer tests designed to directly evaluate eye-hand coordination, ability to copy letters, etc., since this information would be vital to developing a remedial program for the child. It would be inappropriate, however, to evaluate this child's math ability using a test requiring the pupil to write the answers because even if the individual could perform adequately in math, the student would be unable to attain a score reflecting true ability because of the response requirements of the task. The law further requires that complete evaluations be conducted once every three years to ensure that placement and program decisions are made on current data.

Parent access to student records is guaranteed by P.L. 94-142. This provision is included so that parents may (1) be privy to all of the records that form the base for their child's placement, (2) enter any pertinent data of their own, and (3) challenge or request the removal of any records that may lack substance or be pejorative (e.g., contain inaccurate or denigrating anecdotal records). Concurrent with this, anyone who is not considered authorized school personnel (e.g., a researcher) must obtain permission from the child's parents before viewing any records.

Least Restrictive Environment

Education in the least restrictive environment is a concept that looks at program placement alternatives on a continuum of restrictiveness. At the least restrictive end is education in a regular class without supportive services. At the most restrictive end is home-bound or hospital-bound service. Most learning disabled children can be served either through the regular class with special consultative support, through the regular class with resource room support, or through a self-contained special education classroom in a regular school. A very small percentage of learning disabled children need the total environmental support of a special school.

The law states that as children improve they should be moved as quickly as possible toward the normal end of the continuum; any step toward the more restrictive end should be taken only when absolutely necessary. This is done because it is felt that, all other things being equal, it is best for handicapped children's social and emotional well-being to be educated with their peers as much as possible (see Chapter 10 on social-emotional development).

Due process is essentially a set of grievance procedures established to assure an orderly and fair resolution of disagreements. If a parent (or student) does not feel that the school is providing appropriate services, or if the school feels that a parent is presenting unreasonable barriers, either party may call a due process hearing. The session, presided over by an impartial hearing officer selected through a process of elimination by parents and school, is the first step. The decision of the hearing officer is binding unless appealed by either party. An appeal may be made to the state agency in charge of special education services, and from there to civil court if need be. The intent of the due process procedures is to guarantee that neither parents nor school is forced to accept substandard educational services for a child in their care.

Child-find simply indicates that each state and local district must have an approved and viable plan for seeking out and providing service to handicapped children. This may involve public school screening, a mass media advertising campaign, establishing community-based screening centers, and/ or canvassing neighborhoods.

The inservice training provision earmarks money exclusively for the education (or reeducation) of teachers serving handicapped children. This includes those who devote their time exclusively to handicapped children as well as regular education teachers who have such children "mainstreamed" into their classes.

The barrier free concept says that no child may be denied services because of a disability. This usually is discussed in terms of installing ramps or elevators for individuals who use wheelchairs as their primary mode of locomotion. However, it also may involve simply rescheduling a class to a room that is accessible.

Overall, P.L. 94-142 attempts to provide legal safeguards for children who, in the past, have been denied an education because, in the minds of many school leaders, they did not "fit in," or the needed services were "too expensive," or the question was raised (silently or aloud), "Why spend our time and energies on children whose prospects aren't terribly bright anyway?"

Where do IEPs fit in? An IEP is a written document that records the plan for a given child for one year that incorporates all of the provisions just described. An IEP is not a legal contract in that a teacher or school could not be held accountable if a child failed to achieve a goal or objective it specified. It is seen as a program management tool, encouraging responsible long-term planning and facilitating transfer of goals and objectives from placement to placement.

The IEP Process

Section 4, paragraph 19, of P.L. 94-142 defines an IEP in terms of both process and content:

> The term "individualized education program" means a written statement for each handicapped child developed in any meeting by a representative of the local education agency or an intermediate

educational unit who shall be qualified to provide, or supervise the provision of, specially designed instruction to meet the unique needs of handicapped children, the teacher, the parents or guardian of such child, and, whenever appropriate, such child, which statement shall include

(A) a statement of the present levels of educational performance of such child,
(B) a statement of annual goals, including short term instructional objectives,
(C) a statement of the specific educational services to be provided to such child, and the extent to which such child will be able to participate in regular educational programs,
(D) the projected date for initiation and anticipated duration of such services, and
(E) appropriate objective criteria and evaluation procedures and schedules for determining, on at least an annual basis, whether instructional objectives are being achieved.

The law is very specific in stating that an IEP is to be developed through a team effort. At minimum, three persons must be present: parent, teacher, and school representative. The parent(s) or the school may wish to have additional personnel in attendance: professionals involved in diagnosis, parent (or child) advocates, receiving teachers, the pupil (especially at the secondary level), etc. It is recommended, however, that the attendance be limited by two considerations: (1) parents are to be members of the team, and the larger the ratio of school personnel to parents the more likely the latter are to be intimidated into silence; (2) the IEP team is assembled for the purpose of writing an IEP, so it should be small enough so that this task can be accomplished.

Figure 4-1 delineates a generic process by which an IEP is developed. Each step in the process is numerically coded to the descriptions that follow. The process described here contains the bare bones of IEP development, and specifics may vary from state to state, but in general the procedure is as shown. *Box 1.a.* The school notifies the public that screening services are available (as per the child-find provision described earlier). *Box 1.b.* Screening is implemented and a child either is deemed nonhandicapped (exit via *Box 2*) or is referred for further diagnosis (*Box 3*). A child may enter the system directly through the *Referral Box (3)* if a parent or teacher suspects that a problem exists.

Before administering any individualized evaluation instruments, the results of which could be used in a special education placement decision, the school

Figure 4-1 Steps in the IEP Process

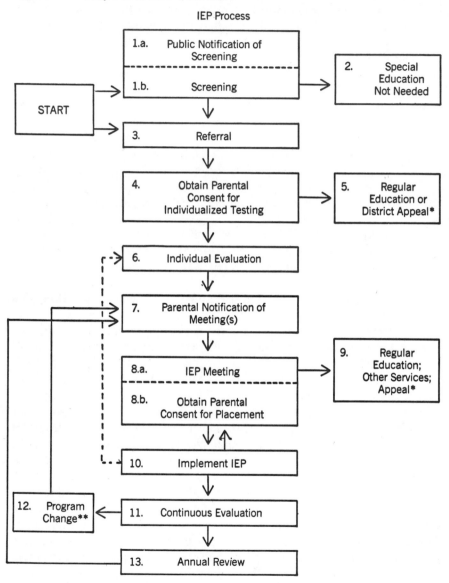

* At the decision points noted, disagreements may be resolved through due process procedures.

** Placement, goal, a short-term objective change.

must obtain parental permission for such evaluation (*Box 4*). If the parents object to the evaluation, the school can either retract their request for evaluation or institute due process procedures (*Box 5*). If the parents agree to the evaluation, it is conducted in *Box 6*.

As the diagnosis nears completion (*Box 7*), the school must notify the parents that a meeting is pending to plan their child's program and that it is incumbent upon them to attend. Efforts must be made to schedule the meeting so as to be reasonably accessible to the parents (in time as well as locale). An IEP meeting can be conducted without parents, but in such cases the school should be able to provide evidence that it made a good faith effort to convince them to attend but they failed to cooperate.

It is at the IEP meeting (*Box 8.a.*) that the program is formulated. This point needs emphasis. In many cases well-meaning teachers may prepare an IEP before the session and present it to the child's parents for approval there. The parents usually are grateful for the teacher's efforts, and everyone departs without realizing the perversion of the law that has occurred. Certainly a teacher should come to each IEP meeting with some idea of the anticipated direction of the child's program. The teacher also should be prepared to take the lead in the actual writing of the IEP. Nevertheless, the law does state clearly that the IEP is to be developed by the parents as well as the other persons at the meeting.

Among the decisions made at the IEP meeting should be the child's placement (*Box 8.b.*). Again, parental permission must be obtained before actual placement can occur. A child who is deemed not eligible for special education services is assigned to regular education (*Box 9*). If either school or parent object to the placement decision, they can appeal to due process (also *Box 9*).

If parents and school are in agreement regarding a special education placement, that occurs and the IEP is implemented (*Box 10*). While not a required part of the law, it is assumed that good teaching practice will be accompanied by continuous evaluation of the student's progress (*Box 11*). If at any time the teacher, parent, or child feels that the program is unrealistic or inappropriate, a new IEP meeting can be called to suggest an internal program change (*Box 12*, back through *Box 7*). In any event, at least once a year each child's program must be reevaluated and updated at an IEP meeting (*Box 13*, back through *Box 7*). Once every three years a complete diagnostic evaluation must be conducted on each child and the special placement reconsidered (reenter *Box 6*).

The Content of an IEP

As indicated earlier, P.L. 94-142 gives only the sketchiest of guidelines for IEP content. Five components are indicated:

1. the child's current level of functioning
2. annual goals, including short-term objectives
3. specific educational services to be provided, including extent of participation in regular class activities
4. dates of service provision
5. evaluation criteria

Each school district is left to develop its own forms (if any) on the level of sophistication it finds most useful. The authors have selected an extremely comprehensive format as a model for purposes of discussion, but readers should be aware that an IEP "form" can be a blank sheet of paper. The form in Exhibit 4-4 originally was printed on noncarbon reproducing (NCR) paper to produce four copies at once, one each for the parents, the teacher's active file, the building file, and the district file. It is useful to go through the form section by section.

I. Student Information—This section simply collects demographic data on a child.

II. Medical Information—This space is not required by federal mandates but makes good sense. It is reasonable to rule out vision and hearing problems before assigning labels indicative of central processing deficits.

III. Level of Current Performance—In direct response to P.L. 94-142, what data are available on the child's current performance? What tests were administered, and when? What were the results? The National Association of State Directors of Special Education (NASDSE) (1976) suggests the following sources of information be considered in generating data to establish the child's current level of educational functioning:

1. School Records: Inspection of cumulative and other available records can be helpful in determining whether or not there are factors that might help to account for the reason for referral, whether or not there seem to be any trends in problem growth, and whether other areas seem to be in need of closer evaluation.

2. Standardized Tests: Standardized tests may be used to obtain information on how one child compares with others. In many cases, standardized tests are required for determination of eligibility. This type of test covers such areas as intelligence, achievement, and personality.

3. Developmental Scales: These compare areas of pupil development within the child and as compared with others. They are especially useful with younger or more severely handicapped children, pinpointing both strengths and weaknesses.

Exhibit 4-4 Form for an Individualized Education Program

I. STUDENT INFORMATION   Date _____

STUDENT NAME _____ SEX _____
      Last   *First*   *Initital*   *M-F*

BIRTHDATE _____ PARENT _____ PHONE _____
     Mo. *Day* *Yr.*

ADDRESS _____ ZIP _____

DISTRICT OF RESIDENCE _____ RECEIVING SCHOOL/AGENCY _____

II. MEDICAL INFORMATION

A. VISION SCREENING _____ ____ ____ _____ _____
         Mo. *Day* *Yr.*   *Examiner*   *Results*

B. HEARING SCREENING _____ ____ ____ _____ _____
          Mo. *Day* *Yr.*   *Examiner*   *Results*

COMMENTS _____

III. LEVEL OF CURRENT PERFORMANCE (Based upon achievement, diagnostic, criterion-referenced testing and teacher observation)

A. ACHIEVEMENT:		
SPELLING LEVEL	TEST	DATE
MATH LEVEL	TEST	DATE
READING LEVEL	TEST	DATE
B. MENTAL ABILITY:	TEST	DATE
C. PSYCHO-MOTOR:	TEST	DATF
D. SOCIAL BEHAVIOR:	TEST	DATE

Exhibit 4-4 continued

E. SPEECH/LANGUAGE:	TEST	DATE
F. OTHER (self-help, vocational, etc):		

IV. PROGRAM ELIGIBILITY [check appropriate item(s)]

___ a.	EMH	___ h.	Deaf D
___ b.	TMH	___ i.	Hard of Hearing HH
___ c.	BD	___ j.	Deaf/Blind DB
___ d.	LD	___ k.	Physical Handicap EH
___ e.	Speech Impaired SI	___ l.	Educ. Handicap EH
___ f.	Visually Impaired VI	___ m.	Early Childhood EC
___ g.	Autistic AUT	___ n.	Other (Specify)

V. PROGRAM PLACEMENT (enter information in columns following listing)

	DATE	DURATION	EXTENT OF PARTICIPATION IN PERCENTAGES
a. Regular Class			
b. Reg. Class w/ Consult.			
c. Reg. Class w/ Supp. Tchng. Treatment			
d. Reg. Class w/ Res. Room			
e. Part-time Spec. Class			
f. Full-time Spec. Class			
g. Residential School			
h. Special Day School			
i. Hospital School			
j. Hosp./Treatment Center			
k. Alternative School			
l. Homebound			

VI. SUPPORTIVE SERVICES [enter item(s) in columns following listing]

	DATE	DURATION	EXTENT OF PARTICIPATION IN PERCENTAGE
a. Counseling			
b. Indiv. Psych. Counseling			
c. Group Psych. Counseling			
d. Speech Therapy			
e. Occup. Therapy			
f. Hearing Aid Evaluation			

Exhibit 4-4 continued

	DATE	DURATION	EXTENT OF PARTICIPATION IN PERCENTAGES
g. Adaptive P. E.			
h. Regular P. E.			
i. Parent-Infant Education			
j. Remedial Reading			
k. Social Work			
l. Braille/Large Print			
m. Orientation/Mobility			
n. Adaptive Equipment			
o. Barrier-free Environ.			
p. Diagnostics			
q. Phsycial Therapy			
r. Aduiological Therapy			
s. Hearing Therapy			
t. Vision Therapy			
u. Phys. Hand./Ment. Hand.			
v. Behavior Therapy			
w. Supportive Materials			
x. Other (Specify)			

VII. PRIMARY LANGUAGE _____

VIII. PLACEMENT COMMITTEE

IX. ANNUAL GOALS: _____

Exhibit 4-4 continued

IX. ANNUAL GOALS (Continued): _____

X.   PARENT INVOLVEMENT

I have been involved in the preparation of this Individualized Plan and:

_____ I am in agreement with it.

_____ I disagree with its contents.

I realize that this is an educational plan and not a binding legal contract.

_____
Signature of parent/guardian

XI. INSTRUCTIONAL OBJECTIVES   EVALUATION   DATE

4. Criterion Referenced Tests: This type of test places the child at a certain level in some area of skill development. It is especially helpful for planning purposes because criterion statements can be used as goals for instruction.
5. Observation: Observational data can focus on a very specific child characteristic, such as interaction with other youngsters, can point out areas in need of further evaluation, and can confirm or reject other information. Observations may be formal or informal and include such things as anecdotal records, interaction analysis, checklists, and rating scales. These observations may take place in any setting, including the home. Observational data are best obtained by those who are close to the child in the normal environment.
6. Interviews: Interviews with the parent, the child, and/or the teacher yield information that lends perspective to other kinds of information. They also pinpoint areas that may be priority needs or strengths.
7. Work Samples: These are similar to criterion referenced testing: they provide information concerning the level of the child in some areas of skill development. They are useful in planning intervention in academic areas.
8. Consultants: These experts may provide information that is not usually available to an educational planner. This may include medical, therapeutic, and family information and may be used to plan services in related areas, define limitations on other planning, or identify areas of major need.

IV. Program Eligibility—Another district option is a checkoff system to indicate which handicapping condition the child evidences.

V. Program Placement—This section also uses a checkoff system to indicate which delivery approach is most appropriate. Note that in this section dates of initiation and duration of service are requested as well as the extent of participation within each delivery option.

VI. Supportive Services—Again in direct response to P.L. 94-142, what services are needed by the child? When will they begin? How long will they last? How much time each week will the child participate in them?

VII. Primary Language—Some districts choose to indicate this in the demographic data section, others in the educational evaluation section, others not at all. This specification makes good sense in terms of evaluating the validity of the test information as well as planning the goals, objectives, and specific curriculum.

VIII. Placement Committee—This is a district option that again makes sense but is not required. If it becomes necessary later to identify who was in attendance at any given IEP meeting, completing this box simplifies the detective work.

IX. Annual Goals—This section is the heart of the IEP: What is this child expected to be able to do one year from now that the individual cannot do today? Annual goals may be stated in broad norm referenced terms: Allister will improve one year in reading comprehension as measured by the Woodcock Reading Mastery Test; or in very specific, criterion referenced terms: Aaron will be able to add two-digit numbers requiring regrouping with 95 percent accuracy. The author's preference is toward the latter whenever possible. Nowhere is it specified that each child must have a given number of annual goals. The exact number of goals should be determined on the one hand by the child's needs and, on the other hand, by what can be reasonably expected in terms of accomplishments given the time frame of the school year and the youngster's rate of growth. A rule of thumb might be that four to five annual goals (one in each of several academic/social/self-help areas) would be a maximum.

X. Parent Involvement—This, too, is a district option. It makes good sense to have the child's parent endorse the IEP at the time of its development, but it is not a requirement established by federal law. Parents are required to endorse any placement decisions, however.

XI. Instructional Objectives—It is not reasonable to assume that the congressional authors of P.L. 94-142 had the traditional instructional objective in mind when drafting the law. First, the traditional view of instructional objectives is that they should be attainable in approximately two weeks to one month. That would mean formulating 9 to 18 objectives per goal per child per meeting. Second, it is unreasonable to expect that on September 15 a teacher can predict with the necessary degree of accuracy how many objectives will be needed by May 15 of that school year, or even whether the objective planned in September will be appropriate in May. What, then, is a reasonable interpretation? The most logical is that the short-term instructional objective is a measurable milestone on the way to an annual goal, and that perhaps four or five such milestones might be an appropriate number. In the original form, Section XI occupied all of Page 4, so that more than one Page 4 could be used, if required. Note, again in direct response to P.L. 94-142, that the evaluation criteria and dates of anticipated completion of objectives are specified on this sheet.

THE USE AND ABUSE OF THE IEP

In closing this section, please permit the author a bit of philosophizing. For all the good intentions and planning that went into the creation of P.L. 94-142 in general and IEPs in specific, it is all just so much paper until teachers and parents take it seriously. If IEPs are regarded as Idiotic Extra Paperwork, they will become just that: an exercise to satisfy certification and review boards, something to dust off once each year in the preparation of next year's dust catcher. If, however, teachers learn to use IEPs as planning tools that they consult on a regular basis to check whether they're on course, they actually can be a time saver and a vital element in providing services to handicapped children.

Summary

In the greater scheme that is an individualized instructional sequence, the starting point is formal assessment, most usually for placement purposes. Following this, the diagnosis is fine tuned through informal diagnostic techniques. These techniques should emanate from a theoretical structure against which behavior can be compared. The diagnosis should lead to a set of descriptors, again based on a theoretical structure that defines the materials needed to attain the desired goal for the child. This chapter has reviewed several retrieval systems designed to match learner characteristics to needed instructional materials according to their various taxonomic perspectives.

The fruit of these efforts should be an educational plan for each learning disabled child outlining the diagnostic results, goals and objectives, and instructional strategies and materials. The federal government has provided special education with a ready format for such fruit in the IEP. The content of IEPs as well as the process by which their content is derived made up the closing portion of this chapter.

The book now plunges boldly forth with a listing of materials (set up according to the authors' taxonomical structure) followed by chapters on program delivery systems.

REFERENCES

Aserlind, L. The special education IMC/RMC network. *Educational Technology,* August 1970, 32–39.

Bower, A.C., & Ritchardson, D.H. A computer-based data bank. *Mental Retardation,* 1975, 13(1), 32–33.

Cawley, J. *Behavior Resource Guide.* Wallingford, Conn.: Educational Sciences, Inc., 1973.

Cross, K. *Computer based resource units.* Buffalo: State University College, Research Development Complex, 1974.

Commission on Instructional Technology. *To improve learning: A report to the President and the Congress of the United States.* Washington, D.C.: U.S. Government Printing Office, 1970.

Gearheart, B. *Learning disabilities: Educational strategies.* St. Louis: The C.V. Mosby Company, 1973.

Gerlach, V., & Ely, D. *Teaching and media: A systematic approach.* Englewood Cliffs, N.J.: Prentice-Hall, Inc., 1971.

Hallahan, D., & Kauffman, J. *Introduction to learning disabilities: A psychobehavioral approach.* Englewood Cliffs, N.J.: Prentice-Hall, Inc., 1976.

Hewett, F., & Forness, S. *Education of exceptional learners.* Boston: Allyn & Bacon, Inc., 1974.

Johnson, D., & Myklebust, H. *Learning disabilities: Educational principles and practices.* New York: Grune & Stratton, Inc., 1967.

Kirk, S., McCarthy, J., & Kirk, W. *Illinois test of psycholinguistic abilities.* Urbana, Ill.: University of Illinois Press, 1968.

Komoski, P.K. The realities of choosing and using instructional materials. *Educational Leadership,* 1978, *36*(1), 46–50.

Laska, E., Logemann, G., Honigfeld, G., Weinstein, A., & Bank, R. The multistate information system. *Evaluation,* 1972, 1, 66–71.

Lehrer, B.E., & Daiker, J.F. Computer based information management for professionals serving handicapped learners. *Exceptional Children,* May 1978, *44*(8), 578–585.

Lerner, J. *Children with learning disabilities: Theories, diagnosis and teaching strategies.* Boston: Houghton Mifflin Company, 1971.

McCarthy, J. Educational material for the mentally retarded: A quandary. *Education and Training of the Mentally Retarded,* 1966, *1,* 24–31.

Minick, B. Personal communication, 1980.

National Association of State Directors of Special Education. *Implementing Public Law 94-142.* Washington, D.C.: NASDSE, 1976.

National Center on Educational Media and Materials for the Handicapped. *Instructional materials thesaurus for special education.* Columbus, Ohio: Ohio State University Press, 1976.

Olshin, G. IMC network report. *Exceptional Children,* 1967, *34*(2), 137–141.

Public Law 94-142 (Education for All Handicapped Children Act of 1975).

Peter, L.J. *Prescriptive teaching.* New York: McGraw-Hill Book Company, 1965.

Popham, W.J., & Baker, D. *Systematic instruction.* Englewood Cliffs, N.J.: Prentice-Hall, Inc., 1970.

Prillaman, D. Diagnostic and prescriptive teaching: Rationale and model. *Council for Exceptional Children Newsletter,* 1968, *1,* 1–4.

Reese, J. An instructional system for teachers of learning disabled children. In D. Sabatino (Ed.), *Learning disabilities handbook: A technical guide to program development.* DeKalb, Ill.: Northern Illinois University Press, 1976.

Sabatino, D. The information processing behaviors associated with learning disabilities. *Journal of Learning Disabilities,* 1969, *1*(8) 440–450.

Select Ed Prescriptive Materials Retrieval System, PMR. Olathe, Kan.: Select Ed, 1972.

Southwest and West Central Educational Cooperative Service Unit, Special Education Services, SEIMC, Montevideo, Minn. Personal communication, 1980.

Vogel, S. Personal communication, 1980.

Woodbury, M. *A guide to sources of educational information.* Washington, D.C.: Information Resources Press, 1976.

Chapter 5

Materials for Learning Disabled Students

Carl R. Schmidt

While the materials available for teaching learning disabled children may be listed in a computerized file with numerous cross-references, there still are many teachers, aides, and parents (believe it or not) who do not have access to such systems. For persons looking for materials, a modest list is presented in this book. The list has been compiled by way of a nationwide solicitation of materials used by federally-funded projects serving learning disabled students. The list has been supplemented by contributions from Dr. Leon Silber of the North Carolina Department of Special Education. The authors wish to thank Dr. Silber and other contributors for their help. It must be stressed that inclusion of a particular piece of material in this chapter should not be construed as an endorsement by the author. There is little in the way of validity information on any commercially available materials, but the fact that they appear on agency lists should lend them some degree of credibility.

This chapter is composed of two sections, a materials listing and a publishers listing. The materials list contains the name of the material and of the publisher, the subject addressed, the approximate difficulty level by grade, the primary input mode (e.g., auditory, visual), the primary response or output required of the student, and the cost of the material.

The materials list is organized as per the Sabatino (1968) list described in Chapter 4 with the following additions:

5.0 Independent Living Skills
5.1 Study Skills
5.2 Home Economics
6.0 Career/Vocational Preparation
7.0 Affective Education

In all cases, an item appears in the most specific category possible. For example, if a particular arithmetic item deals exclusively with numeration, it appears in category 4.41, Arithmetic-Numeration. If, however, the material includes numeration, computation, and measurement in one kit, it simply is classified under 4.4, Arithmetic. Each item appears only once on the list. Therefore, if it cuts across more than one major dimension (e.g., Spelling and Reading) it appears under the one category judged by the author to be most appropriate.

It should be noted that for many of the materials, life can be extended through the use of an adhesive, clear plastic covering such as "Contac" covering, available from most department or hardware stores, or better yet, laminating film from a firm such as Brodert, 1609 Memorial Avenue, Williamsport, Pa. 17705 ($34 for a 22" × 100' roll).

MATERIALS LIST

(Publishers are listed at end of this chapter)

Title/Publisher	Area	Level	Input	Output	Cost
1.0 Motor					
1.1 Gross Motor					
J.A. Preston Corporation					
Circle Balance Discs	Gross Motor	Pre-3	Multi-sensory	Motor	$ 23.15
Foot Placement Ladder		Pre-3			91.60
Twister Board		Pre-3			
Bouncing Tube		Pre-3			47.50
Preschool Climber		Pre-3			
Climbing Ladder		Pre-3			
Rope Ladder		Pre-6			
Doorway Chinning Bar		Pre-6			20.50
Jump Rope		Pre-6			

Title/Publisher	Area	Level	Input	Output	Cost
Constructive Playthings					
Dressing Frames, set of 4 #JC-55	Gross Motor	K-6	Multi-sensory	Gross Motor/ Verbal	22.50
Multiplay Screen #CP-M560					89.95
Developmental Learning Materials					
Dyna-Balance Walking Board	Gross Motor	Preschool K-3	Multi-sensory	Gross Motor	53.00
Weights		Preschool K-6			5.95
Constructive Playthings					
Giant Hollow (plastic) Blocks #ROT-7109	Gross Motor	Preschool Kindergarten	Multi-sensory	Gross Motor	36.95
Childcraft					
Hohner Rhythm Band Set (Primary set) #8R-467 (includes triangle, 2 wrist bells, soprano sounder, 2 ankle bells, 2 pairs sand blocks, crow sounder, tambourine stick, claves, combination rhythm sticks)	Music Gross Motor	Preschool K-3	Auditory	Fine Motor Gross Motor	20.00
Hohner Tambourine (10") #8R-107					7.00

Title/Publisher	Area	Level	Input	Output	Cost
Flaghouse					
Hoppity-Hop V762	Gross Motor	K-6	Multi-sensory	Motor	11.90
Achievement Products, Inc.					
Rocker Balance Square 18″ × 18″ × 5″ AP-205	Gross Motor	Preschool K-3	Multi-sensory	Gross Motor	30.00
Be OK!					
Scooter Board 15½″ × 11⅞″ BK-8156	Gross Motor	Any age	Multi-sensory	Gross Motor	24.95
Carpeted Scooter Board 12″ × 16″ BK-8158					29.95
Be OK!					
Suspension Hammock BK-8109	Gross Motor	Any age	Multi-sensory	Gross Motor	11.50
Skill Development Equipment Co. (SDE)					
Spot Trainer (solid core bolster 20″ × 20″ × 28″) ST-2	Gross Motor (Hand-eye co-ordination)	K-12	Visual	Motor	68.00
Handle Ball 36″ diameter HB-2					89.00

Title/Publisher	Area	Level	Input	Output	Cost
Be OK!					
Swinging Platform 25" × 37" BK-8102	Gross Motor	Preschool K-3	Multi-sensory	Gross Motor	115.00
Childcraft					
Tunnel of Fun #8A-182	Gross Motor	Preschool K-3	Multi-sensory	Gross Motor	15.95
Achievement Products Inc.					
Ultralight folding mats AP-1119	Gross Motor	NA	NA	NA	58.00
Community Playthings					
Unit Building Blocks, half nursery set #G-422	Gross Motor	Preschool Kindergarten	Multi-sensory	Gross Motor	115.00
Teaching Resources Corporation					
Vanguard School Program, Part 1	Gross Motor	Preschool K-3	Visual/ Auditory (game)	Verbal/ Fine Motor	4.50

1.2 Perceptual Motor

Title/Publisher	Area	Level	Input	Output	Cost
Science Research Associates, Inc.					
Beginning to Learn: Fine Motor Skills	Sensorimotor (eye-hand coordination)	Preschool	Tactile Auditory/ Visual	Written/ Verbal	99.50

Title/Publisher	Area	Level	Input	Output	Cost
Teaching Resources Corporation					
Dubnoff Program I	Sensori-motor (eye-hand coordination)	Preschool K-3	Visual/ Auditory (text)	Written	23.95
Vanguard School Program, Part 2			Visual/ Auditory (game)	Verbal Fine Motor	16.95
Pathway School Program 1			Visual/ Auditory (small apparatus)	Gross Motor	18.95
Morrison School Supplies					
Easel Brushes:	Percep-tual Motor (Art)	Preschool K-6	Visual	Motor	
½" (long handle) #EB-3612					13.95 per dozen
¾" (long handle) #EB-3614					14.95 per dozen
½" (short handle) #DL-3252					7.80 per dozen
¾" (short handle) #DL-3254					10.20 per dozen
Finger Puppets: people and ani-mal sets #CV-35				Motor/ Verbal	6.25
Giant Tinkertoy #TT-5300				Motor	38.25

Title/Publisher	Area	Level	Input	Output	Cost

Allied Education Council

Fitzhugh PLUS Programs—Perceptual Training Books	Perceptual (eye-hand coordination)	Preschool	Visual Objects (kits)	Fine Motor	
101					3.60
102					3.60
104					4.15

Developmental Learning Materials

Lacing Boards #133	Perceptual Motor	Preschool K-3	Visual	Motor	4.50
Easy Grip Scissors #361					5.00
Clear Stencils #137					7.00
Stencils: Animals #105, Farm & Transportation #106					4.25 each
Lite-Brite #130					13.50

Childcraft

Large Beads & Strings	Perceptual Motor (Eye-hand coordination)	Preschool & K-3	Visual/ Auditory	Fine Motor	4.00
Colored Beads & Strings (small)					3.50

Title/Publisher	Area	Level	Input	Output	Cost
Beaded Pegs & Pegboard					2.00 (Board) + 4.50 (Beads) = 6.50
Peg Sorting Board					8.00

Developmental Learning Materials

Title/Publisher	Area	Level	Input	Output	Cost
Peglace Board	Percep-tual Motor (Eye-hand coordi-nation)	Preschool & K-3	Visual	Fine Motor	16.95
Lacing Board					4.75

Constructive Playthings

Title/Publisher	Area	Level	Input	Output	Cost
Sand and Water Table	Percep-tual Motor	Any age	Multi-sensory	Fine Motor	
(with top) #A-64					107.50
(without top) #A-65					92.50

Childcraft

Title/Publisher	Area	Level	Input	Output	Cost
Tactile Domino Blocks #86-197	Percep-tual Motor	Any age	Tactile	Fine Motor	14.95

1.3 Body Awareness

Developmental Learning Materials

Title/Publisher	Area	Level	Input	Output	Cost
Body Concept Spirit Masters I & II	Body Aware-ness	Preschool K-3	Visual/ Auditory (text)	Written	3.50 each

Title/Publisher	Area	Level	Input	Output	Cost
Constructive Playthings					
Body Image Puzzle, Oriental Boy #1D-6440	Body Image	Preschool Kindergarten 1st	Visual	Fine Motor	9.95
Developmental Learning Materials					
Large Body Puzzles	Body Awareness	Preschool K-3	Visual (puzzle)	Fine Motor	6.25
Position in Space Posters					
People Puzzles					5.75
Teaching Resources Corporation					
Vanguard School Program, Part 1	Body Awareness	Preschool K-3	Visual/ Auditory (game)	Verbal/ Fine Motor	4.50
Body Position Cards (46)			Visual (card)	Gross Motor	12.95

2.0 Perception

2.1 Visual Perception

Science Research Associates, Inc.					
Beginning to Learn: Perceptual Skills	Perception Visual Discrimination Visual Memory	Preschool K-3	Auditory/ Visual	Verbal	155.00

Title/Publisher	Area	Level	Input	Output	Cost
Developmental Learning Materials					
Colored Inch Cube Designs #111	Visual Perception	Preschool K-6	Visual	Motor	4.50
Large Parquetry #113 and Designs #114					6.50 4.00
Small Parquetry #115 and Designs #116					5.50 3.75
Shapes Dominoes #244					3.00
Shapes Sorting Box #382					12.00
Ann Arbor Publishers					
Perceptual Activities	Perception Visual Figure-Ground	Preschool K-3		Reusable Consumable	4.00 each 3.00 each
Incentives for Learning					
Sequential Cards Level 1 #128 Level 2 #129	Visual Perception	Preschool K-3	Visual	Motor/ Verbal	4.50 each
Developmental Learning Materials					
Size Sequencing Cards	Visual Sequence	Preschool K-3	Visual	Motor/ Verbal	2.50
Sequential Picture Cards, Set I #127					1.60
Sequential Strips #376					3.00

Title/Publisher	Area	Level	Input	Output	Cost

Developmental Learning Materials

Title/Publisher	Area	Level	Input	Output	Cost
Multivariant Sequential Beads #289 and Patterns #290					8.50 3.25
Visual Discriminate Flip Books I, II, III	Perception Visual Discrimination	Preschool K-3	Visual/ Auditory (text)	Fine Motor/ Written	2.25 each

Developmental Learning Materials

Title/Publisher	Area	Level	Input	Output	Cost
Visual Memory Cards	Perception Visual Memory	Preschool K-3	Visual/ Auditory (cards)	Fine Motor/ Verbal Written	
I					1.75
II					2.75
III					4.25
IV					(11.00 all sets)

Teaching Resources Corporation

Title/Publisher	Area	Level	Input	Output	Cost
Vanguard School Program, Part 3	Perception Visual Discrimination	K-3	Visual/ Auditory (text)	Written	16.95

Teaching Resources Corporation

Title/Publisher	Area	Level	Input	Output	Cost
Vanguard School Program, Part 4	Perception Visual Figure-Ground	Preschool K-3	Visual/ Auditory (text)	Written/ Verbal/ Gross Motor	16.95

Title/Publisher	Area	Level	Input	Output	Cost

2.2 Auditory Perception

Developmental Learning Materials

Title/Publisher	Area	Level	Input	Output	Cost
Auditory Perception Training (Memory)	Perception Auditory Memory	K-3 (4-6)	Auditory (tape)	Written	69.75
Buzzer Board			(Instrument Board)	Fine Motor	12.50

Developmental Learning Materials

Auditory Perception Skills Series II	Perception Auditory Figure-Ground	Preschool K-3	Auditory (tapes)	Written	50.75

Imperial International Learning Corporation

Gateway to Good Reading	Perception Auditory Memory	K-3	Auditory/ Visual (text) (tapes)	Motor Written	239.00

Incentives for Learning

Sound Matching #134 (cassettes and pictures)	Auditory Perception	K-6	Visual Auditory	Verbal	13.75

Title/Publisher	Area	Level	Input	Output	Cost
		2.3 Tactile Perception			
J. A. Preston Corporation					
Tactile Board Set	Perception Tactile Discrimination	Preschool K-3	Tactile/ Visual	Motor	34.45
Textured Cubes and Spheres					22.40
Tactile Textures Set					10.40
Tactile Surface Ball					7.75
Teaching Resources Corporation					
Touch-and-Match Textures Set I Set II	Perception Tactile Discrimination	Preschool K-3	Tactile (objects, textures)	Fine Motor	18.95 each
		3.0 Language			
Community Playthings					
Doll House Furniture	Language	Preschool K-3	Multi-sensory	Motor	11.25 each or 54.50 entire set
Living Room Set (D-71) Dining Room Set (D-73) Parents' Bedroom Set (D-74) Child's Bedroom Set (D-75) Kitchen Set (D-76)					

Title/Publisher	Area	Level	Input	Output	Cost
Steck-Vaughan Company Publishers					
English Mastery	Language		Visual (text)	Verbal	2.05 each
Book 1		9			
Book 2		10			
Book 3		11			
Book 4		12			
NASCO					
5-Room Doll House	Language	Preschool K-3	Visual	Verbal/ Motor	33.50
Community Playthings					
Flagg Doll Family	Language	Preschool K-3	Multi- sensory	Motor/ Verbal	12.50 each
White (D-49W)					
Black (D–49B)					
Webster Division, McGraw-Hill Book Company					
The Learning Skills Series: Language Arts	Language Arts (listen- ing, speak- ing, read- ing, writing, gram- mar)		Visual (text)	Written/ Verbal	4.00 each
Acquiring		K-1			
Building		2			
Continuing		3			
Directing		4 across 4 levels			

Title/Publisher	Area	Level	Input	Output	Cost
American Guidance Service, Inc.					
Peabody Early Experiences Kit (PEEK) #6901	Language	Preschool Kindergarten	Visual (text) Auditory (tapes)	Written/ Verbal	285.00
Bowmar					
Reading Incentives	Language	Grades 3-5	Visual (books, films, dittos, auditory tapes)	Verbal/ Written	
Language Program					
Complete Kits for 10					391.20
Complete Kits for 20					782.40
Separate:					
Books					2.52
Reading Kit (record or cassette)					39.12
Bowmar Spirit masters					3.96
Constructive Playthings					
Sculptured Farm Animals #CHC-272	Language	Preschool K-12	Visual	Motor/ Verbal	13.95
200 Animals #CHC-168					13.95

Title/Publisher	Area	Level	Input	Output	Cost

Community Playthings

Woodcrest Refrig- erator #C-51	Language	Preschool K-3	Multi- sensory	Gross Motor	67.50 each
Woodcrest Stove #C-60					
Woodcrest Sink #C-81					

3.1 Conceptual Language

Developmental Learning Materials

Association Picture Cards	Concep- tual Language	Preschool K-3	Visual/ Auditory	Motor/ Verbal	
Set I #124					1.60
Set II #156					1.60
Set III #157					3.25
Same or Different Size Cards #176					1.50
Same or Different Design Cards #212					3.25
Spatial Relations Picture Cards #125					1.60
Size and Shape Puzzle #270					5.00

Communication Skill Builders, Inc.

Concept Box	Concep- tual Language	Ages	Visual/ Auditory	Verbal/ Motor	
#3024-H		3+			13.95
#3082-H		3-8			6.00
#4015-H		3-6			6.00

Title/Publisher	Area	Level	Input	Output	Cost
Milton Bradley Co.					
Goal: Language Development	Conceptual Language	K-6	Auditory/ Visual (text)	Verbal	140.00
Early Childhood Enrichment Series: Unit 2 Learning to Develop Language Skills					
Steck-Vaughan Company Publishers					
Language in Daily Living	Conceptual Language (Functional)	10-12	Visual (text)	Written/ Verbal	1.60 each
Book 1: Verbs and Subjects					
Book 2: Phrases, Clauses, and Sentences					
Book 3: Pronouns, Modifiers, and Verbals					
Book 4: Punctuation and Capitalization					
Frank E. Richards Publishing Company					
Learning Functional Words and Phrases for Everyday Living	Conceptual Language (Functional)	10-12	Visual (text)	Verbal	2.00

Title/Publisher	Area	Level	Input	Output	Cost
Developmental Learning Materials					
Logic Cards	Conceptual Language	K-3	Visual/ Auditory (cards)	Fine Motor/ Verbal	2.50
Association Picture Cards					
I					1.75
II					1.75
III					3.50
IV					3.75
Motive Expressive Language Cards					1.75 each
I					
II					
Category Cards					2.75
Sequential Picture Cards					
I					1.75
II					3.50
III					3.50
IV					3.00
American Guidance Service, Inc.					
Peabody Language Development Kit	Conceptual Language Perception		Auditory Visual Tactile	Verbal/ Motor	235.00
Level P	(Auditory Memory)	3-5			
Level #1	Language	4½-6½			
Level #2	(Expressive)	6-8			
Level #3		7½-9½			
Teaching Resources Corporation					
Sequence Picture Cards Level 1	Conceptual Language	K-3	Visual	Verbal/ Motor	
Set 1 (#85-220)					8.95
Set 2 (#85-222)					5.50

Title/Publisher	Area	Level	Input	Output	Cost
What's Wrong Here (picture absurdities)? Level 1 #85-230					9.95
What's Missing Here? Level 1 #85-210					8.95
Body Position Cards #16-510					13.95

Milton Bradley Co.

Title/Publisher	Area	Level	Input	Output	Cost
Sort-a-Card Game	Conceptual Language	K-3	Auditory/ Visual	Verbal	3.75
Vegetables and Fruits Poster Cards			Auditory/ Visual	Verbal/ Written	6.00
Animals and Their Young Poster Cards					

3.2 Expressive Language

Teaching Resources Corporation

Title/Publisher	Area	Level	Input	Output	Cost
Cognitive Skills: What's Missing?	Language Expressive	K-3	Visual (cards)	Written	
What's Missing? Level 1					8.50
Level 2					6.25

Incentives for Learning

Title/Publisher	Area	Level	Input	Output	Cost
Expression Puppet #153	Basic Skills	Any age	Multi-sensory	Motor/ Verbal	7.50

Title/Publisher	Area	Level	Input	Output	Cost
Teaching Resources Corporation					
Fokes Sentence Builder #86-110	Expressive Language	K-6	Visual/ Auditory	Verbal/ Written	52.00
Parts of Speech Complete #84-100					32.50
Developmental Language Lessons #87-110					46.00
Communication Skill Builders, Inc.					
Games Kids Like #2124-H	Expressive Language (Speech)	K-8	Visual (game)	Verbal/ Motor	15.00
More Games Kids Like #2125-H					
Combination Offer #2024-H					27.00
Developmental Learning Materials					
Homonym Cards	Expressive Language	K-3	Visual/ Auditory (cards)	Fine Motor/ Verbal	2.75
Sequential Picture Cards					
I					1.75
II					3.50
III					3.50
IV					3.00
Logic Cards					2.50
Reaction Cards					2.75
Language Expression Circle					
Motor Expressive Language Picture Cards I, II					1.75 each

Title/Publisher	Area	Level	Input	Output	Cost
Antonym Cards					2.75
Storytelling Posters		K-3	Visual/		5.00
		(4-6)	Auditory		
The Many Faces of Children Posters			(posters)		
The Many Faces of Youth Posters					5.00

Steck-Vaughan Company Publishers

Title/Publisher	Area	Level	Input	Output	Cost
Language Exercises	Expressive Language (Grammar)		Visual (text)	Written/ Verbal	1.90 each
Yellow		1			
Purple		2			
Silver		3			
Tan		4			
Red		5			
Blue		6			
Gold		7			
Green		8			
Review		5-9			

Steck-Vaughan Company Publishers

Title/Publisher	Area	Level	Input	Output	Cost
Language Skill Books 610 720 830 940	Expressive Language (Grammar)	4-8	Visual (text)	Written/ Verbal	.50 each

American Guidance Service, Inc.

Title/Publisher	Area	Level	Input	Output	Cost
Peabody Articulation Decks, Complete Kit #759	Expressive Language (Speech)	K-6	Auditory Visual	Verbal	31.00

Title/Publisher	Area	Level	Input	Output	Cost
Modern Education Corporation					
Spirit Master Language Stimulation Workbooks Verbs (#101) Prepositions (#103)	Expressive Language	K-6	Visual (text)	Written/ Verbal	9.00 each
Milton Bradley Co.					
Story Cards: Tell What Part Is Missing Opposites Flannel Aid	Expressive Language	K-3	Auditory Visual	Verbal	4.00
Modern Education Corporation					
Therapy Kit (Mirror & Pocket Chart) TK-101	Expressive Language (Speech)	Any age	Auditory Visual (text)	Verbal	32.00
Speech Master Therapy Books Sh sounds #106 K sounds #107 G sounds #108 P sounds #109 B sounds #110 T sounds #111 D sounds #112 F sounds #113					9.00 each

3.3 Receptive Language

Title/Publisher	Area	Level	Input	Output	Cost
Steck-Vaughan Company Publishers					
Claws and Paws	Comprehension Vocabulary	1	Visual (text)	Written Verbal	1.60

Title/Publisher	Area	Level	Input	Output	Cost
Gills and Bills		1			
Manes and Reins		2			
Bones and Stones		3			

Caroline School Supply

Title/Publisher	Area	Level	Input	Output	Cost
Task Master Task Cards Intermediate Comprehension Pak	Receptive Language Comprehension Skills	7–12	Visual (game)	Motor/ Verbal	24.00

Caroline School Supply

Title/Publisher	Area	Level	Input	Output	Cost
Task Master Task Cards Junior/Senior High Comprehension Pak	Receptive Language Comprehension Skills	7–12	Visual (game)	Motor/ Verbal	24.00

4.0 Academics

4.1 Reading

Scholastic Book Services

Title/Publisher	Area	Level	Input	Output	Cost
Action Libraries 1–4a	Reading	7–12	Visual (text)	Verbal	44.50 each

New Readers Press

Title/Publisher	Area	Level	Input	Output	Cost
Be Informed	Reading Living Skills	4.7–6.9	Visual	Written	
Single Unit-Set of 10					1.20
(bound)					17.50
(unbound)					12.00

Title/Publisher	Area	Level	Input	Output	Cost
Children's Press					
Challenge to Read Program (6 programs)	Reading (Sports)	Grades 4 & 5	Visual (text) (film)	Verbal	39.95 each
Complete Set			Auditory (cassettes)		239.70
Educational Progress Corporation					
Clues to Reading Progress	Reading	Grades 5+	Auditory (tape)	Written	
Complete Program 1-5123		(deficit in	Visual (texts)		418.50
(Trays 1/2/3)		primary			155.50
1-512 Tray 1		reading			each
1-522 Tray 2		skills)			
1-532 Tray 3					
Imperial International Learning Corporation					
Gateway to Good Reading	Reading	K-2	Auditory (tapes)	Verbal/ Written/	
Auditory Discrimination			Visual (text)	Motor	
Unit 1					75.00
Unit 2					89.00
Unit 3					89.00
Complete Set					239.00
Visual Perception					
Unit 4					89.00
Unit 5					89.00
Unit 6					75.00
Complete Set					239.00
Both Sets					459.00

Title/Publisher	Area	Level	Input	Output	Cost
Love Publishing Company					
Individualized Reading Skills Improvement	Reading	K-6	Visual	Written	
7006 Paper					4.95
7305 Spirit Masters					12.50
Language Instructional Activities					
Book 1 7208					4.95 each
Book 2 7209					
Caroline School Supply					
Kids Stuff—Reading and Language Experiences	Reading & Language	7–12	Visual (text)	Written Verbal	11.00
Caroline School Supply					
Kids Stuff	Reading	K-1	Visual	Written/	11.00
1) Reading and Writing Readiness	Writing Language		(text)	Verbal	each
2) Reading and Language Experiences		1–6			
Bowmar					
Play the Game	Reading	3–5	Auditory	Written	
Book	Sports		(tapes)		2.04
Cassette			Visual		8.10
Spirit Master			(texts)		3.96
Steck-Vaughan Company Publishers					
Read Better	Reading	10–12	Visual (text)	Verbal	2.00

Title/Publisher	Area	Level	Input	Output	Cost
Center for Applied Research in Education					
Reading Correction Kit	Reading (to correct difficulties)	K-9	Visual (text)	Written	13.00
Steck-Vaughan Company Publishers					
Reading Fundamentals for Teenagers	Reading	10-12 (Reading at 3-4 grade level)	Visual (text)	Written/ Verbal	2.00
Steck-Vaughan Company Publishers					
Reading Improvement Activities Book 1 Book 2 Book 3	Reading	 7 8 9	Visual (text)	Written/ Verbal	2.05 each
Scholastic Book Services					
Real Life Reading Skills	Reading Survival Skills	10-12	Visual (text)	Written/ Verbal	50.00 kit
Fearon Pitman Publishers					
Space Police (6)	High Interest-Low Difficulty Reading Material	Reading Level NA. Interest Level 4-8, 9-12	Visual/ Auditory (text)	Verbal/ Written	13.50 set 2.49 each
Pacemaker Classics (8)		RL 2.0-2.5. IL 7-8 9-12(1)	(text/ tape/ films)		

Title/Publisher	Area	Level	Input	Output	Cost
Pacemaker Classics (8)		RL 2.0-2.5. IL 7-8 9-12(1)	(text/ tape/ films)		
Books Only					19.47 series 2.55 each
Multimedia Kit					298.50 39.45 each
Pacemaker Best Sellers (10)		RL 2.0-2.5 IL 4-8			69.75 4 copies 22.50 set of 10 2.49 each
Pacemaker True Adventures (11)		RL 2.0-2.5. IL 4-8			16.20 series 1.62 each
Adventures in Urban Reading (4)	RL NA. IL 7-12				5.16 set 1.41 each

Garrard Publishing Company

Title/Publisher	Area	Level	Input	Output	Cost
Sport Series (22)	High Interest-Low Difficulty Reading Materials	Reading Level 4.0. Interest Level 4-8.	Visual/ Auditory (text)	Verbal	98.56 set 4.48 each
Americans All (27)		RL 4.0. IL 4-8			120.96 4.48 each

Steck-Vaughan Company Publishers

Title/Publisher	Area	Level	Input	Output	Cost
Superstars Series Rock Soul Country Movies Sports	Reading	7-12	Visual (text)	Verbal	1.80 each

Title/Publisher	Area	Level	Input	Output	Cost

Academic Therapy Publications

Typing Keys for Re- mediation of Reading and Spelling	Reading Spelling	K-9	Visual (text)	Motor	6.00

Lakeshore Curriculum Materials Co.

What's Wrong Cards, Set A #REF-50	Reading	K-6	Visual	Verbal	5.95

4.11 Reading—Letter Recognition

Developmental Learning Materials

Alphabet Cards (Manuscript & Cursive)	Reading Letter Recog- nition	Preschool K-3	Visual	Written/ Fine Motor	6.25

Educational Progress Corporation

Audio Reading Pro- gress Laboratory (Level A)	Reading Letter Recog- nition	Preschool K-3	Auditory/ Visual (text) (tapes)	Written/ Verbal	195.50

Science Research Associates, Inc.

Detect Tactile	Reading Letter Recog- nition	Preschool K-3	Tactile/ Visual (game, ob- jects)	Verbal/ Fine Motor	105.00

Title/Publisher	Area	Level	Input	Output	Cost
Milton Bradley Co.					
Giant Alphabet Poster Cards	Reading Letter Recognition	Preschool K-3	Auditory/ Visual	Verbal/ Written	6.00
J. A. Preston Corporation					
Sandpaper Letters	Reading Letter Recognition	Preschool K-3	Tactile/ Visual	Motor	125.68
Plywood Letters Follow-the-Arrow Letter Formation Groovy Letters		K-3			
Educational Teaching Aids					
Sandpaper Alphabet (Lowercase manuscript, Uppercase manuscript, Lowercase cursive, Uppercase cursive)	Reading Letter Recognition	K-3	Tactile	Fine Motor	29.00 each
Continental Press					
Visual Readiness Skills Level 1 Level 2	Reading Letter Recognition Visual Discrimination	Preschool K-3	Visual/ Auditory (text)	Written or Verbal	3.95 each
Seeing Likenesses & Differences Level 1 Level 2					

Title/Publisher	Area	Level	Input	Output	Cost

Visual Discrimination
    Level A
    Level B
    Level C					

4.12 Reading—Word Attack

Garrard Publishing Company

Title/Publisher	Area	Level	Input	Output	Cost
Consonant Lotto Vowel Lotto	Reading Word Attack (Phonics)	K-3	Visual/ Auditory (cards)	Verbal/ Fine Motor	2.75 each

Ann Arbor Publishers

Title/Publisher	Area	Level	Input	Output	Cost
Cues and Signals Series (Cues and Signals IV)	Reading Word Attack (Structural Analysis)	K-6	Visual (text)	Written/ Verbal	4.00

Ann Arbor Publishers

Title/Publisher	Area	Level	Input	Output	Cost
Cues and Signals Series	Reading Word Attack (Phonics)	K-3	Visual (text)	Written Verbal	4.00
Visual Aural Discrimination Book I-V		4-6			

Title/Publisher	Area	Level	Input	Output	Cost
Academic Therapy Publications					
How to Be a Word Detective	Reading (De-coding)	K-6	Visual (text)	Verbal/ Written	3.00
Allied Education Council					
Individual Reading Games	Reading Word	K-6	Visual/ Auditory	Verbal/ Written	
Mott Basic Language Skill Pro-grams	Attack (Struc-tural Analy-sis)		(text) (tapes)		
Semiprogrammed Series					
Book 1607					4.15
Book 1608					4.15
Book 1609					4.15
Book 1610					4.15
Mott Basic Language Skills Pro-grams		4-6			
Classroom Series (Book 600A)					4.15
Ideal School Supply Co.					
Initial and Final Consonants	Reading Word Attack (Phon-ics)	K-3	Auditory/ Visual	Verbal	14.95
Blends and Di-graphs		K-6			
Vowels					6.65
Vowel Enrich-ment					10.75
Phonic Analysis					16.75

Title/Publisher	Area	Level	Input	Output	Cost
Allied Education Council					
Mott Basic Language Skills Programs Semiprogrammed Series	Reading Word Attack (Phonics)	K-6	Visual/ Auditory (text) (tapes)	Verbal/ Written	
Book 1301					59.95
Book 1302					59.95
Book 1303					59.95
Book 1304					59.95
Book 1305					59.95
Book 1306					59.95
Classroom Series					
Books 300a & 300b					4.15 each
Developmental Learning Materials					
Sound Foundations Program (Spelling & Phonics) I & II	Reading Word Attack (Phonics)	K-6	Visual (cards)	Written	19.00 each
The Interstate Printers and Publishers, Inc.					
Sound Wheels No. 1 No. 2 No. 3	Reading Word Attack (Phonics)	K-3	Auditory/ Visual	Verbal	2.95 each
Caroline School Supply					
Taskmaster Task Cards Advanced Phonics Pack Grammar Pack Word Analysis Pack Primary Comprehension Pack	Reading Comprehension Skills	K-6	Visual (game)	Written/ Verbal	24.00 each

Title/Publisher	Area	Level	Input	Output	Cost
Kenworthy Educational Service, Inc.					
UNO-A Phonics Game	Reading	K-3			
Phonic Word Blend Flip Charts	Word Attack (Phonics)	4–6			
Junior Phonic Rummy			Auditory/ Visual	Verbal	1.70 each or
Phonic Rummy Readiness Primary Primary Primary Intermediate Intermediate					9.20 set

4.13 Reading—Word Recognition

Steck-Vaughan Company Publishers

Title/Publisher	Area	Level	Input	Output	Cost
Adult Reading Single Units: 1100 1200 1300 1400 1500 1600 1700	Reading Word Recognition Word Attack Skills	Grade Level: 0–4 Interest Level: Adult	Visual (text) Auditory (tapes)	Written/ Verbal	1.56 each unit
Set of 4 Tapes: 1006					24.00
1 Complete Package					185.00

Garrard Publishing Company

Title/Publisher	Area	Level	Input	Output	Cost
Basic Sight Vocabulary Cards	Reading Word Recognition	K-6	Visual (cards)	Verbal	2.50

Title/Publisher	Area	Level	Input	Output	Cost
Picture-Word Cards		K-3			2.25

Milton Bradley Co.

Title/Publisher	Area	Level	Input	Output	Cost
Paris Word Game Picture Word Game	Reading Word Recognition	K-3	Auditory/ Visual	Motor Verbal	2.50
Picture Word Builder					
Picture Flash Words for Beginners				Motor (written) Verbal	2.25
Educational Flash Words, Group 1 & 2				Verbal	2.25

Developmental Learning Materials

Title/Publisher	Area	Level	Input	Output	Cost
Vocab-Tracks Word-Picture Dominoes	Reading Word Recognition	K-6	Visual (cards)	Fine Motor/ Verbal	3.50 2.95

4.14 Reading—Vocabulary

Steck-Vaughan Company Publishers

Title/Publisher	Area	Level	Input	Output	Cost
Adult Reading: 2100 2200 2300 2400 2500 2600 2700 2800	Reading Vocabulary	4-8	Visual (text)	Written/ Verbal	1.70 each

Title/Publisher	Area	Level	Input	Output	Cost
Allied Education Council					
Mott Basic Language Skills Programs	Reading Vocabulary		Visual/ Auditory (text) (tapes)	Verbal/ Written	
Semiprogrammed Series (Books 1607, 1608, 1609)		4–8			4.15 each
Mott Basic Language Skills Programs					
Classroom Series (Books 300B, 600A)		K-8			4.15 each
Garrard Publishing Company					
Picture Word Cards	Reading Vocabulary	K-3	Visual (cards)	Verbal	2.25
Scholastic Book Services					
Word Mastery with Puzzles and Games	Reading Vocabulary Word Skills		Visual (text)	Written/ Verbal	.95 each
Word Recognition		1 & 2			
Spelling		3 & 4			
Vocabulary Building		5 & 6			

Title/Publisher	Area	Level	Input	Output	Cost

4.15 Reading—Comprehension

Open Court Publishing Co.

Title/Publisher	Area	Level	Input	Output	Cost
Catching On	Reading	2–6	Auditory/	Verbal	2.65 each
Level A-Grade 2	Compre-	K-6	Visual		
Level B-Grade 3	hension		(text)		
Level C-Grade 4					
Level D-Grade 5					
Level E-Grade 6					
Teacher's manual					3.75 each
for each level					

Allied Education Council

Title/Publisher	Area	Level	Input	Output	Cost
Mott Basic Lan-	Reading		Visual/	Verbal/	
guage Skills Pro-	Compre-		Auditory	Written	
gram	hension		(text)		
			(tapes)		
Comprehension		4–8			
Series					
Books 301–					3.15 each
304					
Books 601–					3.50 each
604					
Classroom Series		4–12			4.15 each
(Books 300B,					
600A & B, 900A					
& B)					
Semiprogrammed		K-8			
Series					
Book 1301					3.70
Book 1302					3.95
Book 1303					3.95
Book 1304					4.25
Book 1305					4.25
Book 1306					4.25
Book 1607					4.15
Book 1608					4.15
Book 1609					4.15
Book 1610					4.15

Title/Publisher	Area	Level	Input	Output	Cost
Imperial International Learning Corp.					
Primary Reading Program	Reading Comprehension	K-3	Auditory/ Visual (tapes) (text)	Motor Written	
Intermediate Reading Program		4-6			439.00
The Economy Co.					
Remedial Reading Program	Reading Comprehension	4-12	Visual/ Auditory (tape) (text)	Written/ Verbal	$159.60 kit
Reach					
Barnell Loft					
Specific Skills Series: Complete Secondary Set	Reading Skills by Subarea and Reading Level	7-12	Visual (text)	Verbal or Written	90.00
Barnell Loft					
Specific Skill Series	Reading Skills by Subarea and Reading Level		Visual (text)	Written/ Verbal	
Primary		Pre 1-3			.77
Elementary		Pre 1-6			1.16
Midway		4-9			.90

Title/Publisher	Area	Level	Input	Output	Cost

Developmental Learning Materials

Title/Publisher	Area	Level	Input	Output	Cost
Vocab-Tracks	Reading Compre-hension	K-6	Verbal (cards)	Fine Motor/ Verbal	3.50

4.2 Spelling

Steck-Vaughan Company Publishers

Title/Publisher	Area	Level	Input	Output	Cost
Target: Spelling (180, 360, 540)	Spelling	1-6	Visual (text)	Written/ Verbal	1.65

Science Research Associates, Inc.

Title/Publisher	Area	Level	Input	Output	Cost
Words and Pat-terns The SRA Spelling Series	Spelling	K-6	Auditory/ Visual (text)	Written	
Grade 1					2.15
Teacher's Edi-tion					3.60
Grade 2					2.75
Teacher's Edi-tion					5.35
Grade 3					2.75
Teacher's Edi-tion					5.35
Grade 4					2.75
Teacher's Edi-tion					5.35
Grade 5					2.75
Teacher's Edi-tion					5.35
Grade 6					2.75
Teacher's Edi-tion					5.35

Title/Publisher	Area	Level	Input	Output	Cost
Word Study I and II The SRA Spelling Series		7–8			
Grade 7					2.75
Teacher's Edi- tion					5.35
Grade 8					2.75
Teacher's Edi- tion					5.35

The Economy Company

Title/Publisher	Area	Level	Input	Output	Cost
Continuous Prog- ress in Spelling	Spelling	K-8	Visual (cards)	Written	129.90 kit

Child Service Demonstration Center

Title/Publisher	Area	Level	Input	Output	Cost
I Used to Could Spell Wensday	Spelling	7–12	Visual (text)	Multi- sensory	8.00

Holt Rinehart Winston Inc.

Title/Publisher	Area	Level	Input	Output	Cost
Snoopy's Secret Code Book	Spelling	K-3	Visual (text)	Verbal/ Written	5.50

Developmental Learning Materials

Title/Publisher	Area	Level	Input	Output	Cost
Sound Foundations Program I & II	Spelling	K-6	Visual (cards)	Written	19.00 each

4.3 Writing

Steck-Vaughan Company Publishers

Title/Publisher	Area	Level	Input	Output	Cost
Imaginary Line Handwriting Se- ries	Writing		Visual (text)	Written/ Verbal	
Starting Right		K			2.00
Going Forward		1			1.60
Writing On		2			1.60

Title/Publisher	Area	Level	Input	Output	Cost
Changing Step		2			1.60
New Skills		3			1.60
Carry On		4			1.60
Think and Write		5			1.60
Ventures		6			1.60
Looking Ahead		7 & 8			1.60

Educational Teaching Aids

Title/Publisher	Area	Level	Input	Output	Cost
Sandpaper Alphabet Writing		K-3	Tactile	Fine Motor	29.00 each
Lower Case Manuscript	Manuscript				
Upper Case Manuscript					
Lower Case Cursive	Cursive				
Upper Case Cursive					

Aero Educational Products

Title/Publisher	Area	Level	Input	Output	Cost
Writing Practice Slate, Manuscript Cursive	Writing Manuscript Cursive	K-3 4-6	Visual (text)	Written	1.50 each

4.31 Writing—Manuscript

Teaching Resources Corporation

Title/Publisher	Area	Level	Input	Output	Cost
Dubnoff Program Level 3 Program 3	Writing Manuscript	K-3 K-6	Visual/ Auditory (text)	Written	21.50

Title/Publisher	Area	Level	Input	Output	Cost
Developmental Learning Materials					
Tracing Paper De- signs	Writing Manu- script	K-3	Visual (text)	Written	5.25

4.32 Writing—Cursive

Ann Arbor Publishers					

Cursive Writing
  Level 1
  Level 2
Cursive Tracking
	Writing
	Cursive
		K-6	Visual/
			Auditory
			(text)
				Written	4.00 each

Steck-Vaughan Company Publishers					
Improving Your Handwriting	Writing	10–12	Visual (text)	Written	2.00

4.33 Writing—Expressive

Scholastic Book Services					

Creative Expres-
  sion Books
    Dinosaur Bones
    Jungle Sounds
    Ghost Ships
    Cook Up Tales
    Adventures with
  a Three-Spined
  Stickleback
	Writing	
		
		2
		3
		4
		5
		6
			Visual
			(text)
				Written/
				Verbal
					.95 each

Steck-Vaughan Company Publishers					
Perfecting Reading and Writing Skills	Writing	10	Visual (text)	Written/ Verbal	2.05

Title/Publisher	Area	Level	Input	Output	Cost
Scholastic Book Services					
Real Life Writing Skills	Survival Skills Writing	10–12	Visual (text)	Written/ Verbal	50.00 kit

4.4 Arithmetic

Title/Publisher	Area	Level	Input	Output	Cost
Love Publishing Co.					
Arithmetic Instructional Activities Book 1 7206 Book 2 7207	Math	K-6	Visual	Written	4.95 each
Individual Arithmetic Instruction Paper 7003 Spirit Masters 7304					4.95 15.00
Scholastic Book Services					
Arithmetic Skills Progress Level A Level B Level C	Math	1–9	Visual (text)	Written/ Verbal	3.00 each
Scott Resources Inc.					
Chip Trading Math Lab Kit	Arithmetic Compu- tation Numer- ation	K-6	Visual/ Auditory (text) (chips)	Fine Motor/ Verbal	109.00
Cuisennaire Co. of America					
Cuisennaire Rods (supplemental box of 155 rods) #20030	Math	Any age	Visual/ Auditory	Motor/ Verbal	8.95

Title/Publisher	Area	Level	Input	Output	Cost
Creative Publications					
Desk Top Attribute Blocks #30401	Math	Any age	Visual/ Tactile	Motor/ Verbal	14.95
Caroline School Supply					
Kids Stuff Math	Math	1-6	Visual (text)	Written/ Verbal	11.00
Webster Division, McGraw-Hill Book Company					
The Learning Skill Series Arithmetic Acquiring Building Continuing Directing	Math	1-9 across 4 levels	Visual (text)	Written/ Verbal	4.00 each
Steck-Vaughan Company Publishers					
Mathematics in Daily Living Book 1 Fractions Book 2 Decimals & Percents Book 3 Measurement & Geometry Book 4 Fundamental Algebra	Living Skills Math	10-12	Visual (text)	Written/ Verbal	1.80 each
Steck-Vaughan Company Publishers					
Mathematics Skill Books (5500, 6600, 7700)	Math	4-8	Visual (text)	Written/ Verbal	.50 each

Title/Publisher	Area	Level	Input	Output	Cost
Aero Educational Products					
Math Practice Slates Sets 1, 2, 3, 4, 5, 6	Arithmetic Compu- tation Numer- ation	K-8	Visual (text)	Written	1.50 each
Cuisennaire Co. of America					
Primary Balance #20900	Math	K-3	Visual/ Auditory	Motor/ Verbal	14.50
Scholastic Book Services					
Real Life Math Skills	Math (Sur- vival Skills)	10-12	Visual (text)	Written/ Verbal	.50

4.41 Arithmetic—Numeration

Title/Publisher	Area	Level	Input	Output	Cost
Educational Teaching Aids					
Beginners Math Lab Set No. 2	Arithmetic Numer- ation	K-3	Visual (ob- jects)	Fine Motor/ Verbal	13.40
Ann Arbor Publishers					
Cues and Signals Series, Number Tracking	Arithmetic Numer- ation	K-3	Visual (text)	Verbal/ Written	4.00
Milton Bradley Co.					
Early Childhood En- richment Series Unit 3, Develop- ment of Number Readiness	Arithmetic Numer- ation	K-3	Auditory/ Tactile (text)	Motor	70.00

Title/Publisher	Area	Level	Input	Output	Cost
Ideal School Supply Co.					
Enlarged Place Value Sticks	Arithmetic Numeration	K-6	Auditory/ Visual	Fine Motor	7.50
Modern Computing Abacus			Auditory/ Visual (text)		14.95
Place Value Building Set			Auditory/ Visual		45.95
Garrard Publishing Company					
First Arithmetic Game	Arithmetic Numeration	K-3	Visual/ Auditory (cards)	Fine Motor/ Verbal	3.75
The 10 Game					2.25
Developmental Learning Materials					
Flip-a-Strip	Arithmetic Numeration	K-6	Visual (cards) (stencil)	Fine Motor/ Verbal	5.00
Place Value Stamps					7.00
Science Research Associates, Inc.					
Mathematics Involvement Program	Arithmetic Numeration	K-6	Auditory/ Visual	Written	237.50
Milton Bradley Co.					
Number Concept Cards	Arithmetic Numeration	K-3	Auditory/ Visual	Motor Written	4.00
Imperial International Learning Corporation					
Primary Math Skills Improvement Program	Arithmetic Numeration	K-3	Auditory/ Visual (tape, text)	Motor Written	429.00

Title/Publisher	Area	Level	Input	Output	Cost
Educational Teaching Aids Division					
Unifix Structural Math Materials (ETA Unifix Kit Master Chest)	Arithmetic Numer- ation	K-6	Visual (ob- jects)	Fine Motor/ Verbal	325.00

4.42 Arithmetic—Computation

Science Research Associates, Inc.					
Computapes Grades 1-6 (for set of 6 mod- ules, with 56 tapes)	Arithmetic Compu- tation	4-12	Auditory/ Visual (tapes)	Written	731.00
Grades 7-11 (for set of 5 modules with 46 tapes)					596.85
Instructo/McGraw-Hill					
Desk Tapes (Num- ber Lines)	Arithmetic Compu- tation	K-3	Visual/ Auditory	Motor	
0-10					3.25
0-20					4.50
Learning Resources Associates					
Digitor-Skillmaster	Math	K-9	Visual (text)	Written	1.80
Educational Teaching Aids					
ETA Unifix Kit Mas- ter Chest	Arithmetic Compu- tation	K-6	Visual (ob- jects)	Fine Motor/ Verbal/ Written	325.00

Title/Publisher	Area	Level	Input	Output	Cost
Beginner's Math Lab Sets 3 & 4					13.40
Versa Tiles I & II					13.90
Classroom Learning Labs					143.50 each

Allied Education Council

Title/Publisher	Area	Level	Input	Output	Cost
Fitzhugh PLUS Programs, Number Concepts	Arithmetic Computation	K-8	Visual (kits/objects)	Fine Motor	
Book 203					4.35
Book 204					3.40
Book 206					4.35
Noonan-Spradley Computational Skills Program			Visual/Auditory Verbal	Written	4.75

The Economy Co.

Title/Publisher	Area	Level	Input	Output	Cost
Guidebook to Mathematics	Arithmetic Computation	4-12	Visual (text)	Written	2.19

Developmental Learning Materials

Title/Publisher	Area	Level	Input	Output	Cost
Moving Up in Numbers	Arithmetic Computation	K-6	Visual (cards)	Written/Verbal	22.25
AOT Math Cards, Addition, Subtraction, Multiplication, Division					2.50 each

Milton Bradley Co.

Title/Publisher	Area	Level	Input	Output	Cost
Quizmo (Educational Lotto), Add-Subtract	Arithmetic Computation	K-6	Auditory/Visual	Motor Written	3.75
Quizmo (Educational Lotto), Multiply-Divide					3.75

Title/Publisher	Area	Level	Input	Output	Cost
Garrard Publishing Company					
Say It Addition	Arithmetic Compu- tation	K-6	Visual/ Auditory (cards)	Verbal/ Fine Motor	3.75
Say It Subtraction					3.75
Say It Multiplication		K-8			3.75
Say It Division					3.75
Make One		4-8			2.50
Milton Bradley Company					
Self-Instructional Number Wheels; Addition-Sub- traction, Multipli- cation-Division Mathfacts Games, Addition & Sub- traction (Levels 1, 2, 3, 4, 5)	Arithmetic Compu- tation	K-6	Auditory/ Visual	Motor	18.00 set
Scholastic Book Services					
Word Problems in Math (A, B, C, D)	Math	K-4	Visual (text)	Written/ Verbal	1.00 each

4.43 Arithmetic Measurement

Title/Publisher	Area	Level	Input	Output	Cost
Milton Bradley Company					
Educational Toy Money	Arithmetic Measure- ment	K-6	Auditory/ Visual	Motor Verbal	2.75
International Teaching Tapes, Inc.					
Math Explora Tapes (Group 2)	Arithmetic Measure- ment	K-6	Auditory (text) (tapes)	Motor Written	82.50

Title/Publisher	Area	Level	Input	Output	Cost
Fearon Publishers					
Pacemaker Arithmetic Program	Arithmetic Compu- tation	K-6	Visual/ Auditory (text)	Fine Motor/ Written/ Verbal	
Money Makes Sense	Numer- ation Measure- ment				2.67
Using Dollars & Sense					2.67
Working Makes Sense					2.67
Buying with Sense					3.45
The Cash Box					28.50
Teaching Resources Corporation					
Parts and Wholes Picture Cards	Math	K-6	Visual	Verbal/ Motor	6.50
Developmental Learning Materials					
Time Tracs	Arithmetic Measure- ment	Preschool K-3	Visual/ Auditory	Fine Motor/ Written	2.95
Clock Stamp		Preschool K-6	(cards)		3.95
Coin Stamps		K-3	(text)		
U.S. heads					6.25
U.S. tails					6.50
Canadian tails					6.75
Plastic Clock		Preschool K-3	(ob- ject)		1.25
Linear Measures		K-3	(text)		11.00
Comparison Bal- ance			(ob- ject)		16.95

Title/Publisher	Area	Level	Input	Output	Cost
Ideal School Supply Company					
Two-Faced Clock Dial	Arithmetic Measure-ment	Preschool K-3	Auditory/ Visual (text)	Motor	5.50
Demonstration.Rul-ers		K-6	Auditory/ Visual	Motor/ Written	3.75
Liquid Measure		K-6		Motor/ Written	8.50
Dry Measure		K-6		Motor/ Written	8.50
Playstore Scale		K-6		Motor	17.50
Measurement Chart		K-6		Motor	2.95

4.5 Science

Title/Publisher	Area	Level	Input	Output	Cost
Grolier Educational Corporation					
The Living Earth Vol. 1–20	Science	K-12	Visual (text)	Verbal	169.50

Steck-Vaughan Company Publishers

Title/Publisher	Area	Level	Input	Output	Cost
The Wonders of Science The Human Body Water Life Earth and Beyond Land Animals Matter, Motion, and Machines	Science	10–12	Visual (text)	Written/ Verbal	2.10 each

Steck-Vaughan Company Publishers

Title/Publisher	Area	Level	Input	Output	Cost
Steck-Vaughan Science Series	Science		Visual (text)	Written/ Verbal/ Motor	1.90 each
Do You Know		1			

Title/Publisher	Area	Level	Input	Output	Cost
Things Around You		2			
You Find Out		3			
The World About You		4			
This Earth of Ours		5			
Learning to Use Science		6			
Exploring Our World		7			
Scientific Living Today		8			

Teaching Resources Corporation

Title/Publisher	Area	Level	Input	Output	Cost
Science Sequence Cards Set 1 #85-320	Science	K-6	Visual	Motor/ Verbal	5.75

4.6 Social Studies

Caroline School Supply

Title/Publisher	Area	Level	Input	Output	Cost
Kids Stuff	Social Studies	1-6	Visual	Written/ Verbal	11.00
Kids Stuff Social Studies					

5.0 Independent Living Skills

Janus

Title/Publisher	Area	Level	Input	Output	Cost
Buying a Good Used Car	Living Skills	7-12	Visual (text)	Written/ Verbal	5.00

Title/Publisher	Area	Level	Input	Output	Cost
Janus					
Restaurant Language	Living Skills	7–12	Visual (text)	Written/ Verbal	5.00

5.1 Study Skills

Title/Publisher	Area	Level	Input	Output	Cost
Learning Pathways					
Academic activities for Adolescents with Learning Problems	Study Skills	7–12	Visual (text)	Written/ Verbal	10.00
Scholastic Book Services					
Dictionary Skills Books	Study Skills		Visual (text)	Written/ Verbal	.95 each
A		3			
B		4			
C		5			
Scholastic Book Services					
Doing Research and Writing Reports	Study Skills		Visual (text)	Written/ Verbal	.95 each
A		4			
B		5			
C		6			
Scholastic Book Services					
Library Skill Books	Study Skills		Visual (text)	Written/ Verbal	.95 each
A		1 & 2			
B		3 & 4			
C		5 & 6			

Title/Publisher	Area	Level	Input	Output	Cost
Janus					
Reading Schedules	Study Skills	7-12	Visual (text)	Written/ Verbal	5.00

5.2 Home Economics

Fearon Pitman Publishers					
Getting Ready to Cook	Home Econom- ics	7-12	Visual (text)	Written Verbal	5.00
Fearon Pitman Publishers					
Planning for Your Own Apartment	Home Econom- ics	7-12	Visual (text)	Written/ Verbal	5.00
Fearon Pitman Publishers					
Planning Meals and Shopping	Home Econom- ics	7-12	Visual (text)	Written/ Verbal	5.00

6.0 Career/Vocational Preparation

Educational Progress Corporation					
Career Develop- ment Laboratory	Career Education	Junior & Senior High School	Auditory (tapes)	Written	338.50
Academic Therapy Publications					
Career Education for Children with Learning Disabili- ties	Career Education	6-9	Visual (text)	Written	12.00

Title/Publisher	Area	Level	Input	Output	Cost
Educational Properties, Inc.					
Career Education: New Approaches to Human Development	Career Education	High School/ Adults	Visual (text)	Verbal	8.95
Career Education: What It Is and How To Do It	Career Education	High School/ Adults	Visual (text)	Verbal	
Career Education in Middle/Junior High School		5–9			
Random House, Inc.					
Career Information Kits	Career Education	K-12	Visual/ Auditory Electronic	Verbal	14.49
Fearon Pitman Publishers					
The Job Box	Career Education	Junior/ Senior High	Visual (text)	Written/ Verbal	45.00
Janus					
Janus Job Interview Kit	Career Education	7–12	Visual (text) (kit)	Written/ Verbal	18.00
American Institutes for Research					
Teacher's Guide to Career Education: Primary Grade	Career Education	K-3	Visual (text)	Verbal/ Written	8.25
Teacher's Guide to Career Education: Upper Elementary Grades		4–6			8.25

Title/Publisher	Area	Level	Input	Output	Cost
Teacher's Guide to Career Education: Middle School Grades		7–8			6.75
Resource Book of Sample Lesson Units for Career Education		High School			9.75
Resource Book of Low Cost Materials for Career Education					8.25

Fearon Pitman Publishers

Title/Publisher	Area	Level	Input	Output	Cost
Working Makes Sense	Career Education	7–12	Visual (text)	Written/ Verbal	5.00

7.0 Affective Education

Steck-Vaughan Company Publishers

Title/Publisher	Area	Level	Input	Output	Cost
Human Value Service	Affective Education		Visual (text)	Written/ Verbal	
Teaching Pictures		K-1			21.00
About Me		1			5.50
About You and Me		2			5.50
About Values		3			5.50
Seeking Values		4			5.50
Sharing Values		5			5.50
Thinking with Values		6			5.50

PUBLISHERS LIST

Academic Therapy Publications
1539 Fourth Street
P.O. Box 899
San Rafael, California 94901

Achievement Products, Inc.
P.O. Box 547
Mineola, New York 11501

Aero Educational Products
St. Charles, Illinois 60174

Allied Educational Council
P.O. Box 78
Galien, Michigan 49113

American Guidance Service, Inc.
Publishers' Building
Circle Pines, Minnesota 55014

American Institutes for Research
1791 Arastradero
Palo Alto, California 94303

Ann Arbor Publishers
P.O. Box 388
Worthington, Ohio 43085

Barnell Loft
958 Church Street
Baldwin, New York 11510

Be OK! (Self-Help Aids Catalog)
Box 32
Brookfield, Illinois 60513

Bomar / Noble Publishers, Inc.
622 Rodier Drive
Glendale, California 91201

Caroline School Supply
Box RRR
2619 West Boulevard
Charlotte, North Carolina 28203

Center for Applied Research in
Education
P.O. Box 130
West Nyack, New York 10994

Childcraft
20 Kilmer Road
Edison, New Jersey 08817

Children's Press
1224 West Van Buren Street
Chicago, Illinois 60607

Child Service Demonstration Center
Secondary LD Program
Route 3, Hillside School
Cushing, Oklahoma 74023

Communication Skill Builders, Inc.
815 East Broadway
P.O. Box 42050-H
Tucson, Arizona 85733

Community Playthings
Rifton, New York 12471

Constructive Playthings
12372 Garden Grove Boulevard
Garden Grove, California 92643

Continental Press
P.O. Box 554
Elgin, Illinois 60120

Creative Publications
3977 East Bayshore Road
P.O. Box 10328
Palo Alto, California 94303

Cuisennaire Co. of America
12 Church Street
New Rochelle, New York 10805

Developmental Learning Materials
7440 Naches Avenue
Niles, Illinois 60648

The Economy Co.
P.O. Box 68502
5455 West 84th Street
Indianapolis, Indiana 46268

Educational Progress Corporation
P.O. Box 45663
Tulsa, Oklahoma 74145

Educational Properties, Inc.
P.O. Box DX
Irvine, California 92664

Educational Teaching Aids
159 West Kinzie Street
Chicago, Illinois 60610

Fearon Pitman Publishers
5103 West Pensacola
Chicago, Illinois 60641

Fearon Pitman Publishers
Dept. J.B
6 Davis Drive
Belmont, California 94002

Flaghouse
18 West 18th Street
New York, New York 10011

Frank E. Richards Publishing Company
Box 66
Phoenix, New York 13135

Garrard Publishing Company
Champaign, Illinois 61820

Grolier Educational Corporation
Instructional Systems Division
845 Third Avenue
New York, New York 10022

Holt, Rinehart & Winston, Inc.
Box 3670
Grand Central Station
New York, New York 10017

Ideal School Supply Co.
1100 South Lavergne Avenue
Oak Lawn, Illinois 60453

Imperial International Learning Corp.
Box 548
Kankakee, Illinois 60901

Incentives for Learning
600 West Van Buren Street
Chicago, Illinois 60607

Instructo/McGraw-Hill
Paoli, Pennsylvania 19301

International Teaching Tapes, Inc.
Learning Resources Division
Educational Developmental Corp.
202 Lake Miriam Drive
Lakeland, Florida 33803

The Interstate Printers and Publishers, Inc.
Danville, Illinois 61832

Janus
3541 Investment Boulevard
Suite 5
Hayward, California 94545

Kenworthy Educational Service, Inc.
138 Allen Street
P.O. Box 60
Buffalo, New York 14205

Lakeshore Curriculum Materials Co.
Los Angeles Teachers' Store
888 Venice Boulevard
Los Angeles, California 90034

Learning Concepts
2501 North Lamar
Austin, Texas 78705

Learning Resources Associates
Box 17052
Raleigh, North Carolina 27609

Love Publishing Co.
6635 Villanova Place
Denver, Colorado 80222

MacMillan Library Services
222 Brown Street
Riverside, New Jersey 08075

Mafex Associates, Inc.
90 Cherry Street
Box 519
Johnstown, Pennsylvania 15907

Modern Education Corporation
P.O. Box 721
Tulsa, Oklahoma 74101

Morrison School Supplies
304 Industrial Way
San Carlos, California 94070

NASCO
1524 Princeton Avenue
Modesto, California 95352

New Readers Press
Division of Laubach Literary International
Box 131
Syracuse, New York 13210

Open Court Publishing Co.
P.O. Box 599
La Salle, Illinois 61301

J. A. Preston Corporation
71 Fifth Avenue
New York, New York 10003

Random House, Inc.
School Division
201 East 50th Street
New York, New York 10022

Scholastic Book Services
904 Sylvan Avenue
Englewood Cliffs, New Jersey 07632

Science Research Associates, Inc.
155 North Wacker Drive
Chicago, Illinois 60606

Scott Resources, Inc.
P.O. Box 2121
1300 Blue Spruce Drive
Suite B
Fort Collins, Colorado 80522

Skill Development Equipment Co. (SDE)
Box 6300
1340 North Jefferson
Anaheim, California 92807

Steck-Vaughan Company Publishers
807 Brozos
Austin, Texas 78768

Teaching Resources Corporation
50 Pond Park Road
Hingham, Massachusetts 02043

Webster Division
McGraw-Hill Book Company
1211 Avenue of the Americas
New York, New York 10020

REFERENCE

Sabatino, D.A. The information processing behaviors associated with learning disabilities. *Journal of Learning Disabilities*, 1968, *1*, 440–450.

Chapter 6

Remedial Teaching Techniques in Five Key Areas

*David A. Sabatino
and Pamela Miller*

INTRODUCTION

The purpose of this chapter is to recommend specific teaching techniques in five areas—motor, perception, language, academic remediation, and vocational education—with one section devoted to each field. There are few recommendations of materials or specific teaching apparatus since Chapters 5 and 7 provide an extensive review of these subjects. The effort here is to augment those chapters by suggesting procedures for using some of the materials listed and to clarify initial teaching approaches that go beyond the commercially available instruments. In short, readers could look at the specific instructional procedures as recommended objectives from which to draw, depending upon the specific objective to be accomplished.

Therein, however, lies the call for professional judgment. There are no rules or validated procedures for selecting a specific instructional activity as a recommended enabling step toward a particular objective. The formal and informal diagnostic data described in Chapters 2 and 3 may provide suggestions. The real determination must be in the final analysis, i.e., "someone's" judgment that technique A is the best means of obtaining a certain objective.

Until a complete instructional system is built, with all of the components instructors ever would wish to teach, or until particular materials/approaches are validated for stated objectives, educators remain in the "hunt and peck" era in learning disabilities. The authors apologize for the limited state of the art and hope they can place meaningful objectives at readers' fingertips, if not now, at least in the near future. There is, however, an urgent call for research on instructional utilization.

The five sections in this chapter review selected assessment procedures to describe learner characteristics, objectives, and teaching techniques. The authors also recommend that readers review Chapters 4 and 5. It is important to select objectives and activate a particular instructional procedure or material based on the soundest educational reasoning.

SECTION 1: MOTOR DEVELOPMENT

INTRODUCTION

The authors of Public Law 94–142, the Education for All Handicapped Children Act of 1975, recognized the importance of movement and motor proficiency. Physical education curriculum, unlike most others, was defined and mandated in that act. The physical education curriculum is a direct education service and can be defined as follows:

> development of physical and motor fitness
> development of fundamental motor skills and patterns
> development of skills in aquatics, dance, individual and group games, and sports
> inclusion of special physical education, adapted physical education, movement education and motor development (Wheller & Hooley, 1976).

Legally, learning disabled students can insist on participation in physical education. In P.L. 94–142, ¶121a.14, two types of physical education programs are mentioned: (1) a regular one with nonhandicapped peers, and (2) one designed especially for the handicapped child and included in the Individualized Education Program (IEP). The important aspect is that a desirable pupil–teacher ratio be established and that needed equipment, materials, and physical facilities be made available.

A question of great importance to teachers is: How are the interests and needs of the learning disabled being provided for in physical education? The response may be directly related to the attitudes of school administrators. Several answers are possible for the students:

1. They are excused.
2. They remain spectators. Because special attention and special instruction are sometimes required, the learning disabled are assigned tasks such as keeping score, going for the loose ball, gathering towels, or taking roll.
3. They are excluded, assigned to an area where one continuous adapted or corrective program is conducted on a one-to-one ratio with an adaptive physical education person.

4. They are provided a remedial program and individualized work, but with absorption into a regular physical education class as soon as possible.

5. They are offered an integrated program wherein the learning disabled person is assigned immediately to a regular physical education class and takes part as much as possible, with special instructions when necessary (Wheller & Hooley, 1976).

The opportunities for handicapped children to take part in quality physical education programs are few (Rarick, Widdop, & Broadhead, 1967). It has been shown in Louisiana (Louisiana State Department of Education, Bulletin 1506, 1978) that the majority of handicapped children are taught physical education by regular elementary or special education teachers. Few regular education instructors have had enough professional preparation in physical education to adequately teach movement. On the other hand, few physical educators have received the necessary training in adaptive movement education to teach handicapped children.

Aloia, Knutson, Minner, and Von Seggern (1980), investigating physical education practices, conclude that these teachers must be more familiar with the characteristics of the learning disabled and the educable mentally retarded, and need to be more confident in their ability to teach them.

A RATIONALE

The importance of planned physical education instruction should be understood in relationship to academic endeavors. While most children may learn motor skills in free play, the learning disabled student must receive instruction to build similar skills. Therefore, quality instruction is vital and must be individualized—especially motor skill experiences. Physical education programs for learning disabled students are designed to be remedial, with the goal of returning the child to the regular class environment.

The physical environment of the classroom is an arena in which movement can be encouraged or suppressed (Barsch, 1967; Cratty, 1969). Barsch suggests carpeting an area for creeping and crawling; utilizing "alignment" targets; allowing student participation in bare feet; providing walking and balancing rails, scooter and teeter boards, and plastic balls of all sizes to promote motoric development and, thus, learning.

When instructing a child who exhibits learning difficulties, the movigenic teacher should attempt to develop the pupil's awareness of the surroundings and to promote efficient movement in those surroundings. Touching, seeing, and listening as well as understanding the body in relation to the environment in order to navigate through the surroundings successfully are fundamental. The child should be urged to run fast, walk slow, jump soft, talk loud, walk sideways, color upside down, and color with both hands. Activities involving sitting, kneeling, lying down, and standing can develop a greater understanding of gravitational pull. Sequence, timing, and rate of movement should be practiced in order to shift from one motor movement to another easily, readily, and efficiently. Children should be exposed to all curriculum activities. Movigenics is based on the belief that human learning is highly related to motor efficiency (Barsch, 1967). Thus, the objectives of a movement curriculum include the development and measurement of the student's orientation to learning, including degrees of freedom of bilaterality, flexibility, rhythm, and motor planning.

Motor development, according to Kephart (1960), affects efficient higher thought processes through motor generalization, i.e., the child learns to resist the force of gravity through playing one set of muscles against another—posture laterality. Recognizing the difference in left and right sides permits the child to recognize the difference between *b* and *d*. Kephart's perceptual motor training includes acts such as walking the balance board, jumping on a trampoline, and rhythm activities. Similarly, Cratty (1969) working in the Perceptual-Motor Learning Laboratory at the University of California at Los Angeles, states, "movement games may help children with learning problems, aid active normal children to learn better; and improve the academic progress of the culturally deprived and retarded child." Cratty continues:

1. Movement accuracy is necessary to define the intellect.
2. Motor tasks can elicit optimum levels of arousal, alertness, and activation.
3. Game participation can be used as reinforcement for concept acquisition.
4. Satisfaction gained in physical efforts contributes to a success syndrome.
5. Gross motor movement can be a learning modality through sensory input of the visual, kinesthetic, and tactile for moving through space, i.e., a child jumping from lettered and numbered squares can improve agility [and] recognition of numbers and letters. Or lines, squares, and zigzags may improve his ability to order a series of units.
6. Problem solving can be aided through movement (p. 32).

Cratty believes there are indications that gross motor movement activities can provide a sensory experience to enhance general classroom learning. The start of developmental skills, such as riding a bicycle, dancing, and swimming are cues that a child is developmentally ready to learn "academics."

Movement strengthening, general support, and perceptual motor ability are explored in the primary and intermediate grade levels. The emphasis of movement education is on creativity and problem solving. There is no failure and children are taught to have fun. The process of developing a progression of motor skills integrated with intellectual processes, without fear, tends to develop a better body image carrying over to self-image and better performance in the classroom. Cratty suggests a "failure syndrome" on the playground tends to be generalized in the classroom.

ASCERTAINING MOTOR DEVELOPMENT

Assessment of motor development is necessary to plan an effective physical activity program. The following list of tests and activities may be administered to students to assist in determining their specific motoric deficits or strengths.

The Harvard Step Test

This measures the ability of the heart and circulatory system to recover from vigorous exercises or hard work. The test can be administered to male and female children or adults. A bench is required for the step-ups to be performed during a time period of two to five minutes (depending on age level). The pulse is taken and a fitness formula is calculated for results.

The Standing Broad Jump

This exercise measures power, agility, and strength. A tumbling mat with a tape measure on the side is needed. The child is given three trials to jump with both feet as far forward as possible, swinging the arms as an aid. The farthest jump is recorded.

The Modified Sit and Reach Test

This is an easily administered test of flexibility in which a tape measure is the only equipment needed. The performer sits with legs extended and bobs forward three times, reaching as far as possible each time. The farthest reach on the tape measure is recorded.

Sit-Ups

These should be performed lying on the back with knees flexed, feet flat on the ground. The fingers are interlaced and placed behind the head. The performer curls up, touching the right elbow to the left knee and alternating with the left elbow to the right knee. The number of sit-ups performed without a time limit is recorded.

Flexed Arm Hang

This activity requires static muscular endurance of the upper body. A horizontal bar is needed, adjusted to a height so that the performer cannot touch the floor when hanging from the bar with arms extended. With an overhand grasp, the body is lifted (spotters may assist) until the chin is above the bar, elbows flexed. As soon as the proper position is taken, the time is started. When the chin drops below the level of the bar, the watch is stopped. The number of seconds is recorded as the score.

The Spring-Scale Press and Curl

The performer stands on a wooden platform connected to the spring-scale device. For the curl, the upper wooden bar is grasped with palms facing up, elbows flexed, and forearms extended at waist level. With back and legs straight, the student pulls up as hard as possible. The higher number of pounds for two trials is recorded. The press is done with an overhand grasp with the bar at eye level. The object is to push the bar up as far as possible. Record the greater number of pounds in two trials.

The Nelson Balance Test

A 10-foot balance beam (1¼ inches wide), a stopwatch, nine wooden blocks (four painted red), and a tape measure are needed. The blocks and beam are set in a pattern that the child has to follow, placing the ball of the left foot on the first block while holding the right foot off the floor. The examiner counts five seconds, then the person continues along the path, leaping to the next block while alternating feet. The red blocks indicate a holding of the balanced position for five seconds. The score is the total time of three trials.

The Distance Perception Jump

This requires a tape measure, blindfold, and some type of marker. The child is shown two lines and must "sense" the distance between them. With the blindfold on, the child jumps from behind one line to the next, trying to get the heels as close to the line as possible. The distance between the farthest heel and the second line is measured to the quarter inch and the better of two trials is recorded.

The Nelson Hand Reaction Test

This requires a Nelson Reaction Timer, a desk, and a chair. The student sits with the hand and forearm of the dominant hand resting on the desk. The fingers should extend beyond the table three to four inches. The examiner holds the stick-timer near the top and positions it between the thumb and index finger of the individual, which are held one inch apart. When the stick is released, the student should pinch the finger and thumb together to catch it. Ten trials are given in which the score on the stick above the top of the thumb is recorded. The middle six scores are averaged for the final reaction time.

The Harvey Rhythm Test

This requires two square frames with 15-inch sides, eight blocks 1½ inches square, and something with which to produce beats. The student kneels in front of the frames placed on the floor. There are eight blocks in one frame; the other is empty. The child is asked to put the blocks, one at a time with one hand, into the empty frame in rhythm with given beats. It takes two beats for every block. Several practice tests may be given. The actual test is recorded on a rating scale describing the movement in relation to the beats.

To conclude this section, an overview of objectives and activities is presented to assist the teacher in planning a motor development curriculum for children and youth with special needs.

MOTOR DEVELOPMENT CURRICULUM COMPONENTS

Rhythm

Teaching rhythms involves fundamental movement patterns and various types of dancing set to music or rhythmical beats. An example is to beat a drum or clap hands to form various patterns at different speeds. The teacher should start with a slow regular beat that the children walk in time to in any direction, then speed up the beat to a fast walk, and eventually to a run. As the students learn to move to the beat, irregular beats should be added to accompany combination of movement patterns, i.e., run, run, leap. Eventually, the teacher should let the students create their own movement patterns to a given beat.

Objectives for Rhythm

The classroom work should advance in the direction of enabling the child to:

1. acquire a fundamental sense of rhythm
2. understand changes of direction
3. respond to dynamics (loud, soft) and qualities (vibratory, percussive)
4. perform movements with a partner
5. beat time to music or movement patterns
6. develop rhythmical patterns of walking, running, skipping, sliding, galloping, hopping, and leaping to music or rhythmic beat
7. build self-expression through dancing
8. appreciate music and dance
9. learn to relax
10. create rhythmic patterns
11. build self-concept and self-awareness through rhythmical expression
12. increase balance and coordination.

Low Organized Games

Low organized games have very few rules and allow a great deal of vigorous movement using fundamental skills. Simple team games, tag games, and relays are included. "Squirrels in Trees" is an example. Groups of two children join hands and form trees. The single students are squirrels. There should be more squirrels than trees. On the teacher's signal of "squirrels run," the squirrels run to get into another tree. The extra squirrels also try to get into a tree. A few squirrels are always left without a tree. When all the trees are full, the signal is given again.

Objectives for Low Organized Games

The children in these exercises are becoming able to:

1. learn eye-hand and eye-foot coordination
2. learn to cooperate with others
3. learn to take turns
4. learn to follow directions and rules
5. learn sportsmanship and self-control
6. learn fundamental movement patterns (start, stop, turn)
7. learn basic skills (throw, catch, kick)
8. learn to be leaders and followers
9. increase strength, flexibility, coordination, agility, cardiovascular endurances, and balance
10. learn to work to their ability
11. learn to accept success and failure (win or lose) with appropriate behavior

12. learn to enjoy games and competition
13. improve speed, accuracy, and timing
14. gain confidence and self-control

Developmental Exercise

Many activities can be incorporated into this area. The stress should be on good body mechanics. Body alignment can be improved by walking on a balance beam; by knee dips, i.e., standing on one leg and trying to touch the other knee to the ground; by games that involve starting and stopping on command; and by relays while balancing beanbags on the head or on a foot. Any type of exercise or vigorous movement contributes to body development.

Objectives for Developmental Exercise

Through these activities, children should be able to:

1. improve posture
2. acquire well-balanced muscular development
3. increase flexibility
4. develop efficient movement patterns
5. correct or compensate for faulty development
6. acquire body awareness
7. improve self-concepts
8. be aware of and maintain fitness
9. learn to relax
10. improve weaknesses
11. be aware of and practice good health habits

Flexibility

Flexibility should be accomplished through slow, controlled movements such as bending, twisting, and stretching. Exercise can be made more interesting by using the children's imagination, asking them to climb a "pretend" ladder, write their name "really big" with their leg, kick a pretend football, etc. "Follow the teacher" is useful to teach exercises. For example, the children are told that the teacher wants to try to catch someone not paying attention. The teacher then stands with hands on hips, then to the side; swings one arm up, then the other, both down, etc., adding the legs, step by step, winding up by doing jumping jacks.

Objectives for Flexibility

In these exercises, the students seek to:

1. increase their range of movement
2. acquire efficient movement patterns
3. learn to bend, twist, and stretch
4. develop good health habits
5. develop well-balanced flexibility in opposing muscle groups
6. increase body awareness and limits
7. prevent muscle injury
8. gain body knowledge and control to develop flexibility
9. be able to participate in more activities

Strength

Strength can be developed by increasing the intensity, duration, or rate of the exercises. For example, changing sit-ups from straight legs to bent knees increases the intensity, doing the sit-ups for two minutes instead of one minute increases the duration, and performing a given number of sit-ups in less time than the previous day increases the rate. All of these overload the muscles, a requirement for strength development. Games and stunts, such as tug of war, handstands, and duckwalk also should be included. Circuit training is easy to set up by making five to ten exercise stations combined with running a lap between each station.

Objectives for Strength

The students' goals in these exercises are to:

1. acquire a well-balanced muscular development
2. gain knowledge of how to increase strength overload, frequency, duration
3. prevent injuries
4. learn to work at individual ability
5. acquire body awareness and knowledge of limits
6. increase self-concept
7. develop good health habits
8. increase endurance and resistance to fatigue
9. develop efficient movement patterns
10. develop, through strength, better body alignment

11. be able to participate in more activities
12. improve body weaknesses

Spatial Relationships

Obstacle courses can include all of the objectives for spatial relationships. These involve activities in which the children learn to move under, over, and through objects. A theme or story can be created in which the child follows directions to a destination by crossing bridges (balance beam), climbing mountains (gymnastic horse), walking cliffs (lines on the floor), weaving through trees in the woods (cones), etc. With a little imagination, any gym equipment and facilities, classrooms, and outdoor obstacles can be easily incorporated into a course.

Objectives for Spatial Relationships

Knowledge of these elements can help children to:

1. develop laterality
   a. develop awareness of perception
   b. be able to perform movements on both sides
   c. follow directions
   d. be able to move both hands (arms, legs, etc.) simultaneously
   e. be able to move both hands (arms, etc.) independently
   f. be able to move both hands (arms, etc.) in opposition
   g. acquire body awareness
   h. develop coordination and timing
   i. develop kinesthetic perception
   j. improve the quality of performance
   k. improve balance
2. develop directionality
   a. be able to move from a center point to a designated outside point
   b. be able to follow instructions
   c. know the basic directions (right, left, up, down, front, back, etc.)

Body Awareness

Many of these activities can be used to fulfill objectives for body position in space. Throwing and kicking skills can be developed. Stations that provide targets on the wall, hoops to throw through, cones to kick through, etc., can be set up. Low organized games or relays with balls should be included.

Objectives for Body Awareness

These activities can enhance students' abilities to:

1. increase kinesthetic awareness
   a. acquire awareness of body position
   b. acquire awareness of directionality
   c. be able to adjust body alignment to maintain balance
   d. be able to use kinesthetic sense to compensate for defects in inner ear or eyes
   e. develop awareness for a degree of force for movement
   f. be able to retain or generalize skills learned
2. establish awareness of spatial relationships
   a. be able to judge spaces
   b. know the terms under, over, etc.
   c. follow directions
   d. prevent injury
   e. develop efficient movement patterns
   f. increase coordination
   g. be able to adapt body positions
3. improve hand-eye, foot-eye coordination
   a. develop accuracy
   b. develop timing
   c. increase coordination

Summary

This section has provided a rationale for including movement activities as an integral part of the curriculum for learning disabled students.

SECTION 2: PERCEPTION AND PERCEPTUAL INTERVENTIONS

INTRODUCTION

No other information processing trait has been more vehemently debated than visual-motor perception. The reasons include: (1) an inability to show a relationship between visual perceptual treatment and academic achievement and (2) the lack of reliable, as well as valid, measures to ascertain the trait known as visual perception. These reasons are not conclusive. Therefore, the response of many practitioners—to halt perceptual training activities—has been slightly premature.

What is needed now is an earnest attempt to view perception as a functional process in the natural sequence of human development. This requires:

1. more stable measures of perceptual traits, developed from models employing functional explanations of the processes
2. teachers who are well versed in the complex theories of perceptual and visual-auditory perceptual integration
3. teachers who can develop perceptual curricula to meet specific student needs
4. elimination of motor and language contamination
5. a teaching emphasis more congruent with nature—more specifically:
   a. perceptual training based on objectives designed to improve perceptual development
   b. specific perceptual training directed at modifying either discrimination or memory processes in either an auditory or visual perceptual modality
   c. a strong emphasis on perceptual training in the preschool and early school years
   d. perceptual training when learning efficiency no longer is the question because of serious learning disability
   e. perceptual training as an alternative to persistent tutoring of academic subjects and remediations of academic skill deficits in support of language and other cognitive training
   f. perceptual learning for children with moderate learning disability and most children with severe learning disabilities as an initial objective to badly needed prevocational skills, including functional academics

Perception underlies all new learning where the discrimination and memory processing of neurally coded sensory information occurs. Perception is critical to all theories of learning and, subsequently, to the formulation of intelligence and cognitive style. As a result, it is vital that readers retain a distinction between criticism of the concept of perceptual intervention and criticism of the measurement of that concept.

It is generally held that perception begins in arousal of the nervous system. For example, a change in a child's attention in the classroom, or the startle response, results when an unanticipated sound occurs. Perception is more than a switchboard function for incoming information in the nervous system since it involves acting, reacting, thinking, organizing, and emotionality. Carr has defined perception as "a form of mental activity in which the meaning of present situations, objects, and events is determined, in part, by past learning" (Chaplin & Krawiec, 1960).

To understand what Carr was saying, it is necessary to think for a moment about the difference in "old or previous learning" and "new or novel learning." Even a portion of the distinctive feature of a given stimulus may provide the perceiver with all the information needed to form a complete concept about what already has been experienced. For example, the word "snow" may trigger a complete mental picture of winter, or the letters *c t,* although not a word, place little demand on the experienced reader to visualize *c a t.*

Perception covers so many interactions between people and the environment that it is difficult to define (and measure). In a general sense, perception may be considered the ability to rapidly and accurately order incoming environmental information into meaningful symbols by filtering out unwanted background information. Thus, perception is the discrimination and short-term retention of distinctive features of environmental objects. Perception is a process by which symbols are assigned value, or meaningful experiences, or discarded as unusable environmental data.

PERCEPTUAL FUNCTION

There are several problems in the clinical assessment of perceptual functions (both memory and discrimination):

1. There is the clarity of the trait being taught, i.e., is perceptual-motor training perceptual or a motor learning experience?
2. There are questions about the age at which to urge development of perceptual functions.
3. There is the question of when the trait should be dealt with as a perceptual process distinct from other cognitive processes.
4. There is the issue of whether the state of individuals' descriptive power to elicit measures of that trait has evolved into a fine science. The answer would have to be a resounding "no".

Any understanding of perceptual function should begin by differentiating between the sensory and perceptual processes. The sensory receiving mechanisms are peripheral to the central nervous system and are represented by end organs, primarily the eye and ear. Exactly *how* sensory data are received and interpreted is explained only by theory. Therefore, the measures used to extract perceptual function (or explain its absence) are based on models, paradigms, and theoretical constructs of how that process works. Needless to say, perception is a process of the central nervous sytem and therefore is not directly observable. The measurement of its dimensions is only assumed from an individual's responses. Therefore, a pure measure of what the person perceives rarely has been possible. In fact, generally only a vocal or manual motor response is measured. Therefore, a faulty response or, for that matter, a correct one may deny the examiner a true picture of "perceptual" performance.

Perception is difficult to distinguish from other cognitive processes. Frequently, perception is measured as an aspect of intelligence. For example, Binet (1905) used the concept of perception to define intelligence: "That which is called intelligence in the strict sense of the word consists of two principal things: first, perceiving the exterior world and secondly, reconsidering these perceptions as memories altering them" (p. 93). Pronko (1966) points up the confusion in the vagueness and looseness of perceptual semantics: "The term perception refers to (a) the thing perceived as well as (b) the perceiving of the thing" (Armstrong & Hauck, 1961). Perceptual deficits sometimes are equated with brain damage (Shaw & Cruickshank, 1956), problems in academic achievement (Koppitz, 1958), and emotional difficulties (Clawson, 1959). It may be accurate to state that although what is typically measured is the perception of geometric figures, many reading achievement and other developmental processes probably are ascertained as well in that they are related to the development of visual perception.

Keogh (1962) states that children's representation of their world is dependent on the level of cognitive development at which they currently are functioning. Her study of the *Bender Visual Motor Gestalt Test* (BVMGT) as a reading predictor has supported the proposition that perception is an integral part of the development of intelligence. Normal individuals were found to be superior to retarded children in perceptual development.

Many of the tests used by diagnosticians utilize an individual's production of geometric design after seeing the design. These tests can be regarded properly as visual-motor tasks. To copy the design, the child first must formulate a correct mental image of the figure and then have the motor ability to transfer it to paper. It is quite possible for the individual to have formulated a correct design and yet be unable to translate this visual image to paper properly. For handicapped individuals, it might be desirable to separate the motor functions from the visual task.

Rosenblith (1965), in a series of visual perceptual studies, obtained paired-comparison judgments of simple geometric figures from, among others, brain-damaged children. He found only minimal differences between the performance of the brain-damaged and normal children. Similarly, Sabatino (1969) investigated the auditory perceptual function of brain-injured children. To test the ability of handicapped children to perform auditorily in controlled noise, the test stimuli were mixed with a sound easily distinguished by normal listeners but with difficulty by learning disabled children. Sabatino found that brain-damaged children performed consistently lower (poorer) on this task, suggesting a lower level of organizational and integrational ability.

Thus, perception appears to be an important factor in the learning ability and learning style of handicapped children, but explains only a small part of the total educational process for most, especially those who do not have severe handicaps that create serious learning problems.

VISUAL PERCEPTION

No better example of a visual motor perceptual test commonly used by educators is available than the *Frostig Developmental Test of Visual Perception* (DTVP) (Frostig & Horne, 1964). The DTVP purports to measure five essential processes of the visual perceptual behavioral complex (Maslow, Frostig, Lefever, & Whittlesay, 1964). These processes are designated as (1) eye-motor coordination, (2) figure-ground perception, (3) form constancy, (4) position in space, and (5) spatial relations. Although Frostig does not assume that these five abilities are the only ones involved in the total process of visual perception, she does cite them as having particular relevance to school performance.

Several researchers have attempted to determine the capability of the Frostig DTVP to ascertain five perceptual traits by applying a data evaluation procedure known as factor analysis. The basic principle of factor analysis in this case is a statistical technique used to determine the degree to which subtests measure different abilities. Using this technique, Olson (1968) and Boyd and Randle (1970) report that the five subtests of the Frostig DTVP tap only one factor, thereby suggesting that all five tests measure only one trait. Corah and Powell (1963), Cawley, Burrow, and Goodstein (1968), and Becker and Sabatino (1971) have found that the subtests of the Frostig DTVP essentially measure only two traits. In addition, Becker and Sabatino (1971) provided a maximum opportunity for the five subtests to demonstrate that they measured independent traits and found that the Frostig DTVP measured three specific traits with children of kindergarten age: visual-motor skills, figure-ground perception, and visual discrimination skills.

It is not important that the five presumed independent measures of visual perceptual behavior measure one, two, or three traits as independent traits. What is important is that they do not measure the five perceptual traits named by the test authors as being described in the subtests of the Frostig

DTVP. This fact perhaps best illustrates why many professionals lack respect for such tests. Indeed, the DTVP is not an exception to the rule, for many test developers name traits according to what their instrument is *supposed* to measure.

AUDITORY PERCEPTION

Auditory perception, which should appear to be the corollary of visual perception, remains a relatively unexplored area. The reason is that the auditory process seems more complex, since sound is a more multidimensional stimulus than light. Consequently, physiologically it is more difficult to ascertain when and where the sensory function of hearing begins and ends as well as where auditory perception stops and language learning begins. What, then, constitutes the auditory perceptual process?

Lowry (1970) used the term "auditory-perceptual function" to describe the ability to differentiate each sound of the language from every other. As children develops skill in discriminating sounds, they also must be able to recognize them in all possible phonetic contexts, and later to gain the same meaning from spoken and written work. Children who have difficulty perceiving differences in speech sounds also have problems repeating sequences involving those sounds.

Some children have difficulty in sound recognition, or the selection of relevant from irrelevant auditory stimuli. They suffer from an auditory figure-ground disability. It is assumed that they experience difficulty listening in the classroom. Their behavior often is marked by distraction, short attention span, and lack of response to the auditory stimuli.

Some of the commonly used measures of auditory perception are sound-recognition tests, such as the *Wepman Auditory Discrimination Test* (Wepman, 1968a), the *PERC Auditory Discrimination Test* (Drake, 1965), and the *Boston University Speech-Sound Discrimination Picture Test*. These tests pose speech-sound discrimination tasks that require the child to respond to a pair of words by indicating whether they sound the same or different. Several researchers have questioned the format of having only two response alternatives (Coltheart & Curthoys, 1968), in that a subject has a 50 percent chance of getting the correct response by sheer random guessing. Furthermore, inconsistency in examiners' speech patterns, children's phonetic competence and vocabulary familiarity, the test conditions (extraneous environmental noise), and cultural biases can influence the results.

Snyder and Pope (1970) could not confirm the norms published by Wepman. They found, for example, that 67 percent of their subjects exceeded the cutoff score for auditory discrimination problems as given in the test manual. They believed, however, that with refinements at the age levels with which they were working (6-year-old subjects, N = 204), the Wepman test could be a useful device for the assessment of auditory discrimination, "but the test user should consider discrepancies with norms in arriving at a realistic understanding of his test data" (p. 10).

Possibly criterion cutoff scores, or any results that differentiate one group from another or categorize a child as being deviant, are not necessary. Flowers (1968) suggests focusing on individual differences and believes that certain educational strategies might be more effective than others when the particular subskills, strengths, or weaknesses of a child are known. A number of investigators are trying to specify the type of speech-sound discrimination difficulty a child may have, rather than hypothesizing an organic impairment or merely noting that there is a failure to perform at a level equal to that of the peer group.

Other auditory perceptual tests include the *Goldman-Fristoe-Woodcock Test of Auditory Discrimination* (1970), a pictorial method designed to provide measures of speech-sound discrimination, and the *Lindamood Auditory Conceptualization* (LAC) test (1971), which measures discrimination of speech sounds and the ability to perceive the number and order of sounds within a spoken pattern.

Auditory memory may be measured by the oral direction and oral commissions of the *Detroit Test of Learning Aptitudes* and the rhythming section of the *Screening Test of Auditory Perception* (STAP). Several tests measure digit span—*ITPA Auditory* sequential memory, the *WISC-R,* and the *Stanford-Binet*. Buktenica's (1971) test of nonverbal auditory discrimination (TENVAD) also measures memory of rhythmic patterns. Exhibit 6-1 reports the highest test-retest reliabilities for several commonly administered tests of visual and auditory perception.

AUDITORY PERCEPTUAL INTERVENTIONS

To increase attention and arousal, several gross sound discrimination and listening games can be played. Examples are: *Mother may I, Simon says, Identify that sound,* and *Counting sounds games* to distinguish each time a particular sound occurs.

The basic activity formats of auditory perceptual training include:

1. discrimination of likenesses and differences between speech sounds
2. matching sounds (phonemes and graphemes) to written letters
3. retaining memory for phonemes and sequenced sounds
4. sequencing sounds correctly

Exhibit 6-1 Common Tests of Visual and Auditory Perception

Age Range	Selected Auditory Test	Author	Highest Test-Retest Reliability Reported
5–8	Auditory Discrimination Test	Wepman (1973)	.91
4 & over	Goldman-Fristoe-Woodcock Test of Auditory Discrimination	Goldman Fristoe Woodcock (1970)	quiet .87 noise .81
5–14	Tests of Auditory Perception	Visco (1953)	NA
7–12	Screening Test for Auditory Perception	Kimmel Wahl (1969)	.80
4–6	Kindergarten Auditory Screening Test	Katz (1971)	NA
5–10	Bender Visual-Motor Gestalt Test	Bender (1938)	.55–.69
4–8	Motor Free Visual Perceptual Tests	Colarusso Hammill	.81
4–10	Southern California Figure-Ground Visual Perceptual Test	Ayers	.37–.53
3–8	Developmental Test of Visual Perception (3rd Edition)	Frostig Maslow	.84
2–15	Developmental Test of Visual Motor Integration	Beery Buktenica	.83–.87
1–6	Dennis Visual Perception Scale	Dennis & Dennis	NA
8 & over	Visual Retention Test	Benton	.76

The following strategies are suggested by Wiig and Semel (1976) as methods designed to improve students' awareness of the presence of specific sounds in the environment and to establish associations between sound and sound sources:

- To obtain auditory arousal and recognition of gross environmental noise, the teacher should record or audiotape familiar environmental sounds such as those made by familiar objects or generated in particular environments. Students then are asked to name or identify a picture of the sound source.

- To improve sustained auditory attention and discrimination abilities, the teacher should record or audiotape sounds with controlled differences in pitch, intensity, duration, and quality, identifying one as a target sound. This sound should be presented to the students at irregular intervals, with stimuli of different qualities such as pitch used as an alternative. Students also may be asked to identify the presence of the target sound by raising their hand. They should be presented with a series of tape-recorded taps, asked to count the taps, and indicate the number heard in the series. The rate of presentation may be varied according to the needs of the individual students (Kirshner, 1972).

- To improve student abilities to localize sounds within the environment, one student is asked to sit with covered eyes in the middle of the classroom. Other children may call out the child's name from different directions and different distances. The child in the middle then points toward the caller.

- To recognize a relevant stimulus against a background of competing sounds, the student is asked to perform according to a series of oral directions given against a variety of auditory backgrounds (Semel, 1970).

- To improve auditory sequencing capabilities, the student is presented with a sequence of verbal or nonverbal stimuli such as musical tones, phonemes, syllables, and word sequences. The student is asked to indicate whether the ensuing sound sequence is the same or different, correct or incorrect. For example, students may be asked to rearrange syllables presented in incorrect form so as to form a word, i.e., nic pic becomes picnic.

A number of commercially developed auditory perceptual programs are available. They are listed in Exhibit 6-2.

Exhibit 6-2 Commercial Auditory Perceptual Programs

Source	Program	Price
Product Catalog for the Exceptional Child Outreach & Development Division The Exceptional Child Center Utah State University UMC-68 Logan, Utah 84322	Sound Symbol: sound letter discrimination, elementary grades Blending Sounds: sounding out words in reading, elementary grades	$4.25 5.50
American Guidance Service (AGS) Publishers' Building Circle Pines, Minn. 55014	Sound Makers: discriminating sounds and rhythmic patterns Cassettes and Records: sound identification and sound associations	1.90 tone block stick 2.50 brass bell 29.50 4 cassettes 16.00 7 records
Special Education Materials Inc. 484 South Broadway Yonkers, N.Y. 10705	Auditory Discrimination: skill development for reading readiness	220.00 cassettes 2.50 student response booklets (pack of 30)
Practical Tools Vort Corporation P.O. Box 115524 355 Sherman Drive Palo Alto, Calif. 94306	BCP Methods—Communication Skills: auditory perception, prearticulation, language comprehension, finger spelling	24.95

VISUAL PERCEPTUAL INTERVENTIONS

Visual perceptual discrimination training may begin by asking the child to identify meaningful stimuli from irrelevant background information until the student can recognize them consistently. It also may involve matching geometric forms, then letters, then words, to stimuli that are widely different, and gradually increasing the level of difficulty until the differences are hard to detect.

Visual perceptual memory training may be provided by requiring the student to identify and retain a distinctive feature of one letter, in contrast to other graphemes. The teacher then introduces an interfering task and subsequently asks the child to recognize the initial letter stimulus.

Visual perceptual sequencing is a similar activity except several stimuli are used in the order of presentation.

Visual Perceptual Stimuli and Hierarchical Arrangement

Proper ordering or sequencing of perceptual discrimination and memory training materials is critical. The teacher should begin with gross form recognition, finer form differentiation, letter form and letter discrimination, then finally discrimination of configured forms (letters in words, or word shapes). One of the major pitfalls in perceptual training has been the inability of educators to begin and end a sequence in small, tightly ordered steps, beginning with recognition of divergent forms and ending in looking at words within the forms.

Conceptualizing Visual Symbols

One of the final tasks is to ensure that the perceptual symbol has received a consistent conceptual name. In other words, does every distinctive feature have a name? With some language disabled or impaired children, that will be difficult, but for children who are not so disabled and are adept in language but are perceptually disturbed, the conceptualization of symbols is important. Selected visual perceptual materials are listed in Exhibit 6-3.

AUDITORY-VISUAL PERCEPTUAL INTEGRATION

Reading requires the conversion of graphic symbols into meaningful phonological units. The reading process is more than merely cracking the graphic form code. Each visual symbol must be converted into a meaningful language concept; therefore, it must have an auditory value. In short, a conversion of information from each perceptual channel to the other percep-

Exhibit 6-3 Commercial Visual Perceptual Programs

Source	Program	Price
Special Education Materials Inc. 484 South Broadway Yonkers, N.Y. 10705	"Fit-A-Blob:" for ages 3–7 years; requires keen eye for the relationships of formless objects	$4.75 20 blocks of 10 forms and 2 pads
	"We Learn From Colors and Their Names:" offers brief stories and sing-along tunes about the colors	22.00 two tapes, Spirit Masters, 12 color pictures
	Multisensory Materials for Developing Visual Perception: provides training in locating visual cues, visual recognition and discrimination	220.00 includes 20 tapes, 30 student response booklets, and a teacher's manual
Childcraft Education Corporation 20 Kilmer Road Edison, N.J. 08817	Parquetry: stimulates creativity, visual perception, motor skills, for ages 4–8 years	8.50 set of colored blocks
	200 puzzles: helps form recognition, ages 2–5 years	6.95
Developing Learning Materials 7440 Natchez Avenue Niles, Ill. 60648	Symmetrical matchup: aids visual discrimination	1.75 24 cards
	Design Dominoes: improves visual matching abilities and categorization skills	2.25 7 different black-and-white designs
Teaching Resources Corporation 50 Pond Park Road Hingham, Mass. 02043	Visual Perception Games	29.95
	Lee Body Puzzle: identifies body parts	24.50 16-piece wooden puzzles

tual channel seems to be necessary for reading. How else, in fact, could a person read graphics, or listen to others read, and write the graphic symbol being received aurally? Reading is a dual process that, except for the handicapped learner who may be missing one of the sensory channels or have perceptual deficits, is an integrated function.

Of all the perceptual functions, perceptual integration is the least understood. The result is that applied tests literally do not exist. A number of studies, however, are illustrative of research in the area; one of these is discussed briefly here.

Birch and Belmont (1964) administered a series of cards with three patterns of dots. The examiner first tapped out a pattern. The child was to listen to the tapped pattern, then look at three sets of dot patterns. One set represented the tapped pattern, the others did not. The examiner then required the child to point to the appropriate pattern, that is, the pattern representing the previously tapped sound. Results indicated that children who had the greatest difficulty on this task were the most difficult to teach under remedial conditions of reading instruction. They were found to be unable to deal effectively with tasks requiring judgment of auditory-visual equivalence. Thus, the ability to match visual and auditory patterned information differentiated the good reader from the poor.

In summary, perceptual integration would appear to be the internal stimulation of the opposite modality, i.e., visual perceptual information is received and a signal system translates the meaning to the auditory perceptual modality. Research on the assumed trait is very limited and awaits much dedicated work. It does seem likely that this function holds promise as a predictor of what modality may be used as a unisensory or multisensory receiving mechanism.

IMPROVING AUDITORY-VISUAL INTEGRATION

To assist students to establish a relationship between an auditory stimulus and a visual display the teacher should ask them to match tonal pairs to visual displays representing:

1. duration
2. intensity
3. pitch
4. changes in rate
5. temporal patterns
6. similarities and differences in word pairs

Auditory-visual integration interventions require combining nonsymbolic auditory stimuli with representative nonsymbolic visual information. These procedures may include:

1. Discriminating and matching tonal pairs with visual displays representing their durations:
   Auditory stimulus: long tone — short tone
   Visual display: — —/— —
2. Discriminating and matching tonal pairs with visual displays representing their intensities:
   Auditory stimulus: loud tone — soft tone
   Visual display: ■ □/□ ■
3. Discriminating and matching tonal pairs with visual displays representing their frequencies (pitch):
   Auditory stimulus: upward modulated tone — downward modulated tone
   Visual displays: ╱╲/╲╱
4. Discriminating and matching tonal pairs with visual displays representing changes in rate:
   Auditory displays: fast tone — slow tone
   Visual displays: ⋀⋀⋀⋀∿/∿⋀⋀⋀⋀

The next step in the progression toward the integration of auditory-verbal and visual-symbolic stimuli requires matching between auditory-verbal stimuli and nonsymbolic visual displays. Among possible activities are:

1. Discriminating and matching auditory-verbal sequences with visual displays representing the temporal patterns:
   Instruction: When you hear the word gum,
                           mark the place where you heard it.
                           First, in the middle, or at the end.
   Auditory stimulus: shoe-table-gum.
   Visual display: ____ ____ <u>X</u>
2. Discrimination and identification of the identities or differences (same-different) of the words in the minimal word pair with representative visual displays:
   Auditory stimulus: cat bat
   Visual displays: 0 0/X 0
3. Discrimination and matching of a series of digits, letters, or words of which the majority are identical while one differs, with representative visual displays:
   Auditory stimulus: three-three-three-seven
   Visual display: 0 0 0 X/0 0 0 0

4. Discrimination and matching of an auditory-verbal sequence with visual displays representing similarities and differences in the composition of speech sounds (phonemes):
   Auditory stimulus: gate-rate-date-house
   Visual displays: 0 0 0 0/0 0 0 X
5. Discrimination and matching of minimal word pairs with pictorial displays:
   a. Auditory stimuli: mountain-fountain
      Mark: fountain
      Pictorial displays: two choices
   b. Auditory stimuli: face-race-lace
      Mark: face
      Pictorial displays: three choices
   c. Auditory stimuli: man-pan-fan-can
      Mark: fan
      Pictorial displays: four choices

The procedures designed to establish integration between auditory-verbal and visual-symbolic stimuli may initially introduce additional nonsymbolic visual cues. These facilitating cues may be faded gradually, as in the following steps:

1. Discrimination and matching of minimal word pairs that differ in visual configuration with combined pictorial-written stimuli:
   Auditory stimulus: mountain-fountain
   Visual displays: pictures and configuration outlines
                        for both items.
2. Discrimination and matching of minimal word pairs that differ in visual configuration with visual-symbolic stimuli emphasized for configurational differences:
   Auditory stimuli: coat-boat-goat
   Mark: boat
   Visual displays: configuration outlines for all items
3. Discrimination and matching of minimally paired words with visual-symbolic stimuli:
   Auditory stimuli: tail-mail-pail
   Mark: mail
   Visual displays: printed words

Summary

This section has reviewed the theories related to the development of perception and perceptual integration. This was followed by discussion of the assessment of both auditory and visual perception, providing lists of tests. Finally, specific auditory, visual, and auditory visual perceptual integration objectives and enabled steps (procedures) were offered as examples.

SECTION 3: LANGUAGE INTERVENTION

INTRODUCTION

For the average individual, language is "what comes out of the mouth and works its way into the brain via the ears" (Siegal & Broen, 1976). Language among humans generally is viewed as a common communication tool that usually is taken for granted. Perhaps only those who have had difficulty in acquiring and expressing themselves through language appreciate its importance. Helen Keller's eloquent description of her first realization of language captures the robustness of conceptual learning:

> As the cool water gushed over one hand she spelled into the other the word *water,* first slowly, then rapidly. I stood still, my whole attention fixed upon the motion of her fingers.
> Suddenly I felt a misty consciousness as of something forgotten— a thrill of returning thought; and somehow the mystery of language was revealed to me. I knew then that "w-a-t-e-r " meant the wonderful, cool something that was flowing over my hand. That living word awakened my soul, gave it light, hope, joy, set it free. . . . I left the wellhouse eager to learn. Everything had a name, and each name gave birth to a new thought. (Keller, 1961, p. 34)

The language problems of the hearing impaired are no more severe, only more obvious, than the subtle language and communication deficits of learning disabled students that frequently go undetected. The language problems of the learning disabled pose a difficult diagnostic problem in that they are compensated for and thus hidden. In addition, these problems tend to be multifaceted, defying unitary description. Among the language deficits learning disabled students have been reported to exhibit are:

1. Auditory memory deficits (deHirsch, Jansky, & Langford, 1966; Masland & Case, 1965; Spencer, 1959)
2. Temporal sequencing deficits (Aten & Davis, 1968; Orton, 1937)
3. Auditory figure-ground problems (Flowers & Costello, 1970; Lasky & Tobin, 1973)
4. Reauditorization deficits (Johnson & Myklebust, 1967)

5. Auditory-visual integration deficits (Birch & Belmont, 1964, 1965; Birch & Lefford, 1963; Stamback, 1951)
6. Limitations in symbolization, abstraction, and conceptualization (Johnson, 1968; Johnson & Myklebust, 1967; Myklebust, 1964; Strauss & Kephart, 1955)
7. Deficits in linguistic processing and in the conceptual synthesis underlying adult syntax (Farnham-Diggory, 1967; Menyuk & Looney, 1972; Semel & Wiig, 1975; Wiig & Roach, 1975)
8. Deficits in cognitive logical processing (Wiig & Semel, 1976, p. 23)

Faced with such a mosaic of language-related problems, the classroom teacher must be able to recognize student deficits in language expression and reception. One of the purposes of this section therefore is to present a brief review of the theories of language acquisition and identify language disorders related to specific learning disabilities. The section also provides a framework for language assessment and remediation that can be utilized in the classroom.

THEORIES OF LANGUAGE ACQUISITION

There are two major views of how children acquire language. The first is the behavorial concept that language is learned through imitation. When vocalizations resemble adult speech, parents or other significant persons in the child's life reinforce that inclination to repeat those sounds. As the child develops, reinforcement becomes contingent upon appropriate responding, i.e., cute mispronunciations become less acceptable with age. Thus, language is learned through imitation, then reinforced, shaped, and refined by environmental manipulation.

An alternative view is the psycholinguistic or cognitivist explanation of language development. Where the behavorial learning theorists (Guess, Sailor, & Baer, 1974; Sloane & MacAulay, 1968) suggest that the infant begins with no knowledge of language, the psycholinguistic view is that the child is biologically predisposed to learn and use language (Lenneberg, 1967). Further, Chomsky (1957) argues that the developing human being is capable of observing, extracting, and understanding the rules of language rather than just imitating a series of vocalizations. Central to the cognitivist/psycholinguistic approach is the view that language development follows certain general stages that relate closely to those in cognitive, motor, and speech sound development. It is not the purpose of this section to contribute to the debate between behaviorist and cognitivist factions. However, readers should be aware that certain premises pervade this discussion of language development, assessment, and remediation. It is the authors' view that:

1. Language does not develop in a vacuum.
2. Stages of language development have been shown to be nearly invariant across cultures.
3. Children may progress through these stages at varying rates.
4. Some children do not become users of language in the normal course of development.
5. Teaching language in the developmental sequence native to its occurrence and natural usage may increase the probability of successful functional "rule" learning.
6. Language development is related to the child's general cognitive processing ability

These views should be kept in mind in reviewing the following section on normal language development.

THE PATHOLOGIES OF LANGUAGE

Although the rates at which children advance through language development vary and usually should be no cause for alarm, in some cases problems in progressing may signal a language disability. Descriptions of dysfunctions characteristic of children manifesting language disorders related to learning disability follow.

Expressive aphasia: Symptoms are predominately motor or productive, consisting of an inability to express ideas through spoken or written language symbols.

Receptive aphasia: Symptoms are predominately sensory or receptive, consisting of a disturbance in the ability to comprehend language through spoken and written symbols (Weisenburg & McBride, 1935).

Expressive-receptive aphasia: An approximately equal disturbance exists in both areas (Weisenburg & McBride, 1935).

Global aphasia: All language forms are seriously affected to the degree that it is impossible to use one of the preceding categories.

Agnosia: Loss of the ability to recognize objects or symbols through a particular sensory channel such as vision or hearing is the disability; the loss tends to be specific for words, syllables, letters, or other perceptual symbolic units.

Apraxia: Loss of the ability to execute simple voluntary acts is evident; the loss tends to be specific for elementary units of actions in the expression of language.

In an article titled "Aphasia," Wepman (1968a) offered the following classifications and descriptions of aphasia:

Syntactic: Loss or misuse of grammatical form is the disabling trait. In severe cases, speech will be telegraphic in nature, i.e., "Daughter—home—Monday," for "My daughter will be home Monday." In less severe cases, the final *s* morpheme, *ing* or *ed* endings, or other inflected grammatical forms may be dropped or added inappropriately, i.e., "He put on his pair of shoe." "He added a boating to his collection."

Semantic: Inability or difficulty in substantive word selection is common in such cases. In severe cases, nouns or other substantive words may be omitted or a pronoun substituted. In less severe cases, substantive words inappropriate to the meaning may be supplied. In the least severe cases, words in the same meaning category may be substituted. For example, "See the thing in my hand?" (where the noun *thing* is substituted for the specific word *pencil*); "See the pen in my hand?" (where the word *pen* substitutes for *pencil*) (Wepman, 1968b, p. 22).

Pragmatic: Many words of both syntactic and semantic classes are present but are used inappropriately. Neologisms are substituted for many semantic words. Meaning is lost because the verbal expression is inappropriate, such as, "That man is clipping the kreples."

Jargon: Intelligibility is lost because the verbal utterance is unintelligible. All phonemes seem to be present but rarely are produced in understandable morphemic clusters, i.e., "te da de mo ah too" (spoken with adequate speech inflection as though relating intelligible words to the listener).

Global: Literally no verbal effort is made beyound an automatic expression or two (Wepman, 1951, pp. 41–42).

LANGUAGE ASSESSMENT

To help teachers recognize some of the manifestations of the foregoing language disorders, a checklist is provided in Exhibit 6-4.

Students suspected of having possible language related problems should be assessed further by more formal means. The next section reviews instruments currently available. However, readers should keep in mind the following considerations regarding language assessment:

1. Measurement using formal tests never can encompass all of the complexity, shades, and varied manifestations of language behavior.
2. Assessment of a student's language competence must involve both comprehension and expression.
3. Many standardized language tests assess only the student's receptive or expressive capability, although a number of them have subscales or tests in both modes.

Exhibit 6-4 Checklist for Language Assessment

Yes	No	Language Learning Characteristics

Speech Acquisition

____	____	Student's attempts at verbalization consist primarily of jargon.
____	____	Student repeats words but is unable to use them of own volition.
____	____	Some words are spoken once but not used again or are used inappropriately.

Vocalization

____	____	Student has unusual inflections, intonations, and pitch patterns.
____	____	Student uses improvised sounds in a characteristic manner but not with purpose and intent related to the environment.
____	____	Student does not use gestures while speaking.
____	____	Student may parrot speech of others.

Response to Sound

____	____	Student reactions to stimuli vary a great deal.
____	____	Student responds inconsistently to variations in pitch and frequency of sound.
____	____	Student is limited in ability to select visual and auditory stimuli appropriate to needs.

Affective Behavior

____	____	Student's laughing and smiling lack intensity of feeling.
____	____	Student does not laugh or smile readily.
____	____	Laughter reflects abnormal tonal quality.
____	____	Student does not attend to facial expressions.

4. Since no test is available to measure both areas adequately, data on a student may be obtained from different tests, thereby preventing a simple normative interpretation of results.
5. A student's linguistic ability should not be overestimated on the basis of correct responses to instructions; memory of past experiences and adult (teacher) body language clues can serve to aid in the student's interpretation. (Lamberts, 1979)

In addition, Van Etten and Watson (1977) caution:

1. Few standardized language assessment instruments are available that are appropriate beyond the third grade.
2. Some tests require extensive training to administer and interpret.
3. Data obtained from tests may not be usable by classroom teachers.
4. Some tests are in an experimental edition; the standardized sample may be limited in size, restricted in population, and defined too briefly.

In response to those criticisms, the discussion focus is next on language tests that can be administered and used directly by the classroom teacher.

The Boehm Test of Basic Concepts (BTBC)

This test is appropriate for students in kindergarten through the second grade. Fifty items representing word concepts in pictorial form are presented in groups of three. The students are asked to mark the picture that correctly portrays the concept specified.

The BTBC may be used as either a standardized or criterion referenced test. A class record sheet is provided to allow the teacher to keep track of the child's status and to identify difficulties with particular concepts. Normative data by grade level and socioeconomic status are provided in terms of percent of sample subjects passing each item of the test. In addition, the BTBC is available in Spanish.

The Berry-Talbott Exploratory Test of Grammar

This test is designed to assess the child's knowledge of English inflectional morphology in the context of nonsense syllables. The age level is appropriate for 5 to 8 years. Given a sentence frame by the examiner, the student is required to supply the proper word and its inflection. The 30 response items represent the following morphophonic forms: plurals and possessives of the noun, the third person singular of verbs, the progressive and past tenses, and the comparative and superlative of the adjective. This test is untimed but takes approximately 15 minutes.

Verbal Comprehension Scale (VCS)

This test is similar to the BTBC in that it also measures student concept acquisition. The VCS is for children from 2 to 6 and uses three-dimensional models rather than pictures in four testing situations:

1. A cardboard model of a garage with cars in which 53 concepts are evaluated, e.g., "Take the car *out* of the garage."
2. A tea party setting with male and female dolls and tea set that assesses the student's grasp of pronouns, e.g., "Give *him* a fork,"
3. Boxes and buttons of various sizes and shapes in which the student is asked to perform according to directions, e.g., "Show me the *empty* box," and
4. Various types of dowels, blocks of wood, and a sponge, with the student given such instructions as, "Hand me the *light* one."

The VCS measures 15 concepts or words identified by Boehm but not used in the test, 21 words not included in the BTBC, and another 17 pronouns. For the young school-aged pupil, the BTBC and VCS should provide comprehensive information of the child's concept acquisition.

Assessment of Children's Language Comprehension (ACLC)

This test for ages 3 to 6 measures the student's structural use of language. It focuses on the pupil's core receptive vocabulary development, comprehension of syntactical units, and the consistency of the patterns of syntactical omissions. The elements assessed include agents (girl, boy, dog), actions (eating, sleeping), relations (on, over, above), objects (house), and attributes (little, sad). The test is presented in four parts, beginning with the student's understanding of single elements and increasing to four elements. Standardized data are presented in percentage form.

Elicited Language Inventory

This standardized test was developed by Carrow in 1974. The inventory contains 51 sentences of varying lengths that are composed of several sentence types, such as questions and declarative sentences. The following grammatical categories also are represented: articles, adjectives, adverbs, singular and plural nouns, pronouns, verbs, prepositions, demonstratives, conjunctions, and contractions. The administration and scoring of the inventory take about 45 minutes. The administrative format is innovative. The instructions are tape recorded and the child's response is taped and evaluated. Percentile ranks and age equivalent scores can be derived.

Language assessment of older populations is discussed briefly in Chapter 9 on secondary and postsecondary learning disabled students. The reader is referred to Exhibit 9-1 for an overview of perceptual cognitive tests designed for use with learning disabled youth.

An addition to these measures is the Utah Test of Language Development, which was designed to measure the expressive and receptive verbal language skills of both normal and handicapped children ages 1 to 14. The test consists of 51 items arranged in increasing order of difficulty. Items include recognizing body parts when named, responding to simple commands ("Give me the ball"), naming common objects and colors, repeating digits, copying geometric forms, and decoding written words. The administration time is 30 to 45 minutes. The student's score is converted to language age equivalents in one-year intervals. No standardized scores or percentile ranks are provided.

This review is in no way exhaustive but is intended to suggest the range of possibilities of tests that attempt to sample language behaviors. For a fuller characterization, the tests themselves should be consulted. In the following section, a framework for the development of language intervention strategies is considered.

DEVELOPMENTAL APPROACHES TO LANGUAGE INTERVENTION

Several developmentally based language training strategies have appeared in recent years. These programs have attempted to synthesize behavorial and psycholinguistic models in that data from the latter provide the basis for "what" will be taught while behavioral principles guide "how" instructional procedures will be used.

All of these programs view the cognitive and perceptual development of the student as central to the overall program; however, the degree to which cognitive development is considered varies among programs. Some are syntactically based, in that they train specific vocalizations in a certain order, while others consider the semantic intent of these vocalizations as well as the structural form (syntax).

Bricker and Bricker's (1974) work with the Infant Toddler and Preschool Research and Intervention Project, which was designed to discover instructional strategies that facilitate cognitive development, revealed that young children must master certain prelinguistic behaviors before language teaching procedures can be implemented successfully. Their approach to language intervention therefore is a test-teach system. The child first is located within a sensorimotor lattice structure based upon a Piagetian theory of development. Based upon the child's acquisition of such prelinguistic skills as object permanence, strategies are selected to assist the pupil to move through a particular developmental sequence. When the student has acquired at least some of the prerequisite skills, specific language training procedures are used.

Miller and Yoder (1974) also stress the importance of the cognitive aspects of the child's development in relation to language acquisition. However, rather than attempting to develop cognitive training strategies, they prefer providing the child with an array of experiences designed to assist the student to discover salient relationships within the environment.

Stremel and Waryas (1974) have developed a specific language training program that in many ways is similar to the Miller and Yoder approach. It is divided into three phases of language training—early, carly-intermediate, and late-intermediate. Intervention strategies are ordered according to data obtained by Bloom (1970) and Brown (1973) on the sequence of language acquisition in the normal child.

The Environmental Language Intervention Strategy developed by MacDonald and Blott (1974) also is based on the normal patterns of language acquisition. Brown (1973) reports that normal children's early vocalizations are fairly uniform across languages. The content of such utterances generally is based upon common childhood experiences and characterized by an agent-action-object form. This training program therefore attempts to consider the environmental context in which the child's utterances occur. The training sequence moves from the simple one-word stage for the child with severe language delay to the use of multiword phrases.

A major goal of this approach is the generalization of learned language structures from the training setting to the normal environment. Training sequences take the form of imitation, conversation, then play. In this way, when the child has mastered a task in the training environment, the conversational and play environments can be modified to elicit and thus generalize the learned language structures. Similarly, positive reinforcement moves from verbal praise and token awards in the training setting to less intrusive measures during the conversational and play stages.

In summary, developmental language teaching programs have several commonalities:

1. Teaching strategies are based on the manner in which normal children acquire language.
2. The child's level of cognitive development is viewed as a prerequisite to the effective use of expressive language.

3. Programs use psycholinguistic data as well as principles of behavioral technology.
4. An attempt is made to generalize training gains to new situations and to encourage spontaneous generation of new structures based on those trained.

Other language training programs have been developed in recent years. The major contributors to this area are discussed next.

Orton (1937) describes one of the early approaches to severe writing, reading, and speech disabilities. The cause, he theorizes, was ambivalence of the cerebral hemisphere, which resulted in a delay of normal cerebral dominance. This study prompted Gillingham and Stillman (1936) to reflect upon the use of language training devices to influence children who have reading difficulty. Later, Cole and Walker (1964) published a monograph on reading and speech problems as expressions of specific language disability. This monograph is quite useful as a reference for learning disability teachers. Many speech therapists and language clinicians have developed training procedures for learning disabled children that are based on work with children exhibiting aphasoid language difficulties (Agranowitz & McKeown, 1964).

Gillingham and Stillman (1936) gear their program to children from third to sixth grade who are of normal or superior intelligence and have normal sensory acuity (visual and auditory) but have a tendency to reverse letters or words or to mirror-write, have difficulty in pronunciation, and have been unable to acquire reading and spelling skills by usual school methods. In contrast to functional sight word procedures, in which words initially are recognized by children as ideograms and then dissected by the teacher into letter sounds through phonetic analysis, Gillingham and Stillman's Alphabetic Approach teaches the sounds of the letters first, then builds those letter sounds into words. Their remedial technique is aimed at establishing close association between the visual, auditory, and kinesthetic modalities in the brain.

Myklebust (1968), originally known for his work in the diagnosis and remediation of communication disorders in children, developed a remedial approach to psychoneurological learning disabilities. His aim is to acquire an accurate, differential diagnosis for children with learning disorders and to plan an educational program based on the information gleaned from the diagnostic investigation. Therefore, an accurate appraisal of the brain's capacity to receive, categorize, and integrate information, as well as the intactness of the individual modality systems, is important.

Myklebust and Johnson (1967) outline the fundamental principles that guide the remediation of learning disorders. Some important aspects of the program are individual teaching according to readiness and involvement and to the tolerance level without overloading the sensory systems; using multisensory stimulation; providing training in perception when needed; controlling variables such as attention, rate, proximity, and size as needed; and developing both verbal and nonverbal areas of experience. The total remedial program is designed to facilitate remediation of psychoneural disabilities through structured clinical teaching on deficits in language, reading, and arithmetic.

Myklebust and Johnson establish the following as important educational procedures to be incorporated in language training:

1. Communication input is more important initially than a child's expression.
2. Amplified meaning should be provided for auditory units by structuring, isolating, and timing the presentation of any message until it is comprehended.
3. Simultaneous and repetitious use should be made of selected vocabulary, emphasizing the meaningful words that reflect experiences, teaching the concept, and stressing the auditory configuration or distinguishing characteristics of the word.

Barry (1961) sets her first objective as remediating behavior rather than language. She outlines specific techniques for this difficulty as well as problems in body image and perception—which also are preliminary to language remediation. Like Myklebust, she believes that only deficient areas should be remediated, rather than all areas equally. Barry suggests that six areas of the child's behavior should be explored by the teacher: (1) health history, (2) hearing, (3) language, (4) psychomotor function, (5) emotional and social adjustment, and (6) motoric abilities. Language evaluation consists of an assessment of inner, receptive, and expressive language by having the child play with familiar toy objects such as small figures and furniture. Language training consists of "make-believe" activities, to help the child relate better to the environment; manipulation and play with objects representing the pupil's daily experience; establishment of environmental relationships; and use of the youngster's spontaneous vocalizations as a starting point for further language development.

McGinnis (1963) bases his program on the "association method" that was employed originally with hearing impaired students. It has been adapted by DuBard (1974) to teach aphasics and other language impaired students. The program is designed to: (1) increase attention span, (2) increase word retention, (3) improve the ability to recall words, (4) modify patterns of communication, and (5) provide an opportunity for the successful learning of language and speech. It is a systematic multidimensional approach that includes concept development and the improvement of the student's language structure, sequential language, and learning skills. This program requires the child to acquire precise articulatory ability at the beginning in order to improve recall. As the child masters specific skills with phonemes, more complex sentence units are presented. This is not a packaged program. Teachers must be knowledgeable in phonetics and language development.

Lea (1965) developed a program called the Color Pattern Scheme. In it, words are color coded according to the function they serve in a sentence. Different sentence patterns also are color coded to illustrate syntactic patterns. In the first stage of Lea's program, a 200-word vocabulary is taught. The words also are constructed into sentences emphasizing phrase and sentence patterns. The second stage builds more vocabulary and increases the complexity of sentence construction and of verb tense usage. Unlike programs that teach phonemes or syllabic production first, Lea maintains that it is more practical and effective to introduce whole words—nouns, then verbs, prepositions, adjectives, pronouns, etc. As in McGinnis's program, the written and oral forms of a word are taught simultaneously and a similar format is used for introducing questions and teaching appropriate responses.

Wiseman (1965) utilizes language for both diagnosis and remediation of children with certain types of learning disabilities. His remedial approach is based on the assumption that direct treatment of linguistic deficits can reduce certain forms of learning disabilities. He identifies auditory and visual decoding, association, memory, automatic auditory or visual closure, and vocal and motor encoding as key language abilities in children. Using the *Illinois Test of Psycholinguistic Abilities* (ITPA) as a basis for diagnosis, Wiseman assigns remedial exercises to correct the profiled deficits. The remedial approach is relatively simple, generating exercises to fit each child's individual needs.

Fygetakis and Ingram (1973) believe that language learning is a rule system rather than simply a collection of stimuli and responses. Their study is an application of operant techniques to recent linguistic findings. This is accomplished by systematically introducing a sentence construction one level above the child's present level of functioning. They describe their method as follows:

> In the programmed conditioning procedures, the child makes progressively closer approximations to the target construction by imitating increasingly longer units of the model sentence. When the child has reached the level of imitating the entire construction, the model sentences are systematically faded out as the program progresses. By the end of the program, the child is formulating his

own sentences which exemplify the underlying grammatical relationship (p. 7).

Kaliski Schools (1977) base this program on the work conducted at the institutions founded in 1947 to serve children with specific learning disabilities. This approach is pragmatic in that it first determines how the child learns best. The Kaliski curriculum is composed of nonverbal activities designed to train auditory perceptual characteristics through such activity formats as identification of sounds, matching to sounds, reproduction of sounds, similarities and differences, discrimination of sounds, sequences of sounds, figure-ground differentiation of sound and differentiation of pitch, intensity, and speed of sound. This program also employs Montessori-like sensorial activities, e.g., the child shakes boxes filled with different objects and identifies the box containing the object making the sound that matches an initial sound. Verbal activities include problems in sound-letter discrimination, rhyming, blending, and sounding out short vowels.

LANGUAGE PROGRAMS AVAILABLE IN KIT FORM

Several published language programs target the learning disabled population. Although no prepared program can be expected to provide all of the intervention assistance necessary, the following review details programs that can be helpful in situations in which facilities and personnel are not readily available to develop an individualized program for every student.

Auditory Perceptual Training Program (APT)

Publisher: Alameda County School Department
224 West Winton Avenue
Hayward, Calif. 94544

This program is designed for students in grades 1–3 with auditory perceptual problems and those in grades 2–6 manifesting learning or language problems. The program consists of four units that cover such skills as selective attention, speech-sound discrimination, analysis and temporal sequencing, auditory closure and synthesis, voice identification and attention to intonation patterns, recognition of the number of sounds and syllables in words and phrases, subject-verb agreement, active and passive voice, and complex syntactic structure. The kit includes 39 audio cassette lessons, 43 student booklets, 4 review lessons, and a teacher's manual. A cassette recorder and red and blue markers must be supplied by the user.

M W M Program for Developing Language Abilities

    Publisher: Educational Performance Associates
                 563 Westview Avenue
                 Ridgefield, N.J. 07657

This program is designed for learning disabled students and can be used in a variety of settings. It is based on a model of the ITPA but can be used with or without ITPA diagnosis. The kit includes five copies of workbooks addressing the following areas: auditory and visual reception, visual association, verbal and manual expression, visual memory, and grammatical as well as visual closure. Sound blending is taught via a 33⅓ rpm record. Other materials include: picture cards depicting nouns, verbs, and descriptive words; 15 large stimulus scenes for use in a variety of teaching activities; a wordbook containing 1,018 vocabulary words divided according to function and appropriateness to age level; and a book of 37 stories for use in auditory reception, verbal expression, and auditory association activities. Careful preparation using the teacher's guide is recommended.

Santa Cruz Behavioral Characteristics Progression (BCP)

    Publisher: Vort Corporation
                 385 Sherman Avenue
                 Palo Alto, Calif. 94306

The BCP is designed for autistic, aphasic, and other educationally handicapped children. Language development is only one component of the entire BCP. This program is best described as "a workable management system" in which the teacher charts the student's progress according to 2,400 observable language characteristics. This program is purposively method free, requiring that teachers develop their own strategies for helping the student move from one objective to another.

Sound Order Sense (SOS)

    Publisher: Follett Publishing Company
                 1010 West Washington Boulevard
                 Chicago, Ill. 60607

SOS is designed to develop the auditory skills of both learning disabled and nonhandicapped first and second graders as well as older children with perceptual difficulties. The program includes speech sounds, sound sequence in words, and words in groups as well as the meaning of words, in short: *Sound, Order, Sense.* The kit contains a teacher's guide as well as two pupil response books for each grade level, 160 colorcoded activity cards for each grade level, and one activity record and response book that provides immediate feedback through the use of special markers.

The Syntax Programmer (SYNPRO)

Publisher: Mercury Co., Division of E.M.T. Labs
8564 Airport Road
St. Louis, Mo. 63100

This program targets children with language delays as well as aphasic adults. The focus is on the development of syntactic strings (i.e., sentences, phrases) through the use of multiple cues such as color, shape, pictorial symbols, and printed words. The kit contains a manual and all the components for producing an almost endless number of sentence types. Materials include a unit assembly tray, 19 base pieces, 33 inserts, picture symbols, colored cards, and colored tabs. The selection of words and pictures is left to the user, but the teaching sequence is prescribed.

The DISTAR Language Program

Publisher: Science Research Associates, Inc.
155 North Wacker Drive
Chicago, Ill. 60606

DISTAR is a highly structural program that focuses on such pragmatic concerns as teaching the child the language of instruction, i.e., the language used by the teacher in the classroom. The objectives are to have children acquire the ability to refer to familiar objects in simple, complete sentences, to use these sentences in both the affirmative and negative forms, and to ask relevant questions in a learning situation. The program begins by using words and sentences to make simple language deductions, followed by a deliberate and painstaking drill on language analogies and generalizations. This program is appropriate for preschool and elementary pupils who may be grouped according to performance level for instructional purposes. Lessons of 30 minutes' duration are presented daily. Rewards in the form of take-home activities are provided. Some training of teachers is required before implementing DISTAR.

In addition, the Language Master by Bell & Howell may be used to program lessons in symbols, letters, words, and sentences. Houghton Mifflin has published the *Listen and Do Program,* which establishes auditory-visual association patterns for prereading experiences. *Listen and Think,* by Educational Development Laboratories, is a "developmental program designed to develop the specific thinking skills necessary for good listening . . . and for good reading, too." *The Language Development Experience for Young Children* by Engel, Reid, and Rucher is a similar listening program. The *Echorder,* by RIL Electronics, is a machine for auditory training and language experiences.

Van Etten and Watson (1977) point out that there are problems with commercially available language programs. Specifically, many tend to use a shotgun approach to remediation and thus do not provide the depth of experiences necessary for specific language problems. In addition, commercial programs rarely remediate the same deficits labeled by language tests or inventories. In short, this suggests that it is ultimately the responsibility of the educator to select the intervention methods and strategies that interface best with the youngster's profile of assets and deficits (Wiig & Semel, 1976). To assist the classroom teacher in effecting this match, a review of informal intervention strategies suggested by Wiig and Semel (1976) follows.

THEORY OBJECTIVES AND ENABLING STEPS

Linguistic Processing

To improve knowledge of noun plurals and noun-verb agreement:

1. Ask the student to identify which words in a list of regular and irregular nouns mean one or more than one.
2. Introduce sentence completion exercises in which the student is required to supply a derivational suffix.
3. Require the student to make same-different judgments between the meaning of a root word and a prefix form of the root word.
4. Ask the student to form as many varieties of root words as possible using prefixes and suffixes.

To improve processing of verbs and verb tenses:

1. Establish differentiation between present and progressive tenses using
   a. cloze procedures with multiple choices
   b. cloze or sentence completion procedures requiring spontaneous responses
   c. sentences featuring yesterday, today, or tomorrow as clues to the appropriate tense

To establish the cognitive basis for the comparative form of adjectives:

1. Ask the student to differentiate between two objects that differ in some attribute, e.g., "Which apple is bigger?"
2. Ask the student to choose between correct and incorrect forms of irregular and superlative forms of adjectives using a cloze procedure.
3. Ask the student to correct sentences containing only the root adjectives, e.g., "Which do you like (good) oranges or bananas?"

Syntactic Processing

To improve recognition of word sequencing rules:

1. Ask the student to make correct-incorrect judgments of sentences such as
   a. She in the yard played
   b. She played in the yard
2. Ask the student to rearrange sentences presented in incorrect sequence.
3. Ask the student to differentiate questions from statements.
4. Ask the student to differentiate sentences from sentence fragments.

To establish knowledge of transformational rules:

1. Ask the student to arrange words and phrases into
   a. an active declarative sentence
   b. a contrasting passive sentence
2. Ask the student to transform active declarative sentences to passive and vice versa.

To improve comprehension of interrogatives:

1. Present an oral paragraph followed by a series of questions, i.e., what, who, and which; where and when; why and how; how many; how much; and whose.
2. Present oral sentences and paragraphs followed by a variety of yes-no questions.
3. Ask the student to match question forms to words and phrases, e.g., Does this tell where or when?

To assist interpretation of sentences with conjunctions:

1. Present a sentence employing an and-or conjunction and ask the student to identify the two coordinating ideas.
2. Ask the student to supply the missing conjunction in an oral paragraph using the cloze procedure.

Memory for Sequence

McGinnis (1963) outlined the following procedure for developing memory for sequence in stories:

1. Each child in turn reads a line at a time, turns, and says it from memory.
2. Each child reads the second line, turns, and says it from memory; then, while still taking his turn, he reads both lines and says them from memory. Each child reads the newly added sentence, repeats it, then reads all of them and says them from memory. This routine is carried on until four, six, or perhaps eight lines can be remembered. (p. 131)

Although this procedure may appear extremely rigid to those who acquired language naturally, such routines enable persons handicapped by such deficits to overcome their difficulties.

The Language-Learning Environment

Language is a social phenomenon and thus its development owes much, for better or worse, to the environment and the people in that environment (Berry, 1980). The environment must provide sensorial enrichment in terms of both physical space and proper atmosphere. The following are objectives for the teacher for developing an optimal language learning environment:

1. Promote activities and experiences in the classroom that stimulate students to interact with their peers, i.e., express meanings and feelings.
2. Stress the use of language for pleasurable communication.
3. Capitalize on typical classroom situations as a vehicle for language learning.
4. Encourage students' attentional behaviors by asking them to participate in sustained activities.

5. Foster students' sustained attention by modeling active listening, i.e., when they talk to the teacher, that adult should show genuine interest through eye contact, facial expression, and gestures.
6. Reinforce immediately even the students' qualified success in communication.
7. Increase the sheer volume of talk in the classroom; the classic "no talking" dictum may equal no learning.
8. Encourage students to settle their differences via words rather than fists.
9. Ask students to team up in pairs to tackle a problem or project that requires discussion for successful completion.

This brief overview obviously touches on just some of the areas in which teachers might begin to focus their efforts in language remediation. This section is not intended to substitute for a thorough review of oral language development; rather, it is to serve as a skeletal framework for developing activities to meet the specific needs of students with language deficits in the regular classroom.

Summary

This section has discussed language assessment and remediation procedures from a cognitive viewpoint, i.e., language is seen as part of, and deriving from, a child's general cognitive processing ability. It emphasized the necessity for teacher awareness and assessment of the cognitive prerequisites for language and consideration of the intimate relationship of linguistic ability to mental growth. It describes several developmentally based language programs and a framework for language intervention to help the teacher plan, implement, and monitor the educational activities that are designed to facilitate children's growth or to ameliorate their disabilities.

The lists of objectives and enabling steps in Section 4 are based on the theory in this section. The authors view academic remediation as an extension of language learning.

SECTION 4: ACADEMIC REMEDIATION

INTRODUCTION

This section reviews the academic achievement deficits associated with learning disabilities in reading, arithmetic, spelling, and writing.

READING

Reading may be characterized as a tool subject composed of many subskills. Word recognition, reading vocabulary, and reading comprehension are three broad subskill areas that can be subdivided even further. For purposes here, however, the task is simplified by focusing on reading vocabulary.

Lloyd (1979) has identified four systems for examining the reading process:

1. Formal Reading Skill Assessment

The *Monroe Diagnostic Reading Test* (1932) is an example of a test of reading skills. Errors such as faulty vowels, faulty consonants, reversals, addition or omission of sounds, substitution of words, repetitions of sounds, and addition or omission of words are identified. Reading errors are compared to graphs profiling average error scores.

2. Differential Abilities Assessment

Perceptual-cognition tests can be used to determine the strengths and weaknesses of the traits that underlie the reading process. The commonly administered tests are the *Frostig Developmental Test of Visual Perception* (Frostig, Lefever, & Whittlesey, 1974) and the *Illinois Test of Psycholinguistic Abilities.* Common clinical tests such as the Wechsler Scales also are used (*Wechsler Intelligence Scale for Children-Revised,* 1974).

3. Informal Reading Inventories (IRI)

In contrast to the differential ability measures are the informal reading inventories in which the teacher attempts to identify learner skills by varying extensive referenced materials. Generally, the examiner uses the words, vocabulary level, or passages of the actual material to be taught. The assessment procedure identifies the child's level of skill development in relation to the material. In short, the child's current mastery level is ascertained. That level serves as the basis for any objective that is to be set. The advantages are:

1. Unlike formal tests, the informal assessment approach does not work at the child's frustration level.
2. No special testing equipment is needed; the test material emanates from the teaching material.

3. The teacher may use the material without voiding or violating any norms since there are no norms.
4. By studying the instructional process the teacher:
   a. serves the child's interest in the material
   b. picks up hints on skills needed to accomplish the task
   c. obtains a feeling for the student's response to the reading process
   d. can write a tightly sequenced objective based on actual pilot use of those materials
   e. does not need to use elaborate scoring systems or require special training to administer the test
   f. can determine what the child can do in response to a specific item of material so the objective that follows can specify the time and accuracy for task completion
   g. can estimate more accurately how well a skill has developed according to the materials used
   h. can develop sensitive teaching skills rather than those of simply a test administrator.

4. Behaviorally Based Reading Assessment

Behaviorally based reading assessment is composed of three principal elements: (1) direct, continuous measurement; (2) precisely identified conditions; and (3) individual assessment (Lloyd, 1979).

The task then is to observe or measure a specific reading behavior over time, usually daily. The advantage is that it provides the teacher the opportunity to see the effects of an instructional program immediately. Unlike group tests, there is no reason to wait to the end of the year. Behaviorally based assessment also requires precise identification of the conditions under which the reading behaviors occur.

What to Assess

A review of the literature indicates that several reading skills should be assessed:

1. Sound-symbol relationship
2. Sound-blending skills
   a. long vowel conversions
   b. silent letter conversions
   c. hard-soft conversions
   d. syllabication
3. Left to right progression or special directions

4. Irregular word learning where sound-to-spelling conversions are not in harmony
5. Fluency in converting printed words into speech equivalence
6. Inaccurate decoding in which, if the child does not decode accurately what is read, the printed material will provide irrelevant meaning and deny fluency of presentation, thus failing to become an automatic process
7. Sentence storage in which the child, if unable to recognize the meaning from something just read, must be able to store the sentence
8. Direct comprehension so that each passage read may contain the answer to a direct question phrased by the reader or teacher
9. Indirect comprehension in which the student may need to carry out some additional task before being able to derive an answer to a direct question, i.e., drawing conclusions, interpreting contextual clues, drawing inferences
10. Following directions in critical reading, which requires the student's being able to pursue written guidelines to complex tasks that may include passive storage and indirect comprehension

To ascertain whether a student can follow directions, the teacher should have the pupil:

1. repeat sentences presented orally
2. repeat sentences that have been read
3. answer direct comprehension questions based on material presented orally
4. answer direct comprehension questions based on what has been read
5. answer indirect questions based on orally presented material
6. answer indirect questions based on what has been read
7. follow both simple and complex oral directions
8. follow both simple and complex written directions.

Formal Assessment

Listed next are several individually administered reading tests that were not described in Chapter 2.

The Gilmore Oral Reading Test (Gilmore & Gilmore, 1968) is available in two forms and is composed of paragraphs of increasing difficulty, one for each of ten levels. The first seven paragraphs relate an event and the last three discuss a content area topic. Each selection is followed by five direct comprehension questions. The test can be administered in about 20 minutes and yields three scores: accuracy, comprehension, and rate. The grade level is first through eighth.

The Botel Reading Inventory (Botel, 1970) may be administered to children in grades 1–4. It yields independent, instructional, and frustration levels over three subtests (word recognition, word opposites reading, and spelling placement) and yields an estimate of phonics mastery on one subtest (phonics mastery test).

The Durrell Analysis of Reading Difficulty (Durrell, 1955) is designed for use with learners in grades 1 through 6. It yields seven subscores: oral reading, silent reading, listening comprehension, flash words, word analysis, spelling, and handwriting.

The Gates-McKillop Reading Diagnostic Tests (Gates & McKillop, 1962) yields 28 scores: omissions, additions, repetitions, mispronunciations (reversals, partial reversals, total reversals, wrong beginnings, wrong middle, wrong ending, wrong in several parts, total), oral reading total, words (flash presentation), words (untimed presentation), phrases (flash presentation), recognizing and blending common word parts, giving letter sounds, naming capital letters, naming lowercase letters, recognizing the visual form of sounds (nonsense words, initial letters, final letters, vowels), auditory blending, spelling, oral vocabulary, syllabication, and auditory discrimination.

The Diagnostic Reading Scales (Spache, 1963) are presented at three levels: kindergarten through fourth grades, fourth through eighth grades, and seventh through thirteenth grades. There are subscales for each of the three levels, including word recognition lists, graduated difficulty reading passages, and supplementary tests of phonic knowledge, blending, initial consonant substitution, and auditory discrimination.

Reading Readiness

In 1940 Kirk advocated a mental age of 6 years (chronological age) or more before initiating the reading process. The reason was to ensure that the child had language memory and perceptual skills adequate enough to learn the complex task. To predict when a child is ready to begin word recognition training, a number of formulas have been developed. The difficulty with these formulas is dependence upon intelligence as a single predictor for a complex task such as reading.

Two of the more common formulas are Harris's (1970) and Bond and Tinker's (1967).* The Harris Reading Expectancy formula is:

---

*MA = mental age; CA = chronological age; RA = reading age; R exp A = reading expectancy age.

$$\text{Reading Expectancy Age} = \frac{2MA \times CA}{3}$$

Once the Reading Expectancy Age has been determined, a reading expectancy quotient can be obtained using the Bond and Tinker (1967) formula:

$$\text{Reading Expectancy Quotient} = \frac{RA \times 100}{R \exp A}$$

The difficulty is that for children who fall in the normal range of intelligence (Guszak, 1972), the formula would predict reading success. The search for an easy solution as to when to teach reading has not been answered fully. Most assuredly, vocabulary development equal to, or greater than, the words to be read is important. Otherwise, visual perceptual, auditory perceptual, and perceptual integration development of at least a 6-year mental level are necessary in many cases.

Language disabled children do present many strange reading phenomena. One of these occurs when they comprehend more words than they can pronounce by sight, another when they show sharp preferences for the perceptual mode through which information is presented. For example, a 5-year-old child with an extreme auditory perceptual receptive language deficit that impairs language development had developed a sight vocabulary equivalent to a fifth grade level. How could this occur? The child had relied upon visual perceptual skills to read road signs at age 3, thus compensating for other learning and communication skill deficits.

Word Recognition

Two initial word recognition approaches are (1) sight word (strephics) and (2) phonics:

Strephics

1. Matching Pictures: Pictures that are alike—Dolch Match-Me-Pictures—are paired.
2. Matching Letters: Those that are very different are matched first with the pupil then gradually working toward letters that are highly similar.
3. Matching Words: This exercise is similar to letters; Mill's vocabulary cards may be used.
4. Word Recognition Games
5. Board Games: Clue, bingo, crossword puzzles, and word football are among those available.

6. Track Games: Candy Land, Horse Race, Chutes and Ladders, and Monopoly are useful.
7. Feed-Through Games: These are administered by developing an object or animal word list and administering it through a stimulus background; this is an excellent review technique.
8. Building Word Families: Dolch Picture-Word cards can be placed in a row, with the pictures varied according to one letter difference; this can be used auditorily, too. Initial sight words can involve colors, numbers, or functional vocabulary.

Phonetics

1. Auditory attention, listening training, and gross sound training constitute skills underlying phonetic skill development (see Section 2, Auditory Perception subsection).
2. Discrimination of initial consonants, final consonants, and later medial consonants can be improved by emphasizing grapheme comparisons of two words with one sound variation in the I (initial), M (medial) or F (final) position. A recommended program is the *Auditory Discrimination in Depth* (Lindamood & Lindamood, 1969). Three of its levels are:
   Level 2—Auditory discrimination of speech sounds is delineated.
   Level 3—The sound is associated with the symbol, grapheme to phonics.
   Level 4—The student encodes the sound patterns into graphic representations through the use of letter titles, writing the symbol that represents the sound. Semel's (1970b) *Sound-Order-Sense Developmental Program in Auditory Perception* could provide a transition to sound sequential words.
3. Traditional structured phonics teach short and long vowels with consonants using Hay and Wiig (1967), or Stern and Gould (1965). Sound modeling, emphasizing a one-to-one relationship between phonemes and graphemes, can follow the phonics training.
4. Sequencing sounds by having children listen for correct and incorrect sounds in words is excellent ear training (Winite, 1969). Several beginning reading programs require a corresponding one-to-one grapheme/phonetic relationship. Among these programs are *Words in Color* (Gattengo, 1962), *Psycholinguistics Color Systems* (Bannatyne, 1968), *Open Court Kindergarten Program* (Bereiter & Hughes, 1970), and *Initial Teaching Alphabet* (Pitman, 1969).
5. Distinctive feature training involving sounds in words calls for the child to:

- find a target sound in a pattern of words
- listen for same-different word pairs
- carry out auditory-visual interpretation of sounds by looking at target letters, and letters by looking at target words
- identify target sounds in word triplets
- identify position of the target sound (initial, medial, final)
- reaudit and produce an omitted target sound
- identify the similarity or difference of paired sentences
- identify paired sounds in minimally paired sentences

Reading Vocabulary

Approaches for increasing student vocabulary acquisition include analysis of the semantic features of words and of their structure, study of the context in which they appear, and use of the cloze procedure.

Semantic Features Analysis

In this approach in working with the learning disabled, the teacher should:

- select a category of words

- list in columns those words that fall into a specific category of meaning (differentiate by meaning)

- list in rows those words that have similarities in meaning

- rank synonyms on one feature that they share

- expand word categorizing, adding new words

- list words, one of which is incorrect, then have the child find that one

- have the child "cash words in" by providing a dictionary definition for approval

- use words that are listed with one meaning in a different way

- match definitions of words to sentences, teaching environmental cues for reading

- match sentence definitions against the meaning of pictures or several sentences with similar words but different meanings

- write sentences

- define words by using them in sentences

Structural Analysis

Under this category of vocabulary expansion, the teacher should:

- teach prefixes and suffixes
- teach compound words
- look for little words

Contextual Analysis: Types of Contextual Cues

The context in which words appear can help clarify their meaning. In guiding students with this approach, the teacher should alert them to look for these basic types of clues:

- typographical
- pictorial and graphic
- syntactic
- cloze procedure

Cloze Procedure

The term cloze procedure refers to the practice of having the child read passages in which some words have been deleted. Words may be dropped systematically (every fifth or eighth word, for example) or by design (such as certain parts of speech). The child's task is to read the passage and supply the missing words. To do so, it is necessary to scrutinize the surrounding words, thereby developing the habit of using context. A completed exercise in the cloze procedure follows.

Word Pool

migrate	one
birds	scientists
use	thousands
very	that
die	while

Traditional Cloze Procedure (Sixth Grade Level)
Bird Migration

Bird migration is <u>one</u> of nature's wonders <u>that</u> continues to baffle scientists. Just how are these animals able to <u>migrate</u> such great distances? Scientists have learned that some birds are able to use visual landmarks to navigate while other birds use the sun to guide them. Migration can be very dangerous. Apparently thousands of birds die each year from starvation.

Modified Cloze

As a modification of the cloze procedure, letter clues sometimes are given to make it easier for the child to determine the missing words. Three types, or degrees, of letter clues are shown here, beginning with the easiest (Emans & Fisher, 1967) and progressing to the most difficult, and finally to no clues at all.

Consonant letters (vowels deleted):

1. He had a t_p_wr_t_r on his desk.
2. They flew away in a h_l_c_pt_r.
3. The March day was cold and bl_st_ry.

Reading Comprehension

Reading comprehension is closely related to language. Therefore, the emphasis here is on the fact that reading comprehension is language usage and must begin with linguistic competence.

Linguistic competence involves the following components:

Phonology is recognition of individual sounds and how they are blended to create words. Word blending requires the use of *stress* on word meaning in sentences; *junction,* placing the emphasis on word element, "I scream" and "ice cream"—in short, defining boundaries; and *pitch* emphasis through intonation that can enhance meaning.

Syntactic arrangement is the order of words in sentences to obtain grammatical acceptability.

Semantics is the knowledge of word meanings, the concept usage of a symbol system known as words.

Finally, there are several additional important aspects in teaching comprehension:

Interest: material that is appropriate by age, sex, and grade, something the child wants to learn if it is of interest.

Motivation: the reason within the person to want to read, i.e., to pass a driver's license test; if so the student should be taught the vocabulary from the driver's manual and examined as to ability to comprehend it.

Reading ability: comprehension obviously is at the mercy of the child's capability to read with understanding.

Ordering comprehension difficulty: it is important that words are understood, beginning with those rarely used and continuing to those that are
difficult because of their level of abstractness.

Sentences: meaning may be altered by the relationship of one word to
another; sentence meaning frequently is the relationship of formality and
directness of the message.

Story structure: comprehension of the use of grammar in sentences is
important to understanding the linkage between ideas in the stories, including
thematic information and material from graphic displays.

Reading Comprehension Objectives

The following objectives and enabling steps underlie reading comprehension.

Organization of Words into Meaningful Concepts

The teacher should have the child freely associate all the words that the
pupil can think of related to key words in a sentence or paragraph that is
being read for comprehension.

Class Relations

The instructor should have the child develop semantic maps involving the
relationship of meanings, using examples and property relationships of key
words in the story or sentence.

Related Concepts

The teacher should use concepts related to those being studied to promote
contextual understanding, such as those involving key words in the story. This
activity is excellent for developing dictionary and thesaurus skills. This also
can be enhanced by:

1. associating words already learned with ones the student needs to know
2. drawing on concrete experiences to emphasize the concept
3. using concepts that are known in the passage to augment new information—in short, going from concepts to events.

For example, the relations between concepts in the following sentences can
be represented by a class (*is a*) link and an attribute (*has*) link, respectively.

Leo is a lion.

$$\begin{array}{c}\text{Lion}\\\uparrow\\\text{Leo}\end{array} \quad \text{is a}$$

Leo has a mane.

$$\text{Leo} \xrightarrow{\text{has}} \text{mane}$$

Expanded Semantic Maps

Case grammar may be used to expand the number and kind of relations that can exist in a semantic network. In a case grammar analysis of an event, the first step is to identify the basic action. The second step is to identify the actors: (1) Who is the agent—who caused the action to occur? (2) Who (what) is the object—who was directly affected or who received the action? Some examples may help clarify these relationships:

1. John is gardening.
   Action: gardening
   Agent: John
   Object: none
2. The tea is brewing.
   Action: brewing
   Agent: none
   Object: the tea

In the third step, the story events are organized:

Action	Object
Agent	Purpose
Instrument	Quality
Condition	Recipient
Cause	Time
Location	Truth

Word Level Comprehension

In this approach, the teacher should involve the following elements:
Simple associations through synonyms, antonyms, and classifications of words.
Complex associations using analogies and connotative-denotative classification of occurrences, people, and places in the story.

Ambiguous words and the meanings associated with them, studying them for multiple meanings, homographic value, and homophonous contrasts, i.e., fair-fare.

Looking for the Main Ideas

There are a limited number of ways in which text can be organized. Teachers can vary that organization to facilitate students' development in dealing with the relations between the main idea and details.

First, main ideas can be stated (explicit) or unstated (implicit). Second, main ideas can be stated early in a paragraph or at the end. Third, the main idea-detail relation can be one of two types: label-list or rule-example. A label-list relation is illustrated in Stage 1 below (birds build nests in a variety of places). A rule-example relation is illustrated in Stage 3 (where a bird builds its nest depends upon its main source of food). Main idea instruction can be facilitated if these three factors are combined to generate the following sequence.

Stage 1. Explicit main ideas are stated at the beginning of a paragraph for label-list relations.

> Birds build nests in a variety of places. Robins build nests in trees. Pheasants build nests in bushes. Eagles build nests in rocks.

Stage 2. This is the same as Stage 1 except that the main idea comes at the end of the paragraph.

> Robins build nests in trees. Pheasants build nests in bushes. Eagles build nests in rocks. Birds build nests in a variety of places.

Stage 3. Explicit main ideas are stated at the beginning of a paragraph for rule-example relations.

> Where a bird builds its nest depends upon its main source of food. Because robins eat insects, worms, and other creatures found in wooded areas, they build their nests in trees. Pheasants feed on marsh and field grasses and grains. So they build their nests in grasslands or grainfields. You can find an eagle's nest (called an aerie) high among the arid rocky crags that hide snakes, rodents, and jackrabbits.

Stage 4. This is the same as Stage 3 except that the main idea comes at the end of the paragraph.

Because robins eat insects, worms, and other creatures found in wooded areas, they build their nests in trees. Pheasants feed on marsh and field grasses and grains. So they build their nests in grasslands or grainfields. You can find an eagle's nest (called an aerie) high among the arid rocky crags that hide snakes, rodents, and jackrabbits. Where a bird builds its nest depends upon its main source of food.

Stage 5. Implicit main ideas are unstated in label-list relations.

Robins build nests in trees. Pheasants build nests in bushes. Eagles build nests in rocks.

Stage 6. Implicit main ideas also are unstated in rule-example relations.

Because robins eat insects, worms, and other creatures found in wooded areas, they build their nests in trees. Pheasants feed on marsh and field grasses and grains. So they build their nests in grasslands or grainfields. You can find an eagle's nest (called an aerie) high among the arid rocky crags that hide snakes, rodents, and jackrabbits.

Within each stage, the task can be made easier by giving the students a set of choices. Obviously, then, it can be made more difficult by asking the students to find (or, in Stages 5 and 6, create) the main idea. Set 1 would be appropriate for Stages 1, 2, and 5; Set 2 for Stages 3, 4, and 6.

Set 1:
1. Robins build nests in trees.
2. Birds do things.
3. Last summer.
4. Birds build nests in a variety of places.
Set 2:
1. Robins eat insects.
2. Birds like to eat.
3. Jackrabbits.
4. Birds tend to build nests near their food source.

Teachers are encouraged to use these four factors (explicitness, position of main idea, type of relations, and item format) as an aid in building their own main idea programs or as selection criteria in choosing materials for their students.

Main idea instruction is not an entity unto itself. It is, as is implied, intrinsically related to other comprehension activities such as categorizing. It also is related closely to activities that some would label study skills, such as outlining and summarizing. The educator should consider how an outline of a chapter in a book is devised, with all those indentations with Roman numerals, capital letters, Arabic numerals, and lowercase letters. Essentially this involves placing ideas (propositions) in logical relation to one another. Bigger (more general) ideas occupy farther left positions than do smaller (more specific) ideas. An outline is not unlike a semantic map for a text segment. Later in this section, it is suggested that outlining provides a useful visual model for illustrating to students how main ideas and details fit together.

To teach main ideas, the educator cannot rely on the principle of sheer practice—the more practice activities students complete, the better they will perform. Direct teaching, modeling and feedback, and discussion are necessary. Here are some techniques the authors have found useful.

Understanding Figurative Language:	I'm so hungry I could eat a horse.
Understanding Ambiguous Statements:	The colonel asks the military police to stop drinking on base.
Understanding Causal Relations:	What happened before and what happened after.

Understanding Anaphoric Relationships

Anaphoric relations are encountered more than any of those discussed so far. It is difficult to read more than two sentences without having to deal with one. The previous sentence contains two anaphoric relations—*it* and *one*. *It* refers to the nominal proposition—to read more than two sentences, and *one* refers to the adjective-noun term, anaphoric relations, in the first sentence of this paragraph.

The *Random House Dictionary of the English Language* (1966, p. 53) defines anaphora as, "the use of a word as a regular grammatical substitute for a preceding word or group of words. . . ." Anaphora, therefore, includes all the basic personal pronouns (I, me, we, us, you, he, she, it, they, him, her, them) and demonstrative pronouns (this, that, these, those). But it also includes pro-verbs (not proverbs), such as do, can, will, would, could, should, has, and many nouns that serve the function of pronouns. These findings suggest that (1) systematic instruction in anaphoric structures probably is necessary, and (2) some students and some structures will require more attention than others.

Here are some instructional activities that merit attention.

1. Question Probes

Question probes can be used in written or oral exercises to allow students to practice relating anaphora to their antecedents (words they refer to). However, a note of caution: when the teacher creates written assignments asking, "Who did X," students sometimes will respond, "He did," or "The boy in the story did." To prevent this type of response, the students should be instructed to respond with a name or a noun, and so on.

2. Antecedent Matching

A paragraph or a list of sentences can be constructed with numbers placed over (or in front of) various anaphora. Students are instructed to write the same number over (or in front of) the antecedent for each anaphora:

> John and his cousin went to the fair last week. (1) They had a great time (2) there. First, (3) they took the roller coaster. (4) It was really fast. John got sick. (5) So did his cousin. Then they went to see the gorilla. What a crazy (6) animal! First, it threw peanuts at the crowd. Then (7) it pounded its chest. Then they went on six more rides, but they only liked three of (8) them. John ate four foot-long hot dogs. His cousin ate (9) seven! Finally they went home and were glad to be (10) there.

3. Anaphora Substitution

This is more or less the reverse of the previous activity. Students are instructed to find words to substitute for the italicized words in the paragraph. The task can be made simpler by providing a list of anaphora from which students can select.

> John and his cousin went to the fair last week. *John and his cousin* had a great time *at the fair*. First, they took the roller coaster. *The roller coaster* was really fast. John got sick. So did his cousin. Then they went to see the gorilla. What a crazy *gorilla!* First, it threw peanuts at the crowd. Then *the gorilla* pounded *the gorilla's* chest. Then they went on six more rides, but they only liked three of *the rides*. John ate four foot-long hot dogs. His cousin ate seven *foot-long hot dogs!* Finally, they went home and were glad to be *home*.

This necessarily brief overview is not meant to be all-inclusive. Rather, it is designed to provide readers with an understanding of the basic dimensions of one of the critical skill areas in society—reading. In the following section, mathematics, spelling, and handwriting are reviewed in a similar fashion.

THE ASSESSMENT OF MATHEMATICS

For the purposes of this discussion, mathematics is divided into two processes: calculation and reasoning. Mathematics calculation is the rather mechanical process of addition, subtraction, multiplication, and division. Mathematics reasoning includes the ability to perform the mechanical calculations of arithmetic as well as reading, reasoning, logic, memory, and abstraction conceptualization.

In assessing handicapped pupils it is important first to establish performance levels in terms of mechanical calculation skills. There also is much to be gained by assessing reasoning ability when calculation skills have not been demonstrated adequately. This discussion focuses first on the assessment of computational skills, then proceeds to the reasoning necessary to apply the mathematical skills to real-life problems. Several reviews of the literature on mathematics assessment provide a rather complete description of specific techniques.

One approach is for teachers to use the Brownell and Hendrickson (1950) model to determine the learning difficulty of a task. This model identifies the products of learning along a continuum from zero (0) to some maximum number (N). Four types of learning are discussed: arbitrary associations, concepts, generalization, and problem solving:

1. *Arbitrary associations* are facts that have no meaning, such as the fact that the numeral "2" is equivalent to the word "two," and that both stand for an amount.
2. *Concepts* are abstractions associated with the ability to classify the number property of various sets having other properties as well.
3. *Generalizations* are relationships between two or more concepts. An example provided by Reisman is that "threeness and fiveness" are "eightness." Hence, $3 + 5 = 8$ is a generalization. Generalizations become the means of solving problems.
4. *Problem solving* is learning initiated by a problem and requires an adequate grasp of arbitrary associations, concepts, and generalizations. The typical word problems in most math texts thus are reduced to their simplest form by determining the arbitrary associations that, when understood, form the basis for concept learning. That, in turn, allows for generalizations and finally leads to the ability to solve the problem.

Hyatt and Rolnick (1974) treat mathematics assessment as an evaluation of the child's abilities in terms of Piagetian theory. Specific directions are provided for teacher-administered tests for conservation of length, number, area, and quantity. Examples include the use of Montessori materials and techniques to assess mathematics concepts at the same time that they are being taught. In this way the assessment of mathematics concepts is a continuing process providing constant feedback at each level of presentation difficulty.

This idea is essential to good mathematics assessment and is the basis for most of the better assessment models and techniques. While Hyatt and Rolnick recommend the *Key Math Diagnostic Arithmetic Test* as a commercially available standardized technique that can be used from preschool through the elementary grades, they add that teacher observation of daily performance is the best form of mathematics assessment—especially when the observations are organized by a checklist that relates to behavioral objectives. Hyatt and Rolnick also emphasize heavily the use of readily available, inexpensive materials.

Formal tests that warrant attention are:

The California Achievement Tests-Mathematics is designed for three levels—primary, elementary, and, intermediate. The tests have a section measuring skill with number facts, and operations that provide an adequate survey of skills in fundamentals. The test at each level also has a reasoning section.

The Comprehensive Tests of Basic Skills: Arithmetic is divided into four levels covering grades 2.5–12. The test covers three areas—computation, concepts, and applications, with scores given for each area. The test takes about 70 minutes to administer. Scoring can be either manually or by computer. The test on computation is geared more easily toward low ability readers, who might experience difficulty with the material on concepts and applications.

The Key Math Diagnostic Arithmetic Test is a comprehensive assessment of mathematics skills that covers three major areas with 14 subtests: content (numeration, fractions, geometry and symbols), operations (addition, subtraction, multiplication, division, mental computation, numerical reasoning), and applications (word problems, missing elements, money, measurement, time). The test is intended for preschool through sixth grade and for remedial purposes. There also is an optional *Key Math Metric Supplement*. The entire test can be administered in 30 minutes.

The Design for Math Skill Development is a system for management of elementary school (K–6) mathematics instruction. There are 176 behaviorally stated skill objectives, organized in nine strands: numeration and place value, addition and subtraction, multiplication and division, fractions, geometry, measurement, money, time, and graphs. Pupil profiles are kept on key sort cards that are notched when the skill is mastered. Cards are sorted for grouping purposes. There is a *Teacher's Resource File* of materials keyed to the skills.

The Fountain Valley Teacher Support System in Mathematics is designed to diagnose student deficiencies in mathematics at grade levels K–8 and to provide prescriptions for reteaching. It is criterion referenced, including 785 sequenced behavioral objectives organized in eight strands: numbers and operations, geometry, measurements, applications, statistics and probability, functions and graphs, logical thinking, and problem solving. The tests are on audiocassettes and are organized by grade level.

MATHEMATICAL INTERVENTIONS

To correct or facilitate computational skills, the teacher should:

1. Use manipulative ideas in the development of all operations—addition, subtraction, multiplication, division (Cawley & Vitello, 1972).
2. Correct a computational error that is rule based by having the student talk through the problem while doing it and write down the order of steps followed. Using a procedure of "least corrections," the teacher should propose an alternative algorithm to the student that uses many of the same steps but modifies the one that created the major error (Ashlock, 1976).
3. Correct the student's violation of place value rules, which constitute the major error in all advanced computational experiences, given that the error is not a basic fact. The use of materials such as dienes blocks, Cuisennaire rods, and balance scales can aid in the acquisition of the concept.
4. Adopt a teaching model that uses a systematic interaction of teacher and student behavior, progressing from a manipulative level up through a graphic symbolic level.

MATH REASONING SKILL

In developing the mathematical reasoning skills of learning disabled children, the teacher should:

1. Use pictures and/or manipulatives to represent meaning in problems.
2. Use indefinite quantifiers ("some," "a few," "many," etc.) in conjunction with pictures to represent problems (Schenck, 1973): e.g., This

boy has some toy guns. Another boy has a lot of toy guns. How many guns do the boys have?

3. Use quantitative and qualitative distractors with student selection of relevant information prior to the computation.

4. Use small numbers to minimize the interfering effects of computation on reasoning.

5. Use modified cloze procedures in writing word problems so that the student selects a word rather than a number to complete a problem correctly (Sedlak, 1974):

  The boy has three marbles
  The boy ____ two marbles
  The boy now has five marbles
  a. lost   *b. won   c. saw
  *correct response

6. Not allow the student to use "cue" words to discover the operation of the computation. For example the words "left," "in all," "altogether," and "divided" generally denote the use of a particular operation. When these words are found in indirect problems they provide false cues for the student and result in an incorrect response, e.g.: "Bill had five apples left after eating three. How many did he start with?" Simply following the trick of searching for the cue word of "left" results in the student's subtracting instead of adding. (Cawley, Goodstein, Fitzmaurice, Lepore, Sedlak, Althaus, 1976).

7. Have student cross out extraneous information in the problem.

8. Use set language so that students understand the multiple groupings of information and their respective labels, such as: a dog can be called "dog," "pet," "animal," "four-legged creature," "mammal," etc. depending upon the grouping.

9. Use neutral rather than cued questions so that the student focuses attention on the verbs in the informative statements of the problem to determine the operation (Goodstein, 1974), e.g.: Bill has six apples. He ate two apples.
  How many apples does he have now? (neutral)
  How many apples does he have left? (cued)

10. Give the student one set of information and then ask a series of questions from it that requires the pupil to reorganize the information in different ways in order to get a different concept, e.g.: Bill had two dogs, three cats, five goldfish, four guppies, and a parakeet. The questions:
  a. How many dogs does Bill have? (set identification)
  b. How many fish does Bill have? (simple addition-superordinate)

    c. How many different types of fish does Bill have? (set language)

    d. How many pets does Bill have?

    e. Does Bill have more goldfish or cats?

    f. Does Bill have more goldfish or guppies? (class inclusion)

11. Read each incorrectly answered problem aloud, state the correct answer, write it out, then explain the problem and the answer. This is shown to be an effective sequence of strategies by Blankenship and Lovitt (1976).

SPELLING AND HANDWRITING

Assessment of Spelling

Durrell Analysis of Reading Difficulty (Durrell, 1955) contains two spelling tests—the phonic spelling of unfamiliar words, and a test using words from a graded list. A brief checklist of difficulties in spelling is used for a broad analysis of errors. The test may be used for grades 1 through 6. Norms are given for grades 2 through 6.

Spell Master-Diagnostic Spelling System (1974) is a criterion referenced test designed to pinpoint the student's specific strengths and areas for progress. The criteria are the basic structural and phonic elements of English spelling. There are six levels for grades 1 through 6, and one level for grades 7 and 8. The instrument is scored by recording the number of correct responses and the number of errors. In the misspelled words, specific elements to remediate are identified. The elements tested are correlated to seven basal tests. A *Supplemental Teaching Guide* suggests activities for the instructor as well. The students can correct their own tests. Available from Learnco, Inc., 156 Front Street, Exeter, N.H. 03833.

Spelling Interventions

The ability to discriminate sounds auditorily is requisite to the spelling process. In Language Master, for example, the student is required to make the appropriate sound-symbol correlation by either naming or writing the name of the letter. The child is presented a C-V-C (consonant-vowel-consonant) word and must discriminate the vowel and identify the corresponding grapheme either by writing it on paper or by saying the name into the recorder.

Effective auditory and visual sequential memory skills are necessary for spelling. To encourage development of auditory memory while simultaneously reinforcing phonetic generalization, one activity that has proved successful involves requiring the child to repeat "tongue twisters" from psycholinguistic readers. The length of the sentences is increased as skills improve. To encourage development of visual sequential memory, activities using configuration prompts of the work generally are successful.

Correcting Spelling

The rule of thumb in spelling is obvious to the experienced instructor: no children should be required to spell words that they cannot read. If they are required to do so, they are only sequencing chains of letters that have no meaning to them and have no corrective feedback available. The tack is useless. Therefore, before initiating any spelling activity, sightword mastery should be assessed.

The ability to make the phonological and morphological generalizations necessary to facilitate spelling processes varies with the differences among children. However, some generalizations appear to be more difficult than others. They are loud and soft sounds, vowel-r combinations, and vowel combinations. To remediate difficulties, the teacher should:

1. Provide the students with sets of four words and ask them to circle the correct spelling.

good	doog	goad	gode
bread	breda	braed	brade

2. Use crossword puzzles as effective means of reinforcing phonetic generalizations.
3. Present the children with sentences or paragraphs with missing words or parts of words, as in cloze. Ask them to complete the sentences. A word pool might be provided.
   The b__d flew into the o_ange tr__.

Assessment of Handwriting

Teachers engaged in assessing the handwriting of the learning disabled will find the following materials helpful: *The Ayres Scale for Measuring Handwriting* was designed as a measuring device rather than a standard. The quality of each writing sample is determined by its degree of legibility. It is intended for use in grades 2 through 8, and the writing is evaluated in terms of quality and speed.

The Durrell Analysis of Reading Difficulty is a quick screening instrument indicating speed, letter formation, position of hand, pencil, paper, and body; and height spacing and slant of the letters. The test consists only of copying letters and sentences in one-minute samples.

The Basic School Skill Inventory: Handwriting Subscale assesses a child's handwriting ability on ten different dimensions: left to right, grasp, printing first name, writing position, drawing geometric figures, copying words, drawing a person, copying from chalkboard to paper, staying on the line, and printing last name. The scale is used primarily for screening and readiness purposes. The instrument is norm referenced for ages 4–0 to 6–11, but can be used as a criterion referenced test also. It is available from Follett Publishing Company, 1010 West Washington Boulevard, Chicago, Ill. 60607.

Sequential Testing and Education Programming (STEP) provides sequenced objectives for several developmental levels of handwriting and related abilities. It is based on Osgood's (1957) model and is organized, like the model, by channels and levels and is intended for use from preschool through grade 6. Assessment is criterion referenced. Each objective has suggested activities and is correlated to commercially available teaching materials.

Writing Interventions

Acquisition on Prerequisite Skills for Writing

Commercially prepared or teacher-made manipulatives are useful aids in the development of fine motor skills. For example, activities that require children to identify wooden figures or letters with their eyes closed are effective.

The students' ability to sequence the fine motor movements necessary to form letters (and eventually sequence letters into words) can be enhanced through activities using dot-to-dot figures. These figures should be drawn first on the chalkboard and later, as coordination improves, on ditto sheets.

To enhance the students' ability to understand directional concepts, commercially developed (or teacher-made) activities should be designed that incorporate some of the following commands:

"Draw a line from the top right corner to the bottom left corner."
"Mark a circle in the center of the page."
"Draw a line through the middle of the page from top to bottom."

Corrections of Difficulties in Manuscript Writing

To correct directional errors in manuscript writing, color coding can be used to indicate the initiation and termination points, e.g., green for go and red for stop.

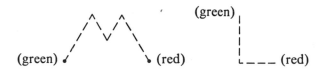

Directionality also can be facilitated by the use of arrows.

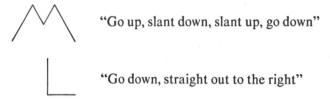

Fine motor sequencing can be developed by encouraging the student to "talk through" the movements necessary to form the letters.

"Go up, slant down, slant up, go down"

"Go down, straight out to the right"

Correction of Difficulties in Cursive Writing

Fading procedures are effective in the development of cursive writing skills. First, the student traces the letter. The intensity of color or shading of the letter then is faded gradually until the student writes the letter with no visual prompt.

The student's violation of spacing rules often constitutes a major error in cursive writing. To correct errors in staying on the line, commercial products can be purchased that are visual (color coded) and tactile prompts.

Practice in a series of cursive strokes is useful in the development of handwriting skills.

ℓℓℓℓℓℓℓℓ ocean waves
ⵔⵔⵔⵔⵔ string of pearls
⌇⌇⌇⌇ snakes

Summary

This section reviewed the academic remediation of reading vocabulary and comprehension, arithmetic calculation and reasoning, spelling, and handwriting. For each area, summary coverage of assessment techniques/instruments, instructional objectives, and specific instructional enabling steps have been provided. The next section examines prevocational and vocational education. It has been specifically prepared as the last section to serve as a contrast to academic remediation.

SECTION 5. VOCATIONAL AND PREVOCATIONAL TRAINING

INTRODUCTION

Adolescents and young adults are faced with increasing social demands requiring that they be able to perceive and interpret verbal as well as nonverbal communication cues. Learning disabled youth who often are hampered by linguistic, perceptual, or logical processing deficits (Wiig & Roach, 1975; Wiig & Semel, 1974) may give inappropriate social responses, show delays in acquiring various social skills, and get into trouble because of their inability to interpret the emotions and intentions of others accurately. (Wiig & Semel, 1976).

Concomitantly, these students may tune out traditional approaches to remediation. To improve the quality of the learning disabled pupils' interpersonal interactions and thus their potential for self-actualization, the teacher must be able to cast language and academic skill development in the guise of career education—an area of great interest to students of those ages.

Career education is defined as the process by which students prepare for various occupational areas through the acquisition of basic academic or vocational performance skills and competencies necessary to perform in the areas of business, industry, the arts, or the professions. The process of career education is multifaceted (Jones, Blaney, & Sabatino, 1975), including prevocational, occupational, and vocational skill development.

2   The first step in this process should be both formal and informal assessment of each student's academic competencies, personal characteristics, and vocational aptitudes and interests (Alpern & Sabatino, 1975).

INFORMAL ASSESSMENT

Informed assessment of student characteristics should include a review of the following factors (Miller, 1979):

1. *Physical Appearance.* The student's physical appearance tacitly expresses the importance he or she places on the experience. Appearance is often a major factor to an individual meeting a student for the first time for the appearance provides information from which to make a judgment about employment desirability.

2. *Punctuality.* Individuals' early or late arrival[s] to a meeting may reflect their attitude toward and the importance they place on an experience.

3. *Oral Communication.* The ability an individual possesses in communicating effectively with others is an essential component in human interaction. Those handicapped by poor fluency, inappropriate vocabulary, and improper syntax frequently experience severe difficulties in working with others and maintaining open channels of communication.
4. *Following Directions.* The individual who can listen and follow work instructions will regularly achieve higher approval than the student who either cannot or will not.
5. *Reliability.* Individuals who assume responsibility for completing tasks in the agreed manner and who can thus be trusted by an employer are not only more employable, but they are more likely to retain the work position.
6. *Cooperation.* In working with individuals it is important that youth not only understand how to work with others, but how to interact with them in a mutually productive manner.
7. *Initiative.* The individual able to identify work needs and assume initiative in accomplishing them is highly prized by most organizations. Those able to assume initiative are self-starters, who not only make a contribution to themselves but also to the employer.
8. *Leadership.* The leader is someone who can determine long- and short-term needs and initiate action that leads to the realization of these needs. The youth who can lead without offending or threatening the employer is an individual who can grow in a work station.
9. *Innovation.* Youth possessing the competency to view alternative strategies and select modes different from those presently being practiced may find him- or herself either applauded or criticized. Such youth must be carefully placed to avoid conflicts.
10. *Flexibility.* Individuals unable to adapt old behavior or adopt new behaviors to meet and resolve new problems frequently come into conflict with those committed to solving the problem.
11. *Social Perceptions.* The youth's perception of his or her community and the values practiced by the individuals who live and work in it will influence the youth's response to specific work and behavioral expectations. Those youths with inaccurate perceptions will face equivalent difficulties in work stations as individuals with rejecting values. (pp. 570–571)

FORMAL ASSESSMENT

By using this information on informal evaluation combined with data from formal assessment procedures, the educator will be better able to identify appropriate training and career goals for each student. Several formal assessment devices are available.

The Kuder Occupational Interest Survey (KOIS)

Publisher: Science Research Associates, Inc.
155 North Wacker Drive
Chicago, Illinois 60606

This test is designed to provide general data on the student's occupational interests. It is appropriate for ages 11 and above. The KOIS is a 100-triad inventory in which the student is asked to choose the most and least preferred activity from three choices. The student's score is then compared to those of individuals involved in 37 occupations and 19 college majors. The assumption is that if a student's score matches that of individuals choosing a specific college major or occupation, that individual also would be suited for that form of endeavor.

The General Aptitude Test Battery (GATB)

Publisher: Bureau of Employment Security
U.S. Department of Labor
Washington, D.C. 20210

This test, for ages 16 and over, is designed to measure capacities to learn various jobs. It produces measures in ten areas: intelligence, verbal, numerical, spatial, form perception, clerical perception, aiming, motor speed, finger dexterity, and manual dexterity. The battery utilizes a multiple cutoff method to determine whether the student passed or failed the minimum qualifying scores for a job or job cluster.

The Differential Aptitude Test

Publisher: The Psychological Corporation

This test is easily administered, scored, and interpreted. It is designed for ages 13 to adult. It measures six areas thought to be indicative of the capability to perform in various occupational groups: verbal reasoning, numerical reasoning, space relations, mechanical reasoning, clerical speed and accuracy, and language usage.

Other formal assessment measures directed at specific populations are:

Mechanical Handyman Test for Maintenance Workers, published by International Personnel Management Association.

Short Occupational Knowledge Test for Carpenters, published by Science Research Associates, Inc.

Short Occupational Knowledge Test for Draftsmen, published by Science Research Associates, Inc.

Bennett Mechanical Comprehension Test, published by The Psychological Corporation, to measure the ability to perceive and understand the relationship of physical forces and mechanical elements.

Following the completion of all phases of formal and informal testing, the teacher should develop prevocational, occupational, and vocational training experiences. This does not require a complete overhaul of existing goals and objectives but simply a change in focus in many classroom activities. The following list of training activities developed by Miller, Sabatino, and Sloan (1975) provides a model for how the teacher might accomplish this task:

1. Provide situations in which the student must follow a complex set of written or oral directions to complete a specific task.
2. Ask a group of students to list common speech errors they hear made by those around them. Discuss how these errors can be corrected.
3. Have two students assume the role of employer and applicant and role play applying for a job. Ask each student in class to provide feedback on the speech and manners of the two.
4. Have students develop and act out skits illustrating the following themes:
   a. a habitually late employee
   b. improper behavior on the job
   c. improper dress on the job
5. Invite experts such as work counselors, tax accountants, and bank officers to demonstrate the proper procedure for filling out forms related to their field.
6. Ask students to practice filling out the following forms:
   a. work permits
   b. Social Security
   c. health cards
   d. bank forms (checking, deposit, and withdrawal)
   e. income tax

Occupational Training Activities

1. Have students list their personal career assets and liabilities.
2. Have students make a comparative diagram of the personality traits helpful to certain jobs.

3. Have students develop a listing of the types of jobs available in their own community.
4. Have students list jobs that are legal and illegal for teenagers to hold.
5. Have students read and report on the biographies of outstanding persons in their field of interest. Have students list the advantages and disadvantages of the careers chosen by the people in the story.
6. Have students research and report on an occupation of interest by interviewing persons in that field. Students should investigate such factors as hours, salaries, life styles, conditions, educational requirements, fringe benefits, etc.
7. Develop a reading vocabulary for each occupation the students study and include these new words in other classroom activities.
8. Invite parents of students who work in various occupations to discuss their work with the class.
9. Take students on field trips to places of employment of occupations being studied and have them write reports on their observations.
10. Ask students to read the want ads in the newspaper and list the common requirements for each type of job listed.
11. Have students write a resume listing the skills and experiences that would indicate they were qualified for a certain job.
12. Have students prioritize a list of occupations according to the following specifications.
   a. their personal preference
   b. their skill level
   c. element of risk involved
13. Have students research and list the types of jobs that have become obsolete in the last 50 years.
14. Have students list the types of jobs that they think will become obsolete in the next 50 years.
15. Have students list the types of skills that will be required of the man and woman of the 21st century.

VOCATIONAL TRAINING ACTIVITIES

Vocational training activities may take two forms: (1) placing students at actual worksites under close employee and educational supervision, and (2) simulating the actual work experience within the school environment. Regardless of which option is used, adequate prevocational skill development and occupational awareness training should provide a foundation for actual student work experiences.

The students placed at actual worksites are provided an opportunity to discover and assess factors associated with specific jobs (Alpern & Sabatino,

1975). Similarly, school personnel have an opportunity to evaluate the students in the field, as well as their preparation efforts and the conceptual framework of the school educational model (Miller, 1975). While functioning in the work environment, students should be provided feedback on the following variables:

Job Aptitude: Does the student possess the cognitive and psychomotor aptitudes that are required by the job? If the student lacks aptitude, what specific skills and overlapping skills are required for improved performance?

Work Judgment: Does the student possess the knowledge to determine when specific operations are to be undertaken and when they are to be delayed? The student should also be assessed on ability to make judgments concerning the appropriate use of equipment and materials associated with the work.

Initiative: The quality and quantity of job performance often is influenced by the individual initiative demonstrated at work. The student who will obtain clarification on work schedule and job responsibilities, or begin new activities, is more likely to succeed than the one who is unwilling to question or try something new.

Adaptability: Can the student alter or change behavior, task direction, or job responsibilities without either disrupting others or becoming disorganized by the changes? The individual capable of adaptive behavior will be able to cope in the changing world better than one who questions why it cannot be the way it was.

Personality Characteristics: As noted earlier, qualities of appearance, social skills, voice, and mannerism can influence the prospective employer's decision in hiring as well as the attitude of colleagues at a worksite. Often the personality characteristic is more influential than competency in the employer's decision.

Temperament and Interests: The student's ability to cope with frustrations, disappointments, patience and/or impatience required by the work situation will affect performance. A student's technical competence to perform a job may fail because the individual's temperament was inappropriate or because of a lack of interest in learning more about the people and the work.

Attitude: The student's attitude toward work and coworkers is a significant variable in the determination of job appropriateness. Attitude is one of the more significant variables to measure in developing accurate performance criteria.

General: Besides these variables, the employer, student, and educator must be aware of general factors such as communication skills, acceptance by others, and personal reliability. Such awareness will help all parties to assess the student's progress and others' reactions. In the classroom, students can be provided with experiences simulating actual work situations. The teacher can:

1. Ask the students to take turns serving as the class receptionist, secretary, or file clerk.
2. Ask students to take turns acting as a salesperson for a classroom store that provides school supplies.
3. Ask students to simulate a courtroom trial in which they assume the following roles: court recorder, court clerk, judge, prosecuting attorney, defense attorney, defendant.
4. Ask students to simulate a banking situation, taking the roles of teller, loan officer, bank president, bank guard, etc.
5. Ask students to simulate a television news broadcast of school-related news by taking the roles of news broadcasters.
6. Ask students to plan a cross-country trip to be taken by
   a. a trucker
   b. a pilot
   c. a bus driver

Summary

Obviously, these activities are not all-inclusive. Rather, they should be used as a guide in planning meaningful learning activities for the learning disabled adolescent—a group of students generally overlooked in the school today (Sabatino & Mauser, 1978). To conclude, it is essential that the teacher always be mindful of the abilities, interests, and needs of each individual student in planning any learning experience. Toward this end, the reader has been presented with guidelines as well as actual examples of assessment and remediation procedures that can be used in academic areas as well as those of motor perception, language, and prevocational skill development.

The modern teacher must recognize that in the absence of laws for learning or an appreciation of the pathology of learning disabilities, reasonable judgment is all that society has to go on currently. May the near future alter that statement.

REFERENCES

Agranowitz, A., & McKeown, M. *Aphasia handbook for adults and children.* Springfield, Ill.: Charles C. Thomas, Publisher, 1964.

Aloia, G.F., Knutson, R., Minner, S.H., & Von Seggern, M. Physical education teacher's initial perceptions of handicapped children. *Mental Retardation,* 1980, *18*(2), 85–87.

Alpern, S., & Sabatino, P.A. *Establishing a meaningful career education plan* (Manual). Springfield, Ill.: Department of Corrections, 1975.

Armstrong, R.G., & Hauck, P.A. Sexual identification and the first figure drawn. *Journal of Consulting Psychology,* 1961, pp. 51–54.

Ashlock, R.B. *Error patterns in computation: A semi-programmed approach* (2nd ed.). Columbus, Ohio: The Charles E. Merrill Publishing Co., Inc., 1976.

Aten, J., & Davis, J. Disturbances in the perception of auditory sequences in children with minimal cerebral dysfunction. *Journal of Speech and Hearing Disorders,* 1968, *11,* 236–245.

Baker, H.J., & Leland, B. *Detroit Test of Learning Aptitude.* Indianapolis, Ind.: Bobbs-Merrill, 1968.

Bannatyne, A. *Psycholinguistic color system: A reading, writing, spelling and language program.* Urbana, Ill.: Learning Systems Press, 1968.

Barry, H. *The young aphasic child: Evaluation and training.* Washington, D.C.: Alexander Graham Bell Association for the Deaf, Inc., 1961.

Barsch, R.H. *Achieving perceptual motor efficiency.* Seattle: Special Child Publications, 1967.

Becker, J.T., & Sabatino, D.A. Reliability of individual tests of perception administered, utilizing group techniques. *Journal of Clinical Psychology,* 1971, *1,* 86–88.

Bennet, G.K., Seashore, H.G., & Wesman, A.G. *Differential aptitude tests.* New York: The Psychological Corporation, 1947–1969.

Bereiter, C., & Hughes, A. *Open Court kindergarten program.* La Salle, Ill.: Open Court Publishing Co., 1970.

Berry, M.F. *Teaching linguistically handicapped children.* Englewood Cliffs, N.J.: Prentice-Hall, Inc., 1980.

Birch, H.G., & Belmont, L. Auditory-visual integration, intelligence and reading ability in school children. *Perceptual and Motor Skills,* 1965, *20,* 295–305.

Birch, H.G., & Belmont, L. Auditory-visual integration in normal retarded readers. *American Journal of Orthopsychiatry,* 1964, *34,* 852–861.

Birch, H.G., & Lefford, A. Intersensory development in children. *Monograph of the Society for Research in Child Development,* 1963, *28*(5, Serial No. 89).

Blankenship, C.S., & Lovitt, T.C. Story problems: Merely confusing or downright befuddling. *Journal for Research in Mathematics Education,* 1976, *7,* 290–298.

Bloom, L. *Language development: Form and function in emerging grammars.* Cambridge, Mass.: MIT Press, 1970.

Bond, G.L., & Tinker, M.A. *Reading difficulties: Their diagnosis and correction* (2nd ed.). New York: Appleton-Century-Crofts, Inc., 1967.

Botel, M. *Botel reading inventory.* Chicago: Follett Publishing Company, 1970.

Boyd, L., & Randle, K. Factor analysis of the Frostig developmental test of visual perception. *Journal of Learning Disabilities,* 1970, *3*(5), 253–255.

Bricker, W.A., & Bricker, D.D. An early language training strategy. In R.L. Schiefelbusch & L.L. Lloyd (Eds.), *Language perspectives—Acquisition, retardation, and intervention.* Baltimore: University Park Press, 1974.

Brown, R. *A first language: The early stages.* Cambridge, Mass.: Harvard University Press, 1973.

Brownell, W.A., & Hendrickson, G. How children learn information, concepts, and generalizations. *49th yearbook of the National Society for the Study of Education, Part 1: Learning and instruction.* Chicago: University of Chicago Press, 1950.

Buktenica, N.A. Auditory discrimination: A new assessment procedure. *Exceptional Children,* 1971, *38*(3), 237–240.

Carrow, E. *Carrow elicited language inventory.* Austin, Tex.: Learning Concepts, 1974.

Cawley, J.F., & Vitello, S. A model for arithmetical programming for handicapped children: A beginning. *Exceptional Children,* 1972, *39,* 101–110.

Cawley, J.F., Burrow, W.H., & Goodstein, H.A. *An appraisal of Head Start participants and nonparticipants* (Research report). University of Connecticut, Contract OEO 4177, U.S. Office of Economic Opportunity, 1968.

Cawley, J.F., Goodstein, H.A., Fitzmaurice, A.M., Lepore, A., Sedlak, R.A., & Althaus, V. *Project MATH: Mathematics activities for teaching the handicapped: Level I and II.* Tulsa, Okla.: Educational Process Corp., 1976.

Chaplin, J.P., & Krawiec, T.S. *Systems and theories of psychology.* New York: Holt Rinehart Winston Inc., 1960.

Chomsky, N. *Syntactic structures.* The Hague: Mouton, 1957.

Clawson, A. The Bender visual motor Gestalt test as an index of emotional disturbance in children. *Journal of Projection Technology,* 1959, *23,* 198–206.

Cole, E., & Walker, L. Reading and speech problems as expressions of a specific language disability. In D. Rioch & E. Weinstein (Eds.), *Disorders of communications.* Baltimore: The Williams and Wilkins Co., 1964.

Coltheart, M., & Curthoys, I. Short-term recognition memory for pitch: Effect of a priori probability on response times and error rates. *Perception and Psychophysics,* 1968, *4,* 85–89.

Corah, N.L., & Powell, B.J. A factor analytic study of the Frostig developmental test of visual perception. *Perceptual and Motor Skills,* 1963, *16,* 59–63.

Cratty, B.J. *Movement, perception, and thought.* Palo Alto, Calif.: Peek Publications, 1969.

deHirsch, K., Jansky, J.J., & Langford, W.S. *Predicting reading failure.* New York: Harper & Row, Publishers, 1966.

Drake, C. *PERC auditory discrimination test.* Sherborn, Mass.: PERC Educational and Research Center, 1965.

DuBard, E. *Teaching aphasics and other language deficient children.* Jackson, Miss.: University Press of Mississippi, 1974.

Durrell, D. *Durrell analyses of reading difficulty.* New York: Harcourt Brace Jovanovich, 1955.

Emans, R., & Fisher, G.M. Teaching the use of context clues. *Elementary English,* 1967, *44,* 243–246.

Farnham-Diggory, S. Symbol and synthesis in experimental reading. *Child Development,* 1967, *38,* 223–231.

Flowers, R. The evaluation of auditory abilities in the appraisal of children with reading problems. In A. Figurel (Ed.), *Perception and reading,* Newark, Del.: International Reading Association, 1968.

Flowers, A., & Costello, M.R. *Tests of central auditory abilities.* Dearborn, Mich.: Perceptual Learning Systems, 1970.

Frostig, M., & Horne, D. *The Frostig program for the development of visual perception.* Chicago: Follett Publishing Company, 1964.

Frostig, M., Lefever, D., & Whittlesay, J. *The Marianne Frostig developmental test of visual perception.* Palo Alto, Calif.: Consulting Psychology Press, 1974.

Fygetakis, L., & Ingram, D. Language rehabilitation and programmed conditioning. *Journal of Learning Disabilities,* 1973, *6*(2), 5–9.

Gates, A., & McKillop, A. *Reading diagnostic test.* New York: Teachers College Press, 1962.

Gattengo, C. *Words in color.* Chicago: Learning Materials, 1962.

General Aptitude Test Battery (GATB). Washington, D.C.: U.S. Department of Labor, Bureau of Employment Security, 1946–1970.

Gillingham, A., & Stillman, G. *Remedial work for reading, spelling and penmanship.* New York: Hackett & Wilhelms, 1936.

Gilmore, J.V., & Gilmore, E.C. *Gilmore oral reading tests.* Indianapolis: Bobbs-Merrill, 1968.

Goldman, R., Fristoe, M., & Woodcock, R.W. *Goldman-Fristoe-Woodcock test of auditory discrimination.* Circle Pines, Minn.: American Guidance Service, Inc., 1970.

Goodstein, H.A. Solving the verbal mathematics problem: Visual aids and teacher planning = the answer. *Teaching Exceptional Children,* 1974, *6,* 178–182.

Guess, D., Sailor, W., & Baer, D.M. To teach language to retarded children. In R.L. Schiefelbusch & L.L. Lloyd (Eds.), *Language perspectives—Acquisition, retardation, and intervention.* Baltimore: University Park Press, 1974.

Guszak, F.J. *Diagnostic reading instruction in the elementary school.* New York: Harper & Row, Publishers, 1972.

Harris, A.J. *How to increase reading ability* (5th ed.). New York: David McKay Co., 1970.

Hay, J., & Wiig, E.C. *Reading with phonics.* Philadelphia: J.P. Lippincott Co., 1967.

Hyatt, R., & Rolnick, N. *Teaching the mentally handicapped child.* New York: Behavioral Publications, 1974.

Johnson, D.J. The language continuum. *Bulletin of the Orton Society,* 1968, *18,* 1–11.

Johnson, D.J., & Myklebust, H.R. *Learning disabilities: Educational principles and practices.* New York: Grune & Stratton, Inc., 1967.

Jones, R.W., Blaney, R.L., & Sabatino, D.A. *Ascertaining vocationally retarded behavior* (Manual). Springfield, Ill.: Department of Corrections, 1975.

Kaliski, L. Auditory-vocal activation: A tool for teaching children with a specific language disability. *Journal of Learning Disabilities,* 1977, *10,* 210–218.

Keller, H. *The story of my life.* New York: Dell Publishing Co., Inc., 1961.

Keogh, B.K. The Bender Gestalt as a predictive and diagnostic test of reading performance. *Journal of Consulting Psychology,* 1962, *26,* 541–546.

Kephart, N.C. *The slow learner in the classroom.* Columbus, Ohio: The Charles E. Merrill Publishing Co., Inc., 1960.

Kimmel, G.M., & Wahl, J. *Screening Test for Auditory Perception (STAP).* Novata, Cal.: Academic Therapy Publishers, 1969.

Kirk, S. *Teaching reading to slow-learning children.* Cambridge, Mass.: Riverside Press, 1940.

Kirshner, A.J. *Training that makes sense.* San Rafael, Calif.: Academic Therapy Publications, 1972.

Koppitz, E.M. Bender Gestalt test and learning disturbances in young children. *Journal of Clinical Psychology,* 1958, *14,* 292–295.

_____. Diagnosing brain damage in young children with the Bender Gestalt test. *Journal of Consultative Psychology,* 1962, *26,* 541–546.

Kuder, G. *Kuder occupational interest survey (KOIS).* Chicago: Science Research Associates, Inc., 1956–1970.

Lamberts, F. Describing children's language behavior. In D.A. Sabatino & T.L. Miller (Eds.), *Describing learner characteristics of handicapped children and youth.* New York: Grune & Stratton, Inc., 1979.

Lasky, E.Z., & Tobin, H. Linguistic and nonlinguistic competing messages effect. *Journal of Learning Disabilities,* 1973, *6*(4), 243–250.

Lea, J. A language scheme for children suffering from receptive aphasia. *Speech Pathology and Therapy,* 1965, *8,* 58–68.

Lenneberg, E.H. *Biological foundations of language.* New York: John Wiley & Sons, Inc., 1967.

Lindamood, C., & Lindamood, P. *Auditory discrimination in depth.* Boston: Teaching Resources Corporation, 1969.

Lloyd, J. Ascertaining the reading skills of atypical learners. In D.A. Sabatino & T.L. Miller (Eds.), *Describing learner characteristics of handicapped children and youth.* New York: Grune & Stratton, Inc., 1979.

Lowry, L.M. Differences in visual perception and auditory discrimination between American Indian and white kindergarten children. *Journal of Learning Disabilities,* 1970, *3*(7), 359–363.

MacDonald, J., & Blott, J.P. Environmental language intervention: A rationale for a diagnostic and training strategy through rules, context, and generalization. *Journal of Speech and Hearing Disorders,* 1974, *39,* 244–256.

Masland, M.W., & Case, L. *Limitation of auditory memory as a factor in delayed language development.* Paper presented at the International Association for Logopedics and Phoniatrics, Vienna, August 1965.

Maslow, P., Frostig, M., Lefever, D.W., & Whittlesay, J.R.B. The Marianne Frostig developmental test of visual perception: 1963 standardization. *Perceptual and Motor Skills,* 1964, *19,* 463–499.

McGinnis, M.A. *Aphasic children.* Washington, D.C.: Alexander G. Bell Association for the Deaf, 1963.

Menyuk, P., & Looney, P.L. A problem of language disorder: Length vs. structure. *Journal of Speech and Hearing Research,* 1972, *15*(2), 264–279.

Miller, J.F., & Yoder, D.E. An ontogenetic language teaching strategy for retarded children. In R.L. Schiefelbusch & L.L. Lloyd (Eds.), *Language perspectives—Acquisition, retardation and intervention.* Baltimore: University Park Press, 1974.

Miller, S.R. *Secondary assessment and programming.* Unpublished paper, 1975.

——————————. Career education: Lifelong planning for the handicapped. In D.A. Sabatino & T.L. Miller (Eds.), *Describing learner characteristics of handicapped children and youth.* New York: Grune & Stratton, Inc., 1979.

Miller, S.R., Sabatino, D.A., & Sloan, C. *An integrated curriculum for chronic disruptive youth.* Springfield, Ill.: Illinois Division of Vocational and Technical Education, 1975.

Monroe, M. *Diagnostic reading examination.* Chicago: C.H. Stoelting, 1932.

Myklebust, H.R. *Progress in learning disabilities* (Vol. 1). New York: Grune & Stratton, Inc., 1968.

——————————. Learning disorders: Psychoneurological disturbances in childhood. *Rehabilitation Literature,* 1964, *25,* 354–360.

Myklebust, H.R., & Johnson, D. *Learning disabilities: Educational principles and practice.* New York: Grune & Stratton, Inc., 1967.

Olson, A.V. Factor analytic studies of Frostig developmental test of visual perception. *The Journal of Special Education,* 1968, *2*(4), 429–433.

Orton, S.T. *Reading, writing, and speech problems in children.* New York: W.W. Norton & Co., Inc., 1937.

Osgood, C.E. A behavioristic analysis of perception and language as cognitive phenomena. In *Contemporary approaches to cognition,* Cambridge, Mass.: Harvard University Press, 1957.

Physical education for the handicapped: Louisiana needs assessment. Baton Rouge, La.. Louisiana State Department of Education, Bulletin 1506, 1978.

Pitman, J. *Alphabets and reading.* London: Sir Isaac Pitman & Sons, 1969.

Pronko, N.H. A critical review of the theories of perception. In A. Kidd & J. Revoire (Eds.), *Perceptual development in children.* New York: International Universities Press, 1966.

Rarick, G.L., Widdop, J.H., & Broadhead, G.D. *The motor performance and physical fitness of educable mentally retarded children.* Madison, Wis.: University of Wisconsin, Department of Physical Education, 1967.

Rosenblith, J.F. Judgments of simple geometric figures by children. *Perceptual and Motor Skills,* 1965, *21,* 947–990.

Sabatino, D.A. Information processing behaviors associated with learning disabilities. *Journal of Learning Disabilities,* 1968, *1*(8), 440–450.

──────────. The construction and assessment of an experimental test of auditory perception. *Exceptional Children,* 1969, *35*(9), 729–737.

Sabatino, D.A., & Mauser, A.J. *Intervention strategies for specialized secondary education.* Boston: Allyn & Bacon, Inc., 1978.

Schenck, W.E. Pictures and the indefinite quantifier in verbal problem solving among EMR children. *American Journal of Mental Deficiency.* 1973, *78,* 272–276.

Sedlak, R.A. Performance of good and poor problem solvers on arithmetic word problems presented in a modified cloze format. *The Journal of Educational Research,* 1974, *67*(10), 467–471.

Semel, E.M. *Semel Auditory Processing Program.* Chicago: Follett Publishing Company, 1970a.

Semel, E.M., & Wiig, E.H. Comprehension of syntactic structures and critical verbal elements by children with learning disabilities. *Journal of Learning Disabilities,* 1975, *8*(1), 53–58.

Shaw, M.C., II, & Cruickshank, W.M. Use of the Bender Gestalt test with epileptic children. *Journal of Clinical Psychology,* 1956, *12,* 192–193.

Siegal, G.M., & Broen, P.A. Language assessment. In L.L. Lloyd (Ed.), *Communication assessment and intervention strategies.* Baltimore: University Park Press, 1976.

Sloane, H.N., & MacAulay, B.D. *Operant procedures in remedial speech and language training.* Boston: Houghton Mifflin Company, 1968.

Snyder, R.J., & Pope, P. New norms for and an item analysis of the Wepman test at the first grade six-year level. *Perceptual and Motor Skills,* 1970, *31,* 1007–1010.

Spache, G. *Diagnostic reading scales.* Monterey, Calif.: California Test Bureau, 1963.

Spencer, E.M. *Investigations of the maturation of various facets of auditory perception in preschool children.* Doctoral dissertation, Northwestern University, 1959.

Stamback, M. Le problème du rhythme dans le développement de l'enfant et dans les dyslexies d'évolution. *Enfance,* 1951, *4,* 480–502.

Stern, C., & Gould, T. *Children discover reading.* Syracuse, N.Y.: L.W. Singer, 1965.

Strauss, A.A., & Kephart, N.C. *Psychopathology and the education of the brain-injured child.* New York: Grune & Stratton, Inc., 1955.

Stremel, K., & Waryas, C. A behavioral-psycholinguistic approach to language training. In L.V. McReynolds (Ed.), *Developing systematic procedures for training children's language.* Danville, Ill.: Interstate Press, 1974. (Asha Monograph 18).

Van Etten, C., & Watson, B. Language assessment: Programs and materials. *Journal of Learning Disabilities,* 1977, *10*(7), 395–402.

Wechsler, D. *Wechsler Intelligence Scale for Children–Revised* (Manual). New York: The Psychological Corporation, 1974.

Weisenburg, T., & McBride, K. *Aphasia.* New York: The Commonwealth Fund, 1935.

Wepman, J.M. *Recovery from aphasia.* New York: Ronald Press, 1951.

Wepman, J.M. Aphasia: Diagnostic description and therapy. *Hearing and Speech News,* 1968a, *36*(1), 3–5.

_____. The modality concept—Including a statement of the perceptual and conceptual levels of learning. In Helen K. Smith (Ed.), *Perception and Reading.* Proceedings of the Twelfth Annual Convention, International Reading Association. Newark, Del.: International Reading Association, 1968b.

Wheller, R.H., & Hooley, A.M. *Physical education for the handicapped.* Philadelphia: Lea & Febiger, 1976.

Wiig, E.H., & Roach, M.A. Immediate recall of semantically varied "sentences" by learning-disabled adolescents. *Perceptual and Motor Skills,* 1975, *40,* 119–125.

Wiig, E.H., & Semel, E.M. Logico-grammatical sentence comprehension by learning disabled adolescents. *Perceptual and Motor Skills,* 1974, *38,* 1331–1334.

_____. *Language disabilities in children and adolescents.* Columbus, Ohio: The Charles E. Merrill Publishing Co., Inc., 1976.

Wiseman, D. A classroom procedure for identifying and remediating language problems. *Mental Retardation,* 1965, *2,* 21.

Chapter 7

Preschool Learning Disabilities

Carl R. Schmidt

INTRODUCTION

Today, special educators have invested heavily in preschool (ages 3–5) education. In fact, a growing national emphasis is on both prenatal and infant (ages 0–3) programs. Preschool programming is an effort to prevent disabilities and/or promote or maximize developmental potential. In the case of learning disabilities, the problem becomes somewhat more difficult at this age because these handicaps commonly are detected by symptoms of academic underachievement, a phenomenon rarely encountered before entering school. Therefore, many preschool educators fail to recognize learning disabilities as a diagnostic entity, speaking instead of high-risk factors or at-risk children.

This chapter begins by looking at the theoretical and historical basis for preschool programs for learning disabled persons and a brief discussion of the peculiar status of their handicaps at that level. Next, trends in identification are presented. A wide variety of philosophical positions exists today among authorities, dictating an equally broad array of programmatic approaches for preschool children who are at risk for school-related learning. The chapter devotes substantial attention to these approaches. Throughout this book, the most critical question the reader should be asking is, "Does the concept (early identification or treatment) work?" Accordingly, this chapter looks at empirical evidence to support early childhood intervention. The chapter closes with a discussion of critical issues related to preschool education for at-risk children. Before embarking upon more general theory, however, it is important to begin with a definition of the characteristics of the children to whom this chapter is dedicated.

HIGH-RISK FACTORS IN PRESCHOOLERS

Children who will need special early intervention to maximize their cognitive and life adjustment potential are considered at risk. Tjossem (1976)

289

refers to three categories of "vulnerability" or levels of risk: established risk, biological risk, and environmental risk. Established risk refers to cases "related to diagnosed medical disorders of known etiology, bearing relatively well known expectancies for developmental outcome" (p. 5). Genetic disorders such as Down's syndrome are included under this category. Biological risk refers to cases in which a history of events during the developmental years (including the prenatal) suggest that a child has suffered "biological insult" such as drug usage by the mother during pregnancy, lead poisoning, disease, etc. Tjossem states that accurate identification of biological sources of developmental delay is particularly difficult. Environmental risk refers to cases in which early life experiences are limiting to the extent that it is likely that developmental delays will result.

It should be noted that these categories are not mutually exclusive and that interactions among the three can increase the probability or degree of developmental delay. This may be especially evident in a situation in which a child evidences an established or biological risk that causes the family or guardians to reject the youngster or to limit their interactions because of lowered expectations.

Despite the problems in defining and planning for preschool learning disabled children, educators must not lose sight of the fact that these children exist and need services. The usual solution to the problem is to avoid categorical labeling until first grade but to provide services under the more general category of at risk or high risk. The term includes a wide range of developmentally disabled children with suspected mental retardation, speech and language deficits, physical and sensory problems, and behavior disorders, as well as potential learning disabilities.

At risk admittedly constitutes a circular definition, but to its credit it has allowed many children to receive needed services that otherwise would have been denied. Paradoxically, the problem of serving at-risk children may become more pronounced as a result of society's increasing ability to provide for premature infants and infants who previously would have died before entering school. Lipsitt (1980) expresses concern that "the very small, very premature babies that are now saved for survival may be in very special jeopardy for nonfatal developmental anomalies such as learning disabilities" (p. 15).

THE CASE FOR EARLY INTERVENTION

Benjamin Bloom (1964) asserts that about 50 percent of any individual's intelligence measured at age 17 has been established by age 4. He continues: "Growth and development are not in equal units per unit of time. For each stable characteristic there is usually a period of relatively rapid growth as well as periods of relatively slow growth" (p. 204).

Bloom is hypothesizing that an individual is most impressionable when experiencing the most rapid developmental growth. Since this period of most rapid developmental growth occurs before the age of 4, that is when the environment, for better or worse, is likely to have its most profound impact. Therefore, one point of view is that if educators wish to have maximum impact on human development with the limited resources available, they should concentrate their efforts on preschool education, especially for children most likely to develop learning problems later.

CRITICAL DEVELOPMENT PERIODS

One of the beliefs that has an impact on the importance of preschool education is that each stage of development may be viewed as a critical period. A critical period refers to a particular developmental time span or time "window" during which a particular skill or ability must be acquired. If the skill—for example, language—is not mastered adequately at this time, it either cannot be acquired at all in later life or it is much more difficult to learn (Bryan & Bryan, 1979). If a problem can be remediated early enough, the snowballing of secondary problems such as poor self-concept or self-fulfilling prophecy can be avoided (Bryan & Bryan).

Kearsley (1980), however, cautions that overzealous identification procedures, in combination with fatalistic attitudes toward prognosis of what may be a temporary developmental lag, can lead to iatrogenic retardation. This condition arises when a child has demonstrated a failure to reach a developmental milestone (usually motor) at the age at which the parent or professional "expected these behaviors would emerge spontaneously" (Kearsley, 1980, p. 174). When the behaviors do fail to appear, inferences of neurological deficits are made, regardless of the fact that when an overly supportive environment is altered, the developmental rate often accelerates to normal.

HISTORY AND LEGAL BASIS

Beller (1973) traces the history of preschool education to the essays of John Locke and Jean-Jacques Rousseau in the 17th and 18th centuries. Locke put forth the notion that children are immature organisms who must be taught the skills and values of adult culture. His directive approach and use of consequent reward and punishment can be seen as an antecedent to the behavioristic thinking of Watson, Thorndike, and Skinner, who believed in classical and operant conditioning procedures, and its adoption by educators of today.

The open classroom school of thought, and discovery learning, have their roots in the writings of Rousseau. He contended that adults should not impose structure and values on children, but rather youngsters should be allowed to investigate their environs and learn through experience. Beller traces Rousseau's impact through Johann Heinrich Pestalozzi, Maria Montessori, and Jean Piaget. It is interesting to note that even today these two positions define the range of philosophical disagreement in preschool education: to what degree should a child, especially one with learning problems, be encouraged to learn through trial and error and to what degree must the teacher provide a structured learning experience? This question becomes particularly relevant in specific program approaches in subsequent pages.

Caldwell (1973) picks up the historic thread in the early 20th century. She identifies three distinct phases in preschool education for handicapped children: forget and hide, screen and segregate, and identify and help. Before 1950 both the preschool and older handicapped were largely ignored. Hence, she calls this period forget and hide. In the 1950s, efforts were made to identify handicapped children, but primarily to segregate them from their peers, or more accurately to remove "the embarrassment" from the teacher of the nonhandicapped. Caldwell sees the post-1950s as an age of relative enlightenment in which society attempts to identify children with an eye toward placement and service for their benefit, not the convenience of the school.

In the late 1950s, the wind shifted. Kirk (1958), working with a preschool mentally retarded population (Binet-Kuhlman IQ of 45–80) in the Midwest, conducted research questioning the effects of early intervention in general and the mutability of IQs in specific. Kirk's population was divided into four groups:

1. Community Experimental (N = 28), preschoolers attending an enriched nursery school environment for six hours per day;
2. Community Contrast (N = 26), children living in the same community but not attending a preschool;
3. Institutional Experimental (N = 15), preschoolers who attended an institutional care program;
4. Institutional Contrast (N = 10), a comparison group of institutionalized children who did not receive such care.

Details on the exact nature of the interventions Kirk used are not available in the literature. Nevertheless, reconstruction of the program from case study descriptions indicates that the Community Experimental group received "individual and small group instruction on cognitive tasks, socialization experiences, total group experiences in music, art, and motor activities, as well as some readiness-type activities" (Rocklage, 1980, p. 12). While Kirk's five-year study may lack contemporary research rigor, the results were timely and had considerable impact on the field (Caldwell, 1970, 1974; Stearns, 1971).

Kirk concluded that the overall effects of the preschool program were positive and that:

> In general, preschool education has some favorable effects in modifying the developmental picture of mentally retarded children, for, on the whole, the preschool experimental groups showed increased rates of growth following educational opportunities at a young age. (Kirk, 1958, p. 205)

Following the publication of Kirk's research, the educational community more readily accepted the concept that IQs could be changed and the public at large became supportive through legislative efforts directed toward the mentally retarded and, later, other handicapped individuals (Rocklage, 1980; Gargiulo, 1980).

In 1965, Head Start was initiated as a summer program designed to interrupt the cycle of environmental deprivation, begetting poor academic readiness, poor academic achievement, limited personal/professional growth options, and parents who provide deprived environments for their children. In retrospect, the expectations of cultural impact for Head Start in its original form were optimistic at best. Happily, the program has expanded considerably in amount of programming, depth of curriculum, and consistency of quality across programs.

From its inception, Head Start has accepted handicapped children into its programs. Before 1973, however, they represented less than 5 percent of its total enrollment. With the passage of the 1972 amendments to the Head Start legislation in Public Law 92-424, the federal government required that a minimum of 10 percent of the total number of children served by the program be handicapped (Klein & Randolph, 1974).

In addition to the Head Start legislation, Congress has appropriated funds through the Handicapped Children's Early Education Projects (HCEEP) starting in 1968. Originally $1 million was expended on 23 projects. By 1978 the appropriation had reached $22 million supporting 215 grants and projects. Congress viewed these funds as seed monies, providing support for up to three years, when it was expected that state and local governments would assume financial responsibility (Maddox, 1978).

Swan (1980) conducted a follow-up study on each of the 23 original projects. Two projects were not funded for the second year and were not included in the study. Of the remaining 21, 18 (89 percent) were operational and funded by two or more other agencies (most commonly local entities in conjunction with state bodies, universities, the United Way, or other grant sources). An additional project was continued but moved across state lines. The majority of the projects actually expanded their services in that time, providing support for the seed money concept.

P. L. 94-142, as passed in 1975, also supports programs for preschool handicapped. It does not mandate preschool services to all handicapped children, as it does for children of school age. It allows for up to 40 percent cost reimbursement for each pupil in the 3-to-5-year-old age range if a state offers such programs. Many special and early childhood educators object strenuously to the fact that handicapped children from birth up to age 3 are denied federal support (Maddox, 1978). As of 1979, only 13 states were mandated to provide full educational programming for handicapped children in the 3–5 age range. Cohen, Semmes, and Guralnick (1979) observe that of these 13, some may not actually be providing service.

Briefly, then, interest in the preschool handicapped has developed from the philosophical treatises of Locke and Rousseau and in the 17th and 18th centuries through periods of relative neglect into the 1960s, when federal support and public interest sparked new life into programs for this age group, both as a subset of culturally disadvantaged children and as a population worthy of attention in its own right.

PRESCHOOL LEARNING DISABILITIES: A CONTRADICTION IN TERMS?

The National Advisory Committee on Handicapped Children (1968) states that learning disabilities are manifested in one or more of the following disorders: "listening, thinking, talking, reading, writing, spelling, or arithmetic" (p. 4). The last four are directly defined by the school experience, and the three others are school related. That is, mild deficits in these areas are likely to go unsuspected and unobserved until the child's relative performance is made obvious by juxtaposition to age peers in a school setting.

The problem doesn't stop there, however. Mercer (1979) enumerates seven problems inherent in identification of preschool learning disabled children. Following is an elaboration on his list:

1. Physicians, the professionals most likely to have an opportunity to identify a learning problem before school enrollment, are reluctant to do so because of the nonmedical nature of the disability. In the absence of a

universal infant educational/developmental screening, physicians come in contact with more preschool children than do any other professionals. Unfortunately, with the exception of a basic psychology course, it is a rare physician or pediatrician who has had any training in education, much less education of the handicapped. Unless a problem is obvious (e.g., a noticeable language delay), is mentioned by a concerned parent, or is related to a known neurological impairment, it is unlikely that a physician will be comfortable extending a diagnosis into the realm of educational problems.

2. Diagnosis of such a problem often is tenuous. "The early warning signals of specific learning disabilities may be very subtle, vary in degree, and occur within a wide range of behaviors" (Mercer, 1979, p. 339). Consider, as an example, an auditory processing dysfunction. The child doesn't realize a problem exists and has never heard anything any other way. A parent who is unaware of a problem is likely to write off the child's inability to follow oral directions as obstinacy, or "a phase he's going through." The problem is more difficult to detect if the child has developed compensatory mechanisms such as operating off visual context cues.

3. The range of normal developmental rates is very broad, making positive identification difficult, and can be affected by a wide variety of factors. Is Jenny late in starting to walk because she has a visual-motor coordination problem, or because she sees little brother carried about and wants that attention too? Momma knows that cousin Harold was late in producing his first sentence. Is baby Alfred following Harold's pattern or does he have an auditory discrimination problem?

4. Because of possible self-fulfilling prophecy effects, professionals often are very hesitant to place a potentially harmful diagnostic label on a preschool child until it can be reliably demonstrated that assignment to such a category has accompanying educational advantages, e.g., valid treatment procedures. The concept of expectancy effect is one of the best documented in the literature (Algozzine, Mercer, & Countermine, 1977; Foster, Schmidt, & Sabatino, 1976). Basically, it says that the very act of labeling children will cause them to behave in a manner consistent with the label, and others as well will treat them as if they were exhibiting the behavior regardless of the actual condition. It is feared that if children are assigned a label so early in life, it may well haunt them for the rest of their educational careers.

5. The prediction studies have been typified by design flaws and ethical constraints. Before it can be said with surety that a child will develop significant learning problems upon entering school, educators must have observed and documented that other children with similar characteris-

tics who have received no services did, in fact, develop such difficulties. If, however, educators noted such characteristics in any child and suspected that a problem might develop, they would be ethically bound to intervene and provide services, but if they intervene, they never can be certain the problems would have developed. Educators are skewered on the horns of the proverbial dilemma.

6. The identification instruments used lack relevance to the classroom teacher in devising instructional objectives. The issue of instruments actually raises two problems: instructional relevance and diagnostic reliability. Tests tend to fall into one of two categories: (1) those used for placement and (2) those used for instructional planning. Placement tests typically are norm referenced and of necessity cover a wide range of ability levels and skill areas. As such they are inappropriate for use in instructional planning. It has been asserted (Nunnally, 1967) that for a test to be used for individual placement decisions, it should have reliability coefficients in excess of .90. For the most part, no test routinely used for diagnosis of learning disabilities even approaches this level of reliability. The problem is further confounded by the fact that tests are more unreliable for younger subjects. For these reasons many preschool programs have gone to criterion referenced measures as a primary diagnostic/monitoring tool (Rocklage, 1980).

7. Diagnoses using historical data (personal history of a child relating to birth trauma, onset of developmental milestones, etc.) often are unavailable or distorted by parents' memories. Developmental checklists are used as supplements to (or occasionally in place of) standardized tests for young children. As noted, however, it is difficult to obtain accurate objective data after the fact. In most cases parents simply do not record developmental milestones (except for "baby's first word," which is written in a baby book and then lost). Further, many parents who already feel guilty about their child's condition may be reluctant to "confess" to events that might have affected their offspring (e.g., drug usage during pregnancy, or a febrile seizure).

In 1973 Keogh and Becker acknowledged many of the problems cited by Mercer (1979). They suggest that:

Effective and early identification is critical and may be accomplished given changes in emphasis and technique. Specification and clarification of the evidence used for identifying problems, as well as broadening the base of identification data, seem promising directions for change. (p. 8)

IDENTIFICATION

At the elementary school level, identification of learning disabled children is facilitated by two factors not present at the preschool level:

1. Since learning disabilities, as previously argued, are defined largely by school-related tasks, the absence of such activities at the preschool level requires that identification rely on other characteristics.

2. Mandatory attendance laws allow children to be compared to their age peers and give educators access to virtually all pupils in a way not possible for preschoolers.

The actual process of identification almost always is broken into two phases: screening and individual diagnosis. In the screening phase, large numbers of children may undergo a relatively gross evaluation to select those in need of the more intense and thorough individual diagnosis. It is at the screening phase that preschool educators are at a disadvantage because of the less "captive" nature of their clientele (see Chapter 2). This poses two major problems at the preschool level: (1) what identification criteria should be established? and (2) what processes might be adopted to ensure identification?

Identification Criteria

In the absence of universal or academically based criteria, it is necessary to turn to characteristics lists. Tarver and Hallahan (1976) list the ten most frequently cited characteristics of learning disabled students and Lovitt (1978) adds an 11th. In Exhibit 7-1, their list appears on the left, a brief definition is in the center column, and common methods of evaluation at the preschool level are on the right.

A behavior checklist is mentioned in several places in the exhibit. To expand on the point, several items adapted from Quinn's (1979) screening checklist follow. While some checklists simply require a yes/no response, others opt for a multiple choice format following a statement (e.g., Always displays behavior, Often, Sometimes, Rarely or Never). As with the Tarver and Hallahan (and Lovitt) lists, not all behaviors or problem areas need to be present for a child to be deemed learning disabled. Quinn recommends as a rule of thumb that if ten or more of the behaviors from her checklist are present, the child should be referred for further testing. In the checklist, she asks, does the child:

- Demonstrate faulty receptive language?

- Use inadequate or immature speech?

Exhibit 7-1 Operationalization of Traits

Trait	Definition	Sample Measurement Approaches
Hyperactivity	continuous motion, the child appears unable to stop moving	behavior checklist
Perceptual motor impairments	inability to coordinate sensory input (i.e., auditory, visual, tactile perception) with (usually) small muscle group expression	copying drawings (e.g., the *Frostig Developmental Test of Visual-Motor Integration*), drawing figures (*Goodenough Draw-A-Person Test*)
Emotional liability	nervous, high strung, easily upset	behavior checklist
General coordination deficits	inability to coordinate large muscle group activities	"Simon says" type activities, throwing, catching, walking balance beam (a formalized measure would be the *Purdue Perceptual Motor Survey*)
Disorders of attention	inability to attend to a task or switch tasks when appropriate	behavior checklist
Impulsivity	overreaction to auditory or visual stimuli	behavior checklist
Disorders of memory	inability to recall information	repeating a sentence or number series, selecting a target picture from a set of pictures after removing the target picture, telling a story about a past event (e.g., "What I saw at the zoo . . .")

Exhibit 7-1 continued

Trait	Definition	Sample Measurement Approaches
Specific learning disabilities	deficit in one or more academic areas	tested by academic readiness tests (if at all) at the preschool level (e.g., *The Jansky Screening Index*)
Disorders of language	inability to understand others or express themselves in a manner appropriate to their age	sentence repetition, verbal analogies (snow is white, grass is ____), grammatic clozure (here is a dog, here are two ____). A common test at this level is the *Illinois Test of Psycholinguistic Abilities*
Equivocal neurological signs	disorders of brain dysfunction, abnormal brainwave patterns	electroencephalogram (EEG); repeating rapid, precise hand movements (e.g., rapidly touching each finger of one hand in order with the thumb of the same hand)
Behavioral disparity	high ability level in some areas, low ability level in others	uneven overall performance across the areas listed above, uneven behavior within a given area (e.g., memory)

Source: Adapted from "Children with Learning Disabilities: An Overview," by S. Tarver and D. P. Hallahan in *Teaching Children with Learning Disabilities: Personal Perspectives,* J. M. Kauffman and D. P. Hallahan (Eds.), and from "Learning Disabilities," by T. C. Lovitt in *Behavior of Exceptional Children: An Introduction to Special Education* (2nd ed.), N. C. Haring (Ed.), both by permission of The Charles E. Merrill Publishing Co., Inc., © 1976 and 1978, respectively.

- Appear to be performing below expectations?
- Forget directions or past events?
- Have faulty size perception?
- Frequently rub the eyes?
- Have poor fine-motor coordination when coloring or drawing?
- Avoid activities that involve eye-hand coordination?
- Seem unusually sensitive to light or noise?
- Act tactually defensive?
- Find it necessary to touch everything in sight?
- Appear to be very afraid of heights?
- Seem to space out occasionally?
- Distract other children?
- Seem to run out of energy easily?
- Have extreme variability in energy levels through the day?
- Lack rhythmic coordination in music?
- Have trouble tying, buttoning, or lacing?
- Have difficulty controlling emotions?
- Bully other children?
- Appear to be an object of bullies?
- Seem to be a loner?
- Seek out older or younger playmates consistently?
- Seem to lack normal caution?
- Seem uncoordinated when running or playing?
- Trip or bump into things frequently?
- Have a high level of distractibility?
- Have directional confusion?
- Have mixed handedness?
- Present a discipline problem?
- Act like the class clown?

- Seem unnecessarily destructive?
- Have low tolerance for frustration?
- Have a short attention span?
- Have a high absentee rate?
- Seem more susceptible to colds than normal?
- Hold pencil or crayon awkwardly?

It must be noted that in completing such a checklist, the key lies in looking at a child's behavior relative to others the same age. For example, it is entirely normal and desirable for very young children to "Find it necessary to touch everything they see." The question should be, "Does the child continue to use a sense of touch to gain information about the environment long after other children of the same age have stopped doing so?"

In an attempt to develop identification criteria for preschool learning disabled children, then, the following has occurred:

1. Starting at the elementary level, learning disabilities have been defined primarily in terms of academic deficits.
2. Concurrent with these academic deficits, however, were several behavioral characteristics, e.g., hyperactivity, coordination problems, social insensitivity, language deficits, and/or perceptual difficulties.
3. Since, by definition, a child cannot be tested for academic achievement before entering school, educators have fallen back on the concurrent characteristics listed in Point 2.

Identification Process

Karnes and Lee (1978) describe four basic approaches to creating a community awareness of preschool high-risk populations (this activity precedes screening):

1. Agency referral: in this, the most common means of referral, children seen by public service agencies often are sent on for screening to other agencies equipped to serve preschool children diagnostically.
2. Media: television, radio, newspaper, fliers, churches, and community bulletin boards are effective means of encouraging parents directly to bring their children to screening centers.
3. School records: upon registration of a child for school, parents are questioned about the existence of younger siblings who might be eligible for screening.

4. Community survey: while a door-to-door survey requires the most staff, it is the most thorough and can be manageable through the enlistment of volunteer organizations.

Once the potential population has been identified, the children must have a screening site. Karnes and Lee (1978) suggest that this site be divided into four stations:

1. Registration: for greeting parents and children and completing forms and name tags
2. Parent interview/sibling play area: for entertaining brothers, sisters, and early arrivals while parents complete behavioral checklists and/or talk with teachers
3. Screening stations: one each for motor, language, and cognitive screening
4. Vision and hearing: acuity testing stations

Screening should be a process that slightly overidentifies children. That is, a higher percentage of children should be identified than are expected to be eligible for services. This is because at this stage, a mistake in the direction of overidentification is neither terribly detrimental to a child nor too expensive for the school district. Missing a child who needs services, however, could have long-lasting effects for one who is in need of service (and could prove costly to the district in prolonged remedial programs).

Formal Screening/Diagnostic Instruments

Formal screening instruments are available, such as the *Developmental Indicators for the Assessment of Learning* (DIAL) (Mardell & Goldenberg, 1975). This instrument was designed for children aged 2½–5½. The DIAL has six subtests:

1. Sensory: this measures visual and auditory acuity.
2. Motor: this is composed of two subtests:
   a. Gross motor: the child is asked to walk a balance beam, throw and catch a beanbag, jump, hop, skip, stand still, and identify body parts.
   b. Fine motor: the child is asked to match designs, stack blocks, use scissors, copy figures and letters, demonstrate finger dexterity, and duplicate a handclap pattern (really an auditory sequence task as well).
3. Affective: ⎫
                ⎬ both affective and social are evaluated through the ob-
4. Social: ⎭ servational checklist.

5. Language: this is tested by word repetition, digit span, description of pictures, and answers to questions.

Lerner (1976) lists six preschool handicapped screening instruments in addition to DIAL but of a similar variety.

Following screening, a more in-depth diagnosis is needed before a decision can be made regarding placement. Although a professional diagnosis certainly cannot rely solely on numbers derived from formal (standardized) published tests, a sample test battery provides guidelines for the types of information of interest and includes national age norms and possibly local, ethnic, or sex norms. Haring and Ridgeway (1967) used eight diagnostic tests following their screening battery:

1. *The Illinois Test of Psycholinguistic Ability (ITPA):* tests visual and auditory reception, association, memory and sequencing, and vocal and motor expression.
2. *The Detroit Tests of Learning Aptitude:* (only 4 of 19 subtests were used) involves pictorial opposites, visual attention span for objects, auditory attention span for unrelated words, and auditory attention span for related syllables. These subtests were chosen as being complementary to the ITPA.
3. *PISCI Auditory Discrimination Evaluation:*
4. *The Wide Range Achievement Test (WRAT):* has items that are listed as "pre-K," but strictly speaking it is more appropriate for older children.
5. *Developmental Test of Visual Motor Integrative:* involves copying line drawings.
6. *Purdue Perceptual Motor Survey:* measures large muscle group coordination, balance, and ocular control.
7. Test of Left-Right Discrimination assesses child's ability to discriminate between right and left.
8. Physical Measurements: include motor strength, muscle tone, range of movement, shape and size of head, tactual and kinesthetic sensory discrimination, postural reflexes, x-ray of hand and wrist bones (a measure of physical maturity), weight and height.

These identification components, while representative, cannot be considered universal. In a statewide survey of Illinois preschool screening programs, van Duyne, Gargiulo, and Allen (1980) found that 77 percent of the agencies responding (74 percent of those surveyed) used standardized screening instruments similar to the DIAL, while 23 percent relied on locally developed instruments. Following screening, 89 percent of the responding agencies reported using intelligence measures, 69 percent developmental scales, and 29 percent tests of specific abilities and language/articulation for diagnostic and placement purposes. As can be seen, even within one state, extreme variability of procedure exists.

If a variety of procedures are employed, which one is most effective in predicting learning problems? Mercer, Algozzine, and Trifiletti (1979) reviewed the literature on validity of early identification procedures. Limiting their analyses to those studies for which it was possible to construct a prediction-performance comparison matrix, they reported:

	Accuracy Rate Range	Accuracy Rate Median
Single Instruments	46–86	75
Battery of Tests	59–92	79
Teacher Perception	70–90	80

Accuracy rate is calculated on the percentage of children identified correctly through current diagnosis as learning disabled who later are classified in the same category (true or valid positives). False positives are children identified as learning disabled who later are classified as nonhandicapped. Similarly, true negatives are children who are classified as nonhandicapped and are so identified, and false negatives are learning disabled children who have been missed by the screening process. The conclusions by Mercer, Algozzine, and Trifiletti include: teacher perceptions appear to be useful and efficient evaluations of school problems; testing in the spring of kindergarten seems to produce the most predictive indexes; socioeconomic status (SES), physical indexes, and developmental histories measured during infancy seem to be strong preschool predictive measures. The distribution of false negative vs. false positive vs. valid positive vs. valid negative varies considerably, depending on the method of analysis.

It is entirely possible that preschool identification of learning disabled children falls into the same category as the flight of bumble bees: the more carefully the topic is studied, the more obvious it becomes that it simply cannot be done. Nevertheless, bees do fly and, to the best of educators' abilities, children with potential learning problems are identified and served. In the words of Cecil Reynolds (1979):

> Early childhood assessment is not only necessary for identifying children at risk for later learning/behavior problems so that they may receive the benefits of preventive experiences, but also to demonstrate measurable gains of the specific intervention program. (p. 178).

The discussion now turns to those specific intervention programs.

RANGE OF PROGRAMS

Preschool programs for high-risk children in general and learning disabled children in specific vary radically in philosophy and structure. Before looking at several programs in detail, some general dimensions are discussed.

Beller (1973) divides programs into two age-sensitive headings, infant (under 3 years of age) and early childhood, which in turn are broken down further. Infant programs include child-oriented, mother-oriented, and group programs.

The child-oriented programs Beller identified are typified by having a tutor go into the child's home for several hours each week to provide language stimulation and preacademic play activities. General findings indicate gains for the infants receiving training, some evidence to support the notion that control group infants declined in language/cognitive skills, and a high correlation between progress and maternal attitude.

The parent-oriented programs involved the tutor's going into the home of a high-risk infant and providing the parents (usually the mothers) with suggestions, and occasionally planned activities, for interacting with the child. The guiding philosophy of these programs is that if a tutor spends an hour each week with an infant, the infant receives one hour of training a week; if an hour each week with a parent, the child receives a solid week of enriched environment. Again, the infants in the experimental groups exceeded those in the control groups.

The group programs for children under 3 brought infants as young as 6 months old to a center for an hour or more each day. The results of these studies indicated that slight developmental gains could be expected from the experimental group, and that no problems in infant-mother attachment were experienced. The latter finding was especially crucial to the public acceptance of preschool programs in light of the findings of physical and mental retardation of infants in orphanages in the 1940s and 50s. Beller concludes his section on infant programs with a call for more detailed and specific measurement of subtle interprogram effects.

Beller (1973) divides early childhood programs into three types: Montessori, educational development, and academic preschool. The first is based on the writings of Dr. Maria Montessori, who in the early 1900s developed teacher education and direct instructional programs for the feeble-minded in Rome (Orem, 1969). The basic principle of the approach is that education must be synonymous with liberty. Free activity is balanced by order and control stemming from the environmental organization, not the teacher's dictates. Her program includes special materials and activities to foster growth in physical, perceptual, motor, intellectual, language, motivation, behavior (social/emotional), and personal areas. Beller questions whether differing interpretations of that approach make comparisons between

Montessori and other programs difficult. He adds that of the comparison studies made, Montessori children tended to be more perceptually oriented and seemed to treat preschool more as "serious business" than did children attending a variety of other preschools.

The educational development center programs are based on the British Infant Schools. The philosophy there is that each child should be allowed to freely explore the enriched environment that is the preschool classroom, and that the role of the teacher is to move in to offer guidance at the "teachable moment." Specific content or materials are not stressed as much as the learning process. This approach also goes by the name "child centered." Beller says that research seems to favor this approach in the areas of creativity, memory, and concentration, but it is inferior to more structured programs in academic readiness.

The last subcategory Beller mentions is the academic preschool originated by Bereiter and Englemann (1966). This is an extremely structured program originally designed as a crash program in language concept and academic remediation. Small group instruction is used and the teacher follows a carefully prepared script. The DISTAR series is a product of this approach. Beller reports mixed results with this program but others (see Karnes and Teska later in this chapter) are more unequivocal in their support.

SOME SPECIFIC PROGRAMS

Perhaps the best way to get a genuine feel for preschool programming for learning disabled children is to look at several activities in detail. Following this, the chapter closes with a discussion of cross-programmatic evaluations.

MECCA

Project MECCA (Make Every Child Capable of Achieving) funded under Title VI G, Public Law 91-230 (1970), is designed to develop early identification and prescriptive education programs for children entering kindergarten with potential learning problems (Rothenberg, 1977). The components of the program are:

- developing screening and diagnostic procedures
- evaluating a multidisciplinary approach to diagnosis and a task analysis approach to early intervention in specific learning disabilities
- parent involvement
- inservice training

- working with advisory consultants from professional groups in Connecticut

- methods, materials and research results dissemination

- replication

- evaluation (p. 10)

The project was initiated in two pilot school kindergartens in Trumbull, a suburb of Bridgeport, Connecticut, in 1973. Children were screened upon registration for kindergarten with the following instruments: *Goodenough Draw-A-Person Test,* as a springboard to elicit a language sample; the *Jansky Screening Index,* designed to predict success in reading; and a sensory vision test. A speech and language clinician rated the speech sample and a psychologist the Goodenough and the Jansky. If a pupil was deemed high risk on any of the measures, parents were offered the option of having their child reexamined and/or entering the MECCA program. School social workers were seen as vital agents in establishing initial contact with parents and generating support for the program as well as gathering information about the home that might have an impact on school performance.

The multidisciplinary team evaluated and synthesized information and created an Individualized Education Plan for the year. Members of the team included the kindergarten teacher, school principal, psychologist, social worker, school nurse, parents, a pupil services administrator, and other specialists as needed.

MECCA's orientation is toward individualized instruction, basic academic readiness skills, recognition of home-school interdependence, and continuous evaluation of each child's progress, with revision when necessary. Learning activities are painstakingly task analyzed, highly structured, and intended to be transferred to academic work, even though many of the tasks appear to be primarily perceptual or perceptual motor in nature.

AECSEP

The *Austin Early Childhood Special Education Program* (AECSEP) is a center-based project for children ages 3–5 identified as physically handicapped (including sensory impairments), mentally retarded, learning disabled, speech or language impaired, or multihandicapped (Austin, Texas, Independent School District, 1976).

Program implementation involves five steps: referral, screening, program definition, program implementation, and program evaluation. Screening includes formal and informal observation in a variety of contexts. Initial program placement is considered a diagnostic step, during which an in-depth evaluation takes place. If formal enrollment is deemed appropriate, placement is made into one of seven classes located in a single building. Placement is based on social maturity, and class size ranges from eight for the least mature, with three teachers and aides, to 20 with four teachers and aides for the most mature.

Classroom schedules include time blocks for large group activites including such elements as story time, music activities, gross and fine motor activities, games, and playtime. Individual and small group activities also are programmed into the schedules.

The program employs a speech therapist, an occupational therapist, a physical therapist, and a parent coordinator. Parent involvement takes the form of coordinated home visits, conferences, newsletters, meetings, a parent library, and counseling in parenting skills. A community coordinator and helping teachers (teacher consultants) also are employed.

AECSEP conducted its own follow-up evaluation of 37 project "graduates," looking at each child's communication skills, social behavior, motor skills, attention, and academic ability. The data suggest that as a result of the programming, the majority of the children were successfully integrated into the Austin public school system.

The Milwaukee Project

Garber and Heber's (1977) basic postulate is that children of mothers with low IQs (under 80) are born as bright as other children but their intellect becomes dulled by constant exposure to a nonstimulating environment. Hence, they take the position that it is the environment, not the child, that is at risk. They selected 40 high-risk families and randomly assigned 20 to an experimental group and 20 to a control group.

Intervention consisted of a maternal rehabilitation program and an infant stimulation program. The former consisted of academic, vocational, and home economics training in classroom settings. Garber and Heber report more success with the vocational aspects than with the homemaking skills.

The infant stimulation program consisted of assigning each infant to a paraprofessional teacher who went to the home to establish rapport as soon as the child was 6 months old. As soon as possible, both child and teacher moved to the Milwaukee Project Center for the instructional day. At approximately 12 months, the child was paired with other teachers and children for "academic" learning. By 24 months, most were in a group with two other children and one teacher. Before 24 months, each child's schedule was established on an individual basis. By about 24 months, the following schedule was in effect:

8:45	Arrival
9:00–9:30	Breakfast

9:30–10:00	First structured learning period
10:00–10:30	Second structured learning period
10:30–11:00	Self-directed activites/free play
11:00–11:30	Third structured learning period
11:30–12:00	Sesame Street
12:00–12:30	Lunch
12:30–1:45	Nap
1:45–2:00	Snack
2:00–2:30	Fourth structured learning period
2:30–3:00	Fifth structured learning period
3:00–3:30	Sixth structured learning period
3:30–4:00	Motor period
4:00	Departure

The morning instruction periods were designed to allow all children to interact with standard equipment and materials in their own way. Afternoon activites centered on the Peabody Language Development Kit.

Garber and Heber (1977) report that upon measuring the experimental and control groups at 54 months of age on the *Illinois Test of Psycholinguistic Ability* (ITPA), the experimental segment achieved a mean score of 45 months. On measures of mother-child interaction, the experimental group children's increased verbal fluency seemed to produce much more constructive parent-child communication. Intelligence was measured by several commonly administered cognitive (intelligence) tests. At the onset of the program, IQs for experimental and control groups were essentially the same. At 24 months, a discrepancy of 23 IQ points favoring the experimental group was evidenced. By 66 months, the discrepancy between the means was more than 30 points (mean of experimental group = 125, mean of control group = 91).

Garber and Heber* followed up the groups in 1977 and found that at least through the age of 5½, the children's IQs and academics either were maintained at a normal level or increased, while the scores of a comparison group (who received the same testing program) sank to levels expected of the neighborhood (borderline subnormal).

Garber (1979) drives the ecology point home again in a later article:

The school psychologist should include in his/her evaluation of the child assessments of the intactness of the family and the quality of the home environment, the attitude of the mother to her children and the value of schooling imparted to the child. (p. 308)

---

*The Garber and Heber studies were longitudinal works with preschool high risk (developmentally disabled) children from inner-city Milwaukee that spanned several years.

CROSS-PROGRAMMATIC EVALUATION

Karnes (1973), in a report summarizing several early childhood studies, outlines an analysis of preschool program success based on the dimension of structure. The study involves a pretest on the Stanford-Binet and the ITPA at age 4 (approximately), a posttest one school year later, and a California Achievement Test, Total Reading Grade Placement Score, toward the end of third grade. Five intervention programs were examined:

1. The traditional nursery school program was the least structured, allowing the child to freely explore the environment while teachers capitalized on informal opportunities to teach.
2. The community integrated program was similarly unstructured but was more balanced on race and SES to provide "good peer language models" for the lower SES handicapped students.
3. The Montessori program, directed by the Montessori Society, was more structured than Models 1 or 2, relying heavily on the students' interaction with directive Montessori materials.
4. The Karnes program was more structured than the Montessori, with activities based on an ITPA model curriculum and including directed play, art, music, study, and snack periods.
5. The most structured program was the Bereiter-Englemann, which featured intensive drill in language, arithmetic, and reading (the initial teaching alphabet).

The first year posttest found that the Karnes program demonstrated the highest scores on the Stanford-Binet and the ITPA, and that both the Karnes and the Bereiter-Englemann were significantly higher than the three other models on these measures. It should be noted, however, that the Karnes program was built around the ITPA model. The third grade reading posttest found the Karnes program on top once again. The report states that the Karnes group was "significantly" superior to the Bereiter-Englemann and to the traditional approach (the only comparison groups available at the time). It is not clear, however, whether the word "significantly" is used in a statistical sense and, if so, at what level.

Combining her own findings with those of several other researchers, Karnes concludes that successful programs are characterized by:

1. a carefully defined approach for teaching young children with a strong theoretical orientation
2. a mode of operation which includes daily allotments of time for continuous inservice training, curriculum development,

daily planning and critiquing of instruction, a high adult-child ratio (one-to-five), and supervision
3. a curriculum for the children which attends to individual needs and fosters the development of (a) cognitive language (b) motivation to learn (c) self-concept (d) social skills (e) motor skills and (f) information processing (p. 59)

Perhaps the most comprehensive attempt to discover the effects of various types of preschool projects is a continuing evaluation of the "graduates" of 11 preschool projects by the Consortium for Longitudinal Studies. The programs have the following in common: (1) they were initiated and completed by 1969; (2) original samples ranged from a N of 92 − 7,895, median 209; (3) subjects were primarily low SES and black; (4) certain research design requirements were met; (5) subjects were followed after the programs; and (6) treatment was explicitly described and standard.

The projects were located in the Eastern and Midwest United States and in urban settings for the most part. Program duration ran from one to four years. Six of the programs were center based, two were home based, and three were hybrids. Some were of a traditional orientation, others were highly academic and structured (Lazar & Darlington, 1978). In their most recent report, Lazar and Darlington (1979) cite robust findings from this large data base:

1. Early intervention programs significantly reduced the number of children assigned to special classes regardless of sex, IQ initially and again at age 6, ethnic background, and family background.
2. Early intervention significantly reduced the number of children retained in grade, again regardless of sex, ethnic background, IQ, or home background.
3. Early intervention significantly increased children's scores on at least fourth grade math achievement, with indications that fourth grade reading might be positively affected as well.
4. Early intervention increased IQ test scores up to age 13, when the differences with the control group become statistically nonsignificant.
5. Early intervention increased mothers' vocational expectations for their children, who were more achievement oriented.
6. The Consortium was unable to discover any program variables either singly or in combination that distinguished a program's capability to prevent special education placement.

Summary

At any given moment in time, in some smoky teachers' lounge in some corner of the globe, the following words are being spoken: "Poor Alexander! If only his learning problem had been caught earlier, it wouldn't have snow-balled into its current appalling dimensions." The name changes, the language changes, even the grade changes, but the lament remains the same. Each of Alexander's teachers, whether they be for eleventh grade or second grade, secretly believes that if someone else earlier in his educational career had done the job properly the poor boy would not be in his current state of disrepair. It is hoped that by taking action at the preschool level, the buck will not have to be passed on. It would be naive to assume that early intervention will solve all of the problems in learning disabilities. The point may never be reached where there will be no "poor Alexanders" who got lost in the shuffle, but through systematic programming and research the gap between "what is" and "what should be" can be lessened.

The case for early intervention still stands and is being validated by projects such as the Consortium for Longitudinal Studies. The single most positive conclusion that can be drawn from this group's massive data base is that early childhood programs for children with learning problems *do* work, and the programs can take a wide variety of forms. Karnes and Teska (1975) have concluded further that, in general, earlier is better. As the field progresses, the sophistication of the measurement process must advance to the point where the system can be fine tuned. For that to happen, the problems must be outlined, as Mercer (1979) has done, and should act as guideposts in research.

The problem of identification is solvable. Workable systems are in place, even if arguments rage concerning why they work. Again, as the "whys" are sorted out, the instructional processes will become fine tuned. It is possible that the definition of learning disabilities in the year 2020 will be devoid of academic dependence. If that is the case, that definition may well emanate from the preschool arena, where academic deficit is not as convenient a construct on which to rely.

REFERENCES

Algozzine, B., Mercer, C.D., & Countermine, T. The effects of labels and behavior on teacher expectations. *Exceptional Children,* 1977, *44,* 131–132.

An overview (Austin Early Childhood Special Education Program). Austin, Texas, Austin Independent School District, 1976. (ERIC Document Reproduction Service No. ED 144 274).

Beller, E.K. Research on organized programs of early identification. In R. Travers (Ed.), *Second handbook of research on teaching.* Chicago: Rand McNally & Co., 1973.

Bereiter, C., & Englemann, S. *Teaching disadvantaged children in the preschool.* Englewood Cliffs, N.J.: Prentice-Hall, Inc., 1966.

Bloom, B. *Stability and change in human characteristics.* New York: John Wiley & Sons, Inc., 1964.

Bryan, J., & Bryan, T. *Exceptional children*. Sherman Oaks, Calif.: Alfred Publishing Co., Inc., 1979.

Caldwell, B.M. The rationale for early intervention. *Exceptional Children*, 1970, *36*(10), 717–727.

——————. The importance of beginning early. In J. Jordan & R. Dailey (Eds.), *Not all little wagons are red*. Arlington, Va.: The Council for Exceptional Children, 1973.

——————. A decade of early intervention programs: What we have learned. *American Journal of Orthopsychiatry*, 1974, *44*, 491–496.

Cohen, S., Semmes, M., & Guralnick, M.J. Public Law 94–142 and the education of preschool handicapped children. *Exceptional Children*, 1979, *45*(4), 279–286.

Foster, G., Schmidt, C., & Sabatino, D. Teacher expectancies and the label "learning disabilities." *Journal of Learning Disabilities*, 1976, *9*(2), 58–61.

Garber, H. Bridging the gap from preschool to school for the disadvantaged child. *School Psychology Digest*, 1979, *8*(3), 303–310.

Garber, H., & Heber, R. The Milwaukee project: Early intervention as a technique to prevent mental retardation. In E. M. Heatherington & R. Parke (Eds.), *Contemporary readings in child psychology*. New York: McGraw-Hill Book Company, 1977.

Gargiulo, R.M. Litigation and legislation for exceptional children: An historic perspective. *ICEC [International Council for Exceptional Children] Quarterly*, Winter 1980, *29*, 1–24.

Haring, N.C., & Ridgeway, R. Early identification of children with learning disabilities. *Exceptional Children*, 1967, *33*(6), 387–395.

Karnes, M. Implications of research with disadvantaged children for early intervention with the handicapped. In J. Jordan & R. Dailey (Eds.), *Not all little wagons are red*. Arlington, Va.: The Council for Exceptional Children, 1973.

Karnes, M., & Lee, R. *Early childhood*. Reston, Va.: The Council for Exceptional Children, 1978.

Karnes, M., & Teska, J. Children's responses to intervention programs. In J. Gallagher (Ed.), *The application of child development research to exceptional children*. Reston, Va.: The Council for Exceptional Children, 1975.

Kearsley, R. Iatrogenic retardation: A syndrome of learned incompetence. In R. Kearsley & I. Sigel (Eds.), *Infants at risk*. Hillsdale, N.J.: Lawrence Erlbaum Associates, Publishers, 1980.

Keogh, B., & Becker, L. Early detection of learning problems: Questions, cautions, and guidelines. *Exceptional Children*, 1973, *40*(1), 5–11.

Kirk, S. *Early education of the mentally retarded*. Urbana, Ill.: University of Illinois Press, 1958.

Klein, J., & Randolph L. Placing handicapped children in Head Start programs. *Children Today*, 1974, *6*(3), 7–10, 36.

Lazar, I., & Darlington, R. *Lasting effects after preschool* (Department of Health, Education, and Welfare Publication No. [OHDS] 79-30178). Washington, D.C.: U.S. Government Printing Office, October 1978.

Lazar, I., & Darlington, R. *Summary report: Lasting effects after preschool* (Department of Health, Education, and Welfare Publication No. [OHDS] 79-30179). Washington, D.C.: U.S. Government Printing Office, September 1979.

Lerner, J. *Children with learning disabilities* (2nd ed.). Boston: Houghton Mifflin Company, 1976.

Lipsitt, L. The newborn as informant. In R. Kearsley & I. Sigel (Eds.), *Infants at risk*. Hillsdale, N.J.: Lawrence Erlbaum Associates, Publishers, 1980.

Lovitt, T.C. Learning disabilities. In N. C. Haring (Ed.), *Behavior of exceptional children: An introduction to special education* (2nd ed.). Columbus, Ohio: The Charles E. Merrill Publishing Co., Inc., 1978.

Maddox, M. Legislative trends concerning early childhood education for the handicapped. In *Report of 1978 Early Childhood Training Seminar*. Springfield, Ill.: State Board of Education, Illinois Office of Education, June 1978.

Mardell, C., & Goldenberg, D. For prekindergarten screening: DIAL. *Journal of Learning Disabilities,* 1975, *8*(3), 140–147.

Mercer, C. *Children and adolescents with learning disabilities*. Columbus, Ohio: The Charles E. Merrill Publishing Co., Inc., 1979.

Mercer, C., Algozzine, B., & Trifiletti, J. Early identification: Issues and considerations. *Exceptional Children,* 1979, *46*(1), 52–54.

National Advisory Committee on Handicapped Children. *Special education for handicapped children,* First Annual Report. Washington, D.C.: U.S. Department of Health, Education, and Welfare, January 31, 1968.

Nunnally, J. *Psychometric theory*. New York: McGraw-Hill Book Company, 1967.

Orem, R. Condensed history of the origins and development of the Montessori method. In R. Orem (Ed.), *Montessori and the special child*. New York: G. P. Putnam's Sons, 1969.

Quinn, J. Learning disabilities can be prevented. *Instructor,* 1979, *89*(2), 196–197, 200.

Reynolds, C. Should we screen preschoolers? *Contemporary Educational Psychology,* 1979, *4,* 175–181.

Rocklage, L. *Strategies for facilitating the transition of handicapped students from the preschool handicapped classroom program to the regular kindergarten classroom setting.* Unpublished doctoral dissertation, Southern Illinois University at Carbondale, 1980.

Rothenberg, J.J. *A learning adventure: Programs developed for early intervention in potential learning problems* (2nd ed.). Hartford: Connecticut State Department of Education, 1977. (Eric Document Reproduction Service No. ED 152 005/EC 103 996).

Stearns, M.S. *Report on preschool programs: The effects of preschool programs on disadvantaged children and their families.* Washington, D.C.: U.S. Department of Health, Education and Welfare, Office of Child Development, 1971.

Swan, W. The handicapped children's early education program. *Exceptional Children,* 1980, *47*(1), 12–16.

Tarver, S., & Hallahan, D.P. Children with learning disabilities: An overview. In J. M. Kauffman & D. P. Hallahan (Eds.), *Teaching children with learning disabilities: Personal perspectives*. Columbus, Ohio: The Charles E. Merrill Publishing Co., Inc., 1976.

Tjossem, T.D. (Ed.). *Intervention strategies for high risk infants and young children*. Baltimore: University Park Press, 1976.

van Duyne, H.J., Gargiulo, R., & Allen, J. A survey of Illinois preschool screening programs. *Illinois Council for Exceptional Children Quarterly,* 1980, *29*(2), 11–16.

Chapter 8

Elementary and Middle School Service and Program Delivery

David A. Sabatino

INTRODUCTION

Historically, programs for learning disabled children grew from work with brain injured (neurologically impaired) and educable mentally retarded children. Alfred Strauss, a psychologist-educator and director of the Cove School for the Brain Injured, a private school that provided significant leadership for perceptually and language impaired brain-damaged children, must be recognized as the modern pioneer of learning disabilities. The leadership and pioneering efforts of the Cove School and the ingenious teaching strategies of persons who worked and studied there are legend. Noted persons such as Laura Lehtinen, Newell Kephart, Samuel Kirk, Raymond Barsch, Heinz Werner, William Cruickshank, and Helmer Myklebust are but a very few who came under the influence of this robust climate for change in psychoeducational thinking.

What was the influence that changed the thinking of an entire field? In a nutshell, before World War II, special education represented teaching those with obvious sensory impairments—visual and auditory—and the mentally retarded. In the years following the war, it became apparent that many children at the upper intelligence limits of the mild mentally retarded range were performing poorly on intelligence tests because of perceptual-language impairments. As a result, special education classes expanded quickly in number to accommodate these students. This phenomenon and the fact that the Veterans Administration had obtained noteworthy success during the war years in returning veterans with severe head wounds to useful lives had an impact on educators.

Note: Graphic and written descriptions of Resource Room Floorplans are provided by Pamela Miller, doctoral student, Southern Illinois University at Carbondale, Department of Special Education.

Educators were aware that there had been a group of children who were too active, too lethargic, or overly distractable and as a result could not maintain attention, and often demonstrated perceptual memory or perceptual discrimination information processing deficits. For years the schools had referred to that population as mentally retarded, emotionally disturbed, lazy, indifferent, academic underachievers, and a whole host of other labels. In fact, these children were hyperactive and restless, but they also were often intellectually bright, seemingly able to learn, but failing to achieve academically.

It is not surprising that a population of bright youngsters who performed poorly presented a professional threat to an educational system that did not understand them, and, as a result, could not help them achieve socially or academically. The public schools attempted to cope with this perceived threat by amplifying the differences these children represented. Labels became a necessary defense mechanism.

The Role of Therapy

Therapy, including educational habilitation, had been successful for teaching academic skills to brain-injured children who were normal in intelligence. The teaching of socialization skills also had proved effective with mentally retarded and normal (intelligence) children known to have brain damage. Strauss and Lehtinen (1947) differentiated children who were familial mentally retarded from those with known brain damage.

The intent of that diagnostic differentiation was associated with the type of educational intervention to be offered. One group was more passive, less hyperactive, not as distractable, and learned social skills much more readily. That population was known to be endogenous, or familial retarded (genetic, or intercellular). The second group was thought to be brain damaged from prenatal, natal, or postnatal accident to the nervous system, or exogenous—damage from outside the cells (neurons) that comprise the brain.

Meanwhile, the diagnostic work leading to placement decisions began to indicate that the two-box model (Reynolds, 1962) that had been operating in special education was not adequate. The principal boxes in the two-box model were: (a) regular classes and (b) self-contained special classes. Efficacy research on self-contained special classes in the mid 1950s to early 1960s (Johnson, 1962; Cassidy & Stanton, 1959; Elenbogen, 1957; Bennett, 1963) generally declared the academic learning of the mentally retarded children placed in self-contained classes to be inferior to matched groups of similar students remaining in regular classes. Conversely, some evidence indicated that social skill development was higher and better for the children in special classes (Cassidy & Stanton, 1959).

There simply wasn't any differentiation of special education services for the various diagnostic categories of handicapped children even as late as the early 1960s. The so-called "efficacy studies" of special classes represented research characterized by serious design flaws. So serious were they that interpretations resulting in statements that one approach to service delivery (self-contained vs. regular class placement) was indeed better than another were at best generalizations.

The truth was that the children in special classes generally had greater behavioral problems and more academic and social deficiencies to begin with than those in regular classes. The real finding was that so-called educable mentally retarded classes were filled with mildly handicapped children with learning disabilities and behavioral disorders. Why?

Work continued in the sorting of children into even greater numbers of diagnostic categories, aided now by the influence of a newly formed parent lobby. In 1962, the Association of Children with Perceptual Disorders, a parent advocate group, was formed on the North Side of Chicago. In 1963, the group became the Association for Children with Learning Disorders. The term "learning disorders" was coined by Sam Kirk. It was adopted by that group of parents and nationally as well. Initially, the parent lobby exerted pressure on state legislative bodies and state departments of special education to develop and fund programs for brain-injured children and, later, those with learning disabilities. They continued these activities until 1969, when the Learning Disabilities Act became a fundable handicapping category under Public Law 91–320.

Civil Rights Involvement

By the late 1960s, support for expanding the two-box model of service and program delivery had become a side issue in the civil rights movement of that era. There was growing national awareness (*Hobson v. Hansen,* 1967) that a large percentage of the children in educable mentally retarded self-contained classes were black. So much so, in fact, that Judge J. Skelly Wright decided to close all (nearly 500) special education classes in Washington, D.C., in 1968.

Research (Zito & Bardon, 1969) had indicated that black retarded students were doing poorly academically in special education self-contained classes. The challenge taken to court was that the traditional practice of testing a child and placing that pupil into a special class was influenced by social, cultural, linguistic, ethnic, and racial variables. Employing a school psychologist as the "gatekeeper" to an educational warehouse known as special education suddenly appeared to be a very bad instructional practice.

As such, it came under harsh criticism, with the courts entering the picture to guarantee a school day in the least restrictive environment. (*Pennsylvania Association for Retarded Children v. Kurtzman,* 1971).

Many of the offshoots from entry by the courts and the increase in litigation followed by legislation were made apparent in P.L. 94-142, the Education for All Handicapped Children Act of 1975. The procedural placement safeguards all were learned through trial and error. They included parental involvement, the interdisciplinary committee approach to placement of the handicapped, and a written educational plan that must reflect each child's programmatic needs. There was no road map for special education. Plans and the future were in response to troubled practices, not a grand design. Special education and programs for children with learning disorders were reactive measures to parents, the times, the courts, legislation, and the obvious unmet needs of the handicapped. Learning disorders were considered to be just another health impairment before P.L. 94-142; afterward, they became a diagnostic entity in their own right with a prevalence rate of 2 percent of all children.

It became obvious that a continuum of programs and services was necessary if the diverse characteristics of all handicapped children were to be met under the guidelines of P.L. 94-142. In response to both social pressures gleaned from the civil rights movement, and educational pressures derived from the courts, resource rooms and special education teacher consultants began to appear as steps in the continuum of programs and services between the traditional self-contained regular classes and the special classes. In short, the two-box model gave way to a series of placement alternatives, a major change in pre-1960s thinking having emerged in mid-decade. Until the middle 1960s, the special education program had been equated with the number of handicapped children in separated special classes. After the middle of the decade, the emphasis shifted to defining the most appropriate practice as a program that entailed placing handicapped children in the least restrictive environment. While not an identical term, the word that caught on was mainstreaming, which became synonymous with maintaining handicapped children in the regular class. The practice believed to be "best" was to place the handicapped children in a regular class and provide them with supportive services.

Supportive services included school psychology, speech and hearing therapy, resource teaching programs, instructional advisement, special education teacher consultants, occupational and physical therapy, remedial programming, adaptive physical education, and vocational programming for special populations. In short, supportive services consisted of everything that was not programs, such as a classroom, but was provided directly to the handicapped school age child.

The idea was that the children could avoid an adjustment into and out of special class if they never were placed there at all. Further, it was reasoned that no one teacher, in a self-contained class, could administer to all the needs of all the handicapped students in a program. Thus, programs were viewed as the means by which instruction was delivered, i.e., self-contained classes for this or that handicapped group. On the other hand, support services were the additional assistance of the helping professions—psychology, as well as speech, occupational, and physical therapy, etc.—in addition to, rather than as a replacement for, the special educator. Interdisciplinary treatment, a theme heralded by many for 20 years (Scranton, Hajicek, & Wolcott, 1978) finally had been implemented in a few of the more aggressive school systems.

This chapter reviews types of programs and services, beginning with a brief definition and description of the resource room and special education teacher consultant. The subsequent sections examine more fully the content of resource rooms as well as strategies used by special education teacher consultants. The emphasis, however, is on systematic structures, not specific instructional approaches. The philosophy represented here is that an array of program delivery capabilities is needed to fit the unique learning style of each handicapped child as contrasted with *shaping the handicapped child to fit an arbitrary program with an undefined set of dimensions.*

In addition, a strong argument is made against developing or delivering special education programs for learning disabled children that depend upon only one discipline. Instructionally, special education is only the base program. The author knows of no learning disabled child who does not also need support services from at least one other discipline. So the argument here advances a rationale for combating the complexities of conditions that handicap human behavior across a wide spectrum of functions as a multidisciplinary effort.

LEARNING DISABILITIES PROGRAMS

The diversity of needs of learning disabled students must be met by an equally variegated set of program options and elements. The continuum of services should include, at minimum, a self-contained class for those with the most pervasive difficulties, a resource room for those with moderate learning problems, and a consultant teacher model for those who have the mildest disorders and/or are in the process of reintegration into regular classes. The assessment class is a seldom used option in most school systems but is worth describing because it provides a valuable transition phase for those requiring an intensive holistic diagnosis before program placement is finalized.

A special education materials library is an essential element of any program. It should be accessible to learning disabilities specialists as well as regular class teachers through the consultant.

Depending on the size of the special education district, a learning disabilities supervisor may be required to coordinate program elements. As is described later, the supervisor must be more of a master teacher and less of a personnel director to be most effective.

This chapter then continues with a description of the salient features of the self-contained class, the resource room, the consultant model, the assessment class, and the materials library. Teacher roles in each program element are described, with a separate section devoted to the supervisor's role. The chapter closes with a brief review of current data addressing the question that brought up the issue of program options initially: can it be demonstrated that one program option is "better" than another, either in general or for specific children? If so, which is best for whom?

Self-Contained Special Education Programs

These may be defined as classes, frequently taught by one teacher, in a self-contained environmental setting. The class must conform to state regulations in terms of equipment, teaching materials, presence of an instructional aide, and class size. The age range, as well as admission criteria for the children, also may come under state regulations.

While self-contained programs do vary across states, a look at the regulations of one state provides an example. In Illinois (Pysh, 1978), the policies covering a self-contained special education class are derived from state regulations and procedures. The class must meet a number of criteria.

It should provide an educational program to learning disabled students whose instructional needs cannot be met in the regular classroom (mainstreamed), using either resource room or special education teacher consultant assistance. It is recognized in the Illinois regulations that when a child requires placement for more than 50 percent of the school day, it is impossible to maintain that student in the regular classroom with supportive services from special education. Children placed in self-contained classes often require a great deal of the support from professionals in other disciplines, such as speech therapists and social workers. The major purposes of self-contained classes are to:

- provide the student with the social and personal adjustment skills necessary to promote school success

- maintain a constant structure within the instructional environment to reduce distractability, hyperactivity, restlessness, poor attention span, and control over the rate of information flowing to the learner
- teach the basic academic and social skills necessary for success in life, i.e., ones not normally taught in resource rooms
- make cooperative arrangements based on adequate communication with parents.

Class size in self-contained programs should be limited to a maximum of ten students because of the severity of the handicapping conditions (type and amount). Teacher aides should be available to work individually with the students. However, the pupils' entire activities are the responsibility of the special education teacher.

Classroom Plan

Every school system is responsible for providing special students with a proper physical setting in an atmosphere conducive to learning. To achieve appropriate building level services for learning disabled students, a school should provide the following:

1. A classroom or learning center should be available solely for learning disabled students. Itinerant teachers (those who divide their time between schools) could share space by alternating days or times with other teachers. Every special classroom should have proper lighting and ventilation, a file cabinet with lock, chalkboards and bulletin boards, proper student and teacher furniture, and sufficient space to accommodate the full range of remediation methods and techniques. Special classrooms should be interspersed among the regular classrooms at the proper age level and should equal them in size and quality.
2. A variety of audiovisual equipment necessary to special education should be accessible to the learning disability teacher.
3. Both learning disability and regular classroom teachers should have access to a materials center.
4. Any other physical facilities provided to special education students should be comparable with those for regular students.

Most other states have similar standards regulating physical facilities and placement procedures.

Curriculum

Students with learning disabilities exhibit a wide range of academic skills and basic behavioral deficits, so the curriculum in self-contained classes will vary from pupil to pupil. Two diagnostic entries of children who may require self-contained programming are (1) those with more frequent behavioral disorders and (2) those with apparent language disorders.

Learning disabled students of elementary and middle school age placed in a self-contained program require a special curriculum for each activity. The curricula should reflect the interest of the age and sex group being taught. Academic, vocational, social, and personal objectives may comprise the major thrust of the program. Other elements can include consumer education, distributive education, prevocational training, health, adaptive physical education, art, and music.

Language development may have a profound effect on the total growth of the learning disabled student. Language disability may range from a mild involvement that is subtle and mistaken for attentional or attitudinal problems, to very severe impairments (aphasia) that may be mistaken for deafness or mental retardation. In the classroom some students may display language impairment, poor listening skills, limited attention, and a hesitancy to enter freely into discussions. They also may have trouble with verbal directions and in retaining verbal materials in a consistent manner.

Students with moderate language impairment often have reading deficits as a result of speech sound discrimination and auditory memory problems. Many learning disabled students have very negative self-concepts. Depending on the age of the student and the degree to which parents and schools have been able to help the pupil develop feelings of self-worth, the emotional problems can range from slight to severe. Accepting the premise that little learning will take place until the student has a positive self-image, it can be realized how extremely important appropriate supportive services are.

These students often display behavioral disorders that present classroom management problems. Appropriate supportive services are essential to help establish behavioral management techniques. If the disruptive behavior is chronic, a review of the child's schedule may be necessary, placing the pupil in a program for those with behavioral disorders.

Flexibility of the Self-Contained Classroom

The benefits of both self-contained special education and regular educational classes can be realized by combining these two structures into one. At this point, however, communication between teachers is a prime factor in determining whether the program can assist the child. Some students may be able to attend regular classes for one or more academic courses in which their interest is high and achievement is satisfactory. When this type of program is planned, it will be necessary for the learning disability teacher to work closely with the academic teacher in program modification so that a student's disabilities will not interfere with successful participation in regular classes (Pysh, 1978, p. 79).

A child may be in a self-contained classroom on a full-time or part-time basis in keeping with the intent of the least restrictive environmental requirements under P.L. 94-142. Again, some learning disabled students may go to a self-contained class for a short time to receive instruction in basic subjects such as math, reading, etc., or they may be based in a homeroom, receiving either all or none of their instruction in a mainstreamed setting.

The intent of a self-contained special education class should be to put itself out of business, at least with the large population of mildly handicapped students who are free of secondary disabling conditions. However, that rarely happens, as there is a seemingly endless supply of children who need the maximum adaption and structure of the curriculum in a self-contained class. Even those severely learning disabled children may be better served by taking them from the self-contained class for at least some activities, i.e., music, art, adaptive physical education, etc.

Generally speaking, a self-contained special education class is recommended for moderate to severely learning disabled children. For the more severely impaired who are in self-contained classrooms, additional special education therapy, such as a resource room, may be advisable, even for the child already placed in the special classroom for the learning disabled or, in particular, for the behavioral disordered. The reasoning behind such a statement is to intensify the therapeutic impact provided a severely handicapped learning disabled child who warrants a self-contained environment. However, if a self-contained class is merely a "holding tank" for relatively undifferentiated students according to the degree of severity, it may not be a justifiable placement option.

Learning Disability Resource Rooms

Learning disabled children displaying mild or moderate disability may not need the restrictive environment of a self-contained classroom. One alternative is for a student to go on a regularly scheduled basis for remediation in one or two academic subjects, work in a basic skill area, cognitive process training, or work in response to social, personal, vocational, or developmental objectives. The student could attend the resource room one day each week, five days a week, or any combination of days required for the length of time (periods) necessitated by the severity of the problem.

What precisely, then, is a resource room? Does it have an identifiable philosophy, physical dimension, and management characteristic? Larsen (1976) acknowledges the resource room to be the most popular placement option. The reasons he provides are (1) the resource room permits children to be mainstreamed in the regular classroom most of the time, and (2) it accommodates noncategorically defined children (nonlabeled) very nicely. He notes that most resource rooms are "cross-categorical" in the way they present instruction, having centers to serve at least three groups, the so-called high incidence handicapped: learning disabled, behavioral disordered, and mild mentally retarded.

Larsen does not mention that resource rooms assist in establishing racial balance in the elementary school. Resource rooms were used to evaluate the difference in 1976 when the Wright decision forced the closing of the racially unbalanced special classes in Washington. The nearly 500 teachers for self-contained rooms were retained that summer for resource rooms.

In answer to the question, what makes the resource room an educationally valuable place, certainly a partial answer is derived from one of Larsen's observations. He notes that the resource room is particularly "appealing" to educators because of its adaptability. It can serve as a short-term diagnostic setting—an instructional center where the child may spend up to 50 percent of the school day. Since it is adaptable, the schedule and instructional activities should be flexibly arranged and offered.

The resource room provides an adaptable setting for making the diagnostic adjustments necessary to serve a variety of categorically handicapped children with an even wider range of severity (mild to severe) in terms of degree of handicapping condition. Finally, each child has a unique type and amount of handicapping conditions in the specific academic skill to be learned, the information processing behaviors to accomplish that education, and social-personal response to the learning task and environment. Many learning disabled children have developed a negative view of themselves in the classroom environment; however, they react quite differently in the resource room.

There is no one simple type of resource room. Instead, resource rooms reflect many different physical arenas and philosophical arrangements. Reger and Koppman (1971) write that a large number of variations exist among their basic themes. This section reviews many of those themes.

The literature has described resource room programs for emotionally disturbed teenagers (Connor & Muldoon, 1967) that represent a combination of public school and community agencies and include special classes and tutoring services for aggressive, withdrawn, or disoriented adolescents. Clark (1969) describes a learning center that helps students and teachers bridge the gap between the broad-based unit curriculum of the pre-1960 era and the current precision of diagnostic-prescriptive teaching. She illustrates how a learning center can make the diagnostic-prescriptive process immediately available to teachers—a system of blending master teachers and school psychologists as a team. The technology and special materials are provided by the learning center. She emphasizes that "the classroom teacher must have more of an 'even chance' at managing the problems of working with children—and this system 'equalized the odds' " (p. 17).

Hillerich (1969) recommends the resource room as a "creative learning center" whose sole objectives are to increase language facility and improve the child's self-concept. He sees the disadvantaged child as requiring not only rich language experiences but also a teacher "who recognized his (the child's) worth, and has time to let him know it" (p. 262).

Comparing the achievements of children served by the resource rooms with those in special classes, Weiner (1969) concludes that the former serves more handicapped children more effectively. He emphasizes the desirability of a widely varied approach as opposed to using any specific technique of instruction.

A prime example of resource rooms used to implement a varied approach to remediation is the Learning Resource Center for Exceptional Children in Sacramento, California (Valett, 1970). The evaluation and programming for each child are the result of consultation among teachers, coordinators, and psychologists rather than the product of one diagnostic assessment or assessor. This multifaceted resource room program includes parent and pupil counseling, parent education, inservice teacher training, and educational therapy.

The Resource Room Staff

The personnel who staff a resource room may range from one coordinating teacher to a team of specialists. The coordinating teacher has been described as a "trouble shooter, problem-solver, consultant, demonstration teacher, and research scientist" (Cienion, 1968). One general criticism of resource rooms has been that the teachers try to be all things to all children, which some educators view as too much of an undertaking for one individual. The following details the role and function of the resource teacher as described by Lewis (1974) and provides examples of how this role is typically implemented based on the earlier views of Cienion (1968).

The Resource Room Teacher

In carrying out the various activities assigned to this function, the resource room teacher:

1. Evaluates children referred and determines the nature of their learning abilities
   - takes part in the screening team for special learning disabilities
   - assumes responsibility for the final evaluation report of each referral
2. Works in an instructional capacity individually or in small groups with the children assigned
3. Teaches six or seven sessions daily, except Friday (a half day)
4. Consults with the students' classroom teachers and other pupil services team members so that all those working with each child are consistent in their efforts (this is a most important role, requiring that sufficient time be allocated for this function)
   - acts as a resource person for all classroom teachers from 8:30 to 9 a.m. and 3:30 to 4 p.m.
5. Provides supportive assistance to the classroom teacher who continues to assume the major responsibility for all the assigned children
   - prepares standby resource lessons for classroom use when a child cannot function within the framework of the regular lesson
   - observes in the classroom in an advisory capacity by invitation
   - confers with the classroom teacher about the progress of the children attending the resource room
   - confers jointly with parents and classroom teachers and initiates separate parent conferences, when indicated
   - initiates the integration of children into the parent class on a full-time basis, when indicated, and serves as supportive resource teacher until the transition is complete
6. Prepares inservice materials when necessary and supervises the work of paraprofessionals and volunteers

The Resource Room Aide

As that list indicates, resource room teachers frequently supervise teacher aides. Lewis (1974) describes the aides' functions as:

1. meeting students at scheduled times in various instructional areas
2. preparing and organizing materials as directed by the learning resource room teacher
3. managing daily records (anecdotal records, organized student files, return of materials and equipment)
4. observing and assessing, under direction, the special learning needs of students
5. completing assigned tasks with children resulting from written directions or conferences with the resource room teacher

6. adapting instructional materials with minimal direction from the classroom teacher
7. assisting in the coordination of information among regular, vocational, special education, and supportive source persons

To recapitulate: The special education resource teacher provides direct services to both individuals and small groups of children, and consultant services to classroom teachers. The resource teacher is responsible for the instructional assessment of the assigned children and the preparation and delivery of individualized developmental and/or remedial programs. In this capacity, the individual may teach six or seven instructional periods a day (9 a.m. to 12 noon, 1 p.m. to 3 p.m.). During the remainder of the school day, the resource teacher fulfills the consultation role of providing regular teachers with instructional objectives for referred children. The individual must not be restricted by a complicated referral procedure and therefore can help school personnel develop strategies for behavior management as problems arise.

To accomplish these objectives, the resource teacher must be equipped with diagnostic, remedial curricula (both special and regular), and organizational abilities. Personally, as well as professionally, this teacher also must possess (1) a realistic self-confidence, (2) self-initiation and self-directedness, and (3) a keen sense of interpersonal skills. That last point refers, in part, to the crucial role this teacher performs as an advocate for the resource room program in a specific school setting.

Procedures for Teachers

Paroz, Siegenthaler, and Tatum (1977) have outlined a potential set of procedures to assist resource teachers in introducing their programs. While these suggestions were aimed at implementation of resource room programs, they certainly apply equally well to initiating any learning disabilities program in a regular school. Initially, Paroz et al., suggest that:

1. all existing services and programs available be reviewed to determine what vital functions the resource room may serve
2. procedures and criteria be established for admission to the resource room and that information communicated to staff, students, and parents; input from staff, students, and parents be elicited on those admission criteria
3. a referral process be developed
4. the resource teacher's assessment role be stabilized with the primary diagnostic providers and assessment committee

5. means of communicating results of assessment to teachers, parents, and principal be established and a continuous evaluation procedure be developed

Paroz et al. (1977) write, "It is imperative that a system for tracking students' progress be developed immediately" (p. 9). They feel it critical to explain to the students why they are attending the resource room and develop a filing system that maintains all necessary placement data, including assessment information and forms for referral, permission to test, and permission for placement. In addition, information from other agencies, or sent to other agencies, along with parental permission to request or send such data, must be filed as legal safeguards under P.L. 94-142.

An additional file monitoring student progress is extremely important, as well as information on conferences and student reevaluation. Further, Paroz, Siegenthaler, and Tatum (1977) recommend that a schedule be developed for each child in conjunction with the classroom teacher and verified by the principal and that an additional list of students receiving services be prepared for teachers and principal.

How should this schedule be developed to best meet the needs of the student? Following are three scheduling options that can be used in a resource room format.

Wiederholt, Hammill, and Brown (1978) introduce a staggered schedule procedure for the teacher. Children report to the resource room for no longer than half an hour at a time but may return two or even more times during the school day. For example, a special teacher's schedule might be:

8:30– 9:00	Preparation
9:00– 9:15	Reading (Three Pupils)
9:15– 9:30	Reading (Three Pupils)
9:30– 9:45	Reading (Two Pupils)
10:00–10:15	Reading (Three Pupils)
10:15–10:30	Mathematics (Four Pupils)
10:30–10:45	Mathematics (Two Pupils)
11:00–11:30	Consultation
11:30–12:00	Lunch
12:00–12:30	Lunchroom duty
12:30–12:45	Spelling (Three Pupils)
12:45– 1.00	Handwriting (Five Pupils)
1:00– 2:30	Assessment and Consultation
2:30– 3:00	Social Studies (Five Pupils)

Barksdale and Atkinson (1971) recommend a sequential activity schedule, where grouping children by objective becomes the differential for how and what they are taught:

8:30– 9:00	Planning and Preparation
9:00–10:15	Instructional Session, Group I
10:15–11:30	Instructional Session, Group II
11:30–12:00	Lunch
12:00– 1:15	Instructional Session, Group III
1:15– 2:30	Instructional Session, Group IV
2:30– 3:15	Conference time with students, parents, regular teachers, other personnel

Hawisher and Calhoun (1975) provide a schedule where the resource teacher can work with two or three students for 30 minutes of individualized instruction daily:

8:00– 9:00	Pre-School Planning
9:00– 9:45	Group A
9:30–10:15	Group B
10:00–10:45	Group C
10:30–11:15	Group D
11:15–11:45	Planning Time
11:45–12:30	Lunch
12:30– 1:15	Group E
1:00– 1:45	Group F
1:30– 2:15	Group G
2:15– 3:10	Post-School Planning

Group E could be divided into two subgroups, E^1 and E^2. E^1 may visit the resource room on Mondays, Wednesdays, and Fridays and E^2 only on Tuesdays and Thursdays. These three schedules do not allow for observation and consultation time in the regular classroom. The resource room teacher must have some organizational and planning time each day, and at least half a day each week for coordination and consultation.

The scheduling and grouping of students with special needs is only one component of a smoothly running resource room program. The room's operational elements are:

1. *Population:* The resource room serves pupils in all grades who are identified by the screening procedures but whose problems are not severe enough to warrant placement in a full-time self-contained class or the assessment class. In the high school, there should be a learning center with equipment to provide reader service, time-recorded lessons, and other types of programmed self-help lessons.

2. *Curriculum:* The resource room teacher provides individualized instruction in perceptual training, language development, motor training, and academic skill development and implements activities for social and personal (emotional) development.

3. *Enrollment:* For any given eight-week instructional block, the resource teacher should serve at least 16 different children in a day, and for the school year, a minimum of 30. The teacher can do this by working two-day schedules for some groups and four-day schedules for others. Children should progress through individualized work into group activities. Generally, the more rapidly this change occurs, the better.

4. *Length of Enrollment:* This depends upon individual progress. Preevaluations and postevaluations are conducted for an eight-week instructional block. These evaluations determine whether a child continues in the resource room for another eight weeks, returns full-time to the regular class, or perhaps is referred for enrollment in the assessment class or other special setting. Daily criterion referenced evaluations serve to validate the instruction void.

5. *Instructional Periods:* Children receive instruction in either one-to-one situations or in groups not exceeding three pupils for any session. Classes are a minimum of 20 minutes and a maximum of 45. Children should be seen, whether on an individual basis or in groups, for at least three instructional periods per week. Massed daily practice is recommended for short periods with some children.

6. *Staffing:* Each resource room is staffed by a certified special education teacher who is trained as a learning disabilities resource instructor (not just a self-contained class teacher). An aide may well be added.

7. *Environment:* A resource room should not be located in a full-sized classroom. There simply is no ideal setting, but broom closets and a corner of the stage are not environments that carry the good practices seal. However, a room with at least 150 square feet of space, plus an area to store materials for the year, is recommended. The room should have all the comfort characteristics of a regular classroom—adequate lighting, ventilation, temperature control—and should receive equal consideration and maintenance. But it should not look like a regular classroom. It should provide the child with a break from that atmosphere. A resource teacher should not have to share the nurses' rooms or the library or work in a "castoff" room in the school basement. The resource room should be easily accessible to children and teachers. A resource room teacher is in a school to help children and support regular classroom educators, and the facilities should help promote such activities. Suggested basic furniture for each resource room includes:

    1 rectangular table
    4 chairs

1 filing cabinet
1 storage cabinet
1 portable chalkboard
1 bulletin board
6 pupil desks

Hawisher and Calhoun (1978) regard space as extremely important. A book room or vacant auditorium, in their opinion and the author's, are used far too frequently when they are grossly inadequate. They recommend a small-sized classroom, with adequate light and ventilation, and well-spaced electrical outlets. The furniture needed is:

1. Teacher's desk and chair, used primarily for planning and the storage of personal items because the teacher will be moving about the room most of the time while attending to students' needs
2. Work tables with chairs, scaled to the size of the students.
3. Student desks with chairs
4. A folding screen or carrels for privacy as required
5. A filing cabinet
6. Shelves and/or storage cabinets for materials
7. Bulletin board and chalkboard for colorful display and instructional aids.

The basic equipment needs of the resource room are identical to those for other classrooms:

1. Tape recorder and one tape player
2. Listening station and earphones
3. Overhead projector
4. Language Master (magnetic card reader)
5. Teaching supplies (paper clips, stapler, paper, rulers, markers, file folders, etc.).

(Hawisher & Calhoun, 1978, p. 80)

Although more will be said about the resource room environment, three things *must* be kept in mind: (1) A resource room must have storage space for records and materials. (2) A resource room *should* be a pleasant place to work, where children want to be. (3) A resource room should be engineered to maximize control over the learning environment.

The last statement requires interpretation: if an educator had the opportunity to visit several hundred resource rooms and was asked to rank them in terms of efficiency of operation, the judgment would reflect their organization. Key questions would be: Are materials readily available where they are needed? Is equipment (tape recorder) at the appropriate teaching station? Are the students' records filed where available? Is there a curriculum plan incorporating the teacher's aide, psychologist, and other support personnel?

A resource teacher, above all things, is mentally and physically well organized. Toward this end, the following section provides diagrams and descriptions of the physical arrangements of several model resource rooms.

THE RESOURCE ROOM AS A PLACE

Four floor plans are shown in Figures 8-1 and 8-2. The first illustrates two model resource rooms at the elementary school level. In Model A, a large resource room contains four group activity centers focusing on academic remediation, perceptual training, language remediation, and perceptual motor development. Space also is provided for a center for audiovisual activities, as well as desks for a teacher and an aide. Model B provides these same features in a condensed and overlapping form to cope with space restrictions.

In Figure 8-2, the two preceding models are adapted for the secondary level student. In Model C, the perceptual motor area has been replaced by space for prevocational training. In other respects, this model possesses the same features as Model A. Finally, Model D, hampered by the same space constraints as Model B, illustrates areas that serve as settings for language remediation and prevocational training, perceptual training, group interaction, and audiovisual presentations.

THE RESOURCE ROOM AS A CONCEPT

Not all special education leaders have accepted the view of the resource room as a place. Reger (1972) is more interested in the systematic impact of the resource room, viewing it as a concept, not a place. Reger argues that the resource room may contribute to the negative ledger by attempting to correct or supplant a "squeaking educational system" by continuing to reinforce regular instructors in avoiding handicapped children. Reger directs his thinking to long-range objectives for the entire school system, attempting to obtain what he calls programs to avoid creating "high risk failure situations" (p. 357). He acknowledges that a resource room program can offer direct services to both children and teachers, but simply feels that that is not enough. The resource room teacher must "effect changes in the educational program through other teachers and local administrators" (p. 357).

Figure 8-1 Elementary Level Resource Rooms

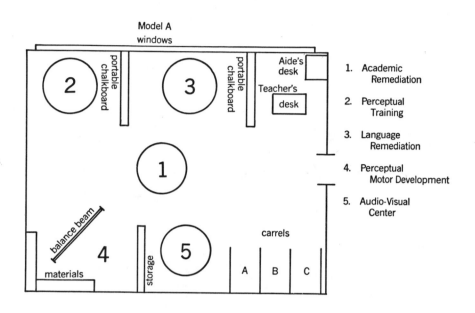

Model A

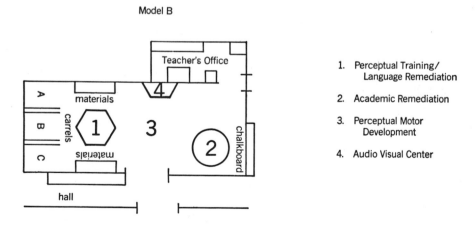

Model B

Source: Pamela Miller, doctoral student, Southern Illinois University, Department of Special Education.

Figure 8-2 Secondary Level Resource Rooms

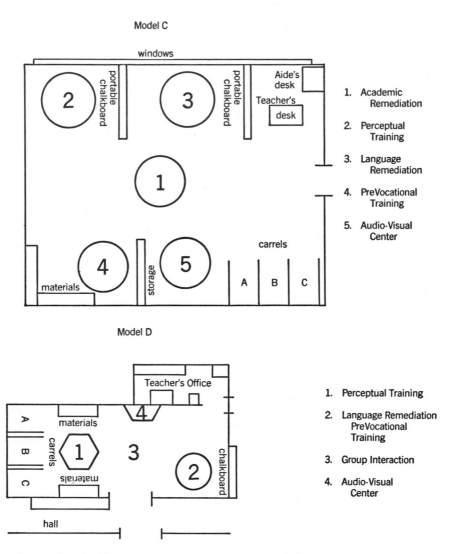

Model C

1. Academic Remediation

2. Perceptual Training

3. Language Remediation

4. PreVocational Training

5. Audio-Visual Center

Model D

1. Perceptual Training

2. Language Remediation PreVocational Training

3. Group Interaction

4. Audio-Visual Center

Source: Pamela Miller, doctoral student, Southern Illinois University, Department of Special Education.

The primary thrust of the resource concept is the establishment of a center where specialists are available to provide unique instructional services to learning disabled students and where professional personnel can help regular classroom teachers establish workable procedures for students. Adelman (1972) criticizes the resource room as too restrictive and overly structured. He strongly advocates revising the resource room from a place to a concept (as does Reger), in order to include a much larger platform for services to handicapped children; hence, it would be "bigger than a room." He sees special education at a critical transition point, facing the task of assimilating various alternative (but not necessarily new) administrative structures, personnel roles, and functions as replacements for those that have fallen into disrepute. To accomplish these objectives, a broader conceptualization than the contemporary resource room is needed. (Adelman, 1972, p. 361)

Adelman regards the resource room as a process for altering the responsibilities of resource room teachers. He sees the teacher involved in planning orderly changes, inservicing other teachers through daily work with students from their classes while attempting to assist those instructors in receiving (attitudinally) handicapped children in their classes. The resource room teacher also is expected to provide materials for the classroom instructor to work with and to demonstrate their use. Adelman views the resource concept as a means of reducing the dichotomy between regular education and special education, which is a critical deterrent to sound program development for learning disabled children.

A conceptual transition is needed to bridge this formidable abyss. If regular and special educators are to communicate meaningfully, that opportunity must be provided. Again, it is the goal of resource programs to keep the handicapped child as near the educational mainstream as possible. Thus, the mission of resource room personnel must be more than that of performing a direct service to children. Those educators must focus on obtaining attitudinal change and demonstrating a better way to do things within the structure of the school system, such as altering the view of teachers, parents, administrators, cooks, and custodians. Reger (1973) emphasizes this mission:

> The mission of a resource room program can be to change the schools. . . . First, a resource room program has a teacher-in-action in the school building setting. This teacher is the primary agent of change; he or she can concretely demonstrate a better way, a new outlook, a different approach. The teacher can show positive results while working in concert with other teachers. The resource room teacher can relate changes in a child in a classroom to altered methods and attitudes, and can suggest that any teacher could do the same—there is no magic, and there is no pathology. . . . Second, the resource room teacher is not tied constantly to one class-

room.... This teacher shares responsibility for children with all other teachers in the building who have children in the program. (p. 16)

It is true that there is a mission to change the system built into the role of the clearly overburdened learning disabilities resource teacher. But that awesome and encompassing role places too much responsibility on any one person to bear if the individual is to continue to see children on a daily basis. Therefore, one alternative is to divide the role of resource teachers into at least two different major functions. The first is to work directly with individual and small groups of children in a direct habilitative and remedial structure. The second is to work directly with teachers, administrators, and parents in the role of change agent strategist. To amplify that distinction, both Wiederholt (1974) and Reger (1973) provide their own perspectives in examining various aspects of the resource room concept.

Wiederholt's Observations on Resource Rooms

- Mildly handicapped pupils can benefit from specific resource room training while remaining integrated with their friends and age mates in regular classes.

- Pupils have the advantages of a total remedial program that is prepared by the resource teacher but may be implemented in cooperation with the regular class teacher.

- Pupils are the recipients of flexible scheduling in that remediation can be applied entirely in their classrooms by the regular teacher with some resource teacher support, or in the resource room itself when necessary; also, the schedule can be altered quickly to meet the children's changing situations and needs.

- Resource rooms are less expensive because the teachers are able to serve a greater number of children than in special class programs.

- More children's needs can be served under the resource room arrangement than by the present system.

- Since the resource teacher is assigned to a particular school (unlike some school psychologists, remedial reading therapists, speech correctionists, or other itinerant staff), this educator is less likely to be viewed as an outsider by the other instructors in the school. In addition, this special teacher probably better understands the programming problems in a particular school.

- Because placement in the resource room is an individual school matter involving the principal, the teachers, and the parents, no appreciable time lapse need occur between the instructor's referral and the initiation of special services for the child.

- Disability diagnoses are not necessary for placement purposes; pupils are not labeled in any way as handicapped.

- Labeling and segregation are avoided; the stigma invariably associated with receiving special attention is minimized.

- Medical and psychological work-ups are done only at the school's request rather than on a screening for placement basis; thus, the school psychologist is freed to do the work that expert was trained to do instead of being relegated to the role of psychometrist.

- Since the resource room will absorb most of the "handicapped" children in the schools, the special classes increasingly will become instructional settings for the "truly" handicapped pupils, i.e., those for whom the classes were intended originally.

- Because young children with mild, though developing, problems can be accommodated, later severe disorders may be prevented.

- Schools large enough to accommodate one or more resource rooms can serve students from neighboring schools. (Wiederholt, 1974, p. 6)

Reger's Observations on Resource Rooms

- Children can be kept in the mainstream of the school. There is no stigma attached in going to the resource room for assistance.

- Children have the dual advantages of receiving both large-group instruction and individual or very-small-group instruction.

- There is greater leeway for flexibility in instructional techniques, for trying alternatives, for varying approaches. The classroom teacher is a major beneficiary of flexibility because of the available feedback from the resource teacher.

- For schools that tabulate "numbers of special children served," for the same amount of money more children can be served in resource room programs than in special classes.

- For schools with "diagnostic centers," the need for such service is greatly reduced; the resource room teacher can provide most such services right in the building. An important feature of such on-the-spot service is that it is connected directly on a continuing basis with the child's instructional program, and the evaluation performed is relevant to the problem(s) involved. Diagnostic centers that primarily perform a labeling function are assets to administrative placement procedures but are of little or no use to the child or teacher.

- There is no need to label children in resource room programs. Such labels certainly add nothing to a teacher's fund of knowledge for instructional purposes. The focus in the program is upon specifically targeted behavior.

- As fewer children with moderate problems need to be placed in special self-contained classes, many who have mild problems who would not have been assigned there can receive assistance. This can become very critical for the child who is just beginning a downward spiral that in a few years could lead to a special class. The preventive aspects of the program are enormous.

- Generally, there is much greater parental and community support for a resource room program than for some other options in the typical school. A parent with a child who displays moderate problems is going to be much happier about resource room placement than about a special class.

Summary

Programming for elementary-aged learning disabled students has set the pace for all of learning disabilities for the last 25 years. Subsequent chapters show how the expansion of services to the preschool and secondary levels (and beyond) may change the form and function of service delivery systems over the next 25 years. The next section of this chapter describes another alternative to the resource room program: the learning disabilities teacher consultant.

LEARNING DISABILITIES TEACHER CONSULTANTS

It should be obvious from the previous discussion that resource rooms represent a range of instructional program delivery capabilities. That range of activities includes many variations on a theme of direct services to handicapped students.

Reger (1972), Adelman (1972), and Wiederholt (1974) view the resource teacher as an out-of-the-classroom instructional adviser, a professional who wears a multitude of hats. McKenzie (1969), Fox (1972), and Sabatino (1972) regard the resource room teaching role as too diverse for one person. Harris and Mahar (1975) attempt to describe how the resource room teacher in a rural setting can be the special education "jack-of-all-trades." Stelleren, Vasa, and Little (1976) have adopted a training model with a broad mission for the sparsely populated, remote, rural state of Wyoming, claiming great success. These latter two approaches would have the resource teacher work with every available handicapped child, from sensory impaired to mildly handicapped, including not so mild behavioral disorders, as a first, last, and only line of defense.

Sabatino (1972) regards "selling" such a broad role to the school as "barbershop" medicine and a severe threat to the competency of tightly focused resource room programs. McKenzie, Egner, Knight, Perelman, Schneider, and Garvin (1970) see a differentiated set of training needs for teacher consultants as opposed to resource teachers, having differing skills if they are to perform sound and appropriate functions. Observations of the critical differences in roles also might suggest that variations in interests and personalities may be evident. In the author's judgment, a noticeable difference in personality, with accompanying philosophical and teaching interests, is evident between resource teachers and learning disabilities teacher consultants. The first want to spend 75 percent or more of their time in direct service, the others 75 percent of their time in instructional advisory activities. One observer noted that the personality of the learning disabilities teacher consultant must be like that of the car salesperson, not afraid to slam doors or kick tires; the analogy is that entry into the sacred ground of the classroom, gym, shop, music, or art room requires an outgoing disposition and ability to work with people in the broadest sense.

Teacher Consultants: Who and Where

In 1972, Sabatino described learning disabilities teacher consultants as strategists who promote the instructional interaction between regular and special educators (usually self-contained, but can be resource room teachers) and the handicapped child. How do they do that? By diagnosing the problem, isolating it as a stumbling block to instruction, and removing, going around, or working in the zone of the academic task or target behavior. Therefore, the function takes place in a resource room, self-contained special class, or regular class. It is hoped that regular class activities would occupy 80 percent of the teachers' time.

The learning disabilities consultant is both an extension of and an alternative to the resource teacher. The operational difference between them is that the latter spends very little time providing direct services to individuals or groups of children and works in support of the regular class teachers, offering instructional and behavioral management techniques. The resource teacher usually works with a limited number of children in just a few buildings, providing direct services to them as a primary function. The consultant is responsible for the diagnostic workups of the assigned children and generally serves in several schools.

In this case, the diagnostic workup includes classroom observation, instructional assessment of what is being taught, and how. Once the consultant has obtained sufficient information for programming the child, this information is discussed with the classroom teacher and they come to a mutual agreement about how the latter can provide for the pupil. The consultant monitors the child's progress and the teacher's implementation of the program by scheduled visitations each week. Once the teacher has the program operating smoothly on a regular basis, the consultant can reduce the visitations to possibly one per month. If the initial operation proves unsuccessful, the consultant and teacher have the option of altering it and recommending or requesting additional services from district and program personnel.

The purpose of the observational periods is to give the consultant more definitive information concerning what the child has been taught and how the material was presented. Once they have completed the classroom observation and instructional assessment, teacher and consultant establish an instructional objective for the pupil. They then initiate a search for an appropriate match between the child's learning characteristics and an instructional material and/or strategy to achieve success through an initial teaching prescription. Thus, the consultant can make fairly specific recommendations to the classroom teacher.

The consultant, unlike the resource room teacher, does not have a specific classroom; instead, the individual obtains needed instructional materials from the program's instructional materials center or borrows them from the resource teacher. Although the consultant's major role is assisting and supporting the classroom teacher, the expert also may provide instructional assistance beyond diagnosis to the resource teacher or the self-contained class teacher.

The Provision of Information

Hawisher and Calhoun (1978) describe how the special educator can consult effectively with the classroom teacher. Their first point is that the consultant should provide meaningful information on classroom management, especially for chronically disruptive students. To accomplish that task they recommend that the consultant and teacher:

1. decide whether it is important to change a behavior
2. consider all possible situations that may elicit undesirable behavior
3. develop a teacher reaction appropriate for those situations
4. internalize the reaction plan

In short, the consultant's role is to help the regular teacher isolate target behaviors, develop a plan for modifying them, create a self-imposed value structure for assimilating stress from the child during the change process, and finally, set up a record system that provides monitoring data to both instructor and student.

Experience has shown that behavioral management (Brophy & Good, 1974) is a critical role for the learning disabilities teacher consultant, so much so that a separate chapter (Chapter 10) is devoted to the topic. However, the consultant must be able personally, and trained professionally, to understand and interact with disruptive behavior effectively. Many learning disabled teachers receive little meaningful information during their professional preparation in the management of children with behavioral disorders. It is one thing to literally plug a child into a prefabricated behavioral management structure. It is quite different to realize that the disruptive behavior is the result of a serious, deep-seated emotional pathology and that the youngster can be either violently aggressive or self-destructively passive, or both.

The message here is that there are other consultants in the school who are professionally prepared to work with behavioral disorders and serious emotional disturbances. While learning disability consultants should be intimate with the principles and practices of contingency management as a tool, they are not crisis teachers for the seriously emotionally disturbed. Role confusion can harm a consultation program.

Direct Remediation

Hawisher and Calhoun's (1978) second point is that consultants may help regular teachers apply direct remediation by assisting them to (1) establish a diagnosis, (2) rule out a developmental curriculum, (3) identify an appropriate instructional procedure, (4) identify and have in their classroom specific instructional materials (taken there by the consultant), (5) effectively use that instructional material, (6) develop a monitoring system, and (7) initiate a weekly or biweekly follow-up to determine its effectiveness.

Their third point is that the consultant may wish to help the regular teacher adapt the instructional environment. They drew from the South Carolina

Middle School Child Services Demonstration Project (1977) a list of six classroom adjustment procedures that appear to be applicable throughout the elementary school age range:

1. Adjust type, difficulty, amount, or sequence of material required by
   a. Giving the exceptional student a lesser amount than the rest of the class: fewer math problems, fewer pages to read, etc.
   b. Giving him only a few questions at a time during testing.
   c. Including in his assignments only that material which is absolutely necessary for him to learn.
   d. Checking and underlining for him textbook passages which contain the most important facts, using markers to tell him where to start and stop the assignment.
   e. Establishing only a few modest goals for this student.
   f. Making certain the child's desk is free from all material except what he is working with.
   g. Taking up the student's work as soon as it's completed.
   h. Keeping the number of practice items on any skill to a minimum.
   i. Giving the student several alternatives in both obtaining and reporting information—tapes, interviews, etc.
2. Adjust space for this child by
   a. Permitting him to do the work in a quiet, uncrowded corner of the room.
   b. Placing him next to a student who can help him when needed.
   c. Letting him choose the area of the room where he can concentrate best.
   d. Separating him from students who are most likely to distract him.
3. Adjust work time for this student by
   a. Giving him more time than other class members to complete assignments.
   b. Setting up a specific schedule for him so that he knows what to expect.
   c. Keeping work periods short, gradually lengthening them as the child begins to cope.
   d. Alternating quiet and active time, having short periods of each, making movement as purposeful as possible.

4. Adjust grouping for this student by
   a. Matching him with a peer helper who can help him understand directions of assignments and read important directions and essential material to him, summarizing orally important textbook passages.
   b. Formulating small work groups of three or four students. Include the exceptional child and make all group members responsible for making certain that each group member completes assignments successfully.
5. Adjust presentation and evaluation modes for a student who is primarily an auditory learner by
   a. Giving verbal as well as written directions, taping important reading material; tape only essential information.
   b. Using published audio tapes with students.
   c. Dictating information into a recorder.
6. Adjust the mode of presentation for a student who is primarily a visual learner by
   a. Flashing cards printed in bold bright colors.
   b. Having him close his eyes and try to visualize the information, seeing things in his mind. (South Carolina Region V Service Center, 1977, p. 13).

The fourth and final point Hawisher and Calhoun (1978) make is that the learning disabilities consultant should:

1. know the student as an individual
2. clarify the goals
3. consider the student's interests
4. analyze the task
5. provide instructional help, not sympathy
6. suggest the appropriate classroom climate

(Brophy & Good, 1974)

Is there a simple rule of thumb for a special education teacher consultant? Montgomery (1978) thinks so. He writes, "The first rule for consultants is to *listen*" (p. 111). He continues with a three-point summary that seems appropriate in closing out this section.

First, take yourself seriously. Consultation is a real job. It can provide your school with an invaluable service if it is undertaken conscientiously. Second, look and listen. Input comes before output.

Watch what's going on in your school. Listen to the concerns of the teachers. Third, learn. There is a lot to know, both about the nature of learning and behavior problems, and about the process of consultation. (p. 321)

The following section provides a more detailed analysis of the skills required of the learning disabilities teacher consultant and the content of a training program designed to develop these competencies.

TRAINING TEACHER CONSULTANTS

Christie, McKenzie, and Burdett (1972) list the type of activities in which the consulting teacher must develop skills in order to manage.

1. The consultant should sell the program as one having merit, a "voluntary" cooperative effort, not as an administrative mandate.
2. The consultant should gain the cooperation of reluctant teachers through parental reinforcement of the program and the principal's help, but most of all by selling good work to children that teachers identify as being beneficial.
3. The consultant, if that fails, should draw on the principal's administrative skill to work directly with the handful of teachers in most buildings who are reluctant to take advantage of consulting services. Christie, et al. (1972) describe eliciting the principal's assistance with reluctant teachers:

   > To date, this problem has been solved only when the building principal has insisted on total staff participation and has made working with the consulting teacher a condition under which new teachers are hired. While this may result in involving some teachers of the "reluctant" variety, it does at least provide for initial interaction (p. 4).

4. The consultant will find it exceedingly important to provide inservice with groups of teachers by building as well as by grade level. Inservice must continue, with the daily direct consulting contacts between the special adviser and the regular teacher.
5. The consultant provides regular educators with encouragement, emotional support, and verbal compliments, routing still more praise through other teachers, parents, and principals. The regular teacher's work must be reinforced in a multidirectional effort as information is obtained that progress is being made.

6. The consulting teacher should provide direct diagnostic help to the regular educator, identifying the specific tasks to be developed instructionally or behaviors to become targets for intensive modification.
7. The teacher consultant who expects to see different instructional approaches in the regular classroom probably will find it necessary to provide the materials and provide inservice on their use.

Christie et al. (1972) list eight additional important considerations:

1. defining target behavior in measurable terms
2. measuring behavior reliably
3. following teaching/learning procedures precisely
4. collecting, recording, and graphing data daily
5. identifying possible reinforcing consequences in the classroom
6. writing instructional objectives
7. responding to changes in the behavior of the child
8. involving parents in the education process. (p. 6)

While these are important, they also reflect using a strong behavior management approach. The author's position is that the special education teacher consultant also must draw equally, if not more so, on instructional approaches. What becomes intensely important is a means of ordering or organizing the curriculum changes that the consultant recommends.

McKenzie, Egner, Knight, Perelman, Schneider, and Garvin (1970) describe one early program to prepare special education teacher consultants. The training took two academic years and one summer. The curriculum incorporated the following aspects:

1. Principles of behavior modification
2. Application of these principles to meet the needs of handicapped children in regular classrooms
3. Precise daily measurement and monitoring of a child's progress to ensure that contingencies, methods, and materials are effective
4. Procedures for training parents and teachers in the principles and application of behavior modification techniques
5. Research training to increase skills in devising and evaluating education tactics
6. Development of supplementary materials suited to the particular needs of handicapped learners
7. Methods of advising elementary school teachers in the management and education of handicapped learners. (p. 139)

Ten regular teachers were selected by five school districts to enter the program. The teachers were released one day each week for courses during the first year of study and for practicum as resource teachers in the second year of study. The program was stabilized as a master's degree offering at the University of Vermont the following year.

Christie et al., conclude that training efforts require support for financial reimbursement, university flexibility in developing programs, and local school district administrative assistance, especially that of the principal.

RESOURCE ROOMS: DO THEY WORK?

It should be remembered that the reason for developing resource rooms was the record of mediocre achievement (Cegelka & Tyler, 1970) demonstrated by mildly handicapped children in self-contained special classes. In 1969, Weiner reported that such children being seen for short periods in a resource room performed better academically and socially than those in self-contained classes. Later, Sabatino (1971) reported that a summer resource room program was more effective than a self-contained catch-up program for children seriously perceptually and cognitively handicapped.

Empirical support for noncategorical, categorical, short-term, and long-term resource rooms continued into the 1970s (Sabatino, 1971; Galvin, Quay, Annesley, & Werry, 1971; Deno, 1973). Even so-called contradictory data did not impede progress in resource rooms; they simply showed that such rooms and self-contained classes generated about the same progress (no significant differences). Rodee (1971), Tilley (1970), and Jenkins and Mayhall (1976) indicate that the answer to the effectiveness of the resource room resides in the extent to which it is developed. Well-developed programs are highly successful; poorly developed ones report results equivalent to self-contained classes.

Part of the issue of development is in relation to placement factors or to the severity of the handicap. Obviously, in a well-developed special education program, a resource room should produce better results than a self-contained class. Why? Theoretically, the children in it are not as severely handicapped. The point is that, generally speaking, resource rooms are no better or worse, on either academic or social adjustment variables, than are self-contained classes. Educators rarely are sure of the differences, if any, in populations. What then would they hypothesize in response to teacher consultants? Once again, consultants demonstrate academic achievement gains and social/behavioral adjustments similar to those of resource teachers (Miller & Sabatino, 1978). One highly beneficial side effect has been significant improvement in communication and the on-task behavioral responses of mainstreamed children influenced by teacher consultants.

Neither Found Superior

Miller and Sabatino (1978) write that academically, neither the teacher consultant nor the resource room has emerged as a service delivery model clearly superior to the other. Both represent definite improvements over the absence of any special education support (i.e., control subjects). However, it could be argued that the consultation model was surprisingly effective, since academic gains were on a par with the direct service approach. That is, regular teachers seemingly became as effective in instructing special children in their classes as resource teachers were in intensive classes out of the mainstream. This seems to provide tentative support for the consultation model, especially in view of the short duration of the period (six months for academic measures and three months for observational measures).

A review of teacher-pupil interaction as a spinoff of special education teacher consultant programs may be more meaningful than the academic achievement gain. Significant increments in several teacher behaviors were found for consultant programs (greater acceptance of feelings, increased praise and encouragement, more imparting of information, reduced criticism, increased communication with students), which probably would be accepted by most persons as desirable attributes of the classroom instructor's behavior.

It should not be shocking that positive teacher behavioral change is found since the focus of the consultant programs is on improvement through continued inservice training in the regular classroom. One aspect of that continued inservice certainly must be providing regular teachers with an alternative to their traditional responses to learning disabled children.

Response Not Dramatic

Miller and Sabatino (1978) report that student behavior change is not dramatic in response to the special education teacher consultant program. This may be accounted for in at least two ways.

1. The behavioral levels of students appear to be appropriate throughout the study; that is, perhaps the teachers sought no radical change in behavior.
2. Teacher change in response to the consultants' influence must have been gradual. It thus is doubtful that the change in teachers' behaviors was sufficiently consistent, or of long enough duration, to alter the students' conduct effectively.

An administrative question appears in the thought that the number of teachers with whom the special education consultant is able to work might be greater than the number of children with whom the resource teacher can work. In fact, careful scrutiny indicates that the teacher consultant model, when done effectively, is very time consuming. Conceivably, the required amount of consultant time might diminish as regular teachers acquire basic skills with handicapped students.

However, a washout of this effect should be expected in optimal practice, since the constant flow of new teaching processes and materials assures new topics for continual inservice training. In the absence of keeping these professionals "mainstreamed" technically and directing their energies appropriately, a consultant could run the risk of becoming more teacher supervisory than instructional advisory. Thus, any attempt to implement the model must ensure both the continuing skill development of the consultant and adequate contact time with the regular teacher.

Finally, the parallel academic gains coupled with improved teacher behaviors suggest utility in having both models in operation within a continuum of services. The data support increased instruction in the regular classroom, thereby promoting many of the goals of mainstreaming through education in the least restrictive environment, improved regular teacher skills, and attenuation of the effects of labeling.

OTHER ALTERNATIVES

The Model Learning Disabilities Continuum

One of the themes conveyed in this chapter is the necessity of developing the administrative structures for a total learning disabilities program. It is important that each component be understood clearly and that alternatives to existing programs be permitted to develop, if not encouraged. The whole of the program must be larger than the sum of its parts.

If local school district special education directors offer only regular education classes to their constituents, then children will have to be bent to fit programs. The school psychologist will have to force-fit children to accommodate the program's faulty and limited dimensions. Planned program reentry and planned program entry (mainstreaming) of handicapped children into regular education will not occur. The opportunity for a child to recycle through a regular program for a period of time, supported by a learning disabilities resource teacher, will never be attempted. If a child is to find help in a resource room or through a learning disabilities strategist, and if the gravity of the pupil's handicap warrants an assessment class placement, then a fully developed continuum of services and programs should be spelled out in detail from the inception of the program.

Before describing the service alternatives for learning disabled children, it is necessary to clarify the role of the program supervisor. This individual is responsible for the coordination of learning disabilities programs and services with district efforts and with other agencies and professional services as needed. This includes:

1. describing and explaining the program's operational procedures and responsibilities to elementary school faculty and auxiliary personnel
2. coordinating the program's services with those existing in the district, e.g., elementary guidance counselor, reading specialist, speech therapist, and elementary supervisor
3. organizing and implementing screening procedures for identifying and assisting the program's teaching staff in diagnosing individual problems and in implementing appropriate intervention strategies
4. coordinating data collection activities for use in program monitoring
5. coordinating the selection and requisition of instructional materials and teaching supplies
6. assisting in the development and implementation of curriculum
7. helping in planning and presenting inservice workshops for the base elementary school teachers
8. assisting in dissemination of information concerning efforts with local parent-teacher groups and other interested community service organizations
9. acting as an ambassador or liaison between the district and program personnel and a supervisor or monitor of activities and progress

The Assessment Class

Assessment classes are designed to diagnose individual problems to provide comprehensive educational programs for each child. These include motor training, perceptual training, language activities, development of academic skills (reading, arithmetic, spelling, writing), academic remedial activities, and modification of inappropriate classroom behavior patterns.

Assessment class teachers are responsible for keeping the regular classroom teachers informed of the progress of these children. This can be accomplished through informal talks, regularly scheduled conferences, and progress reports. Assessment class teachers also are responsible for preparing both the child and the regular teacher for the pupil's reentry into the regular classroom. It is important that both teachers cooperate in this effort so that the transition is smooth and that specific instructional or management strategies begun in the resource room will continue in the regular classes.

The operational aspects of the assessment class are:

1. *Population:* This encompasses elementary pupils who have been identified by the screening program and whose problems are of such a nature as to warrant intensive educational intervention.
2. *Curriculum:* Individualized informal assessment is provided, using direct remedial materials from reading, arithmetic, spelling, and writing. Appropriate supplemental activities involving visual and auditory perception, language, and motor training also are important. The modification of inappropriate classroom behaviors and the development of positive self-concepts are emphasized.
3. *Enrollment:* Six pupils should constitute the maximum enrollment, depending upon the number of teachers and aides—and the role of the latter.
4. *Length of Enrollment:* This class is not a permanent placement for any child. The pupil is reevaluated on a schedule of six-week instructional blocks, when it is decided whether the child remains for another six-week block or returns to the regular class with resource room support.
5. *Staffing:* At least one learning disabilities teacher and one teacher aide are required; two teachers are ideal.
6. *Ancillary Services:* The teacher has supportive services from the school psychologist and program supervisor and the district's guidance counselor and speech therapist. The delivery of these services is of prime importance and, therefore, receives priority over other requests.

Although the assessment class serves a smaller number of children than the typical special class, it should be housed in a classroom with 450 square feet of space so that the teacher can implement learning and skill centers for both small group and individual instruction and provide time-out and free play areas. The teacher and aide should not have to lose valuable time setting up and putting away materials and equipment as activities change, as they would in a smaller room without work stations. The classroom should have work tables for each learning center, pupil desks for individual work, and folding screens and carrels to provide privacy for the children as they require it.

The basic furniture for implementing the ideal assessment class would be:

 2 rectangular tables
 4 round tables
24 chairs
 1 storage cabinet
 1 filing cabinet

2 storage shelves with rollers
4 folding screens
2 mobile carts for audiovisual equipment

Special Education Instructional Materials Center

It would be desirable, although financially unrealistic, for each teacher to have all the instructional materials necessary to provide a full range of instructional strategies to learning disabled children. Since this is impossible, a program should establish a central (or beyond, in a large city) Instructional Materials Center to support the roving resource teachers and strategists. The center supplies duplicates of materials used occasionally with some children. In this way, the program can provide (1) each teacher with basic equipment and materials necessary for day-to-day operation of services, and (2) a support system for retrieval of additional materials. The center also permits the learning disabilities teachers to supplement regular classroom activities by providing materials to the teacher there.

A simple library system can be used to classify and catalog the materials in the Instructional Materials Center. Thus, the teachers can retrieve materials with ease as they need them. It is highly desirable, however, to employ a librarian/secretary to catalog and index the materials and to facilitate teachers' use of the center.

The approximate cost of implementing a center would be:

Furniture (work table, chairs, filing cabinets, storage cabinet, shelves)	$ 500
Instructional materials (programs, kits, workbooks, etc.)	$4,000
Audiovisual equipment	$ 500
	$5,000

After the initial year of operation, the cost of maintaining the center would be approximately $2,000 to $3,000 for replacement of consumable supplies and the purchase of additional materials. In developing a budget for implementing a learning disabilities program, additional funds (approximately $1,500) should be included to cover personal travel expenses for the resource teachers, and particularly for the strategist.

Thus far, various service delivery options as well as the roles, competencies, and training of personnel have been described—in short, the "who" and the "how" but not the "what" in terms of the content of a resource room program.

This section, while not a cookbook as to what to teach, examines systems for determining class content. The number of materials and approaches for delivering information to learning disabled children is voluminous. What is needed is a systematic means of viewing the learners, contrasting their characteristics with specific instructional materials and environments. The learning disability teacher is faced with selecting materials and determining how to present them. Since most materials or techniques are not validated, it is anyone's guess as to what to use. To that end, the author offers several instructional (program) models to help in selecting appropriate enabling steps. These models are not meant to replace teacher judgment, which is the only element at this point that has even face validity.

DUNN'S MODEL

Dunn (1968) includes several step-by-step diagnostic procedures in developing a sound diagnostic procedure. He recommends beginning with a detailed psychoeducational study of the child to determine which behaviors are faulty and the current skill level. A sequential program then is designed to move the child forward from that functioning point to the next. The type and number of reinforcers to be used, administered under selected conditions, are established. Next, the instructional materials are selected. The method is task analyzed in a similar sequential process. The different modalities for reaching the child are investigated to determine learner preference or learning styles.

The instructional program becomes the principal diagnostic device in the task analysis procedure; thus, Dunn establishes what he calls "diagnostic teaching." He notes, "Failures are program and instructor failures, not pupil failures. . . . This diagnostic procedure is viewed as the best available since it enables us to assess continuously the problem points of the instructional program against the assets of the child" (p. 12). Next, the teacher produces a prescription in written response to the problem points that have been identified. In short, Dunn has developed what is commonly referred to as diagnostic-prescriptive teaching, which is specifying an instructional procedure (materials or techniques) in response to a strength or weakness diagnosed from observation or measurement of the child's response to the curriculum.

In essence, what Dunn (1968) suggests is a paradigm or pattern for assessment that provides for continuous use of data derived from the interaction of child to academic task. In addition, he suggests a beginning taxonomy for the development of specialized programs of study for children with learning disorders. Potential areas for remediation include modifying the environment, motor development, sensory and perceptual training, cognitive and language development, speech and communication training, personality development, and vocational training.

Environmental Modifications

Interventions in this category involve altering the student's learning or living environment in order to restore the pupil who deviates from the expected level of achievement to "scholastic homeostasis" (Algozzine & Sutherland, 1977). Remediation strategies in this category might consist of foster home placement, improved community conditions, out-of-school activities, parent education, public education, better cultural exposure, and modifications of the actual physical properties of the classroom. This last means a learning environment free of visual and auditory distractions and provision for individual work study areas, as well as such basic properties as appropriate lighting and acoustics. In short, the optimal setting is one that is both supportive and motivating.

Smith, Neisworth, and Greer (1978) have written of the physiological effects of the classroom environment. The headings they examined were:

Illumination: A brightness ratio of 3 to 1 (Haywood, 1974) is recommended between the task area and the surrounding space. A brighter light is recommended for reading areas and a softer light where less emphasis is placed on eye usage. There has been speculation that fluorescent lighting increases hyperactivity (Arehart-Treichel, 1975) but the evidence has not been well supported.

Temperature: American classrooms are among the warmest in the Western world. Aggressiveness, mood, and interaction tend to increase with temperature changes. Student energy output seems to increase as the temperature decreases.

Noise: Reviews of noise and its influence on learning indicate that reasonable levels do not disrupt performance for nonlearning disabled students. Studies (Cohen, Glass & Singer, 1973; Bronzaft & McCarthy, 1975) found that children in constant noise did not perform as well. Sabatino (1969) and Flowers (1968) report that noise does deteriorate the performance of learning disabled pupils in listening tasks. Strauss and Lehtinen (1947) report undesirable effects from background noise on learners.

Color: Room color has been demonstrated to be related to feeling; generally speaking, light pastels (except pink) are recommended. Dark colors absorb too much light.

Personal Space: There is evidence that where a child sits (center or edge of the room) and the amount of space the pupil has (personal space vs. crowding) influence ability to do seat work. One of the real issues is personal-social acceptance and seating. Where should the recently mainstreamed child be seated? It may be wise to seat the child in the front and center of the room, with maximum space. The purpose is to reduce anxiety by giving teacher identity and permitting peer relationships to develop slowly and positively. Secondary students with histories of school failure depend on others for support when confronting academic tasks.

Motor Development

Under this category, intervention may consist of activities to facilitate the early stages of psychomotor development, progressing to the fine and large movements necessary for acquiring vocational skills.

Gross motor experiences involve the student's use of the whole body. The purpose is to facilitate the control of body movements and develop more effective body awareness and spatial orientation. Specific suggestions for activities include the child's skipping, bouncing, or hopping in rhythmical patterns, walking backward and forward across a balance beam, and drawing self-pictures in a variety of spatial settings such as a room or an auditorium.

Fine motor activities consist of developing eye-hand coordination (cutting with scissors) and training in ocular control (eye movement). Activities for eye movement training are presented in detail by Kephart (1971) as well as Getman, Kane, Halgren, and McKee (1968). An example of such intervention is to have the child follow a moving object with the eyes—ocular-pursuit training (Lerner, 1971).

Sensory and Perceptual Training

Intervention in this area involves teaching children to organize and convert bits of input from various sense modalities such as vision, hearing, and touch into meaningful units of awareness. Potential areas for remediation related to vision include the child's ability to see the general overall figure as well as the details, to perceive spatial relations, to discriminate one object from another, to distinguish an object from its background, and to recognize an object seen previously.

Auditory modality dysfunctions concern the child's ability to recognize a difference in phoneme sounds, store and recall what has been heard, remember a sequence of items presented orally, and blend single units of sound into a complete word.

Haptic perceptual problems involve tactile and kinesthetic skills. Tactile perception is obtained through the sense of touch via the fingers and skin surfaces. Kinesthetic skills help the child differentiate between objects through body movements and muscle feeling. Teaching strategies include visual (matching geometric shapes); auditory (identifying environmental sounds); and haptic (matching texture to object) activities. To facilitate a child's cross-modal abilities, i.e., transfer or integration of two or more perceptual areas, a game such as Simon Says may be played. In this way the child receives input via the auditory modality and transfers or interprets these commands motorically.

Cognitive and Language Development

Intervention in this area assists learning disabled children in acquiring and storing knowledge as well as generating and evaluating information. Sensory motor training, perceptual-motor, perceptual discrimination, perceptual memory, and language intervention strategies are viewed by special educators as cognitive training activities (Sabatino, Miller & Schmidt, in press). Cognitive training is not academic remediation, the point being that this may not apply directly to the aquisition of academic achievement skill or academic product learning.

Speech and Communication Training

Systematic exercises in speech and language include activities to stimulate overall language and to improve mild to moderate speech disorders such as articulation, pitch, loudness, quality, and duration. Activities for improving skills in verbal expression include helping the child in (1) building a speaking vocabulary, (2) producing speech sounds, (3) learning linguistic patterns, and (4) formulating sentences (Lerner, 1971).

Personality Development

Programs in this area involve developing insights into self, the effects of others on self, and an individual's effect on others. Personality development also includes development of social interaction skills to assist the handicapped individual in forming peer, authority, and other relationships, including work skills.

Vocational Training

Intervention involves continuing emphasis on developing good work habits, independence, reliability, and social skills. At the secondary level, vocational programming becomes even more crucial as the student prepares to enter the work force. The emphasis in this area is to ensure that the youth possesses both the academic and social skills required to obtain and hold a job.

QUAY'S MODEL

Quay (1968) suggests a conceptual framework that cuts across categorical boundaries and permits the assessment, grouping, and instruction of exceptional children on educationally relevant variables. Quay's model is composed of variables related to the learning process that can be manipulated in the classroom. The exceptional student is viewed in terms of characteristics within the parameters of input, response, and reinforcement. The input parameters involve the student's sensory acuity, orientation to task, perceptual function, and storage (memory) capabilities as they are related to visual, auditory, and tactile modalities. The response functions include dexterity, orientation, organization, and delay expressed through motor and verbal modalities. There also are elements such as a reinforcement parameter, acuity, orientation, and delay effect (long-term memory), each of which is related in amount and ratio to the social and informational modalities (the receipt of information).

Quay presents a scheme concerned with the fundamentals of the learning process in which specific remedial procedures are linked directly to diagnosis. For example, he notes that the acuity in all senses—vision, hearing, and tactile—might be a point of initial observation or measurement of input considerations. Then the diagnostician is concerned with the response counterpart, which might be dexterity or the ability to respond accurately and appropriately. The third component, reinforcement, involves orientation toward the stimulus so that the child may respond. Orientation, according to Quay, is a reinforcer but also assists the student with the input function of receiving and perceiving sensory stimuli as well as forming a response to those stimuli.

Quay's information processing plan provides information relevant to the remediation of the learner in the areas of perception—the ability to generate the required response to incoming perceptual information and storage and to retain stimulus data for future use.

Information also is provided on the status of the instructional intervention in the form of its effect: the capacity of a reinforcer actually to enhance appropriate learning behavior; delay and amount of reinforcement; when and how much reinforcement is applied; and the ratio, a frequency with which the students' correct responses are reinforced.

The input, response, and reinforcement model is shown in Exhibit 8-1. It may be seen that the above categories are enhanced further by the inclusion of modalities on the ordinate of the figure. The result is an organizational schema for the collection of student performance data in an organized manner that assists in identifying areas of strength or weakness in the individual child. This, of course, is a primary concern of measurement on the Individualized Education Program (IEP).

Information processing models such as Quay's, which describe learning procedures, are not new. Neisser (1967), Broadbent (1958), and Simon (1967) are only a few of the scientists who have directed their life's work toward the belief that information is processed in a systematic manner. Unfortunately, while most scientists will agree that information does flow into the central nervous system, there is no agreement on how it is processed. Although such models have great appeal, there generally is only tentative evidence to support their premises. The value of any information processing model may lie more in its abilities in organization, hypothesis formulation, and testing than its capability actually to represent a (any) learning event. Quay's work sensitizes the user to view information to be learned as water being channeled into irrigation ditches, thence to be fed into specific areas of a large field. The information must be controlled vigorously by the teacher, with firsthand knowledge of where it is to go and what it is to do if it is to be learned. The theory is that learning from a neurologically different nervous system requires systematic control over the environment and the information, with knowledge of where the difficulties for learning exist.

CATERALL'S MODEL

Caterall (1970) describes a model of service delivery that has many practical implications for intervention. Its major aspects are the directness of approach (direct or indirect intervention) and the focus of approach (the environmental or personal interaction plane). The taxonomy described by Caterall assists the diagnostician in considering the many influential factors of learning. Among them are the role of the teacher, the role of support personnel, the classroom environment, and the directness or indirectness of the intervention.

Caterall provides the following definitions that have relevance both in measurement and instruction:

    a. Things that can be done around the student—Environmental Interventions

Exhibit 8-1 Parameters, Modalities, and Functions of Quay's Learning Characteristics Structure

	PARAMETERS													
	Input				Reponse				Reinforcement					
	FUNCTIONS				FUNCTIONS				FUNCTIONS					
MODALITIES	Acuity	Orien-tation	Percep-tion	Failure to Store	Dexter-ity	Orien-tation	Organi-zation	Delay	Acuity	Orien-tation	Effect	Delay	Amt.	Ratio
Visual														
Auditory														
Tactile														
Motor														
Verbal														
Primary														
Social														
Information														

Source: Reprinted from "The Facets of Educational Exceptionality: A Conceptual Framework for Assessment, Grouping, and Instruction" by H. C. Quay in *Exceptional Children* by permission of The Council for Exceptional Children, © 1968.

b. Things that can be done to the student—Installed Interventions
c. Things that can be accomplished by the student—Assigned Interventions
d. Things that can be done with the student—Transactional Interventions (p. 5).

An example of environmental interventions is special class placement; installed intervention involves changing or adding reinforcers to increase or stabilize a behavioral response; indirect assigned intervention (not a direct academic objective) is the completion of social role playing designed to help the student to handle "real" social situations; transactional intervention involves direct student-interviewer relationships such as contact-schedule production of assigned lessons or desired behavioral response.

In general, Caterall's (1970) taxonomy is straightforward and easy to understand (Exhibit 8-2). Its use seems quite practical in formulating student IEPs.

SABATINO'S MODEL

The Sabatino (1968) model describes learner characteristics, showing that environmental stimulation begins as sensory input in the receptors, where it is coded neurally for transmission to the perceptual centers. Perception is the interpretation of sensory information into meaningful units for further relay to the language reception centers. In these centers, language is formed into symbolic conceptual units. The higher centers must be able to receive, express, associate, and mediate symbolic conceptual units in a systematic manner if language is to be used normally.

The model implies that the integration, sequencing, and storage (memory) of perceptual information is from both visual and auditory input. Perception follows, and arousal occurs as the interconnection between a meaningful perceptual input is related to the appropriate units of the language centers in the central nervous system. This last point has important educational implications: a lack of arousal may be the reason that certain information cannot maintain a child's attention and therefore is not directed into the symbolic conceptual centers where it can be "learned." Figure 8-3 is a graphic display of the Sabatino information processing model.

From a practical standpoint, this model results in a systematic assessment procedure using a descriptor system, the purpose of which is to ensure that most academic and nonacademic behaviors that can be described are in fact described. The basic description may suggest that the behavior is within a

Exhibit 8-2 Caterall's Three-Stage Diagnostic Teaching Plan

WHAT	WHO	HOW
STAGE I Identifying skills for group instruction based on the following: A. Demands of core program B. Analysis of "Hard Data"	TEACHERS AND READING SPECIALIST	Core program material
STAGE II Individualized implementation of in-class program based on the following: A. Pupil response B. Teacher observation of pupils in group C. Reading Specialist observations of pupils in group D. Analysis of appropriate instructional sequence	Classroom teacher individualizes according to pupils needs within classroom Consultation with the reading specialist may be necessary	Selected supplementary materials according to mode and need of pupil. Techniques: Utilize a variety of materials —manipulative, paper-pencil, observational, combination.
STAGE III Specific Prescription using supplemental services based on the following: A. Pass-fail test data B. Classroom Response C. Prerequisite Skills	READING SPECIALIST	Implementation of specific skills by reading aide or tutors using selected materials chosen by Reading Specialist

Source: Reprinted from "Taxonomy of Prescriptive Intervention" by C. D. Caterall by permission of *Journal of School Psychology,* © 1970.

Figure 8-3 Sabatino's Information Processing Model

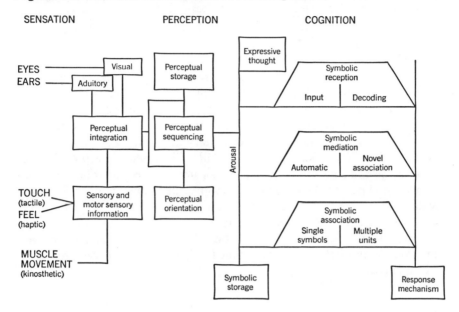

Source: Reprinted from "The Information Processing Behaviors Associated with Learning Disabilities" by D. A. Sabatino by permission of *Journal of Learning Disabilities*, © 1968.

normal range for that particular child's age or is inhibiting the pupil's function in that and related areas of performance.

The psychoeducational diagnostician using similar systems should view it as a pilot does a preflight checkoff of an aircraft. The research to date (Ryckman & Wiegerink, 1969; Sabatino, 1968) suggests there are at least four areas that must be described in this checkoff: visual perception, auditory perception, perceptual integration, and receptive-expressive language. Since these four information processing behavioral complexities must be addressed with a stimulus input, and while the exact nature of the component traits of each complex behavior is not clear, Sabatino's stimulus response descriptor system assists the diagnostician in classifying learner characteristics. The system has four major classifications:

1. motor—nonacademic behavior
2. perceptual—nonacademic behavior
3. language—directly related to nonacademic and academic behaviors
4. academic—academic remediation

These four were selected because they make it possible to sort learner characteristics for classification, study, and assignment to instructional materials. Motor disabilities are the most basic and the most difficult to remediate in regard to academic achievement. Perceptual training may show some transfer to academic learning but it is primarily to provide for the classification of perceptual information, storage, and integration of visual or auditory received material. Language learning is related directly to academic learning, for without language there is no basis for learning academic subject matter. However, language training (as in the case of vocabulary development) does not mean that reading vocabulary also will increase automatically. Finally, direct academic remediation of achievement skills provides the richest increase in skill growth but does not improve coordination, balance, perception, and possibly new language. In short, educational prescriptions can provide the training of a specific academic or nonacademic behavior. The professional judgment of the educator is required to determine the conduct that needs the most attention. To facilitate the judgment process, a system identifying many of the more important human learning characteristics is provided in Exhibit 8-3.

FROSTIG'S MODEL

There are five standardized tests that comprise the battery given by the Marianne Frostig Center of Educational Therapy: the *Frostig Movement Skills Test Battery,* the *Marianne Frostig Developmental Test of Visual Perception,* the *Wepman Test of Auditory Discrimination,* the *Illinois Test of Psycholinguistic Abilities* (ITPA), and the *Wechsler Intelligence Scale for Children* (WISC).

These assessment instruments yield information about the child's educational programming and remediation in the following areas: awareness of the outside world, body awareness, eye-hand coordination, balance, strength, flexibility, visually guided movement, auditory discrimination, auditory figure-ground perception, auditory closure, recognition and discrimination of auditory sequences, eye-motor coordination, figure ground perception, space perception, perception of spatial relationships, receptive and expressive language, use of symbols, organization and association of perceptions and concepts, use of imagery and memory for sequences, verbal comprehension, and attention and concentration. An analysis of the abilities assessed by four of the five standardized instruments is presented in Exhibit 8-4.

Frostig (1976) views the assessment of the child's basic abilities as the first step in providing an educational program that will maximize the pupil's psychological functions and, thus, academic abilities.

Exhibit 8-3 A Descriptor System for Classifying Learner Characteristics

1.0	MOTOR
1.1	Gross
1.11	Coordination-Balance
1.12	Strength-Endurance
1.2	Perceptual-Motor
1.21	Eye-Hand Coordination
1.22	Directionality
1.3	Body Awareness
2.0	PERCEPTION
2.1	Visual
2.11	Discrimination
2.12	Memory
2.13	Integration/primary visual input
2.2	Auditory
2.21	Discrimination
2.22	Memory
2.23	Integration/primary auditory input
2.3	Tactile
3.0	LANGUAGE
3.1	Conceptual
3.11	Concrete
3.12	Functional
3.13	Abstract
3.2	Expressive
3.21	Vocabulary
3.22	Syntax
3.3	Receptive
4.0	ACADEMICS
4.1	Reading
4.11	Letter Recognition
4.12	Word Attack
4.121	Phonics
4.122	Structural Analysis
4.13	Word Recognition
4.14	Vocabulary
4.15	Comprehension
4.2	Spelling

Exhibit 8-3 continued

4.3	Writing
4.31	Manuscript
4.32	Cursive
4.4	Arithmetic
4.41	Numeration
4.42	Computation
4.43	Measurement

MEEKER'S STRUCTURE OF INTELLECT

One model of cognitive abilities was developed specifically to provide greater accessibility to practicing educators on the Structure of Intellect (SOI). Guilford and Hoepfner's (1971) SOI model of intellectual aptitudes or learning characteristics was designed to teach students *how* to learn. The rationale is quite simple. Information is piling up too fast to be learned in rote manner. The nature of human intelligence, at least as it is measured, requires the integration of human abilities. Teaching the curriculum as commercially printed is a secure thing to do, and a traditional requirement of most schools. To teach human abilities—that is reasoning, memory, problem solving—is much more difficult and requires the instructor to go beyond the role learning of this or that assumed task. Meeker (1969) writes, "One goal of cognitive therapy is the realization of a student's learning potential, and the process requires some measure of his abilities and some concrete means of exploiting his strengths and developing his weaknesses. . . . Cognitive Therapy, for all of its practical *saliency* and patently direct approach, is not a generally well-developed practice in the educational system" (pp. 6–7).

Guilford and Hoepfner's work is an extension of Thurstone and has been validated by a host of researchers using factor analytic methods. The model proposes a number of operational byproducts. Thus, every intellectual activity may be characterized in terms of the type of operation that is used, the content involved, and the product that results. Figure 8-4 delineates the three categories that recognize the Structure of Intellect cube as well as its subclasses within each category. What is important to note is that each intellectual act requires one cell from all three categories. Hence, CFU, or *C*ognition (C), as an operation may be *F*igural (*F*); it also could be *S*ymbolic, se*M*antic, or *B*ehavioral, and under the Products classification it could involve *U*nits, *C*lasses, *R*elations, *S*ystems, *I*nformation, or *I*mplications. That point is made in Figure 8-5.

Exhibit 8-4 Frostig's Model Analysis of Standardized Tests

The Frostig Movement Skills Test Battery	Frostig Developmental Test of Visual Perception	Illinois Test of Psycholinguistic Abilities	Wechsler Intelligence Scale for Children
Bilateral eye-hand coordination and dexterity. Eye-hand and fine motor coordination involving crossing the midline of the body. (Children with learning difficulties are frequently deficient in this ability). Visual-motor coordination involving aiming and accuracy.	Eye-hand coordination (necessary for handwriting, drawing, arts and crafts, manipulatory and self-help activities). Ability to focus visually on relevant aspects of visual field and "tune out" irrelevant background. Ability to see sameness of essential form despite changes of	Auditory reception Visual reception Manual expression Verbal expression Auditory association Visual association Grammatic closure Auditory sequential memory Visual sequential memory Visual closure Auditory closure (optional)	General background of knowledge acquired from experiences in the cultural environment. Ability to determine essential relationships (usually of an abstract nature) between two objects or concepts. Ability to concentrate and exert a mental effort utilizing abstract numer- Ability to distinguish essential from nonessential details from a visually perceived object from everyday life. Ability to arrange cartoon-like pictorial sequences to make a meaningful story (requires planning and anticipating sequential and causal events). The ability to an-

Exhibit 8-4 continued

The Frostig Movement Skills Test Battery	Frostig Developmental Test of Visual Perception	Illinois Test of Psycholinguistic Abilities	Wechsler Intelligence Scale for Children
Ability to flex spine, back muscles, and hamstring ligaments. Leg strength. Running speed and ability to make quick stops, changes of direction, and changes of body position. Speed and agility in changing body position from a lying to a standing position.	image on retina. Has implication for learning to identify letters presented in various prints. Ability to discriminate position, ability to differentiate letters such as d and b, w and m. Ability to see spatial relationships of objects to one another, related to ability	Sound blending (optional)	ical concepts and arithmetic operations. Verbal comprehension, verbal fluency, and word knowledge acquired from environmental experiences. Common sense and judgment regarding the socially accepted action in a given situation. Immediate audi- alyze an abstract pattern into its parts and to reproduce the parts into an anticipatory image of the whole (requires visual-motor coordination and nonverbal abstract reasoning). The ability to assemble parts of a known or imagined object into a

Abdominal muscle strength. Ability to maintain dynamic balance. Static balance with eyes open. Static balance with eyes closed. Arm and shoulder girdle muscle strength.	to perceive the sequence of letters in a word.	tory sequential memory (requires attention and concentration).	meaningful whole (requires visual organization, flexibility, and the ability to integrate new clues). The ability to learn a new task requiring visual-motor coordination, visual memory, concentration, and speed. The ability to plan ahead to reach a goal in a paper-and-pencil maze (requires visual-motor coordination, planning, and delay of impulsive action).

Source: Reprinted from *Education for Dignity* by Marianne Frostig by permission of Grune & Stratton, Inc., © 1976.

Figure 8-4 Guilford and Hoepfner Structure of Intellect Model

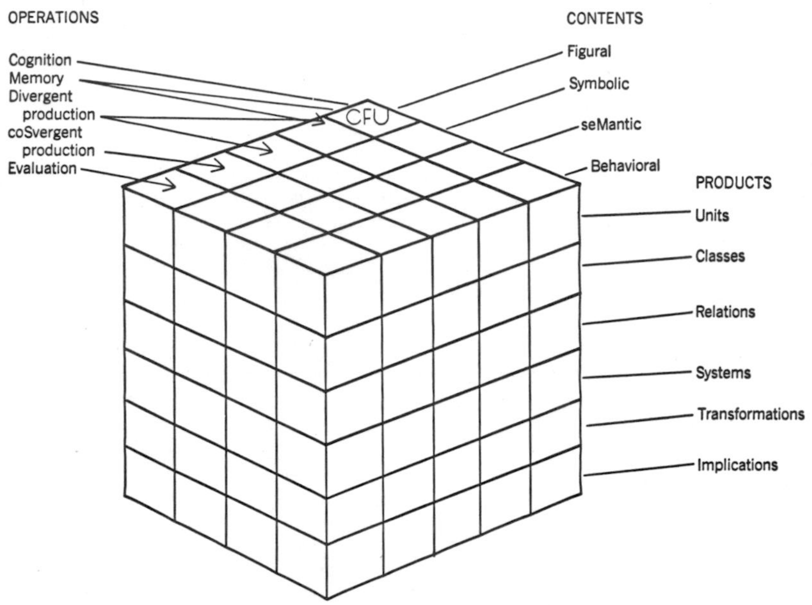

Source: Reprinted from *The Analysis of Intelligence* by J. P. Guilford and R. Hoepfner by permission of McGraw-Hill Book Company, © 1971.

Complete characterization of an intellectual ability is achieved in terms of the possible subclass differentiation on each of the three major dimensions. "Operations" is differentiated five ways: *C*ognition, *M*emory, *D*ivergent *P*roduction, con*V*ergent *P*roduction, and *E*valuation. Figure 8-5 demonstrates the breaking apart of the major slices (operations) of the matrix cube. *C*ontents and *P*roducts are identical components in each of the major operations. "Contents" is differentiated by four subclasses: *F*igural, *S*ymbolic, se*M*antic, and *B*ehavioral. "Products" is differentiated by six subcategories: *U*nits, *C*lasses, *R*elations, *S*ystems, *T*ransformations, and *I*mplications. The complete schema is represented by a three-dimensional classification array of 120 predicted cells or categories of intellectual abilities (Meeker, 1969, p. 9).

It is important for educators to recognize that information processing terminology and the aptitudes described by learning theorists generally are

Figure 8-5 Operations, Contents, and Products of Guilford and Hoepfner Structure of Intellect

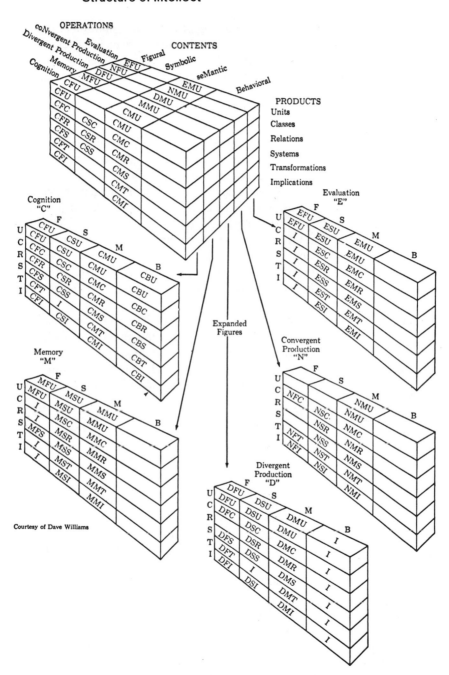

PRODUCTS
Units
Classes
Relations
Systems
Transformations
Implications

Expanded
Figures

Courtesy of Dave Williams

Source: Reprinted from *The Structure of Intellect: Its Interpretations and Uses* by M. N. Meeker by permission of The Charles E. Merrill Publishing Co., Inc., © 1969.

one and the same. Using Guilford and Hoepfner's own definition of the major categories and subcategories that explain the Structure of Intellect, a careful reading of the definitions (Exhibit 8-5) is highly recommended.

These six cognitive skills are behaviorally defined in terms of their component subtasks:

Knowledge: Consists of cognizance of specific terminology and facts; understanding of methods related to conventions, trends and sequences, classifications and categories, and criteria and methodology; and acquaintance with principles, generalizations, theories, and structures of a universal and abstract nature.

Comprehension: refers to the translation, interpretation, and extrapolation of information.

Application: is viewed as a single unitary skill involved in all problem-solving situations, and thus is not defined in terms of subtasks.

Analysis: is composed of abilities such as the identification of salient features or elements and awareness of significant relationships and organizational principles.

Synthesis: refers to the production of unique communications, strategies for operations, and abilities to determine abstract relationships.

Evaluation: is the highest order cognitive skill; utilizes all prior skills and criteria in decision making both from internal evidence and external criteria.

Bloom's taxonomy has been widely used for curriculum development. Organized instructional units can be developed to teach children how to acquire knowledge and comprehension skills, apply this information in the form of specific projects, and finally analyze, synthesize, and evaluate any educational product that results.

Although Bloom's taxonomy has been utilized frequently with gifted children (emphasizing the higher thought processes of analysis, synthesis, and evaluation), it also has application to evaluating the thinking processes of learning handicapped children and in planning specific remediation of cognitive deficiencies. For example, if a student exhibits an inability to synthesize input adequately, Bloom's taxonomy allows the development of activities ranging from simple puzzle construction to a recombination of abstract relationships.

Exhibit 8-5 Definitions for Structure of Intellect

DEFINITIONS OF CATEGORIES

Operations:

Major kinds of intellectual activities or processes; things the person does with the raw materials of information, information being defined as "that which the person discriminates."

Cognition:

Immediate discovery, awareness, rediscovery, or recognition of information in various forms; comprehension or understanding.

Memory:

Retention or storage, with some degree of availability, of information in the same form [in which] it was committed to storage and in response to the same cues in connection with which it was learned.

Evaluation:

Reaching decisions or making judgments concerning criterion satisfaction (correctness, suitability, adequacy, desirability, etc.) of information.

Convergent Production:

Generation of information from given information where the emphasis is upon achieving unique or conventionally accepted best outcomes; it is likely the given information (cue) fully determines the response.

Divergent Production:

Generation of information from given information where the emphasis is upon variety and quality of output from the same source. Likely to involve what has been called transfer. This operation is most clearly involved in aptitudes of creative potential.

Exhibit 8-5 continued

Contents:

Broad classes or types of information discriminable by the organism:

Figural: Shapes like trees, forms, or concrete objects, and most of them would be recognized or comprehended as visual or kinesthetic forms or totalities.

Symbolic: If the stimulus material is learned in the form of a numeral, a single letter, or a note of music; if the kind of stimulus is distinguishable from a figural one, it is called a symbol.

Semantic: Semantics refers to words and ideas where an abstract meaning is so associated in the individual's repertoire of knowledge that its external referent calls up the internally associated stored word.

Behavioral: Behavioral is perhaps the most intriguing from the psychologists' point of view. Behavior is both a manifestation of a response and a stimulus.

Products:

The organization that information takes in the organism's processing of it.

U—Units: Figures, for example, can be processed singly, in which case it is a unit which is being perceived; that is, one figure, or one symbol, or a single word idea is a unit.

C—Classes: There is a hierarchy inferred in the products dimension, for in a sense each subsumes the preceding one. For example, classes follow units. It is valid to suppose that before one can make classifications or perform a classifying task, one would have to perceive the units to be classified.

R—Relations: Relations or connections between the content involved—relations between figures, or between symbols as in deciphering a code, or relations between words or ideas (semantics). . . . Many of the materials developed for the Montessori

Exhibit 8-5 continued

schools teach relational aspects. One example is a set of wooden cylinders in which varied materials are sealed. When the child rattles them he is asked to match two that sound alike. An auditory task is involved here when the student is asked, and at the same time he is being taught, to discriminate auditory differences—a task which can be accomplished successfully only if he understands the differences in relationships such as loud and heavy and soft or high and deep so that he can match similar sounds. Kinesthetic tasks and olfactory tasks can be devised as well. Many items in high-school group IQ tests are exclusively relationship tests—relations between sequences of numerals or geometric figures. Some tests actually formulate the student's score into an IQ score, yet relations between figures are the only ability being tested. The IQ score goes into the record as a permanent indication of the student's academic potential, and counseling judgments are made accordingly. Suffice it to say that intelligence is much more complicated than a single IQ score based on results of any one or two abilities or any one test result.

S—Systems: Systems may be composed of figures, symbols, or semantics. A system can be mathematical, as in arithmetic, or composed of numerals written as words where the subject must comprehend the idea of a sequence of arithmetic operations necessary for solution.

T—Transformations: It [sic] labels a more abstract ability. If a task requires that redefinitions or modifications of the existing information be made into other information, it means that the person is in some way transforming the original material. This kind of ability may demand visual, auditory, abstract, or motor flexibility and has been found to characterize people who have been termed creative.

I—Implications: The final and most abstract ability category across the model is implications. The ability to foresee consequences involved in figural problems can be demonstrated visually, vocally, or by motor expression. Maze tracing, a task most commonly found in IQ tests, is testing the ability to see implications in figural material. (Meeker, 1969, 13–36)

Exhibit 8-6 Bloom's Cognitive Taxonomy

MAJOR COMPONENTS IN BLOOM'S TAXONOMY

The following levels comprise the cognitive taxonomy:
1. *knowledge,* including the ability to:
   a. recall, remember
   b. recognize a given object or idea when it is presented
2. *comprehension,* including the ability to:
   a. predict
   b. generalize
   c. interpret
3. *application,* including the ability to:
   a. apply or use ideas in appropriate ways
4. *analysis,* including the ability to:
   a. detect fallacies
   b. detect interrelations
   c. detect cause and effect
5. *synthesis,* including the ability to:
   a. create
   b. propose new solutions
6. *evaluation,* including the ability to:
   a. judge on the basis of criteria

Source: Reprinted from *Taxonomy of Educational Objectives, Handbook I: Cognitive Domain,* B. C. Bloom, Ed., by permission of David McKay Company, Inc., © 1956.

VALETT'S MODEL

Valett (1978) also classifies development into a six-level basic learning abilities classification system (Exhibit 8-7). Cognition begins on Level 3, and includes Levels 4 and 5. The structure proposed by Valett may be viewed as a systematic means of planning remediation for learning disabled children. It is developmental, beginning with gross motor in Level 1 and continuing through conceptual skills in Level 5. Moreover, it provides the diagnostician a road map of activities and a structure for ascertaining sensory, perceptual, and cognitive function (with some attention paid to social skill development).

This model can be used as a framework for investigating and remediating task difficulties and skill deficiencies in any of the basic learning abilities. Valett also augments this model with a curriculum guide, *The Remediation*

Exhibit 8-7 Critical Features of Valett's System

BASIC LEARNING ABILITIES

Level 1: Gross motor development

- Rolling (controlled)
- Sitting (erect)

- Crawling (smoothly)
- Walking (coordinated)
- Running (course)
- Throwing (accurately)
- Jumping (obstacles)
- Skipping (alternately)
- Dancing (eurythmy)
- Self-identification (name awareness)
- Body localization (part location)
- Body abstraction (transfer, generalization)
- Muscular strength (sit-ups, leg-ups, bends)
- General physical health (significant history)

Level 2: Sensory-motor integration

- Balance and rhythm (games, dance)
- Body-spatial organization (mazes)
- Reaction-speed dexterity (motor accuracy)
- Tactile discrimination (object identification)
- Directionality (right-left, etc.)
- Laterality (hand-eye-foot)
- Time orientation (lapse and concept)

Level 3: Perceptual-motor skills
Auditory

Visual

- Acuity (Snellen chart)
- Coordination and pursuit (tracking)
- Form discrimination (association)
- Figure-ground (differentiation)
- Memory (visual recall)

Visual-motor

- Memory (designs)
- Fine muscle coordination (designs)
- Spatial-form manipulation (blocks)
- Speed of learning (coding)
- Integration (Draw-A-Man)

Level 4: Language development

- Vocabulary (word knowledge)
- Fluency and encoding (use and structure)
- Articulation (initial, medial, final)
- Word attack skills (phonic association)
- Reading comprehension (understanding)
- Writing (expression)
- Spelling (oral, written)

Level 5: Conceptual skills

- Number concepts (counting)
- Arithmetic processes ($+ - \times \div$)
- Arithmetic reasoning (problem solving)
- General information (fund of knowledge)

Exhibit 8-7   continued

- Acuity (functional hearing)
- Decoding (following directions)
- Vocal association (imitative response)
- Memory (retention)
- Sequencing (patterning)

- Classification (relationships)
- Comprehension (common sense reasoning)

Level 6: Social skills

- Social acceptance (friendship)
- Anticipatory response (foresight)
- Value judgments (ethical-moral sense)

Source: From Valett, Robert E.: Developing cognitive abilities: Teaching children to think, St. Louis, 1978, The C. V. Mosby Co.

of Learning Disabilities (1974). This guide describes developmental-remedial prescriptive lessons, commercial programs, and material resources.

Summary

This chapter has reviewed the types of service and program delivery structures used principally in the elementary schools. The review examined self-contained classes, resource rooms, and special education teacher consultant services for learning disabled children. A few of the less well-known programs, such as assessment classes and learning centers (material centers) also were discussed.

The chapter fails to do two things.

First, it fails to bring support services into the program because it is difficult to cover all the options available when speech and hearing, language, occupational, and physical therapists are added and when psychologists, social workers, nutritionists, and remedial educators are brought to bear in harmony with the learning disability program. The chapter did relate the inability of the special education teacher either to be a one-person band or to work in a single program dimension, i.e., as a resource teacher calling that effort a learning disability program. A learning disability program is a continuum of activities and services that focus all the helping (human resources) disciplines on the child as needed in an interdisciplinary team relationship.

Second, the chapter doesn't say what to teach. This text is against "the approach" or the cookbook style of compendium. What learning disabilities practitioners don't need is a theory, model, or set of constructs for viewing the learner and developing a program to match the child's characteristics. In the last section (on content models), the authors have done that.

Exhibit 8-8 Summary of Diagnostic/Remedial Models

	Dunn	Quay	Sabatino	Frostig	Meeker	Valett
Motor Development	Early stages of psycho-motor development to fine and large motoric development necessary for vocational training	Dexterity of motoric response to input from sense modalities	Sensory (tactile, haptic, kinesthetic) and motor sensory information	Awareness of outside world, body awareness, eye-hand coordination, balance, strength, flexibility		Gross motor development including self-identification, body localization, body abstraction, muscular strength, general physical health
Perceptual Training	Ability to adequately receive, organize, and convert information from sense modalities (hearing, sight, touch) into meaningful	Acuity in all senses— vision, hearing, and touch. Orientation toward a sensory stimulus in order to receive, perceive, and	Perceptual (auditory/visual) integration. Perceptual storage, sequencing, and orientation	Visually guided movement, eye-motor coordination. Auditory and visual discrimination, figure perception, and audi-	Discriminating figural, symbolic, semantic, and behavioral stimuli through senses. Organizing and processing units,	Sensory motor integration including balance and rhythm, body spatial organization, motor accuracy, tactile discrimination, directionality, laterality, time orientation, visual acuity, coordination, form discrim-

Exhibit 8-8 continued

	Dunn	Quay	Sabatino	Frostig	Meeker	Valett
	units of awareness	respond to sensory stimuli adequately		tory and visual closure, space perception	classes, relations, systems of information, transforming existing information, foreseeing consequences	ination, figure ground, and memory. Perceptual motor skills, including acuity, decoding, vocal association, memory, sequencing
Cognitive Training	Intervention consists of assisting child to acquire and store knowledge as well as generate and evaluate information	Organization and storage of information	Symbolic reception, mediation, association, storing, storage of information as well as expressive thought	Recognition and discrimination of auditory sequences; use of symbols, organization, and association of perceptions and concepts: utilization of imagery,	Discovery, awareness, rediscovery or recognition of information in various forms, memory, convergent and divergent production, evaluation	Conceptual skills: number concepts, arithmetic processes, reasoning, information, classification, comprehension

Communication Training	Stimulation of overall language ability, improve mild to moderate speech disorders	Dexterity, orientation, organization, and delay of verbal response	Receptive and expressive language related to academic learning	verbal comprehension, attention and concentration; memory for sequences	
Social and Personal Development	Instruction concerned with insights into self and others and in assessing the self's effect on others	Orientation toward relevant stimuli and responding in an appropriate fashion	Academic-social environmental relationships	Receptive and expressive language	Social acceptance, anticipatory response, value judgments

Exhibit 8-8 continued

	Dunn	Quay	Sabatino	Frostig	Meeker	Valett
Vocational/ Self-Help Skills	Intervention emphasizes good work habits, independence, rehabilitation, and social skills necessary to obtain and maintain a job					
Academic Remediation			Achievement skills related to academic areas			

The authors must be forgiven if they cannot tell readers what to do—remember, there are no clear-cut rules of learning. We recommend readers develop a process that makes sense and base instruction on that, using good judgment and also a great deal of consultation and improvisation.

To conclude, Exhibit 8-8 is offered as a summary of the Diagnostic Remediation Models. The intent in reviewing the principal characteristics of these models is to encourage readers to fill gaps in developing their own systematic procedure for describing learner characteristics and for devising remedial activities that are logically complete in meeting instructional objectives.

REFERENCES

Adelman, H.S. The resource concept: Bigger than a room! *Journal of Special Education,* 1972, *6,* 361–367.

Algozzine, R.F., & Sutherland, J. Nonpsychological foundations of learning disabilities. *The Journal of Special Education,* 1977, *11*(1), 91–98.

Arehart-Treichel, J. The good health shining light. *Human Behavior,* 1975, *4*(1), 16–23.

Barksdale, M.W., & Atkinson, A.P. A resource room approach to instruction for the educable retarded. *Focus on Exceptional Children.* 1971, *3*(4), 12–15.

Beery, K.E., & Buktenica, N.A. *Developmental Test of Visual Motor Integration.* Chicago: Follett Publishing Co., 1967.

Bennett, A.A. *A comparative study of the progress of subnormal pupils in the garden and in special classes.* New York: Columbia University, 1963.

Bloom, B.C. (Ed). *Taxonomy of educational objectives Handbook I: Cognitive domain.* New York: David McKay Company, Inc., 1956.

Broadbent, D.E. *Perception and Communication.* New York: Pergamon Press, 1958.

Bronzaft, A.L., & McCarthy, D.P. The effect of elevated train noise on reading ability. *Environment and Behavior,* 1975, *7*(4), 517–528.

Brophy, J.E., & Good, T. *Teacher-student relationships: Causes and consequences.* New York: Holt Rinehart Winston Inc., 1974.

Cassidy, V., & Stanton, J. *An investigation of factors involved in the educational placement of mentally retarded children: A study of differences between children of special and regular classes in Ohio.* Columbus, Ohio: The Ohio State University, 1959.

Caterall, C.D. Taxonomy of prescriptive intervention. *Journal of School Psychology,* 1970, *8,* 5–12.

Cegelka, W.J., & Tyler, J.L. The efficacy of special class placement for the mentally retarded in proper perspective. *Training School Bulletin,* 1970, *6*(5), 1–18.

Christie, L.S., McKenzie, H.S., & Burdett, C.S. The consulting teacher approach to special education: Inservice training for regular classroom teachers. *Focus on Exceptional Children,* 1972, *4*(5), 1–12.

Cienion, M. Some aspects of a learning resource room. In J. I. Arena (Ed.), *Successful programming: Many points of view.* Pittsburgh: Association for Children with Learning Disabilities, 1968.

Clark, P. The magic of the learning center. *California Teachers' Association Journal,* 1969, *65,* 16–20.

Cohen, S., Glass, D.C., & Singer, J.E. Apartment noise, auditory discrimination, and reading ability in children. *Journal of Experimental Social Psychology,* 1973, *9,* 407–422.

Connor, E.M., & Muldoon, J.F. Resource programming for emotionally disturbed teenagers. *Exceptional Children,* 1967, *34*(4), 261–265.

Deno, E. *Instructional alternatives for exceptional children.* Arlington, Va.: The Council for Exceptional Children, 1973.

Dunn, L.M. Special education for the mildly retarded: Is much of it justified? *Exceptional Children,* 1968, *35*(1), 5–22.

Elenbogen, M.A. *A comparative study of some aspects of academic and social adjustment of two groups of mentally retarded children in special classes and regular grades.* Unpublished doctoral dissertation, Northwestern University, 1957.

Flowers, R. The evaluation of auditory abilities in the appraisal of children with reading problems. In A. Figurel (Ed.), *Perception and Reading,* Newark, Del.: International Reading Association, 1968.

Fox, W. Consulting teacher program. In L. Schwartz, A. Oseroff, H. Drucker, & R. Schwartz (Eds.), *Innovative non-categorical and interrelated projects in the education of the handicapped.* Washington, D.C.: U.S. Office of Education, 1972.

Frostig, M. *Education for dignity.* New York: Grune & Stratton, Inc., 1976.

Galvin, J.P., Quay, H.C., Annesley, F.R., & Werry, J.S. An experimental resource room for behavior problem children. *Exceptional Children,* 1971, *38*(2), 131–137.

Getman, G.N., Kane, E.R., Halgren, M.R., & McKee, P.W. *Developing learning readiness,* St. Louis: McGraw-Hill Book Company, 1968.

Guilford, J.P., & Hoepfner, R. *The analysis of intelligence.* New York: McGraw-Hill Book Company, 1971.

Harris, W.J., & Mahar, C. Problems in implementing resource programs in rural schools. *Exceptional Children,* 1975, *42*(2), 95–99.

Hawisher, M.R. & Calhoun, M.L. *Mainstreaming the learning disabilities adolescent: A staff development guide.* Lancaster, S.C.: South Carolina Region V Educational Services Center, 1977.

Hawisher, M.R., & Calhoun, M.L. *The resource room: An access to excellence.* Lancaster, S.C.: South Carolina Region V Educational Services Center, 1975.

——————————. *The resource room: An educational asset for children with special needs.* Columbus, Ohio: The Charles E. Merrill Publishing Company, Inc., 1978.

Haywood, D.G. Psychological factors in the use of light and lighting in buildings. In J. Lang, C. Burnette, W. Moleski, & D. Vackon (Eds.), *Designing for human behavior.* Stroudsburg, Pa.: Dowden, Hutchinson, and Ross, 1974.

Hillerich, R. L. The creative learning center. *Elementary School Journal,* 1969, *69,* 259–264.

Hobson v. Hansen, 269 F. Supp. 401,497 (D.D.C. 1967).

Jenkins, J.R., & Mayhall, W.F. Development and evaluation of a resource teacher program. *Exceptional Children,* 1976, *43*(1), 21–29.

Johnson, G.O. Special education for the mentally handicapped—a paradox. *Exceptional Children,* 1962, *29*(2), 62–69.

Kephart, N.C. *The slow learner in the classroom.* Columbus, Ohio: The Charles E. Merrill Publishing Co., Inc., 1971.

Larsen, S.C. Learning disabilities specialist: Role and responsibilities. *Journal of Learning Disabilities,* 1976, *9*(8), 498–508.

Lerner, J.W. *Children with learning disabilities: Theories, diagnosis, and teaching strategy.* Boston: Houghton Mifflin Company, 1971.

Lewis, A.L. A resource room program for learning disability pupils. *Academic Therapy,* 1974, *10*(1), 93–100.

McKenzie, H.S. *The 1968–1969 yearly report of the consulting teacher program* (Vol. 1). Burlington, Vt.: University of Vermont, 1969.

McKenzie, H.S., Egner, A.N., Knight, M.F., Perelman, P.F., Schneider, B.M., & Garvin, J.S. Training consulting teachers to assist elementary teachers in handicapped children. *Exceptional Children,* 1970, *37*(2), 137–143.

Meeker, M.N. *The structure of intellect: Its interpretations and uses.* Columbus, Ohio: The Charles E. Merrill Publishing Co., Inc., 1969.

Miller, T.L., & Sabatino, D.A. An evaluation of the teacher consultant model as an approach to mainstreaming. *Exceptional Children,* 1978, *45*(2), 86–91.

Montgomery, M.D. The special educator as consultant: Some strategies. *Teaching Exceptional Children,* 1978, *10,* 110–112.

Neisser, V. *Cognitive psychology,* New York: Appleton-Century-Crofts, Inc., 1967.

Paroz, J., Siegenthaler, L.S., & Tatum, V.H. Model for a middle-school resource room. *Learning Disabilities,* 1977, *10*(1), 1–9.

Pennsylvania Association for Retarded Children v. Kurtzman, 343 F. Supp. 279 (E.D. Pa 1971).

Pysh, M.V. *The learning disabilities manual recommended procedures and practices.* Illinois State Board of Education, 1978.

Quay, H.C. The facets of educational exceptionality: A conceptual framework for assessment, grouping, and instruction. *Exceptional Children,* 1968, *35*(1), 25–32.

Reger, R. Resource rooms: Change agents or guardians of the status quo? *Journal of Special Education,* 1972, *6*(4), 355–359.

—————————. What is a resource room program? *Journal of Learning Disabilities,* 1973, *6*(10), 607–614.

Reger, R., & Koppmann, M. The child oriented resource room program. *Exceptional Children,* 1971, *37*(6), 460–462.

Reynolds, M. A framework for considering some issues in special education. *Exceptional Children,* 1962, *28*(7), 367–370.

Rodee, M. *A study to evaluate the resource teacher concept when used with high level educable retardates at the primary level.* Unpublished doctoral dissertation, University of Iowa, 1971.

Ryckman, D.B., & Wiegerink, R. Factors of the Illinois test of psycholinguistic abilities: A comparison of eighteen factor analyses. *Exceptional Children,* 1969, *36*(2), 107–113.

Sabatino, D.A. The information processing behaviors associated with learning disabilities. *Journal of Learning Disabilities,* 1968, *1*(8), 444–450.

—————————. The construction and assessment of an experimental test of auditory perception. *Exceptional Children,* 1969, *35*(9), 729–737.

—————————. An evaluation of resource rooms for children with learning disabilities. *Journal of Learning Disabilities,* 1971, *4*(2), 84–93.

—————————. Resource rooms: The renaissance in special education. *The Journal of Special Education,* 1972, *6*(4), 335–347.

Sabatino, D.A., Miller, P.F., & Schmidt, C.R. Cognitive training: Can intelligence be altered? *The Journal of Special Education* (in press).

Sabatino, D.A., & Hayden, D.L. Information processing behaviors related to learning disabilities and mental retardation. *Exceptional Children,* 1970, *37*(1), 21–29.

Scranton, T.R., Hajicek, J.O., & Wolcott, G.J. Physician and teacher as team: Assessing the effects of medication. *Journal of Learning Disabilities,* 1978, *11*(4), 205–209.

Simon, H.A. An information processing explanation of some perceptual phenomena. *British Journal of Psychology,* 1967, *58,* 1–12.

Smith, R.M., Neisworth, J.T. & Greer, J.G. *Evaluating educational environments,* Columbus, Ohio: The Charles E. Merrill Publishing Co., Inc., 1978.

Stelleren, J., Vasa, S., & Little, J. *Introduction into diagnostic-prescriptive teaching and programming.* Glen Ridge, N.J.: Exceptional Press, 1976.

Strauss, A.A., & Lehtinen, L.E. *Psychopathology and education of the brain-injured child.* New York: Grune & Stratton, Inc., 1947.

Tilley, B. *The effects of three educational placement systems on achievement, self-concept, and behavior in elementary mentally retarded children.* Unpublished doctoral dissertation, University of Iowa, 1970.

Valett, R.E. The learning resource center for exceptional children. *Exceptional Children,* 1970, *36*(7), 527–530.

——————————. *The remediation of learning disabilities* (2nd ed.). Belmont, Calif.: Fearon Publishers, Inc., 1974.

——————————. *Developing cognitive abilities: Teaching children to think.* St. Louis: The C. V. Mosby Company, 1978, 37.

Weiner, L.H. An investigation of the effectiveness of resource rooms for children with specific learning disabilities. *Journal of Learning Disabilities,* 1969, *2*(4), 49–55.

Wiederholt, J.L. Planning resource rooms for the mildly handicapped. *Focus on Exceptional Children,* 1974, *5*(8), 1–10.

Wiederholt, J.L., Hammill, D., and Brown, V. *The resource teacher: A guide to effective practices.* Boston: Allyn & Bacon, Inc., 1978.

Zito, R.J., and Bardon, J.I. Achievement motivation among Negro adolescents in regular special education programs. *American Journal of Mental Deficiency,* 1969, *74,* 20–26.

Chapter 9

Secondary and Postsecondary Educational Aspects of the Learning Disabled

David A. Sabatino

INTRODUCTION

It has been contended (Sabatino, 1978) that there is an absence of realistic information with which to alter the attitudes of secondary teachers and principals regarding mildly handicapped (high incidence) youth. It appears quite evident that handicapped elementary school age children benefit from the efficient delivery of well-developed special education programs. However, adolescent handicapped persons are not viewed by educators as requiring the same concentration of adaptive curricula or supportive service delivery. It is necessary that little handicapped children incapable of caring for themselves be provided service, at least in the eyes of the child-oriented teacher in the self-contained classroom.

Some educators reason that if opportunity is provided to adjust handicapping conditions in the elementary school, then those students who don't appear to be different physically or mentally should "outgrow" and respond favorably to the secondary academic arena, without the necessity for additional program adjustments. The inability of secondary teachers to see youth positively when they fail to learn or give evidence of other negative experiences in social and extracurricular activity indicates to these instructors that the students do not take advantage of the privilege to learn. Teachers maintain their prejudicial views concerning pupils' indifference, and continue overt measures to stop the students (*stop out* as opposed to *drop out*) from attending school. To be realistic, many secondary handicapped youths must face the attitudes of educators who are centered on subject matter, excluding from their consciousness the students who fail to achieve in the secondary academic setting.

One state superintendent of public instruction stated that if every handicapped junior or senior high school student who dropped out or was stopped from attending school the previous year suddenly appeared on the doorstep, there would not be enough money in the state educational budget to provide programs for them (Cronin, 1977). Such a public admission from a politically astute educator must have a strong message to teachers concerned with the priority of special education programs for adolescents.

Elementary vs. Secondary: The Gap

Data collected by the National Center for Educational Statistics (NCES) before the passage of Public Law 94-142 in 1975, and again in 1979, showed a sharp contrast between (a) the number of elementary and secondary handicapped students served, and (b) a fairly consistent gap in services for elementary as opposed to secondary.

The data indicate that handicapped children served nationally in the 1970–71 school year totaled 3,158,000; following the passage of P.L. 94-142, the enrollment jumped about 20 percent—to 3,777,106. That is a total gain for both elementary and secondary students of more than half a million handicapped served nationally. Proportionately, the incidence of handicapped students in both elementary and secondary school in that period remained constant at 10.7 percent (Grant & Lind, 1979). However, the figures for those receiving services tell quite a different story. In 1975, 5.9 percent of the secondary students, or half of the estimated total handicapped population, were receiving services (Grant & Lind, 1975). In 1978, the figure for secondary students still was only 5.9 percent, still roughly only half of the potential population, while elementary students in programs surpassed 90 percent. (These data are based on the U.S. Bureau for Education of the Handicapped annual report to Congress for 1978.) The NCES data raise a question deserving an answer. When P.L. 94-142 requires services to *all* handicapped children to age 21 (by 1981), why hasn't the gap between elementary and secondary program development closed more rapidly?

Regular educators, including administrators, convey the impression that providing special education services to the young is an appropriate action that coincides with the predominant ideologies and social philosophies of the nation. On the other hand, providing services to physically large, secondary age adolescents capable of purposeful decision making and, in particular, of norm violating behaviors, does not fit the country's social-moral views of youth.

The development of programs for mildly handicapped secondary students also is viewed as a relatively low educational priority (Scranton & Downs, 1975). That view is widely espoused by secondary teachers who treat school and academic learning as a privilege, not a right. Many secondary teachers fail to see learning or behavioral disabilities in mildly handicapped students, referring to them instead as indifferent manipulators who are lazy and undisciplined. The attitude fosters benign neglect, driven by an "us *v.* them" feeling.

Many secondary classes are taught with an "I present it, you learn it, or else" attitude by the teacher, which is supported by the principal. Evidence for such generalities may be drawn from the fact that 85 percent of the referrals for service to school psychologists are from the elementary school level (Hohenshil, 1975). Studies on attitude indicate the elementary teachers are child oriented by and large, while secondary teachers are subject centered, which may explain why two-thirds of the programs for handicapped children are in the elementary schools (Martin, 1972).

The Peer Problems

Another factor contributing to the absence of program development in the secondary schools is the attitude of regular students in making it impossible for handicapped pupils to feel at all comfortable with, and accepted by, their peers at a time in their lives when such recognition is critical.

Prejudicial attitudes among peers frequently are unkind to learning disabled adolescents who are earmarked by poor scholarship and behaviors that draw unfavorable attention to them, especially those who are unfortunate enough to be labeled in order to receive specialized services. A discriminating vocabulary, which changes every few years, delineates the secondary student with learning and behavioral disorders as a "retard" or "tard," "nummy," "wacko," "flake," and "speckie." These identifiers are not exactly terms of endearment. Socially and athletically, the learning disabled individual frequently is trapped in the lower track classes, where greater belligerence and indifference to teachers—and reciprocal disinterest by teachers—are evident.

As one mother who also was an elementary teacher put it, "I know he has a severe academic problem, I've always known it. But he has always gotten along just beautifully in school, and with his friends. Now his classmates are not the group he wants to be with, and they also resent him, which causes him to hate school." The problem she addressed was that her son was not invited to attend parties, to date, or to associate with children of like culture, finding himself among streetwise peers who disdained him as much socially and personally as he did them. The adjustment difficulties of bright (but not academic), socially attuned, learning disabled adolescents placed in low performance tracks on the basis of poor academic performance are now legend (French, 1958).

There simply are no data available on peer acceptance of secondary learning disabled students. Assumptions, drawing on research derived from elementary mentally retarded and learning disabled children, would indicate that at the younger ages, peer rejection can be expected (Gottlieb & Budoff, 1972). Bryan, in two studies (1974, 1976), found that fourth grade learning disabled children received significantly more votes on a scale of social rejection, and fewer votes on a scale of social attraction, than comparison pupils. Is it possible to assume that older children are even more rejecting? Data collected by Sabatino (1974) suggest that older youths are not more critical than those of elementary age but their self-perceptions are more sensitive to rejection. Adolescence is a time when youths abandon the primary social structure (home) to find identity with peer groups. If that identity is stifled by rejection, social sensitivity may result in overwhelming anxiety, depression, and the need to express aggression or withdrawal from the social situation.

What results is a belief, which is advanced in this chapter, that adolescent learning disabled youths cannot be classified and compared programmatically with handicapped elementary age children. It is the author's point of departure that these adolescents have assigned such importance to social interaction that academic learning, or the absence of it, may influence that relationship. For that reason, this chapter makes no attempt to depict the learning disabled adolescent as a sweet child, wronged by a system that doesn't understand. Rather, it presents syndromes that evidence symptoms associated with secondary youths indicating that truancy, aggression, dropouts, drugs, delinquency, gang affiliation, and depressive withdrawal must be viewed as important social personal aspects of self-concept, affecting the will to achieve. These are important ingredients to consider in these adolescents' school program. That is not to say that every learning disabled child has a primary or secondary behavioral disorder. But, it is a safe bet that more than half of them do. And, if you don't believe us, ask a secondary learning disability teacher, if you can find one. There are only a few out there.

Career Goals and Possibilities

What are the career goal possibilities for learning disabled adolescents as they reach for adulthood? Vocationally, educationally, personally, and socially, are learning disabled children scarred for life? Why has the Rehabilitation Act of 1973 (P.L. 93-112) failed to include learning disabled children as clients for services when visually and hearing sensory handicapped, orthopedically handicapped, emotionally disturbed, and the mentally retarded qualify for vocational training and (for the first three groups) special assistance for college preparation? Is it someone's belief that learning disabled students with superior intelligence but with perceptual-language disabilities that result in academic achievement deficits cannot benefit from vocational rehabilitation services, or is it a matter of cost?

The military also have academic standards for officers and selected entrants into specialized training that exclude many learning disabled children. If failure in school is experienced for a number of years, are indelible marks imprinted for life on adolescents reaching for adulthood in a society that fails to understand their dilemma? Is it possible that an individual's entire outlook for the full span of the adult years is flavored by the school years, and especially the secondary school years? If so, where is the answer for secondary youths and postsecondary adults who have experienced, and continue to have, learning disabilities?

The length of this chapter alone may be a single indicator that the issues associated with the secondary school age learning disabled and their emergence into adulthood have no simple answers. One of the predominant themes running through the literature is that little, indeed very little, longitudinal work following a child from first identification to adulthood has been reported. Certainly, an absence of information may be part of that problem, evidenced in why so many gaps exist between the quality and quantity of elementary and secondary programs.

Therefore, the next section examines some of those gaps, with the later sections attempting to narrow and bridge those gaps. The absence of unique program models for learning disabled children in secondary programs has prompted a review of those available.

A program principle does underlie the chapter. That is, most secondary programs for learning disabled children currently draw heavily on academic remediation. One finding in a follow-up work of secondary age youth into adulthood is that two postschool groups clearly are visible. One group looks as if its members have had histories of "brain difference" to explain learning disabilities. They have failed to catch on through years of sustained academic remediation or to profit from life's skills or functional teaching once they have reached 14 or 15 years of age (puberty). Members of the other group failed for fairly mechanical reasons, i.e., too many family relocations, resulting in changes in schools; poor health; an accident causing prolonged school absence; or a poor start in class. Remediation seems to be effective and as a group these individuals do catch up and continue to grow academically long after the remediation has stopped.

Two groups, then, can be said to exist—a catch-*up* one and a catch-*on* one, requiring that different programs be offered. It is the author's contention that the only valuable program for catch-*on* students is a completely integrated curriculum where personal, social, academic, and vocational objectives are met by accompanying programs.

GAPS IN SECONDARY PROGRAMMING

Gaps may exist in the information and attitude of people and in the perceived need, implementation, and development of programs within an organization. What is important, if gaps are to be narrowed or bridged, is an understanding of *why* obstructions exist. Earlier, it was noted that the preponderance of services to learning disabled children occurred in the elementary schools. That occurrence should be examined as a fact, on its surface value alone. It might be deduced correctly from this that learning disability is an elementary age handicapping condition with a history and tradition not shared at the secondary level.

An Elementary Age Hardship

Learning disabilities have a tradition, in fact a very strong history, suggesting that they occur early in life but fade from existence at entrance into adolescence. Where did such a belief emanate and why is it perpetuated?

The answer to the first part of the question is not difficult to find. Learning disabilities began to be recognized in the work of Strauss and his students and colleagues (Vernon, Cruickshank, Kephart, Kirk, Barsh, and others), most of whom were associated with the Cove School for the Brain Injured in Racine, Wisconsin. In other words, the learning disabilities movement is deeply rooted in the work of the experts who focused on children with so-called minimal brain damage (Clements, 1966). In addition, it was a common belief that perceptual impairments, so commonly associated with minimal brain damage, were outgrown by the time (age) youths entered adolescence (Strauss & Lehtinen, 1947).

The evidence for such a belief was derived from the fact that perceptual impairment is difficult to measure after the age of 12 (Vernon, 1959). As may be recalled from Chapter 1, the National Advisory Committee for Handicapped Children (NACHC) in its 1968 definition capitalized on the language of "the basic psychological processes," which include conditions such as perceptual handicaps, minimal brain dysfunction, developmental aphasia, etc. The resulting dependency on a "perceptual deficit" as a key identifier of learning disabled children was restricted by the age limitations placed on the common perceptual tests. This, in turn, resulted in restricting the age at which children no longer seemed to be learning disabled because they no longer were perceptually impaired. Therefore, until very recently, it simply was assumed that learning disabilities were "outgrown" by adolescence because of the cycle begun by the inability of perceptual tests to measure the trait in children over 12.

It now appears that with diagnostic instruments more sensitive to measuring perceptual developmental deficits in older children and the inclusion of the term "language" adding a (perceptual-language) cognitive deficit, that belief of a few years earlier can be seriously challenged (Carroll, 1970). Put another way, young children depend primarily upon their perceptual world. As they grow in cognitive structure, they shift dependence from the perceptual symbolic to cognitive conceptualization, relying more on language. That shift occurs in the years 10 to 13 (Piaget, 1963). Recent research emphasizing language development and functional usage indicates that adolescents and adults known to have been learning disabled during childhood use language as adults in a manner unlike those who were nonimpaired as children. The complexity of measuring perceptual development, which is highly related to language, i.e., auditory discrimination or memory, rarely is measured in older children. In fact, Goodman and Mann, in their 1976 text on secondary learning disabled children, in Chapter 3 on "The Process of Determining Process," list nine perceptual-cognitive tests that may be used to measure basic psychological process in secondary age children. Of those nine, only one measures anything beyond memory for digits. More serious, however, is the fact that none of the nine have sufficient test-related reliability to make them useful for diagnostic purposes with secondary students. Exhibit 9-1 provides an expanded list of tests, drawing on Goodman and Mann but adding reliability data to each.

There is, then, a historic reason for not including adolescents in the group originally thought to be minimally brain damaged. Operationally, however, programs for secondary educationally handicapped youth, using that term in a broader sense than learning disabilities, may have been slow to take root because of the snowballing effect that the adolescent period can have on children with poor school histories.

In short, there is evidence to suggest that the premature withdrawal of services and programs for learning disabled youth upon entrance to junior high school has had a devastating effect. Some of the problems associated with poor school performance (academic and social) merit examination. The factors worthy of attention are: truancy, dropouts, vandalism and violence, delinquency, and ultimately poor adjustment to adult life, all of which seemingly relate to poor academic performance and are symptomatic of a youth who has given up on achieving in school.

Widening the Gap: The Behavioral Aspects

There are some obvious facts and facets under the rubric of secondary learning disabled youth that present a mosaic that is most difficult to interpret. It has become obvious that most adolescents with high frequencies

Exhibit 9-1 Perceptual-Cognitive Tests

Name of Test	Publisher & Copyright	Level	Contents	Reliability
Detroit Tests of Learning Abilities	Bobbs-Merrill (1968)	Children & Adults	Pictorial absurdities; verbal absurdities; pictorial opposites; verbal opposites; motor speed and precision; auditory attention span; oral commissions; social adjustment; visual attention span; orientation; free association, memory for designs; number ability; social adjustment; broken pictures; oral directions; likenesses and differences	Test-retest 0.96
Developmental Test of Visual-Motor Integration	Follett Educational Corporation (1967)	2-15	Figures and designs to be reproduced	Test-retest 0.83-0.87
Bender Visual Motor Gestalt Test (BVMGT)	American Orthopsychiatric Association (1946)	4 & over	Designs to be copied	Test-retest 0.55-0.69

Exhibit 9-1 continued

Name of Test	Publisher & Copyright	Level	Contents	Reliability
Memory-for-Designs Test	Psychological Test Specialists (1960)	8.5–adult	Simple straight-line designs to be reproduced from memory	Split half 0.92
Benton Test of Visual Retention	Psychological Corporation (1955)	8–over	Memory for designs and sequence of designs	Test-retest 0.85
Elizur Test of Psychoorganicity— Children and Adults	Western Psychological Services (1969)	Children & Adults	Drawings, digits, blocks	NA
Minnesota Percepto Diagnostic Test	Clinical Psychology Publishing (1962)	5–20	Gestalt designs to be copied	Test-retest 0.37–0.60
The Minnesota MAST (Motor Accuracy and Speech Test)	Special Education Materials	Preschool to adult	Motor tasks	NA
Wechsler Memory Scale for Adults	Psychological Corporation (1945)	Adults	Personal and current information, orientation, mental control, logical memory, memory span, visual reproduction, associate learning	NA

Exhibit 9-1 continued

Name of Test	Publisher & Copyright	Level	Contents	Reliability
Developmental Test of Visual Motor Integration	Follett Publishing Company (1967)	2–15	Perceptual motor closure, recognition of similarities and differences	Test-retest 0.83–0.87
Quick Test	Psychological Test Specialists (1962)	2–adult	Perceptual-verbal intelligence test	Interform reliability 0.60–0.96
Specific Language Disability Test	Educators Publishing Services Inc. (1968)	11–14	Perceptual motor functioning, visual and auditory discrimination, visual and auditory memory, visual motor discrimination, comprehension	NA
Woodcock-Johnson Psychoeducational Battery	Teaching Resources, The New York Times Company (1979)	Preschool to adult	Verbal ability, reasoning, perceptual speed memory, scholastic aptitudes achievement and interest level	Cluster score— 0.90–0.95

Exhibit 9-1 continued

Name of Test	Publisher & Copyright	Level	Contents	Reliability
Tests of Auditory Perception	Educational Activities Inc.	5–14	Auditory discrimination	Test-retest 0.75–0.89
Inventory for Language Abilities	Educational Performance Associates (1972)	4–18	Auditory and visual reception, auditory and visual association, verbal and manual expression, auditory memory, visual and auditory closure, sound blending	NA
Quick Neurological Screening Test	Academic Therapy Publications (1977)	4–18	Emotional intellectual sensorimotor development, muscle coordination, readiness for number concepts, auditory visual perception	NA

Source: Adapted from *Learning Disabilities in the Secondary Schools: Issues and Practices* by L. Goodman and L. Mann by permission of Grune & Stratton Inc., © 1976; Reliability column added by D. A. Sabatino.

of behavioral disorders, serious enough to draw attention to the act (truancy, delinquency, dropouts, and chronic in-school disruptive youth) evidence long histories of poor class achievement. Some authorities (Frease, 1973) have viewed the problem as a chicken and egg dilemma. They sense that if a student is truant, drops out, or attempts to manipulate the system through norm violating conduct, those acts in themselves will lower the youth's academic achievement substantially. The more common view (Sabatino & Mauser, 1978) is that poor academic achievement, and an almost endless array of other problems—of which truancy, dropping out, and delinquency are but a few—represent symptoms that may have a common cause. One of them is learning disabilities (Keldgold, 1969).

The speculation that learning disability is one of the major contributors to school-related problems grows from evidence from class records of troubled adolescents. Morgan (1979), in a study of the incidence of handicapped children in juvenile delinquent facilities across the United States, finds that 44 percent of the incarcerated adolescents sampled evidenced long histories of pronounced academic underachievement.

In another such study, Burke and Simons (1965) examine reasons for truancy. They find that 76 percent of the youths who were chronically truant were reading far below grade level and 59 percent had normal IQs. The most frequent reason given for being truant was a lack of interest in school (47 percent). However, a review of school records indicated that 92 percent had histories of chronic disruptive behavior. The others were characterized by (a) inadequate school adjustment, and (b) repeated grade failure. Of these youths, 73 percent had failed at least two different times. From the 90 percent of the truant group who went on to drop out of school altogether, 95 percent had long court histories.

Douglass (1969) in a conclusive study on dropouts characterizes them as having:

1. academic records of poor school achievement (rarely do they exceed fourth grade reading skill)
2. family background of low economic and cultural status that differentiates them from others (currently the highest percentage of dropouts are youths with Hispanic cultural-linguistic characteristics)
3. poor school achievement despite continued "social" promotion
4. records of absenteeism
5. lack of membership in organized school activities
6. poor verbal abilities in relation to nonverbal abilities
7. records of chronic disruptive behavior in school
8. peer group drawn from among similar students
9. attitude toward school ranging from distrust to disdain

In response to the last point, as stated earlier, it must be remembered that many youths are stopped from going on to secondary school. In fact, some researchers believe that as many students are stopped as voluntarily drop out (Empey & Erickson, 1966). French (1969) found that in a group with measured IQs in excess of 110, 20 percent disliked school and 18 percent were asked to leave. That phenomenon of stopping youths, in one way or another, from attending secondary school was reported in a 1915 classic study on truancy. Washington (1973) studied 56 high school students from the Midwest. His data indicated that financial worries, need for jobs, low grades, and trouble at home were the most common problems.

Delinquency and Learning Disabilities

A number of disciplines now are interested in the relationship between delinquency (formal ajudication by the courts) and learning disabilities. There is nothing very new about the assumed relationship. It was reported first as early as 1926, when Percival noted that 99 percent of those who could not pass first grade were locked into a failure mode the rest of their school careers, which ultimately terminated in antischool behavior. Years later, Roman (1957) observed what she called the reading-related triad: reading failure begets truancy, and truancy begets delinquency.

Fabian (1955) reported that 83 percent of a group of problem readers (10 percent of the general school age population) evidenced serious social-personal maladjustment. Klasner (1972) estimated that the range of proportion of pupils with severe reading problems among asocial children ranged from a low of 20 percent to no less than 83 percent.

There is neither a theory to account for the difference nor an operational program that can claim inordinate treatment success at the secondary school level. Generalities remain in vogue simply because data from longitudinal macroresearch have failed to emerge. The chapter on preschool programming (Chapter 7) noted an interesting parallel between the data now available on so-called high risk preschool children and what is evidenced in the school and community adjustment of secondary school age youth.

What are the causes or, better yet, what are the theoretical contributors to that multiplicity of symptoms associated with educational disabilities in adolescents? The truth is, they are numerous; they vary from youth to youth, depending on the type and amount of intervention during earlier years; parental, school, and self-expectancies during adolescence; and the emotional support base and personal reinforcement during crisis. There is evidence that some youths enter school with known minimal brain damage (Keldgold, 1969), evidencing an early lack of academic success and the strong necessity for special educational and parental (home) management. Since that has been demonstrated with youths known to have epilepsy (Taylor, 1969), the potential may exist for a wide range of children to experience early school failure because of cognitive deficit(s) other than intelligence.

The author again takes the position that there is more than one way to look at the group of children with learning disorders; that these individuals are, indeed, a population who experience underachievement and, therefore, academic failure. Moreover, many of these children have normal intelligence but show perceptual-language (cognitive) deficits. Some authorities have difficulty with that statement because of the present-day limited capability to measure or observe these perceptual motor traits, especially in older children.

The Self-Fulfilling Prophecy

From the perspective of the student, once school success is impaired, a self-fulfilling prophecy is set in motion. Its theme is that academic achievement is difficult; therefore, the child focuses on attention-getting conduct or resorts to withdrawn behaviors. Thus, the theory of an aggressive-withdrawn behavioral continuum seemingly has merit.

Gruhn and Krause (1968) compared 73 handicapped high school age students with a nonhandicapped group. They found that the handicapped students saw themselves as different and became extremely rigid in their views of themselves; there also was a noticeably reduced level of aspiration. Mulligan (1969) reported on a study demonstrating that 60 percent of a group of poor, almost nonreaders, yielded high frequency outputs of antisocial behaviors. Yamamoto, Lembright, and Corrigan (1966) related self-concept to social personal adjustment with various populations of children and youth. They noted that, in general, youths with lower self-concept scores were frustrated, unhappy, and often hostile.

Coopersmith (1967) determined that age was not a factor but that, from preschool to college age, social acceptability related positively to emotional adjustment and negatively to anxiety. Thus, early poor achievement in school sets into motion what may be hypothesized to be lowered self-concept, lowered expectancy of performance, a fear of failure based on previous failure, and more frequent aggressive or withdrawn behavior.

Youths experiencing academic difficulties literally give up on themselves in school, and sometimes express the hostility caused by that failure against the school—the so-called alienated youth syndrome. Many of these youths begin expressing norm violating conduct through increasing truancy, dropping out or being stopped out by the schools, and/or becoming highly aggressive, joining gangs, and displaying violent, vandalistic behavior. The incidence of learning disabled youth in a population of ajudicated children runs quite high in lower socioeconomic communities. Frease (1973) found that while youths from higher socioeconomic classes might display behavior similar to lower levels, in fact, they might become more involved in the destruction of property—and they stayed in school far longer.

Frease advances several reasons for the problems associated with the similarity between lower-class and middle-class students. The common antecedent is that both groups were experiencing academic difficulty in school. The second reason is that when middle-class youths experience poor school achievement, no matter what the reason, this has direct social implications. Certainly, many youths, especially males, fail in school.

It is more than pure speculation that the pressure of home and school alike are greater for middle-class youth. Frequently, a middle-class youth failing the system takes refuge in lower-class attitudes, dress, and rebellious mien, with the primary resentment against the school and other adult authority. Frease (1973) indicates that if individuals perceive themselves as relatively worthless, or poor students, and as objects of derision, it is quite likely that they will behave accordingly. With this category of individual, poor school and work performance would be expected. Since the areas of school and work are so inexorably bound together in an industrial culture, performance in one often is correlated positively with action in the other.

Oppenheimer and Mandel (1959) report that youngsters do manifest symptoms of social-emotional maladjustment before entering kindergarten. They conclude that pupils likely to experience later emotional problems could be identified at the first grade level. Lambert and Bower (1961) report that 90 percent of elementary school age students identified as being potential norm violators by teachers were found to be so labeled by clinicians, too. Public school teachers do have the ability to reliably detect propensities for violating norms early in the child's life. It must be remembered, however, that only a third to a half of all youth committing chronic disruptive acts do come to the attention of the court. The group that does come before the courts generally commits the same offenses as those who do not come to trial. Many learning disabled youths display aggressive behavior as an expression of frustration directed against the school.

Aggressive Behaviors

The focus on learning and behavioral disorders as a cluster is for good reason. Efforts to determine differences and similarities in a primary-secondary diagnostic interplay between learning and behavioral disorders meet stiff resistance. To the secondary educator, however, those differences may not be realistic. A passive child with a learning disability is one thing; an aggressive, acting out, threatening, potentially explosive, disruptive youth, who may inflict personal harm, is quite another.

Youths who are motivated by unmet emotional needs are characterized as low academic achievers with poor self-concepts. A significantly recurring relationship between self-concept and academic achievement has been verified to some extent (Brookover, Erickson, & Joiner, 1967). Shaw, Edson, and Bell's study (1960) of achievers' and underachievers' self-perceptions indicates that male achievers feel relatively more positive about themselves than their underachieving counterparts. In a closer look at underachievers, Taylor (1964) lists the following as personality traits: they are self-derogatory, have a depressed attitude about themselves, have feelings of inadequacy, and tend to have strong inferiority feelings. A general unhappiness with their personal situation may lead them to seek peer acceptance and high self-esteem through violent acts.

One factor faced by practically all norm violating youths no matter what the reason or symptom is the search to fulfill unmet emotional needs. Those who exhibit manifestations of personal emotional problems have a low trust level. Their interpersonal commitments and communication skills are very low, and they share little satisfactory emotional involvement with others. For example, known secondary vandals evidence minimal ability to demonstrate sympathy toward others, to stand alone when necessary, to have close friends, or to be aggressively constructive. This inability to relate to others is supported by Goldman's study (1960) of the Syracuse Public School System, where he attributed a high rate of alienation to the following factors: frequent staff turnover, authoritarian administration, and highly formal interpersonal relations.

Many norm violating youths experience personal crises, have difficulty meeting academic and social competition, and face recurring, severe academic underachievement. The response of many to their disastrous social and academic experiences in class is to display such unacceptable behaviors as vandalism, truancy, and aggression, ending the unpleasant experience by dropping out of school. Handicapped youths who traditionally have been placed in special education programs are not usually involved with such activities. Yet at the secondary level, behaviorally disordered, learning disabled, and mildly mentally retarded students have accumulated histories of school difficulties.

School problems may be expressed in the overt attention getting of aggressive behavioral responses, causing the secondary handicapped student to look, act, or appear to be indistinguishable from the chronic disruptive or norm violating youth. In summary, secondary chronic disruptive/norm violating youths in social or academic difficulty with the schools may be handicapped, may have histories of school failure, may have been dropped or stopped from school attendance, or may be chronically truant.

Lambert and Bower (1961), in a longitudinal study of the 22 percent of the secondary student population displaying behaviors that brought them to the attention of guidance counselors in California schools, determined that the same group was in trouble five years following graduation from high school. That is, they were representing the group in society whose members are chronically unemployed, have frequent turnover in marriages, are seen in outpatient mental health clinics and drug and alcohol abuse programs, and end their lives in accidental deaths or suicides.

It should be clear that not every youth who drops out, is truant, delinquent, or manifests aggressive behaviors, including vandalism and violence, is learning disabled. But it should be equally evident that 76 percent of school nonattenders read below grade level, 73 percent have failed two or more grades, while 59 percent have normal intelligence. There is evidence that at least 50 percent of most youths in trouble in the secondary schools certainly appear learning disabled. There are those (Smith, 1978) who seemingly do not care if a precise diagnosis is derived. They tend to lump most mildly handicapped into a very broad educationally handicapped category. It is not necessary to agree or disagree with them. It is important to recognize that just under 30 percent of those in secondary school are not realizing much success in or from education, and at least 13 percent of them are handicapped in a sensory, physical, mental, or social sense. An additional 17 percent have a serious educational handicap.

Therefore, while not all the educationally handicapped can be considered emotionally or behaviorally disturbed, the lack of secondary school interventions for those having such problems will result in about 59 percent being unsuccessful in life's achievements without some type of support programs (Barone, 1977). Data supporting Barone's conclusion were drawn from a five-year follow-up study by the U.S. Department of Labor, whose data yield the following conclusions:

> 525,000 (21%) will be either fully employed or enrolled in college.
> 1,000,000 (40%) will be underemployed and at the poverty level.
> 200,000 (8%) will be in their home community and idle much of the time.
> 650,000 (26%) will be unemployed and on welfare.
> 75,000 (3%) will be totally dependent and institutionalized (Barone, 1977, p. 6).

At least one very real issue is that not much has changed in the last ten years. The problem is recognized, it does exist, yet little is done. In 1977, Hoyt in HEW wrote:

> Within the existing educational systems across the nation ... otherwise able students experience difficulty in learning to read. ...

A student's initial failure in learning to read can have enormous consequences in terms of emotional maladjustment, tendency toward delinquency, likelihood of becoming a drop-out, and difficulty in obtaining employment. The economic loss to the nation . . . is incalculable (p. 8).

A gap exists now, it has since the beginning of compulsory education in this country in the 19th century. It would appear that in that undifferentiated mass of humanity that is not achieving in the secondary schools, a group of learning disabled youths are worthy of more than they have been given.

Behavioral Management Strategies

The preceding section focused on behaviors that draw unfavorable attention. The youths might be expressing frustration, fear, anger, hurt, or any powerful emotion against a school situation that is producing discomfort. The school officials' response frequently is overreaction. When the youths' initial emotional impact hits a soft and understanding, but firmly believing, surface that expresses as powerful a belief and confidence in the person as that individual has doubts, the emotionality tends to dissipate.

However, most initial student emotionality triggers a similar attitude in those (such as educators) who see or feel the abuse or attack, or witness the emotion in action. Emotionality begetting emotionality increases the tempo and inadvertently reinforces students in disbelieving in their role in the system, and ultimately in themselves.

It is extremely important that readers not confuse the perceiving of another's emotion in an open, receiving, and comfortable stance with the understanding and the love theme that some persons advocate. There is a sharp difference between accepting the person and accepting the behavior. Most individuals have difficulty enough focusing on the two entities and distinguishing between them. Therefore, to shroud the whole atmosphere in a blanket of love is an ultimate practice of self-denial that only a few can accomplish. Not many possess the maturity, insight into human nature, and belief in self necessary in the presence of threat.

Love and understanding may be steps on the same continuum but even so, they are distinctly different. Love is the ultimate feeling of acceptance for another person, and few can achieve the reduction in threat necessary to accomplish that emotion when confronted by a loud voice, fiery temper, and explosive personality whose fist is raised and who breathes hostility. Confrontation produces doubts, and if there still is a reasonable question whether an explosive out-of-hand situation will result, it is difficult to express the emotion of love, as in "I love you." In the face of that threat, the first objective is to calm the atmosphere by being concerned for the individual, soft in tone, and quieting in manner, and reassuring the frightened or the aggressive person that the situation is not out of control. At the same time, attempts must be made to (a) verbally break through the emotion or, if that fails, (b) restrain the individual softly, with comforting hands on shoulders, (c) move the hands to the upper arms while bringing the person into closer physical contact. If physical explosion is evident, then the advantage is the educator's in being able to restrain the person, whose acts require understanding, logic, or thought, not an expression of love.

Obviously, this description is directed at a most forceful and outwardly aggressive situation. The majority of disruptive behaviors in secondary schools are troublesome but not nearly as emotionally charged as the one described. The point of discussion here on more severe symptoms such as aggressive behaviors is that they do occur. The learning disability teacher must recognize that:

1. the students the educator sees stand a much higher probability than those not seen of being brought to the attention of the school, nonschool helping agencies, and ultimately the courts;
2. they must know how to manage human conflict or even provide meaningful suggestions to other educators, although their primary training has not been with disruptive youth (they are not crisis teachers).

Learning disability teachers in the secondary school are in the role of a first line of defense with both students and faculty. As special educators, they must have some knowledge of developing behavioral control.

Therefore, several so-called behavioral management techniques are listed and described briefly. Additional information is available on these procedures from other sources. To begin, however, in the resource room, learning center, or self-contained classroom for learning disabled children in secondary schools, one behavioral and academic management technique remains highly effective. That process is called contracting (DéRisi & Butz, 1974; Jesness & DéRisi, 1973).

Contracting

A behavioral contract is a written, legal looking document that details what the student will do and, if that is done, the positive consequences (privileges). It also stipulates the penalty if responsibilities are not met. Contract clauses should cover how the teacher will monitor and record these responsibilities. Recordkeeping is required to maintain an accurate picture of contract compliance. Contracts can be written on tasks that will be learned or conduct that will be maintained. Exhibit 9-2 is an example of a behavioral contract.

Exhibit 9-2 Example of a Behavioral Contract

_____ Privileges and responsibilities deal

Effective from _____ to _____

Responsibilities	**Privileges**
1. _____	1. _____
a)	a)
b)	b)

Bonus

Penalty

2. _____	2. _____
a)	a)
b)	b)

Bonus

Penalty

This deal is scheduled to be renegotiated on _____ _____

Details of responsibilities and privileges are spelled out on the attached sheet. This deal suits me and I agree to take part in it.

_____   _____

_____, counselor

Rules of Positive Reinforcement

The only sure measure for reducing the inadvertent reinforcement of negative behaviors is to observe and record the conduct and the consequences in a particular learning environment. The teacher's principal task is to identify and isolate positive reinforcers, linking them to behaviors that deserve support. Positive reinforcers may be as simple as a smile or a warm and friendly comment, or as complex as a daily performance grade for completion of work assigned. Adolescents generally respond to social reinforcers that fall under the rubric of adult and peer recognition.

Group management procedures can be engineered where the adolescent receives much-desired social attention from other meaningful authorities and—especially important—peer recognition. When the group recognizes on-task behavior at regular intervals and disregards off-task conduct, providing punishment if necessary (generally through the denial of privileges), it can eliminate the sometimes positive short-term effects but frequently detrimental long-term influences of punishment, reprimands, ridicule, and criticism by adults. It doesn't take adolescents long to learn the manipulative skills necessary to provoke a teacher and to maintain an adversarial relationship, setting the entire environment into an off-task relationship.

Peer Recognition, Peer Tutoring

These are very effective elements in behavioral management. Peer recognition generally requires that the group develop and police the rules. Frequently, behavioral courts are arranged where the group responds to any violation of its rules. It is far better to provide adolescents the self-control they do indeed desire and work with them in putting their systems into operation than to remain the authority figure. Challenges then are made to the group, and not to the authority, and the group (not the authority) will respond.

There is one principle that must be considered, however: if a behavioral court is convened and the teacher is named the defendant, the teacher must respond to the group. To do otherwise is to offer an inappropriate model by declaring the teacher above the rules of the group. Group activities must be structured and considerable work devoted to organization and written rules. Of all the effective practices, using peers as tutors has demonstrated consistently good benefits. Peers may be older students, athletes, students with recognized abilities, future teachers, or just plain paid tutors. The reinforcement value of learning for peer reward is unmatched.

Modeling

This factor assumes that the adolescent lacks the skills necessary for dealing with a particular situation. First, teacher and student must decide on the specific behavioral and training skills required for successful performance in the situation. (Physical appearance, facial expressions, and verbal behavior must be considered.) When the important skills have been isolated, the adolescent and the teacher must agree on a reasonable approach to handle a situation (identify the skill to be learned).

The second component involves repeated demonstrations of each of the required skills. These may be performed live, be videotaped, or involve filmed models; demonstrations by several models probably are preferable. For each skill that is modeled, a rationale in terms of its importance to the ability to be learned should be given. A discussion of the fine points in performing this skill can be helpful. Finally, typical mistakes in performing each skill are pointed out and also may be modeled and critiqued by the student (or group).

The third step is guided practice under practical conditions. Adolescents who are reluctant to perform a new skill may need to see it and to learn sequential steps or solutions. Practice, correction, and repractice continue until performance is mastered.

At each step of the way, approval for correct performance and other kinds of positive reinforcement should be provided. A good idea is to videotape practice sessions so the adolescents can monitor their own performances. For complex skills, successive approximations are accepted temporarily, with successively more perfect approximations required (behavioral shaping). This component of reinforced modeling is not an unstructured role-taking situation, but planned, guided practice in appropriate skill development.

After component skills are quite familiar and the entire adaptive behavior pattern can be performed with ease, further practice takes place in more realistic situations (Sabatino & Mauser, 1978).

Premack Principle

As detailed by Gardner (1977), this concept suggests that enjoyable activities serve as activity reinforcers for compliance on tasks that the child would choose less frequently. (See Chapter 10.) Some teachers in resource rooms have provided "high interest, low vocabulary books" to stimulate learning. Others have provided mixed activities such as building model cars, listening to music, talking softly to friends, or even being read to as highly desirable efforts to follow less preferred ones. The use of the Premack principle thus allows the educator to select the reinforcers that are most appropriate for each individual. Sitting idly, looking at magazines, being included in a peer group, shooting basketball, listening to jazz records, drawing, eating, and talking with the teacher are examples of possible high preference activities.

"As soon as we clean up the mess, we'll listen to your favorite record" represents an application of this rule for children who have a high preference for music and a low desire to clean up. "Those of you who finish your geometry problems may spend your break time with the headsets listening to the new records" proved a valuable contingency in a class of emotionally disturbed adolescents (Gardner, 1977, p. 226).

Aversive Stimuli

These are any stimuli that are unpleasant or associated with discomfort. Removal of aversive stimuli strengthens behavior and therefore is considered a *negative reinforcer*. Punishment and negative reinforcers are not the same thing. A negative reinforcer could be the escape and avoidance that occurs when an adolescent must take any unfinished assignment to the learning disability teacher for completion. The youth may be uncomfortable doing class reports in biology class and may fail to complete them just to be able to do the work and make the report in a safer, more comfortable environment. This behavior of avoiding the biology classroom is reinforced negatively by the regular and special educator.

Negative reinforcement increases the strength of a given behavior by permitting avoidance, and punishment is an aversive consequence that follows (not precedes) a behavior. The major point to remember is that the use of aversive stimuli frequently reinforces inappropriate behavior, i.e., permitting the pupil to leave the biology classroom to complete work in the resource room. Aversive stimuli also generalize from one situation to another, i.e., from biology to English. Therefore, positive reinforcers become more difficult to place behind appropriate behavior as such conduct diminishes.

Prompting and Fading

Adolescents frequently know appropriate responses to situations but display inappropriate behaviors. A teacher may cue an appropriate response by providing visual or auditory signals or physical interaction. A youth may enter the secondary resource room in a euphoric state, having just been a contributing party to a disruption in the corridor. The resource room teacher may be wise to see the manic state and catch the youth's glance, with an "I recognize your state" look. If that fails, it may be necessary to suggest "where were we yesterday," an auditory cue. If necessary, the teacher may have to greet the youth at the door and act as an escort to the seat.

Chaining

Complex behaviors, which require more than one-step learning, may require forward and backward chaining as shaping procedures leading to a completed task capability and compliance. Forward chaining begins by identifying the sequence of steps necessary to achieve a desired task or advance a behavior capability. Backward chaining requires the teacher to assist the youth with the preliminary steps, preparing for the final step or completion of a behavior. An example would be eliminating three choices in a four-choice examination.

Counterconditioning or Desensitization

This is the process by which a painful or threatening fear associated with a behavior or task is removed. A common problem faced by secondary teachers is the threat of failure associated with a student's previous inability to learn. The fear of learning skills overcomes the ability to try. Therefore, a process must be undertaken where the learning task is broken into tightly sequenced steps. Each procedure requires extinction of the fear associated with it until the threat imposed is disassociated from the task. The key is that a positive emotional response, stronger than the threat, be imposed with each step in the learning process. Assuming that Staat (1975) is correct in observing that a child cannot be both relaxed and anxious at the same time, one technique of desensitization is called progressive relaxation.

Progressive Relaxation

This process begins by assisting the youth to enter an anxiety-free state, generally by talking about pleasant things. Once the youth has learned to associate the environment with relaxation, a progressive procedure of relaxing toes, feet, legs, and body can be evoked, until the thought or fear-producing stimulus is completely out of mind. At that point, relaxation should be sustained for weeks, and sometimes months, gradually working the fear-producing stimuli back into the relaxation scheme until their anxiety-producing characteristics are lost.

Emotive Imagery

In this form of desensitization (Lazarus & Abramowitz, 1962), feelings of self-assertion and accomplishment that are induced through discussion and identity with heroes, real or imaginary, are used to overcome old fear patterns. Biographical and autobiographical stories of great men and women who overcame learning disabilities provide an excellent approach.

Finally, techniques for controlling threats and a threatening environment by managing behaviors are helpful. However, the goal of restoring self-control in on-task behavior is critical. Long (1974) advanced a sensible approach to understanding a self-control curriculum. Initially, it requires the teacher to understand that the disruptive behavioral expression represents the student's present solution to the situation that the youth senses cannot be resolved otherwise. Thus, the youth creates and maintains conflict by perpetuating a negative reaction to a situation that the student feels is beyond coping with successfully. Thus, a self-fulfilling prophecy is maintained, with the student sensing an inability to cope, then demonstrating that inability.

The Breaking of the Cycle

The teacher, according to Morse (1976), must interfere with the cycle, breaking it into three dimensions: (1) support of self-control, (2) situational assistance, and (3) reality and value appraisal. Dembinski (1979) has isolated teacher interference under three headings.

Support of Self-Control

1. Signal Interference: These are teacher cues such as staring, snapping a finger, tapping the chalk, or clearing the throat.
2. Planned Ignoring: The teacher intentionally ignores a behavior.
3. Interest Boosting: The teacher draws a student's wandering attention back to the work at hand.
4. Humor: The teacher makes an amusing comment about the day's activity, or tells a funny story.
5. Proximity Control: The close physical presence of a teacher may enable a student to regain control.

Situational Assistance

1. Hurdle Help: The teacher offers the student the help needed to grasp the concept or skills involved, rather than focusing on misbehavior. It is important to note that the teacher's assistance is appropriate for learning social as well as academic skills by helping the student before frustrations begin.
2. Restructuring the Class Setting: Sometimes it may be more profitable to alter the teaching environment. The key to restructuring classroom activities is whether the change will facilitate the learning process.
3. Routines: Students exhibiting maladaptive behavior need and benefit from structure.
4. Removing Distracting Objects.
5. Antiseptic Bouncing: This technique simply calls for a teacher to send a student out of the room to cool off and regain self-control before returning to class. Sending the student on an errand or to another teacher or principal with a note explaining the situation enables the

student to save face with classmates and spares the teacher the problem of having to cope with temper flareups.

6. Physical Restraint: Sometimes a student erupts aggressively and physical restraint is the only course of action open to the teacher. Restraint exercised by an adult on a student must be protective and not counteraggressive. The youth must be reassured that no one will be hurt but simply that the student must be restrained until control is regained. Policies and techniques regarding restraint vary. Teachers should be aware of local policies for their own and their students' protection.

Reality and Value Appraisal

Morse (1976) has suggested several short-term reality goals for use in life space interviewing (LSI). Dembinski (1979) explains five steps in LSI.

1. Reality Rub-In: Help the student see it like it is. The goal is to increase the student's acceptance of reality and his role in a chain or sequence of events.
2. Symptom Estrangement: Reduce value of self-defeating symptoms or problem behaviors. The goal is to increase the student's discomfort about his present maladaptive behavior.
3. Massaging Numb Value-Areas: Help reinforce or identify potential values within the student for more constructive behavior. The goal is to increase the student's commitment to positive behavior values.
4. New Tool Salesmanship: Help the student to identify and appreciate alternative ways of behaving. The goal is to strengthen the possibilities for utilizing new behaviors.
5. Manipulating the Boundaries of Self: Help strengthen the student's resistance to group contagion. The goal is to help the student become constructively independent. (p. 135)

Again, it is not the intent of this section to provide the teacher with a cookbook approach to coping with disruptive behaviors. The intent merely is to augment the belief that (a) many of the students in secondary learning disability programs display behaviors that are disruptive enough to interfere with learning, (b) a goodly number of such students will evidence serious difficulties in obtaining a successful school experience even with emotional support or behavioral management, depending on the severity of the emotional/behavioral disorder, (c) learning disability teachers are just that and must not become holding tanks for seriously emotionally disturbed or chronic disruptive students unless school and community support personnel are working in a team relationship with them.

Secondary Learning Disabled Students: Characteristics

It would be useful if the next few pages were filled with a description of distinct characteristics found in learning disabled adolescents. In Chapter 2, a discussion of the modern-day morass associated with defining learning disabilities probably left some confusion. That confusion stems mostly from the fact that learning disabilities are defined more frequently by what they are not than by what they are. Gallagher's (1972) classic analogy defining nonhorse, before defining horse, reflects how most authorities regard learning disabilities. An example occurs in Goodman and Mann's (1976) attempt to define adolescent learning disability by excluding what it isn't. There is an inordinate overlap between their views on a definition, and the so-called federal definition devised by the National Advisory Committee on Handicapped Children (NACHC) in 1968 (see Chapter 1). Goodman and Mann (1976) contend that learning disabled adolescents are not:

1. visually, auditorily, or orthopedically handicapped with sensory or physical disabilities
2. mentally retarded, which means their IQs are at least dull normal (IQ 85 and above)
3. either socioeconomically, culturally, or linguistically deprived, depressed, or different enough to produce an academic underachievement
4. brain damaged, wherein the injury to the brain results in clinical manifestations of behavior (they note that a learning disabled person's most pronounced behavioral syndrome results in an inability to master academic achievement skills)
5. emotionally disturbed
6. casualties of the educational system
7. youths who failed to adjust satisfactorily to the pressures of junior or senior high school—in essence, they are youngsters who upon making the transition into secondary school initiate a pattern of failure that they had not displayed previously.

While the author agrees with several of the parameters outlined by Goodman and Mann, he believes their focus remains on the preadolescent child, not the adolescent youth.

Agreement between Goodman and Mann's seven points and the 1968 definition actually prohibits argument on items that state that the youth not be sensory, mentally, or physically handicapped. The presence of these handicaps does not exclude a learning disability. For example, there are most certainly blind and deaf children (primary handicaps) who have a secondary handicapping condition, i.e., a learning disability. Mental retardation does exclude learning disabilities, except that the clinician administering standardized tests must recognize that older learning disabled youths with language deficits perform poorly on verbal measures of intelligence. It behooves the examiner to ensure that nonverbal conceptual measures of cognitive function are ascertained.

The author agrees that influences of depressed socioeconomic, family, cultural, and linguistic differences require special study. Again, however, he does not agree that a minority child cannot be learning disabled, or in fact a child from a socioeconomically depressed home cannot also be learning disabled.

Learning disabilities should be distinguished from serious handicaps such as clinical brain damage and emotional disturbance. The only difficulty is that it is not inconceivable to envision a child with a long history of learning disability who displays greater frequency of behavioral adjustment problems each year in a reaction to both academic and social failure. In the secondary school, the extent of this behavioral problem, as determined by its frequency, would cause the student to be labeled as chronic-disruptive. The difficulty in diagnosis and the resulting labeling are a direct reflection on the socially relative nature of the definition of emotional disturbance. At what frequency of occurrence (output) are serious emotional disturbances and behavioral disorders differentiated? The author believes that a primary learning disability, as evidenced by a perceptual-cognitive interference with information processing behaviors, is the essential ingredient, as described in Chapter 2.

Dimensions of Language Problems: Secondary-Level Issues

Generally, the work of the secondary diagnostic team is tracing the history of the learning disability and determining the presence of a perceptual-cognitive handicap in information processing behaviors, especially those associated with language conceptualization. McCullough (1968) has identified some of the language aspects associated with reading. Mauser (Sabatino & Mauser, 1978) lists her ideas.

1. *Word Form:* The reader must be able to decode the symbols by sight methods, sound methods, or by contextual clues to arrive at the English sound patterns.
2. *Sentence Order and Structure:* The reader must observe the role of the word in the order and structure in the sentence.
3. *Word Meaning:* The reader must determine the meaning a specific word should have, given its form, its role in the sentence, and the suggestions of its meaning from the larger environment, such as previous sentences, physical setting, etc.

4. *Sentence Meaning:* The reader must arrive at the meaning of the sentence in view of the sound, order, function, meaning of its parts, and suggestions from the larger environment.
5. *Sentence Function:* The reader must determine the kind of idea the sentence offers and its role in the pattern of thoughts around it.
6. *Evaluation and Interpretation:* The reader must measure the author's style and views against self-experience, filtering them through a cognitive and affective sieve. Interpretation includes the intonation that the readers possess and an understanding of the author's intention. Readers must go beyond what the author has said, applying their own thought processes to the ideas, both as they meet them and after they have finished reading them.
7. *Use:* The reader must use both the ideas gained and those generated from the reading. Some of these uses occur while reading or may motivate the student to read in the first place. Some of the ideas appear later in dreams and memories.

Allen (1964) offers a detailed outline for examining language experiences (Sabatino & Mauser, 1978).

1. *Sharing Experiences:* the ability to tell or illustrate something on a purely personal basis.
2. *Discussing Experiences:* the ability to interact with what other people say and write.
3. *Listening to Stories:* the ability to hear what others have to say and relate to their experiences.
4. *Telling Stories:* the ability to organize one's thinking so that it can be shared orally or through dictation in a clear and interesting manner.
5. *Dictating:* the ability to choose, from all that might be said, the most important part for someone else to write and read.
6. *Developing Speaking, Writing, and Reading Relationships:* the ability to conceptualize reading as speech that has been written.
7. *Making and Reading Books:* the ability to organize one's own ideas into a form that others can use, and the ability to use the ideas that others have shared through books.
8. *Developing Awareness of Common Vocabulary:* the ability to recognize that our language contains many common words and patterns of expression.
9. *Expanding Vocabulary:* the ability to expand one's vocabulary through listening and speaking, followed by writing and reading.
10. *Writing Independently:* the ability to write one's ideas and present them in a form for others to read.

11. *Reading Whole Books:* the ability to read books for information, recreation, and improvement of reading skills on an individualized and personalized basis.
12. *Improving Style and Form:* the ability to profit from listening to and reading well-written material.
13. *Using a Variety of Resource Materials:* the ability to recognize and use many resources in expanding vocabulary, improving oral and written expression, and sharing.
14. *Studying Words:* the ability to find the correct pronunciation and meaning of words and to spell the words in writing activities.
15. *Improving Comprehension:* the ability through oral and written activities to gain skill in the following directions: understanding words in the context of sentences and paragraphs, reproducing the thought in the passage, and reading for general significance.
16. *Outlining:* the ability of briefly stating ideas in the order in which they were written or spoken.
17. *Summarizing:* the ability to express the main impression, outstanding ideas, or details of what has been read or spoken.
18. *Integrating and Assimilating Ideas:* the ability to use reading and listening for specific purposes of a personal nature.
19. *Reading Critically:* the ability to determine the validity and reliability of statements.

ORAL LANGUAGE

O'Reilly (1971) lists the major skills identifiable in reading that relate to functional language by examining the semantic phonology, syntax, and morphological rules of oral language. The teacher should help the student to develop:

1. Oral language skills in semantics
   a. Utilize a vocabulary appropriate to the learner, home and family, school and play activities, community, and environment.
   b. Interpret, classify, and relate objects, pictures, and spoken words.
   c. Use vocabulary appropriate to needs and emotions.
   d. Interpret number concepts.
   e. Compare diverse situations.
   f. Establish and describe sequences of events.
   g. Determine cause and effect and predict outcome.
   h. Use new words.
   i. Relate and interpret experiences.

2. Syntax-related language functions
   a. Identify and construct substitutions for parts of speech (nouns, verbs, pronouns, adjectives, adverbs) in simple sentences.
   b. Identify and construct multiple substitutions of parts of speech (nouns, verbs, adjectives and adverbs) in simple sentences.
   c. Recognize and use complete sentences (past, present, and future forms).
   d. Identify and construct sentences with compound subjects, verbs, adjectives, adverbs, or pronouns.
   e. Identify and use subordinators and coordinators.
   f. Identify and use prepositions.
   g. Identify and use determiners.
   h. Use auxiliary words.
   i. Identify and construct transformations.

3. Morphological language-related functions
   a. Identify and form plurals.
   b. Use correct verb forms.
   c. Use contractions.
   d. Use compound words.
   e. Use positive, comparative, and superlative forms of adjectives.
   f. Use verbs to form agents.
   g. Use inflected endings.

At the secondary level, assessment must provide for two types of decision-making data to derive educational programming. One aspect should provide information on: (a) motivation to achieve, (b) self-perceptions, (c) aspirations and expectancies, and (d) anxiety. Achievement motivation and self-concept were addressed in Chapter 2. A list of usable instruments is provided in Exhibit 9-3. The second aspect should include observations and measurement of behavioral characteristics. There are any number of commercially prepared observation devices. The names, companies, age ranges for usage, and reliability are provided in Exhibit 9-4.

The critical features to be ascertained are the student's frequency of behaviors and whether those behaviors are on-task or off-task. Critical behaviors that may be observed are listed in Exhibit 9-5.

Exhibit 9-6 is a form of observational device that provides classroom data on verbal and nonverbal behaviors and the student's on-task and off-task responses to the teacher. In short, it offers a means of determining the interaction between classroom climate and the student.

Teacher and student target behaviors are defined in the observational device in Exhibit 9-7.

Exhibit 9-3 Achievement Motivation Scales

Name of Test	Author	Age Range (years)	Traits Measured	Available from	Cost	Reliability
Aberdeen Academic Motivation Inventory	N. Entwistle	12–15	Noncognitive measure of school achievement. Items relate to drive, school attitudes, and scholastic expectations	North Entwistle School of Education Univ. of Lancaster University House Lancaster, England	Unknown	Test-retest 0.83
Achievement Motivation Test for Children (Prestatie Motivatie Test Voor Kinderen PMT-K)	H. Hermans	9–15	Four subscales: Achievement motive, debilitating anxiety, facilitating anxiety, social desirability	Swetz and Zentlinger Keizesgracht 487 Amsterdam, Netherlands	$30 test booklet, answer form, scoring keys, manual	Reliability coefficients range 0.80–0.90
Achievement Motive Questionnaire	W. Robinson	13+	Three variables: Achievement motive (Q Ach), motive to achieve (Q Ach+), and motive to avoid	W. Robinson MacQuare University North Ryde, N.S.W. Australia 2113	Unknown	NA

Instrument	Authors	Age	Description	Source	Availability	Reliability
Achievement-Related Affect Scale	D. Solomon J. Yaeger	8–15	failure (Q Ach–). No age norms available. Based on assumption that achievement motivation consists of behavioral striving for success and feelings associated with success and failure.	D. Solomon Psychological Services Section Montgomery County Public Schools 850 Hungerford Dr. Rockville, Maryland 20850	Unknown	Internal consistency reliability 0.47
Children's Achievement Motivation Scale	B. Weiner	6–14	Differentiates individual with high and low achievement needs. Items measure the kind of affect (hope or fear), direction of behavior (approach or avoidance), preference for risk (intermediate vs. easy or difficult)	Dept. of Psychology University of California 405 Hilgarde Avenue Los Angeles, Calif. 90024	Unknown	NA

Exhibit 9-3 continued

Name of Test	Author	Age Range (years)	Traits Measured	Available from	Cost	Reliability
Children's Preference, Orientation, and Motive Scales	D. Solomon A. Kendall M. Oberlander	8–15	Six measures: 1. personal expression vs. structured role orientation 2. fear of failure 3. intrinsic motivation 4. class characteristics, preferences ("open" vs. "traditional") 5. locus of instigation (initiation of action) 6. task preference, generality-specificity	D. Solomon Psychological Services Section Montgomery County Public Schools 850 Hungerford Drive Rockville, Maryland 20850	No charge for one copy	Reliability coefficients 1 = .54 2 = .46 3 = .66 4 = .53 5 = .69 6 = .66
Junior Index of Motivation (JIM scale)	J. Frymier	12–18	Likert-type scale measures students' desires to do good work in	Publications Sales Office Ohio State University	$3.75: 100 copies $1.50: manual	Test-retest 0.70 Split half correlation 0.83

Name	Author	Age	Description	Address	Physical description	Reliability / Validity
Michigan State M-Scales	W. Farquhar	12–18	Battery of 4 tests designed to measure academic motivation: The Generalized Situational Choice Inventory; The Preferred Job Characteristics Scale (work aspiration); The Word Rating List (self-concept); The Human Trait Inventory (personality inventory)	W. Farquhar 439 Erickson Hall Michigan State University East Lansing Michigan		Variance Reliability 0–94 males 0.93 females Subscale Reliability ranged from 0.68–0.92 males 0.60–0.93 females Validity: total scale prediction .56—males .40—females
Motive-Attitude Intensity Scale	R. Sumner	12–17	Motive and attitude with the dimension of intensity 7 classes of educational attitude: parents, teachers, friends, self,	R. Sumner Guidance & Assessment Service N.F.E.R. The Mere Upton Park Slough	54 p: manual 1 pp: answer sheet 33 pp: scoring stencils 7 p: questionnaire	Test-retest range from 0.66–0.81—attitude scales; 0.72–0.81—motive scales 0.91—total test

school
20 Lord Hall
124 West 17th
Columbus, Ohio
44113

Exhibit 9-3 continued

Name of Test	Author	Age Range (years)	Traits Measured	Available from	Cost	Reliability
			curriculum, organization, material	Berkshire, England		
			5 classes of educational motive: reward, self-realization, intellectual stimulation, enjoyment, social conformity			
			4 levels of intensity: receiving, responding, valuing, commitment			

Exhibit 9-4 Behavior Observation Scales

Name of Test	Author	Age Range (years)	Traits Measured	Available from	Cost	Reliability
Devereux Adolescent Behavior Rating Scale	G. Spivack	13–18	Unethical behavior, deviant-resistive, domineering-sadistic, heterosexual interest, hyperactive, expansive, poor emotional control, need approval and dependency, emotional distance, physical inferiority-timidity, schizoid withdrawal, bizarre speech, cognitive bizarre action	Devereux Foundation Press Devon, Pennsylvania 19333	$4.50 per 25 scales & manual	.42 interrater .82 test-retest

Exhibit 9-4 continued

Name of Test	Author	Age Range (years)	Traits Measured	Available from	Cost	Reliability
Pupil Behavior Inventory	R. Vinter R. Sarri D. Vorwaller W. Schafer	12–18	Classroom conduct, academic motivation, socioemotional, teacher dependence, personal behavior	Campus Publishers 711 N. University Avenue Ann Arbor, Michigan 48104	$2.50 per 100 forms $2.15 per manual	NA
A Process for In-School Screening of Children with Emotional Handicaps	N. Lambert E. Bower	5–9 9–12 12–18	3 ratings: teacher, peer, and self. Behavior ratings of pupils by teacher K-12, peer rating K-3, 3–7, 7–12, self-rating K-3, 3–7, 7–12	Educational Testing Service (Atlanta Office) Suite 100 17 Executive Park Drive Atlanta, Georgia 30329	$10.00 complete set	NA
Behavior Problems Checklist	J. Feldhusen J. Thurston	6–18	Socially approved behavior and aggressive-disruptive classroom behavior	J. Feldhusen Educational Psychology Section Purdue University SCC-G, West Lafayette, Indiana, 47907	Unknown	May be obtained from author

Name	Authors	Age	Description	Source		Reliability
School Behavior Profile	B. Balow R. Rubin	5–18	Teacher rates child's behavior as observed in routine school activities	B. Balow Department of Special Education University of Minnesota 55455	Unknown	Split half .96
Hurewitz Quick Scoring Behavior Rating Scale	P. Hurewitz	3–21	Social habits, relationship with adults, emotional response, work habits and achievement, general physical appearance and health, use of crafts and creative media	P. Hurewitz Education Department Herbert H. Lehman College Bedford Park Boulevard Bronx, New York 10468	Unknown	NA

Exhibit 9-4 continued

Name of Test	Author	Age Range (years)	Traits Measured	Available from	Cost	Reliability
Hahnemann High School Behavior Rating Scale (HHSB)	G. Spivack M. Swift	12–18	Reasoning ability, originality, verbal interaction, rapport, anxiety production, general anxiety, quiet, withdrawal, poor work habits, lack of intellectual independence, dogmatism-inflexibility, verbal negativism, disturbance-restlessness, expressed inability	Hahnemann Community Mental Health, Mental Rehabilitation Center 314 North Broad Street Philadelphia, Pa. 19102	$2.00 manual scale 50 for $7.50	NA

Exhibit 9-5 Behavior Problem Checklist

CRITICAL BEHAVIORS TO BE OBSERVED

The teacher should check to determine whether the student:

1. Is restless and unable to sit still
2. Is attention-seeking, with showoff behavior
3. Stays out late at night
4. Doesn't know how to have fun, behaves like a little adult
5. Is self-conscious, easily embarrassed
6. Has fixed expression, lacks emotional maturity
7. Is disruptive, tends to annoy or bother others
8. Has feelings of inferiority
9. Steals in company of others
10. Is boisterous, rowdy
11. Dislikes school
12. Belongs to a gang
13. Has short attention span
14. Is inattentive to what others say
15. Engages in fights
16. Is loyal to delinquent friends
17. Indulges in temper tantrums
18. Is reticent, secretive
19. Is hypersensitive, feelings easily hurt
20. Suffers anxiety and chronic general fearfulness
21. Is irresponsible, undependable
22. Is prone to excessive daydreaming
23. Is disobedient, has difficulty in disciplinary control
24. Is uncooperative in group situations
25. Is passive, suggestible, easily led by others
26. Is clumsy, awkward, has poor muscle coordination
27. Is impertinent, sassy
28. Tends to drowsiness
29. Uses profane language, swearing, cursing
30. Is irritable, hot tempered, easily aroused to anger
31. Has frequent physical complaints, e.g., headaches, stomach aches
32. Is an underachiever (at least two classes below grade level)
33. Should be recommended for special education program

Exhibit 9-5 continued

34. Shows that school adjustment has interfered with school place-
    ment
35. Is possible school dropout
36. Has difficulty in math
37. Should carry a special label (categories such as learning
    disability)
38. Is a slow learner
39. Lacks respect for others

NARROWING THE GAP

One of the predominant issues in the secondary education of learning disabled adolescents is what happens to them as adults. That issue usually is raised as a two-part question: (1) What is the outcome if they do not receive appropriate intervention? (2) What data are available from adults who did receive interventions during their high school years?

In the former case, little research exists on the effects of intervention at any period during the school years. Robinson and Smith (1962) did a ten-year follow-up on 44 students seen in their University of Chicago Reading Clinic. All their former students had graduated from high school, 27 had graduated from college, three were in master's degree programs and two were enrolled in doctoral degree programs. Two of the differences were that Robinson and Smith's students (1) were from higher socioeconomic status homes and (2) received intervention into their junior and senior high school years.

In a follow-up study of adults some 12 years after they were seen initially at the Bellevue Hospital Mental Hygiene Clinic in New York, there still was evidence of neurological and perceptual dysfunction. The work reported by Silver and Hagen (1964) did reveal an additional finding of considerable importance that is fairly consistent with the work of others: the more serious the reading problem in the early elementary years, the more involved it becomes in adult years. Balow and Bloomquist (1965) reported on a sample of 32 males studied at the University of Minnesota Psycho-Educational Clinic from 1948 to 1953. Ten to fifteen years later, the men were 20 to 26 years of age. Selection of the sample was based on sex, age, clinical diagnostic classification, intelligence, and amount of retardation in reading. Balow and Bloomquist note

> that reading trouble had hindered them in academic work and that
> their own efforts had been the important element in improving their

Exhibit 9-6 Teacher-Student Classroom Observation Form

KEY						600	

+ was observed	
− was *not* observed	
± was observed in part	(Please check appropriate response)
? questionable	
O suspected observation but no opportunity to be observed	

+	−	+	?	O	Other	
						TEACHER BEHAVIORS:
						1. Accepts Feelings
						2. Praises/or/Encourages
						3. Accepts/or/Uses Ideas of Pupils
						4. Asks Questions
						5. Gives Information
						6. Gives Directions
						7. Criticizes/or/Justifies Authority
						8. . . . communication

+	−	±	?	O	Other	
						ON TASK STUDENT BEHAVIORS:
						1. Student Talk-Response
						2. Student Talk-Initiation
						3. Silence
						OVERT OFF TASK STUDENT BEHAVIORS:
						1. Verbal
						2. Phsyical Nondirective
						3. Physical Directive

Exhibit 9-7 Teacher-Student Target Behaviors

OBSERVATION SCALE

Teacher Behaviors refer to any activity, verbal or nonverbal, that relates to classroom activities. The teacher:

1. *Accepts feelings* of the child in nonthreatening manner.
2. *Praises* or *encourages* child's behavior and effort to continue.
3. *Accepts* or *uses a child's idea* or thought by clarifying it, building it, or relating it to other ideas.
4. *Asks questions* about an idea, event, or behavior, intending the child to respond.
5. *Gives information* about things, events, and ideas.
6. *Gives directions* verbally, indicating what child is or is not to do.
7. *Criticizes child,* justifying teacher authority and expecting child to change.
8. *Initiates no communication* with child in a two-minute period when it would have been possible or appropriate (when students are expected to work independently or teacher is fully involved with a different group of pupils).

On-Task Student Behaviors refer to any activity, verbal or nonverbal, that relates to designated task materials, events, and/or ideas. The pupil:

1. *Responds verbally* to another child or teacher regarding task-related materials.
2. *Initiates talk* with another child or teacher about task-related materials.
3. *Attends nonverbally* to task-related activity such as listening, writing, reading, or constructing for a continuous two-minute period.

Overt Off-Task Student Behaviors refer to any activity, verbal or nonverbal, that is *not* related to designated task material. The pupil:

1. *Talks* with another person about something other than the task.
2. *Fidgets physically* and *nonpurposefully,* wanders around room, daydreams, etc., for continuous two-minute period.
3. *Engages physically* and intentionally in nontask activity.

---

reading skills. . . . Many appeared to have a negative and slightly defeatist attitude about life in general. Only three of the thirty-two are married. (p. 48)

They did attain average adult reading proficiency (approximately tenth-grade level), graduate from high school, reveal mild behavioral disorders, and were employed in a wide range of occupations, with a disproportionate number in semiskilled and unskilled jobs.

Carter (1964) found that students who entered high school having obtained grade level reading proficiency tended to continue their education, whereas a group one or more years retarded in reading at the time of high school entry did not continue formal education, evidenced poorer high school adjustment, and obtained significantly poorer employment as attested by earning power.

Howden (1967) studied 57 adults who had completed school some 9 years earlier. The subjects studied were in their late 20s and early 30s. They were known to be poor childhood readers. As adults they performed less well than average or good readers on all sections of the standardized reading tests administered to them. The adult socioeconomic status of these poor childhood readers again was lower than that of the two better reading groups. One obvious fact is that adults, who as children were in poor reading groups, accumulated less formal education by the time they reached maturity. Another finding: poor childhood readers who became average adult readers were brighter and performed better on reading and intelligence tests in elementary school than did children found to be illiterate as adult readers.

Preston and Yarington (1967) reported an eight-year follow-up of 50 children enrolled in the University of Pennsylvania Reading Clinic. They ranged in age from 6 to 17 when first seen; 46 had received remedial instruction, four had not. Their IQs ranged from 53 to 126. Preston and Yarington found that retarded readers generally took longer to complete their formal school experience. Obviously, the delay is caused by failures. As would be expected, the disabled readers did appear to represent a larger percentage of dropouts from high school and their corresponding rate of unemployment was much higher. Unlike earlier studies, this one found that subjects with severe reading disabilities, as a group, paralleled the general population, reading with sufficient accuracy to graduate from high school, enter college, and obtain jobs in management.

A more optimistic follow-up study was completed by Rawson (1968). He studied the adult accomplishments of a group of 56 males who had attended a private school in Pennsylvania for at least three years. Twenty had severe reading disabilities and 16 had mild problems. Their median IQ was 131. The vast majority of the families were upper class. Specialized instruction was provided if needed.

Twenty-three years later, all but ten of the subjects were functioning occupationally in the upper two socioeconomic classes. There was no significant difference in highest educational level reached between the boys and their fathers, nor was there any difference among the three groups of boys classified according to severity of reading difficulty. Each of these 56 received intervention as needed and 48 earned college degrees. It would appear that the availability of intervention through the elementary and adult years is critical and that bright students with high parental expectations, even those with severe reading disabilities, progress normally if given the opportunity for remediation.

Hardy (1968) followed 35 males into adult life some years after their remedial experience. The length of remediation was three to fifty months, with more than half having received help for ten months or longer. The reading skill of Hardy's subjects had improved from the point of referral, but 60 percent still were 20 months or more below grade level. Forty percent were retarded 20 or more months at point of referral, while 23 percent were retarded at the same level at exit as when they were dismissed from remediation. A negative relationship existed between reading skill development, number of grades repeated, and chronological age. Hardy concluded that if the programs requiring reading were custom tailored, and vocational programs were offered, the severely disabled readers were able to make adequate progress. However, 30 percent of the readers with severe problems had extensively limited self-concepts, although job adjustment was reported satisfactory in almost all cases.

Frauenheim (1978) drew a conclusion that the learning disabled reach a plateau in reading development where little progress is made with great difficulty after that level is achieved. He based that statement on a follow-up of 40 severe reading disabled, diagnosed as dyslexic in childhood. All of his subjects had been seen in a mental health residential facility some ten years earlier. He found no relationship between the amount of special reading help and adult reading outcome.

His statement is dangerous for several reasons. It can cause a continuation of the belief, if not the practice, that remediation should cease when progress stops. The maximum amount of remediation for Frauenheim's subjects was five years. Even then, the type of intervention is unknown. What if the 40 subjects had been (a) free of emotional problems, and (b) the remediation had continued?

Herjanic and Penick (1972) in a review of the research to that date drew six conclusions:

1. The samples were small and strongly influenced by intelligence and high socioeconomic factors.
2. There were no control groups.

3. Controls on amounts of remediation were not offered.
4. Follow-up research looked at restricted output measures of the adults studied, i.e., reading, vocational, academic success.
5. Many of the children studied also were sent to the clinic conducting the follow-up work because they had a number of learning and behavioral disorders.
6. Children in follow-up studies rarely were separated into mild and severe reading disorder programs.

That means that data from long-term research are nonexistent as to the type and amount of intervention at elementary, junior, and senior high levels. It also means that information denoting when remediation began (what age or grade) is not available. Nor can it be said that remediation is better on a sustained basis than "as needed."

What generalities can be drawn as a summary?

• Intelligence is important. It would appear that brighter children compensate, if they fail to learn to read, better than students of average ability (Eisenberg, 1966).

• Most adults with severe reading disorders also have other deviant behaviors, i.e., emotional adjustment problems, court records, etc. (Katzenbach, 1967).

• The greater or more frequent a display of behaviors other than poor reading, the poorer the progress (West, 1967).

• There are controversial data generated from follow-up studies of childhood disabled readers. There are studies that suggest that continued remediation greatly reduces reading disorders. There are studies that suggest mild problems seem to disappear while severe problems linger. Most certainly, severity and socioeconomic considerations tend to be closely related. They seem to interrelate with when to interpose remediation and how much to provide.

• Silver and Hagen's (1964) data tend to indicate that when the severe group is divided into a known neurological subgroup, evidence on the existence of the problem continues into adult years.

• There seems to be some evidence that if there are remediation and family support, including belief in the child and the pupil's future, a more positive outcome is evident. At least, special and regular educators do *not* have any data suggesting that remediation is either nonessential or that the adult lives of severely reading disabled children are predetermined losses. On the contrary, persistent remediation and planned entry into each step or stage of adult activity seem to bear positive results.

The emotional lift of knowing that working with severely learning disabled youth can be viewed as a most worthwhile investment is certainly worth the tedious, expensive, frequently heart-rending short-term effects of such efforts.

LEARNING DISABILITIES IN ADULTS

Cox (1977), in relating an account of two young adults with learning disabilities, draws a most interesting conclusion. She sees work with secondary age youth and adults as going back into their vivid memories, assisting them to understand incidents, memories, feelings. She believes that one aspect of working with youths is to reassure them that the mistakes inherent in the educational system do not reflect on them as being different or dumb and that many of the errors were in fact professional. One type of training Cox feels is important for adults with learning disabilities is in assertiveness. She believes that learning disabled adults must be taught to assert themselves in productive ways because the childhood realities of growing up with such a handicap tend to be ego-destroying and counterproductive to the confidence necessary to attain life's goals. There is evidence to indicate that adults thought to have learning disabilities as children are marked for life.

What conclusion could be drawn from the follow-up studies of children and youth who received intervention during their school years? In their early adult years? Howden (1967) summarizes the follow-up work by saying these individuals may be "... illiterate, poor readers, or average readers as adults" (p. 136). Much of the answer depends upon the nature of the original etiology, which may well have produced a symptom—in the cases just presented, severe reading retardation. In cases where reading (or other academic subjects) was depressed in function because of (presumed) brain dysfunction, remediation improves academic achievement performance but the person still is confronted with severe reading disability. In cases where the reading disability is secondary to any number of nonneurological types of problems such as learning, social adjustment, health, or too-frequent school moves, reading tends to be normal or at least near normal in the adult years. Once again, it is the difference between the catch-*up* and catch-*on* groups described earlier.

Frauenheim (1978) studied 40 adult males who had received intensive special educational services at the Hawthorn Center in Michigan. They were seen initially when they were 8 to 15 years old (X = 11-6). The follow-up work some ten years later found the age range of the adults to be 18 to 25, with a mean age of almost 22 years.

The adults ranged from 1.5 to 8.4 in reading grade level scores. The 8.4 reflected one person; the next score was 6.6. Ninety-two percent of the group read below the fifth grade level, 63 percent below the fourth grade. In short, in ten years, 1.3 years of reading progress was demonstrated by the group. Frauenheim then examined the remediation, which he found ranged from 2 to 24 semesters, with 10.6 the mean. That suggests that the subjects, on the average, had received five years of remediation. The average age at which remediation began was 9 years, with a range of 7 to 13 years.

Spelling and arithmetic errors persisted at a significantly low level. The subjects in this sample had neurologic impairment and it was Frauenheim's opinion that as adults these persons responded more poorly than any other group studied. He concluded that dyslexia, caused by neurologic impairment, must be viewed as a "restricted continuum" of reading performance where individual variations were unrelated to the amount or times of initial intervention.

The results of Frauenheim's work suggest that the etiology may have more to do with the outcome than once was thought. Certainly, however, until other follow-up studies are completed, the principal conclusion is that there is a phenomenon known as severity. It would seem that some children fail to learn to read because the teaching-learning act is not well synchronized. Examples are the first grader who gets off to a poor start because of a fear of school, health problems, a recent household move, or other reason that imposes a social, emotional, or mechanical inhibitor between the learner and the instruction. Given catch-up type of intervention (remediation), this group seems to continue to improve and show normal or near normal adult achievement. Diagnostically, it may be that this catch-up group profits from remediation via a basic developmental curriculum where the subjects are presented repetitively and with additional learning clue or cues—a remedial curriculum, if you will, provided by a remedial reading teacher.

That is not necessarily true for handicapped children who comprise the catch-on (learning disabled) group. Learning disability suggests a neurological organizational difficulty in how the nervous system receives and arranges information. The learning disabled child is handicapped in an educational sense. The data presented here, although not complete and not particularly representative of well-designed research, suggest that if treated as a catch-up remedial group, the catch-on learners will evidence very poor progress. Even over a ten-year period, five years of remediation do not provide earthshaking results on skill development.

Does that mean that learning disabled children should not be provided remediation? No, it simply means that a more comprehensive intervention base of cognitive training may be warranted in the early years. However, no intervention, at any time, guarantees progress with every group. Youths with learning disabilities because of neurological impairment need help in catching on. That means they are unlike their catch-up counterparts. Remediation must include long-term cognitive training process, with less recordable progress in most cases. There are breakthroughs now and again, but they are so infrequent that they should be disregarded. As Mann (1976) once noted, special education is a ground game where most of the gains are made in small yardage.

The remaining question that must be asked is how long in the school life should remediation continue? The reason for the question is that some educators have maintained that the basis for continuing special education or remediation rests upon progress. If the child makes progress, then the course of remediation is continued. If a high school student does not progress, then thinking turns toward a nonacademic alternative. Silberberg and Silberberg (1969) describe a person who was a very competent automotive mechanic but whose employment was terminated on more than one occasion when he was confronted with reading tasks on the job. Diamond and Bredrosian (1970) summarize the serious problem of adult nonreaders as persons having major barriers in meeting initial requirements, which remain one of the causes of occupational turnover. The Silberbergs (1978) reported on examination of 30 job application forms. Their findings indicate that even in the simplest format, a job application may require recognition and comprehension of more than 80 words. They recommend that remediation continue into adulthood and that environmental (specific job) adaptation of the skills needed for some type of employment training (tape recorders, handheld calculators, etc.) can reduce the risk of poor reading.

How long should remediation continue? It requires a continuous and sustained effort, even into adult life. What then should characterize a secondary and adult program for learning disabled students?

BRIDGING THE GAP TO THE LEARNING DISABLED

Secondary students with special needs receive communiques from the environment about their role in life, as we all do. Theirs, however, goes like this:

"You're a loser. Dummy! You can't do it. Why try? Drop out. Get lost! Die!"

They are then continually asked, "Do you get the message?" Thousands of youths do get the message annually, from kindergarten to the day they graduate, or drop out, or are stopped out. Why?

The position in this chapter is that neither the information available to regular educators to date (their preservice or inservice training), the prevailing attitude of the secondary school as a social organization, nor the type and amount of specialized service delivery have been conducive to the development of appropriate alternatives for secondary students requiring special considerations.

Siefferman, using a transactional analysis model (Harris, 1973) illustrates the basic four modes used to identify the position in which a person may be found in relation to another individual or to the organization. The four life positions are:

I'm not OK—you're OK.

I'm not OK—you're not OK.

I'm OK—you're not OK.

I'm OK—you're OK.

The theory on personality development being advocated simply advances speculation that by the time most adolescent learning disabled students reach secondary school, they have been well reinforced to feel they are "losers." In fact, they have been made to feel that their inability to learn engenders peers and teachers to feel they're "not OK." Such a simplistic view explains little of what is, has happened, or will happen, nor does it suggest what is needed programmatically. However, it does indicate clearly why these students may display strong emotional feelings and passive apathetic reactions (withdrawal).

What is happening out there? In a 1979 study, Deshler, Lowrey, and Alley sampled 98 secondary learning disability teachers in all the states except Louisiana and Hawaii. The responses clearly indicate what would be expected: a predominant focus on remediation of academic subject areas in self-contained classes. Nearly 92 percent of the service delivery was offered in such classes, with 90 percent of the instructional program devoted to language arts and mathematics skills remediation.

One interpretation is that secondary special education programs offered to secondary youths are based on an elementary learning disability model. The reasons are that most learning disability teachers in secondary schools were trained to work in elementary schools; rarely has training been differentiated (Miller, Sabatino, & Larsen, 1980).

Data to support that belief (Learner, Evans, & Meyers, 1977) can be extrapolated from a questionnaire survey sent to an unreported number of secondary learning disabilities teachers (the definition of learning disabilities was not included in the study) in the Chicago and Denver areas. The teachers were asked to rank, in the order of most to least importance, their basic philosophy in what their work with learning disabled children should accomplish. They rated remediation and academic skill using special education material as first and equally important. Teacher prevocational and vocational skills was ranked least important.

The survey originators erroneously identified the major problem facing secondary special educators as "the paucity of appropriate materials for both academic skills and vocational preparation . . ." (p. 10). This author's position is that materials are available. They are the technical vocabularies emanating from shop manuals, scientific areas of interest, and in particular the students' interest, for which the real world has provided ample information to be learned. The teacher's job, be it a secondary learning disability instructor or any educator, remains:

1. finding an incentive to promote learning
2. sequencing the material to be learned into small enough steps (informational units) that it can be learned

In short, the major problem remains interest and adaption/adoption of material the students feel they need to learn. Ensminger (1976) put his finger squarely on the problem when he noted "at the secondary level, emphasis has traditionally been placed on mastery of content areas to fulfill requirements for graduation" (p. 5). That problem can be called traditional rigidity, which has fixed the high school curriculum in terms of Carnegie units of study, not in terms of information necessary, important, or even interesting in promoting life skills.

The issue then rises: How is material typically delivered to secondary age students? The two primary means are textbooks and lectures. Both of these make assumptions about the basic academic and cognitive skill level of the learner. Textbooks require reading skills and lectures need listening skills. If these skills are not present, then a learning disability most assuredly must exist.

Academically, then, the author recommends that the curriculum be modified for learning disabled students. Ensminger (1976) has made positive suggestions that are worthy of reproduction (Exhibit 9-8).

THE BROKERAGE FUNCTION

Chapter 8 emphasizes the resource teacher-instructional adviser role of the elementary-middle school learning disability teacher. The importance of achieving a successful service delivery capability was related directly to the impact that learning disability teachers have in establishing and maintaining productive relationships with other educators. The importance of that function in the elementary-middle school in contrast with the secondary schools is indeed a day-to-night difference. The strength of that belief is evidenced in the statement that any secondary learning disability teacher not maintaining a working relationship with regular, other special, and vocational educators in a team effort probably is locked away remediating. The author's view of remediation as a viable element in secondary schools is that it should occur only in relationship to a student's interest and in support of other meaningful academic, social, personal, and vocational goals.

Exhibit 9-8 Two Proposals for Adapting Curricula

CURRICULUM MODIFICATION FOR SECONDARY LEARNING DISABLED STUDENTS

1. Substitution of courses
   a. Credit should be given for completing an individualized course in English, math, reading, history, science, etc., under the supervision or direction of a regular class teacher, tutor, or learning disabilities specialist in any setting where the student works, i.e., learning resource center, resource room, etc.
   b. Substitutes are alternative courses such as business math for algebra, vocational basic electronics for physical science, etc.
2. Waivers of courses
   a. Waiver of a course on which a severe disability can have a negative impact and substituting a course in a related area of strength is an excellent solution for avoiding failure.
   b. Examinations should be administered in such a manner as not to penalize the student.
3. Alternatives for testing and evaluation (any one or combination of the following)
   a. Objective instead of essay tests
   b. Oral instead of written tests
   c. Retests in the same or an alternate form
   d. Tests with readability level adjusted to student
   e. Frequent short testing on short units of material
   f. Extra credit projects or bonus questions
   g. Projects to demonstrate proficiency in lieu of tests
   h. Adjustment of time factor to give additional time to complete test
   i. Cues in the form of additional information, i.e., spelling or list of words from which to choose
   j. Review and/or narrowing the scope of material to be studied for the test
4. Parallel courses—a regular course paired with any one of the following:
   a. Course individually programmed to fit the needs of the particular student.
   b. Course-directed study by the regular classroom teacher.
   c. Project-centered course perhaps taken outside the building, i.e., social science project carried out in conjunction with the county department of family and children's services.
5. Alternatives for choice of major already available in many high schools:
   a. Business education
   b. Occupational education
   c. General studies program

Exhibit 9-8 continued

   d. College preparatory program
   e. Distributive education (work-study programs)
6. Joint enrollment with private schools specializing in services for the learning disabled or half-day programs for students unable to tolerate a full-day program.
7. Course credit for experience study programs such as:
   a. Summer jobs
   b. Summer travel

CLASSROOM MODIFICATION BY LEARNING DISABILITIES OR CLASSROOM TEACHER

1. Instruction in the classroom
   a. Modification of course requirements by reducing scope of material to be covered
   b. Adjustments through use of individualized instruction:
      (1) Learning packets
      (2) Programmed materials
      (3) Independent study
      (4) Contracting
      (5) Competency-based instruction

Source: Adapted from *A Handbook on Secondary Programs for the Learning Disabled Adolescent: Some Guidelines* by E. E. Ensminger.

The purpose of a broker (adviser) function is to mediate among those who impart the school experience to the student with the goal of establishing an integrated curriculum. The integrated curriculum is discussed in the next section. By definition, it is the development of a custom-tailored school program in which the role responsibilities of all persons working with the student are oriented to the integrated curriculum plan. The secondary learning disability teacher may take on the role of caretaker for the plan, determining its efficiency, its effectiveness, and its usefulness or purpose.

The instructional adviser should be far less an advocate, attempting to obtain compliance or attitudinal change by fiat or mandate. The program can be right, the approach wrong. When that happens, social organizational pressures stiffen and passive sabotage is initiated. Instead, the learning disability teacher should be an active team member, a coordinator of the management plan, if that function is required, but not a policeman or specialist.

As a team member, the adviser must win the support of the administration. Therefore, the roles of all team members and their central purpose in building a custom-tailored program must be defined. It cannot simply be assumed that everyone will accept such innovative ideas with open arms—especially administrators and, in particular, high school principals who tend to feel that one more change will result in chaos.

Next is dialogue with department heads, seeking their endorsement. It is wise to "sell" programs as making good sense, recognizing the wise counsel of principals and department heads in the process. The adviser (broker) should acknowledge all input from others, then act on whatever improves the operation, in this case the integrated curriculum.

Next comes work with team members and support personnel. It is essential that they all feel their work is important and that the purpose of that work is stated clearly. Contingency plans can be beneficial, as can second order objectives to either the plan or the program.

The purpose of the brokerage function is to ensure that a sound management plan is in place. That plan, when it constitutes an integrated curriculum, will have four distinctly separate objectives that then are brought together as an integrated whole, each in support of the other:

Academic: what are the objectives for each academic area?

Vocational: what are the career goals of the student, and how are they being explored or developed through career education and career placement?

Social Development: what survival skills or social relationship skills are being developed, and how?

Personal Development: what are the personal growth behaviors of the student and how is development being encouraged and reinforced when manifested in improved basic life management skills?

INTEGRATED CURRICULUM

An individually custom-tailored secondary school program leading to graduation, based on the career goals and interests of the student, can be constructed successfully through an integrated curriculum. An integrated curriculum is exactly what its name implies: a mutually supportive relationship among all facets of the school's possible offerings, adapted or adopted so the student can reach goals through specific objectives in each of four program areas: (1) personal, (2) social, (3) academic, and (4) vocational.

ACADEMIC PROGRAMMING

Much has been said in this chapter concerning academic objectives and goal statements, with a strong stand taken against the current overdependence on remediation. It should be clear that remediation has several operational definitions. What is referred to here is academic remediation, or teaching clinical reading for the 1,001st time in an attempt to achieve that major breakthrough that will gain the person curricular normalcy.

The answer lies in that most difficult to make decision where the functional teaching of life's survival skills overrules remediation of a subject area or basic skill. That decision is difficult because teachers hate to give up hope that academic normalcy can be achieved. The author believes that as early as age 12 the functional teaching of technical vocabulary to meet vocational needs takes on far greater importance than remediating academic skills or tool subjects.

Remediation, when used to denote the reteaching of a regular secondary subject such as English, math, social science, biology, etc., should be called tutoring. Tutoring is recommended when the regular teacher and special educator have agreed upon a plan, knowing that with a particular amount of support, the student can profit and learn in the least restrictive setting using the regular curriculum or a slightly adapted version. It is not uncommon to teach word recognition and vocabulary (word meaning) using the technical vocabulary from biology, for example, in a secondary learning center (resource room).

The academic portion of the integrated curriculum is both (a) supportive and (b) developmental. The curriculum can be developed to support the functional learning necessary to meet career educational goals when reality dictates that the student will not profit from the developmental route. The developmental curriculum is the content normally taught in a particular subject area. It can be adapted for a student with a deficit in listening, visual recognition, language expression, or reading. It also can be supported by remediation. It is not unusual to have a student work on a developmental curriculum without support in some subject areas, with remedial support in others, and with supportive fashion program modifications in still others. Therein lies the strength of having the total program under one plan or integrated.

Exhibit 9-9 lists the high priority objectives for the academic curriculum by subject area. It should be noted that the objectives emphasize high priority, basic, functional academic skills and knowledge. Continual emphasis is placed on competencies exhibited by the student.

VOCATIONAL PROGRAMMING

The intent of any vocational objective is to further delineate the career planning process. Three formal/informal task-oriented counseling and assessment situations are discussed: career information centers, job stations, and vocational assessment. The goals are to (a) stimulate interest for career

Exhibit 9-9 High Priority Objectives for Academic Curriculum

TOP OBJECTIVES LISTED BY SUBJECT AREA

1.0 *Language Arts:* language arts include reading, writing, speaking, listening, and related study skills. The objectives are:

    1.1 Reading, and reading and interpreting written communication
    The student will be able to:
        1.11   Identify letters and sounds
        1.12   Identify word forms
            1.1021 Use root words
            1.1022 Use prefixes and suffixes
            1.1023 Use synonyms, antonyms, homonyms
        1.13   Read and follow directions
        1.14   Identify main ideas
        1.15   Derive word meaning from context
        1.16   Distinguish fact from opinion
        1.17   Read with comprehension
        1.18   Skim for main ideas
        1.19   Scan to locate information / data
        1.110 Read to prepare reports
        1.111 Read graphs, charts, tables, etc., efficiently
        1.112 Relate reading to personal experience
        1.113 Identify writing styles for themes
            1.1131 Entertain
            1.1132 Persuade
            1.1133 Inform
            1.1134 Compare bias vs. evidence
        1.114 Read and analyze reports
            1.1141 General
            1.1142 Technical, i.e., income tax
            1.1143 Reviews

    1.2 Writing
    The student will be able to:
        1.21   Write legibly
        1.22   Identify and write sentences
        1.23   Use language correctly
        1.24   Capitalize and punctuate correctly
        1.25   Organize sentences into paragraphs
        1.26   Develop sentence variety—length, order, kind
        1.27   Use appropriate word choices

Exhibit 9-9 continued

1.2 Writing (continued)
       1.28   Write simple directions and explanations
       1.29   Apply rules of syllabication
       1.210 Complete forms
       1.211 Write resumes and summaries
       1.212 Write letters—applications, claims, complaints, inquiries
       1.213 Write a report
       1.214 Prepare a written argument, pro and con
       1.215 Spell functionally in writing

1.3 Oral communication
The student will be able to:
       1.31   Use voice, gestures, and eye contact effectively
       1.32   Participate in general conversation
       1.33   Participate in group discussion
       1.34   Ask questions for clarification
       1.35   Make announcements
       1.36   Give explanations
       1.37   Give brief reports
       1.38   Participate in an interview

1.4 Listening
The student will be able to:
       1.41   Listen to and follow directions
       1.42   Use listening behaviors—eye contact, body posture, verbal patterns
       1.43   Listen to complete ideas
       1.44   Identify main ideas
       1.45   Identify speaker's purposes
       1.46   Extract information by listening
       1.47   Consider effects of listening
       1.48   Consider other's point of view, consider change
       1.49   Identify bias
       1.410 Relate information to personal situation

1.5 Use material to study effectively
The student will be able to:
       1.51   Use dictionary and thesaurus effectively
       1.52   Use index and table of contents
       1.53   Use library card catalog, resources
       1.54   Use encyclopedia and other reference texts
       1.55   Use media resources
       1.56   Use audiovisual aids, resources
       1.57   Locate sources of information

Exhibit 9-9 continued

2.0 *Mathematics:* The following objectives are directed toward utilizing basic mathematics effectively:

 2.1 Solve problems using basic mathematics functions
 The student will be able to:
  2.11 Identify, read, and write whole numbers
  2.12 Understand place value
  2.13 Round off numbers
  2.14 Add and subtract sets of numbers
  2.15 Solve problems using addition and subtraction
  2.16 Multiply and divide pairs of numbers
  2.17 Solve problems using multiplication and division
  2.18 Estimate answers
  2.19 Factor whole numbers

 2.2 Solve problems using basic functions with fractions
 The student will be able to:
  2.21 Read and write fractions
  2.22 Write equivalent fractions
  2.23 Add and subtract fractions
  2.24 Multiply and divide fractions
  2.25 Solve problems using basic functions with fractions

 2.3 Solve problems using ratios and proportion
 The student will be able to:
  2.31 Define and write ratios
  2.32 Define and write proportions
  2.33 Solve problems in either ratio or proportion

 2.4 Solve problems using decimals
 The student will be able to:
  2.41 Identify, read, and write decimals
  2.42 Round off decimals
  2.43 Change decimals to fractions/fractions to decimals
  2.44 Add and subtract decimals
  2.45 Multiply and divide with decimals
  2.46 Solve basic problems using all basic functions with decimals

 2.5 Solve problems using percent
 The student will be able to:
  2.51 Identify, read, and write percentages
  2.52 Calculate percentage and solve typical problems
  2.53 Change: Fractions to decimals/decimals to percent
  2.54 Solve problems with percent

Exhibit 9-9 continued

2.6 Solve problems using time, distance, weight, area, and volume
  The student will be able to:
    2.61 Identify, read, and write units of time
    2.62 Identify units of length
    2.63 Solve problems using basic functions with units of length
    2.64 Identify and solve problems using units of area
    2.65 Identify and solve problems using units of volume and capacity
    2.66 Identify and solve problems using units of weight
    2.67 Learn the metric system

  2.7 Solve problems using geometry
    2.71 Identify and draw lines and plane figures
    2.72 Identify three-dimensional objects
    2.73 Identify and measure angles
    2.74 Perform constructions
      2.7401 Bisect lines
      2.7402 Draw perpendiculars
      2.7403 Bisect angles
      2.7404 Draw equivalent angles

  2.8 Solve problems using tables and graphs
  The student will be able to:
    2.81 Read and draw simple graphs
      2.8101 Line
      2.8102 Bar
      2.8103 Circle
    2.82 Read and construct tables with data

  2.9 Solve basic business problems
  The student will be able to:
    2.91 Understand currency
    2.92 Solve problems involving borrowing money
    2.93 Solve problems involving mark-up, margin, profit and loss
    2.94 Solve problems involving list price and discount
    2.95 Solve problems involving commission
    2.96 Solve problems involving personal finances (see also management of personal finances, Exhibit 9-12)

3.0 *Social Studies:* The social studies may be coordinated with units of study in each of the other areas; however, basic study of certain objectives should occur:

  3.1 Study communities and characteristics
  The student will be able to:
    3.11 Understand community structure
    3.12 Understand state organization
    3.13 Understand federal government organization

Exhibit 9-9 continued

3.1 Study communities and characteristics (continued)
    3.14 Understand the basic needs of all people
    3.15 Understand the need for laws and citizenship
    3.16 Understand the need for public services
    3.17 Understand the economic structures of society
    3.18 Understand and locate sources of consumer information
    3.19 Understand the purpose, structure, operation, and responsibilities necessary to participate as a productive citizen
    3.110 Utilize maps and globes to read and locate information data, geography, topography, etc.

  3.2 Review basic disciplines of study in the social sciences
    The student will be able to:
    3.21 Understand the basic social science disciplines
    3.22 Understand an overview of American history
4.0 *Science/Health:* The student should be exposed to basic areas of science and health.

  4.1 General science
    The student will be able to:
    4.11 Understand basic body function and structure
    4.12 Apply first aid
    4.13 Understand common illness
    4.14 Understand effects of drugs, alcohol, narcotics on the body
    4.15 Apply principle of heat/cold to life situations
    4.16 Apply principles of mechanics to life situations
    4.17 Understand principles of electricity/make repairs
    4.18 Understand problem of environment
    4.19 Solve problems using scientific procedures and methods
    4.110 Gather, analyze, and interpret information to seek answers to problems
    4.111 Understand weather and climate

  4.2 Physics, chemistry
    The students will be able to:
    4.21 Identify and measure heat and temperature
    4.22 Understand reflection and refraction
    4.23 Understand speed and sound
    4.24 Use and understand measurement
    4.25 Define and measure force and energy
    4.26 Define and understand work and mechanical advantage
    4.27 Identify friction
    4.28 Understand basic machines and their functions
    4.29 Understand principles of electricity
    4.210 Understand basic forms of matter
    4.211 Relate and apply chemistry to food compounds
    4.212 Relate and apply chemistry to fuels/lubricants

Exhibit 9-9 continued

4.3 Biology
      The student will be able to:
      4.31   Identify life processes of organisms
      4.32   Understand and describe life processes of people
      4.33   Understand structure and function of simple plants and animals
      4.34   Explain relationship between organisms and their physical environments
      4.35   Identify food dependency and relationships
      4.36   Understand problems of ecology and environment
      4.37   Understand basic genetics

planning by exposing youths to the world of work in an organized, systematic manner; (b) obtain additional career planning information by bringing the youths into contact with specific information under various job titles; (c) determine specific career interests, strengths, and weaknesses through exposure to the world of work under structured learning conditions. The rationale for this three-phase process is that the youths will be aided in decision making concerning their future career plans when they understand the demands of various types of work, attempt to test their aptitudes in job simulation stations, and try out various positions in a protected training environment.

A student's experiences in these three areas must be planned and coordinated carefully. If a youth spends time in a career information center, that time must be directed by the individual's current vocational thoughts and plans. The job titles of interest should be pursued in determining how well this person is suited for work that at first glance "looks good" in the books in the career information center. It is not wise to have a youth attempt every task at a job station. The individual should choose those that reflect aptitudes the youth is sure of at that point. Finally, work stations should not be used as merely a means for a youth to earn money, to get out of school, or to assist someone because an extra hand is needed.

A work station is structured to provide coordinator, work station supervisor, and the youth useful information for career decisions. The youth's performance should feed back as much information as possible on abilities and attitudes. Work stations are directed vocational experiences and, as such, are not described in this chapter.

CAREER INFORMATION CENTERS

A career information center is a library of written, recorded, and graphically displayed materials concerning jobs. The holdings should be easy to use;

whenever possible, they should be presented with audiovisual aids. They should not require a high level of reading skills, which could cause a potential problem for nonreaders. The physical dimensions of the room are not critical. They should promote a feeling of informal use, and materials should be displayed to permit browsing. Even more important, however, is to have some type of teacher coordinator available to provide technical assistance. That person need not be a trained librarian. In fact, a youth on work station assignment could handle that role for other students in the center if a professional librarian were nearby to assist. A secretary or paraprofessional could handle this task with ease. It is important that the person be sensitive to the students who may be clumsy in their initial explorations of work information.

The mission of the career information center is to stimulate curiosity about jobs. Therefore, the entire atmosphere should provide the youths with an impetus for thinking about:

1. the vast number of jobs
2. different characteristics of different jobs
3. what it is they like and dislike about a given job
4. why they selected a particular vocation

One last note is the recognition that there are a vast number of jobs available. One of the first principles in developing a realistic career education plan is to select jobs that are meaningful. One procedure is to assist the youth in using the *Dictionary of Occupational Titles* (*DOT*) which is used by the U.S. Employment Service and others and is issued annually in two volumes containing 21,750 different jobs. It is overwhelming even for an adult to search the pages and note the number of different job titles; therefore, youths must be introduced to the *DOT* and given the opportunity to explore it with assistance until they uncover positions of interest. The *DOT* utilizes the three major determinants of *Data, People,* and *Things* as the variables that must be considered when deciding if a job could be suitable. *Data* provide information about the job. *People* involve those already at the job site as well as interpersonal relationships, and *Things* are the materials, tools, and characteristics of the position.

HOW TO USE A CAREER EDUCATION CENTER

The youth should be introduced to the career education center by the counselor or teacher. The youth also should be introduced to the secretary or librarian managing the center. The youth should be encouraged to browse freely and should be provided with directed searches if uninterested in just browsing.

Job Stations

A job station is a means of providing the student with simulated work tasks under controlled conditions in the classroom. The purpose is to assess the vocational, academic, and social skill development, identifying areas that need further refinement through the integrated curriculum.

It should be emphasized that this assessment process serves as a continuing part of the career educational process. That is not to say that the assessment cannot take place at given time intervals and for specified amounts of time, because it can. Career planning and assessment do not mean vocational assessment or planning alone, but rather all the factors that contribute to preparedness for the world of work. Simply put, a youth can't be taught vocational preparation with any degree of success by teaching the components in an isolated one-shot manner.

The job station is a work sampling procedure that has five main goals:

1. By observing student performance and behavior on a series of standardized work samples, a trained vocational evaluator can assess job-relevant variables including skills, interests, attitudes, and physical capacities.
2. By establishing a core set of work samples that are representative of a wide range of occupational areas and job requirements, the evaluator can expose students to a comparable set of vocationally relevant experiences.
3. By producing work samples in a direct, hands-on operation, the student can experience what it is like to perform specific work tasks and to acquire information about reactions to carrying out these jobs.
4. By providing opportunities to choose the jobs the student would like to perform, the vocational evaluator creates a situation in which the individual understands immediately the consequences of a choice.
5. By providing the student with an opportunity to indicate reactions to performance and behavior on work samples, and following this up with the evaluator's analysis, a learning situation for developing self-evaluation abilities is established.

The potential value of using work samples in job stations is to develop standardized methods of reporting behavior in a situation that is commensurate with a real position. At present, however, more evidence is needed that differences in performance on work samples are related to variations in performance on the actual job. Vocational education topics and suggested objectives are outlined in Exhibit 9-10.

Exhibit 9-10 Vocational Education Topics

SUGGESTED OBJECTIVES

1.0 *Career Awareness:* This refers to the understanding of the characteristics of the world of work that determine life career decisions. The objectives relating to career awareness are that the student will be able to:
1.1 Understand the variety and complexity of careers in the world of work
1.2 Understand the relationship of careers to social goals, functions, and needs
1.3 Identify the characteristics of the preparations for various careers
1.4 Understand that "career" involves progressive stages of preparation
1.5 Understand the relationship of career to life style

2.0 *Economic Awareness:* This refers to the perception of the relationship of the economic processes in the environment to an individual's life career decisions. The objectives relating to economic awareness are that the student will be able to:
2.1 Relate career roles to life style and personal economics
2.2 Recognize the social and economic benefits of careers
2.3 Recognize nonoccupational means of acquiring wealth
2.4 Relate personal economic status to social economy

3.0 *Decision Making:* This refers to the skill of applying knowledge to a rational process of career choice. The objectives relating to decision making are that the student will be able to:
3.1 Relate career goals to the process of making career decisions
3.2 Identify, gather, and apply information
3.3 Identify and select alternatives and use them in making decisions

4.0 *Beginning Competence and Skill Awareness:* This refers to both awareness and acquisition of the skills necessary in the performance of tasks relating to a career. The objectives relating to this topic are that the student will be able to:
4.1 Identify objectives, specify resources, outline steps of action, perform the steps, and evaluate the action
4.2 Identify tools required for tasks of industry and commerce
4.3 Identify the interpersonal relationships involved in various career roles
4.4 Perform entry level tasks
4.5 Acquire in-depth skills for entry into relevant occupations

Exhibit 9-10 continued

> 5.0 *Employability Skills:* This refers to the social and communication skills
> appropriate to career placement. The objectives relating to employabil-
> ity skills are that the student will be able to:
>   5.1 Understand the implications of working in independent, team, and
>   supervised situations
>   5.2 Relate individual interest and aptitude information to occupations
>   5.3 Demonstrate work habits and attitudes necessary for entering
>   occupations of interest
>   5.4 Demonstrate skills to seek and obtain a job
>
> 6.0 *Attitudes and Appreciation:* This refers to feelings toward the social and
> economic environment in relation to life roles. The objectives relating to
> this topic are that the student will be able to:
>   6.1 Recognize responsibilities involved in accepting a job/task
>   6.2 Recognize differences in the environment and exhibit the ability to
>   be tolerant and flexible. .

PERSONAL DEVELOPMENT

Personal development is a counterpart to social development and has long
been recognized as inseparable as a major objective in shaping a meaningful
program for a learning disabled student. Improved personal-social development enables all persons to feel better about themselves and to relate to
others; it also promotes the independence so avidly sought and so highly
valued. The following objectives act as a guide to the team of educators
planning and implementing efforts with learning disabled youth. It frequently
is difficult to choose a simple objective in this priority area. That choice must
be approached and emphasized carefully and thoroughly by all staff
members. The importance of this area of development in youth with specialized learning and behavioral problems remains critical if a successful student
is to exit high school equipped for life.

The personal-social objectives again are presented as potential miniunits of
instruction. However, close coordination is expected between educators and
counselors. The objectives are shown in Exhibit 9-11.

SOCIAL DEVELOPMENT

Most youths have had experiences with and have studied the facets of
social development that enable one to be an effective person in society.
However, data and clinical observation (Bryan, 1977) indicate that learning

Exhibit 9-11 Personal Development Program

PERSONAL AND SOCIAL OBJECTIVES

1.0 *Attain a Sufficient Understanding of One's Self*
    The student will be able to:
    1.1 Attain a sense of body
    1.2 Identify interests
    1.3 Identify abilities
    1.4 Identify emotions
    1.5 Identify personal needs
    1.6 Understand physical self
        1.61 Physiological development
        1.62 Human sexuality

2.0 *Obtain Positive Self-Confidence, Self-Concept*
    The student will be able to:
    2.1 Express feeling of self-worth
    2.2 Understand how others see him or her
    2.3 Accept criticism
    2.4 Develop faith in self

3.0 *Desire and Achieve Socially Responsible Behavior*
    The student will be able to:
    3.1 Understand character traits needed for acceptance by others
    3.2 Exhibit acceptable behavior in public
    3.3 Develop and understand respect for the rights and properties of others
    3.4 Recognize and follow instructions, rules
    3.5 Identify personal roles in many situations
    3.6 Understand cultural and multicultural values

4.0 *Choose, Develop, and Maintain Appropriate Interpersonal Relationships*
    The student will be able to:
    4.1 Know how to listen and respond to others
    4.2 Understand how to make and maintain friendships
    4.3 Understand appropriate heterosexual relationships
    4.4 Understand how to establish close relationships

5.0 *Achieve Independence*
    The student will be able to:
    5.1 Understand the impact of one's behavior on others
    5.2 Understand the need for self-organization
    5.3 Develop goal-seeking behavior
    5.4 Strive toward self-actualization

Exhibit 9-11 continued

6.0 *Make Good Decisions, Solve Problems*
The student will be able to:
6.1 Differentiate bipolar concepts
6.2 Understand the need for goals
6.3 Consider alternatives
6.4 Anticipate consequences
6.5 Know where to find advice

7.0 *Communicate Appropriately with Others*
The student will be able to:
7.1 Recognize emergency situations
7.2 Understand the need to and be able to read effectively
7.3 Understand and be able to communicate effectively in
7.31 writing
7.32 oral speech
7.4 Understand subtleties of mass and/or personal communication

disabled youth generally are less developed than their age peers in personal management skills. Therefore, high priority objectives (in terms of utilization in counseling or work in the resource room) are stated here to guide both students and educators.

Social Development Objectives

These objectives are presented for consideration as miniunits of study and/or topics for individual or small group counseling. Both major objectives and the enabling steps are presented in the form of competencies. The objectives are outlined in Exhibit 9-12.

The Big Bandaid

The length of this chapter should indicate that comprehensive coverage of adolescent and postschool aspects of learning disability requires entire books, not just a chapter. Several excellent books are available on secondary aspects of learning disabilities and the author encourages reading them. However, it is difficult to stay current. At the time of this writing, many new and unresolved issues loomed, i.e., statewide competency testing, a lack of vocational rehabilitation services to learning disability students, limited number of colleges that will enroll secondary learning disabled students, an absence of secondary counselors trained to work with learning disabled adolescents, and limited career information centers for nonreading or poor reading populations. These are but a few examples.

Exhibit 9-12 Personal Management Program

COMPETENCIES TO BE ATTAINED

1.0 *Managing Personal Finances*
The student will be able to:
1.1 Identify money and make correct change
1.2 Make wise expenditures
1.3 Use bank facilities for
    1.31 Money exchange
    1.32 Bank accounts
    1.33 Savings accounts
    1.34 Safety deposits
    1.35 Credit / loans
1.4 Maintain financial records
1.5 Calculate and pay taxes
1.6 Understand Social Security payments and benefits
1.7 Understand retirement and fringe benefits
1.8 Understand purpose and function of insurance programs
1.9 Understand purpose and function of Worker Compensation

2.0 *Selecting, Managing, and Maintaining a Home*
The student will be able to:
2.1 Select adequate housing
2.2 Maintain a home
2.3 Use basic appliances and tools
2.4 Maintain household and household goods

3.0 *Caring for Personal Needs*
The student will be able to:
3.1 Select appropriate clothing for
    3.11 Work situations
    3.12 Social situations
    3.13 Leisure time activities
3.2 Exhibit proper grooming
3.3 Understand and exhibit basic hygiene
3.4 Demonstrate knowledge of physical fitness
3.5 Demonstrate knowledge of good nutrition in
    3.51 Eating skills
    3.52 Meal planning
    3.53 Food purchases
    3.54 Food preparation
    3.55 Food storage
    3.56 Sanitation
3.6 Demonstrate knowledge of personal health care
3.7 Demonstrate knowledge of health care services

Exhibit 9-12 continued

4.0 *Participating in Family Life*
    The student will be able to demonstrate knowledge of:
    4.1 Sexual relationships
    4.2 Responsibilities involved in marriage
    4.3 Responsibilities in child care, especially
        4.31 Personal care
        4.32 Psychological development
        4.33 Intellectual development
        4.34 Social development
    4.4 Family safety procedures and practice
    4.5 Family planning

5.0 *Purchasing and Caring for Clothing*
    The student will be able to:
    5.1 Exercise judgment in clothing purchases
    5.2 Exercise care of clothing in
        5.21 Cleanliness
        5.22 Storing
        5.23 Repairing clothing

6.0 *Engaging in Civic Activities*
    The student will be able to understand:
    6.1 Basic local government
    6.2 Basic laws and law enforcement
    6.3 Basic American government
    6.4 Personal rights and responsibilities as a citizen
        6.41 Due process
        6.42 Legal process—rights and responsibilities
        6.43 Municipal services
        6.44 Registration and voting procedures
    6.5 Selective Service System

7.0 *Utilizing Recreation and Leisure Time*
    The student will be able to:
    7.1 Participate in individual and group activities
    7.2 Know activities and available resources
    7.3 Understand recreational values
    7.4 Use recreational facilities in the community
    7.5 Plan activities wisely
    7.6 Plan vacations

8.0 *Adapting to Mobility, Transportation*
    The student will be able to:
    8.1 Demonstrate knowledge of traffic rules and safety practices as
        8.11 Pedestrian

> 8.12 Vehicle operator
>   8.121 Bicycle
>   8.122 Automotive
> 8.2 Demonstrate knowledge of responsibilities of a car in
>   8.21 Automotive ownership
>   8.22 Automotive purchases
>   8.23 Automotive insurance, liabilities
>   8.24 Legal aspects
>   8.25 Work and leisure
> 8.3 Demonstrate knowledge and use of various means of transportation, public and private

This chapter has focused on the goals of the secondary program from three standpoints.

First, the position taken here is that the current service delivery model is based on the elementary level. This is grossly unfair to the student, the program, the future of this nation—in short, learning disabled youth are a major national resource who become a wise investment or a tragic, neglected waste. Remediation of academic skills is but one instructional strategy. In a pointed criticism of the current programs, Schoolfield (1978) laid the issues wide open in a hard-hitting paper. His 12 issues are worthy of much discussion, in the classroom or elsewhere.

1. The drive to bring students up to level as manifested through documented "success" cases and parental pressure.
2. The need to follow the curriculum and make grade reports based upon computerized printouts.
3. The need to mainstream or keep the youngster in tune with his peer group in the event he is dropped from the learning disabilities program.
4. The requirement to write objectives to fit a predetermined goal and then fit the child into these objectives.
5. The inadequacy of diagnostic data in that it presents a picture but not a portrait.
6. The limited availability of resource help while planning techniques or materials, which would in fact require hours of presentation if we really expected them to be successful.
7. The inability to escape from the routinized and impersonal aspects of the secondary environment.
8. The lack of supportive personnel to work with students needing more attention than the modified elementary model can provide.

9. The reputation of the learning disabilities program as a place for outcasts and the unworthy.
10. The inappropriate placement of learning disabled students caused by the lack of more appropriate alternatives.
11. The lack of trained personnel to implement on-going student program changes based on progress, failures, and personal needs from day to day or from year to year.
12. The reliance upon state guidelines which do not guarantee quality, success, or an ultimately saleable skill. (Schoolfield, 1978, p. 425)

Second, the chapter proposed that an integrated curriculum be developed that brings into play the total school program that interacts with the student. To achieve that, four objectives are necessary:

1. *Academic Program Goals:* objectives in support of the student's academic status, career level of achievement, and vocational career goals, predicted on the youth's interests.
2. *Vocational Program Goals:* occupational career objectives based on the aptitudes, interests, and vocational program potentialities available to the student.
3. *Social Skill Development Goals:* objectives directed at overcoming any social awkwardness initiated and reinforced by the learning disability, particularly where peer and authority relationship skills are necessary to achieve a life management plan.
4. *Personal Development Goals:* Social-personal objectives related to the development of skills necessary to achieve positive, realistic feelings for self.

Third, a service delivery system is proposed that brings learning disability teachers out of the confines of the self-contained classroom, and even the resource room, and places them in a coordinating or brokerage function in the junior and senior high school. The coordinating role involves the counselors, teachers, vocational educators, community agency personnel, and support services needed to mount an integrated curriculum approach for secondary students.

Summary

To summarize, the author is in complete agreement with the concluding statements made by Lindsey and Kerlin (1979). In particular, reading remains the major academic difficulty, with diagnosis for etiology a less than productive exercise since there is no agreement on the definition (the population cannot be defined except as a program is being structured), nor are there data from well-designed research on the nature of the reading disability. Finally, many factors exist in secondary schools that complicate the delivery of service in an integrated and coordinated plan. Little (at best) usable data exist to guide the user on instruction and behavioral management methods of choice, or the most efficient or effective service delivery mode.

Secondary special education is a vast new frontier where only a few true pioneers have forged, with more hope than science.

REFERENCES

Allen, R.L. Better reading through the recognition of grammatical relations. *The Reading Teacher,* 1964, *18*(3), 194–198.

Balow, B., & Bloomquist, M. Young adults ten to fifteen years after severe reading disability. *Elementary School Journal,* 1965, *66,* 44–48.

Barone, S. Career education and the handicapped. In R.D. Bhaerman (Ed.), *Career education and basic academic achievement: a descriptive analysis of the research.* Washington, D.C.: U.S. Office of Education, May 1977.

Brookover, W.B., Erickson, E.L., & Joiner, L.M. *Self-concept of ability and school achievement III: Relationship of self-concept and achievement in high school.* (U.S. Office of Education, Cooperative Research Project No. 2831.) East Lansing, Mich.: Michigan State University, Office of Research and Publications, 1967.

Bryan, T. Peer popularity of learning disabled children. *Journal of Learning Disabilities,* 1974, *7*(10), 621–625.

―――――――――. Peer popularity of learning disabled children: A replication. *Journal of Learning Disabilities,* 1976, *9*(5), 307–311.

―――――――――. *Social behaviors of learning disabled students.* Paper presented at the Association for Children with Learning Disabilities conference, Washington, D.C., March 1977.

Burke, N.S., & Simons, A. Factors which precipitate dropouts and delinquency. *Federal Probation,* 1965, *29,* 28–32.

Carroll, J. The nature of the reading process. In H. Singer & R. Ruddell (Eds.), *Theoretical models and processes of reading.* Newark, Del.: International Reading Association, 1970.

Carter, R.P. *A descriptive analysis of the adult adjustment of persons once identified as disabled readers.* Unpublished doctoral dissertation, Indiana University, 1964.

Clements, S.D. *Minimal brain dysfunction in children.* (National Institutes of Neurological Diseases and Strokes Monograph No. 3, U.S. Public Health Service Publication No. 1415). Washington, D.C.: U.S. Government Printing Office, 1966.

Coopersmith, S. *The antecedents of self-esteem.* San Francisco: W.H. Freeman, 1967.

Cox, S. The learning-disabled adult. *Academic Therapy,* 1977, *13,* 79–86.

Cronin, J. State Superintendent of Illinois Office of Education. Address to Professors of Special Education in Illinois Colleges and Universities, 1977.

Dembinski, R. The reliability of the self-control behavior inventory. *Behavioral Disorders,* 1979, *4*(1), 137–142.

DeRisi, W.J., & Butz, G. *Writing behavioral contracts.* Champaign, Ill.: Research Press Co., 1974.

Deshler, D.D., Lowrey, N., & Alley, G.R. Programming alternatives for LD adolescents: A nationwide survey. *Academic Therapy,* 1979, *14,* 389–397.

Diamond, D.E., & Bredrosian, H. *Industry hiring requirements in the employment of disadvantaged groups.* New York: New York University School of Commerce, 1970.

Dictionary of occupational titles. Washington, D.C.: U.S. Department of Labor, Employment and Training Administration, U.S. Employment Service, 1977.

Douglass, H.R. An effective junior high school program for reducing the number of dropouts. *Contemporary Education,* 1969, *41,* 34–37.

Eisenberg, L. Reading retardation I. Psychiatric and sociologic aspects. *Pediatrics,* 1966, *37,* 352–365.

Empey, L.T., & Erickson, M.L. Hidden delinquency and social status. *Social Force,* 1966, *44,* 546–554.

Ensminger, E.E. *A handbook on secondary programs for the learning disabled adolescent: some guidelines,* 1976. (ERIC Document Reproduction Service No. 102 454).

Fabian, A.A. Reading disability: an index of pathology. *American Journal of Orthopsychiatry,* 1955, *25,* 319–326.

Frauenheim, J.G. Academic achievement characteristics of adult males who were diagnosed as dyslexic in childhood. *Journal of Learning Disabilities,* 1978, *11*(8), 476–83.

Frease, D.E. Delinquency, social class, and the schools. *Sociology and Social Research,* 1973, *57*(4), 443-449.

French, E.G. Effects of the interaction of motivation and feedback on task performance. In J.W. Atkinson (Ed.), *Motives in fantasy, action and society.* Toronto: Van Nostrand Co., 1958.

French, J. *Characteristics of high ability dropouts.* National Association of Secondary School Principals Bulletin, 1969, *53,* 67–79.

Gallagher, P.A. A synthesis of classroom scheduling techniques for emotionally disturbed children. In E. Meyer, G. Vergason, & R. Whelan (Eds.), *Strategies for teaching exceptional children.* Denver: Love Publishing Co., 1972.

Gardner, W. *Learning and behavior characteristics of exceptional children and youth.* Boston: Allyn & Bacon, Inc., 1977.

Goldman, N. School vandalism: A sociopsychological study. *Education Digest,* 1960, *26,* 1–4.

Goodman, L., & Mann, L. *Learning disabilities in the secondary schools: Issues and practices.* New York: Grune & Stratton, Inc., 1976.

Gottlieb, J., & Budoff, M. Attitudes toward school by segregated and integrated retarded children: A study and experimental validation. *Proceedings of the 80th Annual Convention of the American Psychological Association,* 1972, *1,* 713–714. (Summary).

Grant, W.V., & Lind, C.G. *Digest of educational statistics.* Washington, D.C.: Department of Health, Education, and Welfare, U.S. Office of Education, 1975.

——————. *Digest of educational statistics.* Washington, D.C.: Department of Health, Education, and Welfare, U.S. Office of Education, 1979.

Gruhn, H., & Krause, S. On the social behavior of physically handicapped children and teenagers. *Problème and Ergebnisseder Psychologie,* 1968, *23,* 73–86.

Hardy, M.I. *Clinical follow-up study of disabled readers.* Unpublished doctoral dissertation, University of Toronto, Canada, 1968.

Harris, T.A. *I'm ok—You're ok.* New York: Harper & Row Publishers, Inc., 1973.

Herjanic, B.M., & Penick, E.C. Adult outcome of disabled readers. *The Journal of Special Education,* 1972, *6*(4), 397–410.

Hohenshil, T.H. Call for reduction: A vocational educator views school psychological services. *Journal of School Psychology,* 1975, 13, 58–62.

Howden, M. *A nineteen-year follow-up study of good, average, and poor readers in the fifth and sixth grades.* Unpublished doctoral dissertation, University of Oregon, 1967.

Jesness, C.F., & DeRisi, W.J. Some variations in techniques of contingency management in a school for delinquents. In J.S. Stumphauzer (Ed.), *Behavior Therapy with Delinquents.* Springfield, Ill.: Charles C. Thomas, Publisher, 1973.

Katzenbach, N. DeB. *Task force report: Juvenile delinquency and youth crime.* Washington, D.C.: U.S. Government Printing Office, 1967.

Keldgold, R. Brain damage and delinquency: A question and a challenge. *Academic Therapy,* 1969, *4,* 93–99.

Klasner, E. *The syndrome of specific dyslexia.* Baltimore: University Park Press, 1972.

Lambert, N.M., & Bower, E.M. *Bower's two-step process for identifying emotionally handicapped pupils.* Princeton, N.J.: Educational Testing Service, 1961.

Lazarus, A.A., & Abramowitz, A. The use of "emotive imagery" in the treatment of children's phobias. *Journal of Mental Science,* 1962, *108,* 191–195.

Lerner, J.W., Evans, M.A., & Meyers, G. L.D. programs at the secondary level: A survey. *Academic Therapy,* 1977, *13,* 7–19.

Lindsey, J., & Kerlin, M. Learning disabilities and reading disorders: A brief review of the secondary level literature. *Journal of Learning Disabilities,* 1979, 12(6), 408–415.

Long, H.B. Perspectives of the continuing education unit. *Adult Leadership,* 1974, *22,* 268–270.

Mann, D. *Intervening with convicted serious juvenile offenders.* Santa Monica, Calif.: The Rand Corp., 1976.

Martin, M.Y. Advancing career education. *American Education,* 1972, *8,* 25–30.

McCullough, C. Reading and realism. *Proceedings of the Annual Convention of the International Reading Association,* 1968. (Summary).

Miller, S.R., Sabatino, D.A., & Larsen, R.P. Agreement between university and local administrators of special education on selected issues in the professional preparation of secondary special educators. *Exceptional Children,* 1980, *46*(5), 344–352.

Morgan, D.I. Prevalence and types of handicapping conditions found in juvenile correctional institutions: A national survey. *The Journal of Special Education,* 1979, *13*(3), 283–295.

Morse, W. The crisis or helping teacher. In N. Long, W. Morse, & R. Newman (Eds.), *Conflict in the classroom* (3rd ed.). Belmont, Calif.: Wadsworth Publishing Co., Inc., 1976.

Mulligan, W.A. A study of dyslexia and delinquency. *Academic Therapy,* 1969, *4,* 177–187.

National Advisory Committee on Handicapped Children. *First Annual Report.* Washington, D.C.: U.S. Office of Education, 1968.

National Center for Educational Statistics (NCES). *Digest of education statistics.* Washington, D.C.: U.S. Government Printing Office, 1979.

Oppenheimer, E., & Mandel, M. Behavior disturbances of school children in relation to the preschool period. *American Journal of Public Health,* 1959, *49,* 1537–1542.

O'Reilly, R.P. *A system of objectives in reading,* (Manual draft). New York State Education Department, 1971.

Percival, W.P. *A study of the causes and subjects of school failure.* Unpublished thesis. Teachers College, Columbia University, New York, 1926.

Piaget, J. *Origins of intelligence in children.* New York: W.W. Norton & Co., 1963.

Preston, R.C., & Yarington, D.J. Status of fifty retarded readers eight years after reading clinic diagnosis. *Journal of Reading,* 1967, *11,* 122–129.

Rawson, M.B. *Developmental language disability: Adult accomplishments of dyslexic boys.* Baltimore: Johns Hopkins University Press, 1968.

Reading disorder in the United States: Report of the Secretary's National Advisory Committee on dyslexia and related disorders. Washington, D.C.: U.S. Department of Health, Education, and Welfare, 1969.

Robinson, H.M., & Smith, H.K. Reading clinic clients—ten years after. *Elementary School Journal,* 1962, *63,* 22–27.

Roman, M. *Reaching delinquents through reading.* Springfield, Ill.: Charles C. Thomas, Publisher, 1957.

Sabatino, D.A. *Neglect and delinquent children,* Educational Development Center report. Wilkes-Barre, Pa.: Wilkes College, 1974.

——————. Norm violating secondary school youth: Demographic findings. In D.A. Sabatino & A.J. Mauser (Eds.), *Specialized education in today's secondary schools* (Vol. 1), Boston: Allyn & Bacon, Inc., 1978.

Sabatino, D.A., & Mauser, A.J. (Eds.). *Specialized education in today's secondary schools.* Boston: Allyn & Bacon, Inc., 1978.

Schoolfield, W.R. Limitations of the college entry LD model. *Academic Therapy,* 1978, *13,* 423–431.

Scranton, T.R., & Downs, M.C. Elementary and secondary learning disabilities programs in the U.S.: A survey. *Journal of Learning Disabilities,* 1975, *8*(6), 394–399.

Shaw, M.C., Edson, K., & Bell, H.M. The self-concept of bright underachieving high school students as revealed by an adjective checklist. *Personal and Guidance Journal,* 1960, *39,* 193–196.

Silberberg, N.E., & Silberberg, M.C. Myths in remedial education. *Journal of Learning Disabilities,* 1969, *2*(4), 302–307.

Silver, A.A., & Hagen, R.A. Specific reading disability: Follow-up studies. *American Journal of Orthopsychiatry,* 1964, *34,* 95–102.

——————. Maturation of perceptual dysfunction in children with specific reading disability. *The Reading Teacher,* 1966, *19*(4), 253–259.

Smith, S.L. *No easy answers: The learning disabled child.* Rockville, Md.: Department of Health, Education, and Welfare, National Institute on Mental Health, 1978.

Staat, A.W. *Social behaviorism.* Homewood, Ill.: The Dorsey Press, 1975.

Strauss, A.A., & Lehtinen, L.E. *Psychopathology and education of the brain-injured child* (Vol. 1). New York: Grune & Stratton, Inc., 1947.

Taylor, R.G. Personality traits and discrepant achievement: A review. *Journal of Counseling Psychology,* 1964, *11,* 76–81.

Taylor, D.C. Aggression and epilepsy. *Journal of Psychosomatic Research,* 1969, *13,* 229–236.

Vernon, M.I. The perceptual process in reading. *The Reading Teacher,* 1959, *13*(1), 2–8.

Washington, R. A survey-analysis of problems faced by inner-city high school students who have been classified as truants. *High School Journal,* 1973, *56,* 248–257.

West, D.J. *The young offender.* New York: Penguin Books, 1967.

Yamamoto, D., Lembright, M.L., & Corrigan, A.M. Intelligence, creative thinking, and sociometric choice among fifth grade children. *Journal of Experimental Education,* 1966, *34*(3), 83–89.

Chapter 10

Adolescent Social-Personal Development: Theory and Application

David A. Sabatino
and Patrick J. Schloss

INTRODUCTION

A number of excessive and deficit social and emotional behaviors have been associated with the presence of learning disabilities.

Poremba (1974) contends that most delinquents in the United States are learning disabled youth who have not been served. As many as 85 percent to 90 percent of delinquents display learning disabilities as opposed to 20 percent to 25 percent of the school population. Jacobson (1974) provides more modest figures, placing 50 percent to 80 percent of delinquents in the learning disability group. Jordan (1974) found 81 percent to be learning disabled.

Compton (1974) assessed the incidence and type of learning disabilities, noting a general pattern of 75 percent having a sudden drop in achievement coupled with truancy before the sixth grade. Hodgenson (1974) also reported a highly positive statistical relationship between reading failure and antisocial, aggressive behaviors. Morgan (1979) conducted a survey of some 200 juvenile correctional agencies in all 50 states and U.S. territories to ascertain the known incidence of handicapped incarcerated youth. He found that 42.4 percent of the youths were handicapped according to the categories delineated in Public Law 94-142, with the prevalent diagnoses being educable mental retardation, serious emotional disturbance, and specific learning disabilities.

Several investigations have reported an association between neurological dysfunction and delinquency. Fitzhugh (1973) reports that court-referred delinquents performed significantly poorer than the general population on a battery of neuropsychological tests. Fitzhugh concluded that neurological dysfunction may be associated with delinquent acts through an adolescent's reduced ability to succeed in school. Berman and Siegal (1976) administered a neuropsychological battery to adjudicated delinquent males and a nondelinquent control group. The delinquent group performed significantly worse on all but one subtest. These and other studies support the association between neurological dysfunction and nonadaptive social behavior.

Bryan (1976) offers two explanations for the coexistence of learning disabilities and behavior disorders: (1) either of these disorders can produce the other; (2) children who have difficulty comprehending printed material also may have problems in understanding people. Bryan, Wheeler, Felcan, and Henek (1976) and Bryan and Bryan (1977) present data that supports these contentions. Their research demonstrates that (1) learning disabled children are not good people readers, (2) their responses in social interactions reflect an insensitivity to the feelings of others, and (3) they often are disliked by their peers.

Auerbach (1971) describes an approach to learning disabilities that emphasizes the social context in which the child develops. The author argues that ". . . the child's disability affects mainly his parents and then teachers, school officials, and professionals in such a way that their efforts to help him are thwarted by the same complex of symptoms (failure, anxiety, hyperactivity, emotional liability, etc.) as those of the child's disability." (p. 87) Auerbach argues that effective intervention with the learning disabled child must concentrate on the ecosystem in which the youth is expected to function.

Whether disabilities derive from known or inferred neurological dysfunctions or from the influence of the learning environment, the importance of social and emotional development strategies in an educational program is paramount. As Lerner (1971) states ". . . a lack of sensitivity to people and poor perception of social situations . . . affects every area of the child's life. This is probably the most debilitating learning problem the child can have" (p. 247). It is the purpose of this chapter to explore the relationship between learning disabilities and social-personal adjustment factors and to present an approach to developing motivating and monitoring social competency behaviors with learning disabled children and adolescents.

BEHAVIORAL CHARACTERISTICS

The school experience can be relevant, or boring, frustrating, or fulfilling for any child. The common responses of learning disabled children and youth generally speaking are reactions of frustration to the educational environment and those in it, both student and teacher. That frustration may be displayed by students' anger at (aggression) or passive withdrawal from learning and teachers when basic reading, writing, spelling, and arithmetic skills (tool subjects) are so inadequate that they are unusable for purposes of daily living. More importantly, academic achievement may be so weak that skill deficiencies actually multiply as the youth grows older.

As learning disabled students attempt to learn, and fail, they also cannot meet their own expectations for achievement. This lowers their expectation for future success until a generalized fear of failure dominates their attitudes and behaviors. Response generalization to other social, academic, and school-related activities is inevitable and a pattern of learned helplessness results. One of the principal aspects of that syndrome is that motivation to achieve deteriorates, negating self-concept and self-reliance. The result is a student who

1. generally feels noncompetitive and is fearful of failure in academic settings
2. generally feels inadequate in response to the expectations of others, having limited feelings of self-worth (self-concept)
3. generally feels anxious, responding in an aggressive-passive behavioral continuum in a rigid, nonappropriate manner, evidencing a self-fulfilling prophecy of continued misconduct

The end product is a person with limited motivation to achieve who is practicing learned helplessness. It is worthwhile examining at least five partial explanations for some of the symptomatic behaviors that accompany the learning disability syndrome: (1) limited (poor) relations with significant others, (2) inappropriate response to social cues, (3) feelings of inadequacy for self, (4) lack of achievement motivation, and (5) learned helplessness.

RELATIONSHIPS WITH SIGNIFICANT OTHERS

That subhead could well read "Disruptive Relationships with Significant Others." The nature of learning disabilities is such that children's comparison of self with others frequently leaves them with a sense of inferiority unless those inadequacies can be compensated for or offset by success in other areas.

A simple case in point: persons who fail to achieve something expected of self and manifested by others begin to question themselves and develop a greater incidence of off-task academic behaviors. Many of those behaviors are socially unacceptable, resulting in a further separation between those individuals and others.

The presence of behaviors that draw unfavorable attention to the child, that are not readily explainable, and that tend to be unresponsive to standard teaching practices and general classroom reinforcement principles generally are viewed by the teacher simply as off-task behaviors.

Children's off-task academic behaviors may be prompted by self-perception (Bryan & Bryan, 1975). Although there are data to suggest that students' ratings of themselves do not agree with their teachers' (Richmond & Dalton, 1973), the self-fulfilling prophecy has been shown repeatedly (Archibald, 1974) to affect actual performance on academic achievement tasks.

Bryan (1974) investigated peer reactions of 84 learning disabled children in regular classes in sixty-two third, fourth, and fifth grade classrooms. A sociometric scale was used to ascertain peer popularity and peer rejection. The data indicated that when learning disabled children were compared to randomly selected classmates of the same sex and race, they were rejected to a significant degree by their peers who were not so afflicted. Learning disabled girls were rejected considerably more frequently than any other group. The research notes that peers of such children report them to be highly anxious, sad, frightened, seldom having a good time, and generally socially neglected. Later Bryan (1976) replicated the study with all-white subjects only. The results were stable over time, with the peer rejection continuing.

There is evidence (Siperstein, Bopp, & Bak, 1978) that children without learning disabilities do accept those who are affected into the group on nonacademic as opposed to academic tasks. As a group, however, the learning disabled are neither viewed as sociometric stars nor placed in social isolation any more than nondisabled children.

INAPPROPRIATE RESPONSES TO SOCIAL CUES

People are judged "good" or "bad" in a socially relative sense based upon their capability to comply with the rules of the social order. Not all rules are written or even spoken. Therefore, compliance is provided by cues from a leader, the gang, a group, in any given situation. It already has been established (in the introduction to this chapter) that learning disabled children are not as perceptive as others in reading or interpreting social cues.

The question that must be asked is: If learning disabled children display inappropriate behavior, does it influence their total personality development? The answer is yes, because personality has been defined as the construct describing the aspect of a unified, complex, organized person. Personality is considered to be stable when the characteristic modes of behaving, or interpreting the world in which people live, is consistent. One of the key behavioral characteristics of learning disabled children is that they do not react consistently even to similar stimuli in the same environmental situation.

The point is that the social situation shapes and even teaches behaviors, reinforcing or negating them until they comply with the "rules" of the social order. That assumption is one explanation as to why learning disabled children respond inconsistently, fragmentedly, and poorly to social cues. It does not require a leap in logic to speculate that their view toward self resulting from poor understanding of social cues, and inappropriate responses to social situations, would in turn reduce their concept of self—at least on academic and related tasks in the school environment. The next section examines the self-concept, locus of control, achievement motivation, and learned helplessness of learning disabled students.

INADEQUATE CONCEPT OF SELF

Brookover and Erikson (1975) divide self-conceptualizing behaviors of students into four major categories:

1. role requirements for self
2. self-concept (perception) of ability to execute the role requirements
3. intrinsic value to self of role performance
4. instrumental value to self of role performance

A role provides identity, and that identity determines the view of self. Certainly, the expectancy theories of Atkinson (1964) (discussed in the section on Achievement Motivation) and Rotter (1966) are examples of individuals' self-concept of their abilities. The instrumental value to self establishes the value and expectancy for reward, while intrinsic value places a personal meaning on the worth of task and person.

To measure the task relationship of self-concept, Boersma, Chapman, and Maguire (1978) studied both general and academic self-concept. Third grade and sixth grade children were asked about their self-perception of abilities in general, their skills in arithmetic, reading, spelling, and writing, their attitudes toward school satisfaction, and their confidence in their academic ability. The results indicated that learning disabled children had lower self-concepts of ability than the nondisabled in all academic subject areas except penmanship and neatness. The correlation between general school satisfaction and any specific academic achievement subjects was not statistically significant. However, the difference between the two types continued from third through sixth grades. The academic self-concept did reveal a statistically significant difference between the two by the third grade, remaining consistent through the sixth grade.

Predictions concerning future performance indicated that learning disabled children had lower expectations than others for academic achievement (reading, spelling, and math). The results suggested that actual experience played an important role in the children's estimates of themselves.

Larsen, Parker, and Jorjorian (1973) find a greater discrepancy between real self-concept and ideal self-concept measures for both the third grade and fourth grade learning disabled in comparison to the nondisabled. Rosser (1974) reports that fourth grade learning disabled students display lower self-concept test scores than the others on ideal vs. real self. Most learning disability teachers comment on the poor self-concept of their students and their capability to idealize their performance in off-task activities. Exhibit 10-1 lists published self-concept instruments.

In conclusion, the following generalities on self-concept and academic achievement may be drawn:

1. Lowered self-esteem or a more negative self-concept does appear to characterize learning disabled children in contrast to those not so disabled. Self-concept does seem to be a highly unstable measure, especially for first and second graders.
2. Self-concept seems to be fixed toward school tasks by third grade and remains fairly stable after that.
3. Information on one's condition seems to raise self-concept.
4. There seems to be little relationship between specific academic underachievement factors and specific views of self.
5. In sum, self-concept and academic achievement share a modest relationship with identifiable learning disabled populations. The meaning of that relationship is only speculative at present. However, initial research would indicate that the variables that have an impact on self-concept also may affect several other critical factors such as age of recognition of the problem, information on the problem, and the amount of control children feel they have in given situations. In short, self-concept may reflect social learning for a task with regard for the people involved.

The next section discusses a concept that examines the student's feelings of control over the immediate environment.

LOCUS OF CONTROL

As an extension of his social learning theory, Rotter (1966) hypothesized that predictions for an individual's need to achieve could be based on what he termed *locus of control*. This concept involves a referenced continuum running from internal to external control over a person's own behavior in a given situation. The situationally sensitive theme developed by Rotter suited his theory of social learning extremely well. The theory provided the user an explanation of behavior by observation of its interaction between person and environment. In short, internal control refers to the perception of being in control of the situation and consequently one's own actions. On the other

Exhibit 10-1 Self-Concept Descriptive Instruments and Procedures

1. **About Me**
   Age: 8–14 years
   Obtainable from: James Parker (author)
   Box 374
   Cordele, Georgia 31015
   Cost: Send self-addressed stamped envelope.
   Description: This is a self-reported, numerical rating scale designed to measure: A, the self in school; B, the self as achieving; C, the self; D, the physical self; and E, the self in relation to others.
   Reliability and Validity: This test was presented to 31 sixth graders on a test-retest basis. An agreement of 64.2 percent was obtained between the two administrations.

2. **The Adjective Check List (ACL)**
   Age: Grades 9–16 and adults
   Obtainable from: Consulting Psychologists Press Inc.
   577 College Avenue
   Palo Alto, California 94306
   Cost: $2.50 per manual, $3 per specimen set, postage extra, available in Booklet Form, IBM Format, or NCS Format.
   Description: This is a 300-item test that can be scored for 24 variables. These include measures of personal adjustment, counseling readiness, and scales for self-confidence, self-control and liability.
   Reliability and Validity: A mean test-retest reliability coefficient of .54 was obtained for a sample of 100 men.

3. **Coopersmith Self-Esteem Inventory** (SEI)
   Age: 9 years to adult
   Obtainable from: Self-Esteem Institute
   1736 Stockton Street
   San Francisco, California 94133
   Description: The SEI is available in two forms. Form A consists of 58 items that make up five subscales. These include General Self, Social Self-Peers, Home-Parents, Lie Scale, and School-Academic. Form B is briefer and is not broken down into subscales.
   Reliability and Validity: Total scores of Forms A and B correlate 86. Further reliability and validity data are provided in the Self-Esteem Institute Newsletter.

Exhibit 10-1 continued

4. **How I See Myself Scale** (HISMS)

   Age: Grades 3–6 and 7–12

   Obtainable from: Florida Educational Research and Development Council
   College of Education
   University of Florida
   Gainesville, Florida 32601

   Cost: $1 per manual, postpaid.

   Description: The HISMS is for the measurement of groups, not individuals. The Secondary Form provides seven or eight scores for grades 7–9 and seven or nine scores for grades 10–12. The number of scales is determined by grade and sex. These include teacher-school, physical appearance, autonomy, academic adequacy, physical adequacy, interpersonal adequacy, emotions (girls), attitudes toward peers (boys), body build (girls), and language adequacy (boys).

   Reliability and Validity: At the secondary level a median test-retest reliability coefficient of .70 was obtained.

5. **MSW Self-Esteem Inventory**

   Age: Adolescents

   Obtainable from: Pehlon J. Malouf (author)
   319 MBH
   University of Utah
   Salt Lake City, Utah 84112

   Description: This test consists of 50 statements about self that require true-false responses and 22 adjective pairs that follow semantic differential procedures. Provided are three scores reflecting self-esteem: student competency, personal adequacy, and personal satisfaction.

   Reliability and Validity: Test-retest coefficients for 58 tenth grade students were .90 and for 35 college students, .91. Construct validity is evident in the coefficient of .70 between student competency scores and teacher ratings for 76 tenth grade students.

6. **The Offer Self-Image Questionnaire for Adolescents**

   Age: 14–18 years

   Obtainable from: Daniel Offer (author)
   Michael Reese Medical Center
   2959 South Ellis Avenue
   Chicago, Illinois 60616

Exhibit 10-1 continued

Cost: 50¢ per test and answer sheet, postpaid; scoring service, 25¢ per test.

Description: This test provides .11 scores. Included are: impulse control, emotional tone, body and self-image, social relationships, morals, sexual attitudes, family relationships, mastery of external problems, vocational-educational goals, psychopathology, and superior adjustment. Separate forms must be used for males and females.

Reliability and Validity: No reliability or validity statements were obtained.

7. **The Piers-Harris Children's Self Concept Scale (The Way I Feel About Myself)**

Age: Grades 3–12

Obtainable from: Counselor Recordings and Tests
   Box 6184 Acklen Station
   Nashville, Tennessee 37242

Cost: 1 to 99 tests, 23¢ each; 60¢ per key, $1 per manual, $1.50 per specimen set, postage extra.

Description: This test consists of 80 first person declarative statements to which the child responds "yes" or "no." Half of the statements are worded to indicate a positive self-concept, the other half a negative self-concept.

Reliability and Validity: The internal consistency of the scale ranges from .78 to .93 and retest reliability from .71 to .77, based on a population of 1,183 children in grades 4–12.

8. **Primary Self-Concepts Test**

Age: 10–13 years

Obtainable from: R. J. Andrews
   Schonell Educational Research Center
   University of Queensland
   St. Lucia, 4067, Australia

Description: This test contains 51 adjectives and 25 descriptive statements in a four-choice response format. The six subscales consist of: self as striving for success, self as tense, self as socially adequate, self as hostile, physical and psychological self-worth, and self as conforming. Norms for each subscale are in the form of percentiles.

Reliability and Validity: The test-retest reliability coefficient is .86 with six weeks intervening between test administrations.

Exhibit 10-1 continued

9. **Self-Appraisal Scale**
   Age: 8–14 years
   Obtainable from: Judith W. Greenburg
                      City College of the City University of New York
                      Convent Avenue and 138th Street
                      New York, New York 10031
   Description: This test is designed to measure personal and academic self-concepts. There are 24 items with a three-choice response format describing the frequency with which the concept fits. The test provides four competence factors: personal, social, academic, and nonintellectual.
   Reliability and Validity: The split half reliability of the scale is .77.

10. **Self-As-Pupil Q-Sort**
    Age: 9–15 years
    Obtainable from: Edward A. Wicas
                       School of Education
                       University of Connecticut
                       Storrs, Connecticut 06268
    Description: This test is designed to measure the concept of actual self-in-role and of ideal self-in-role to explore the adequacy of performance in school. The subject is required to sort 50 items into a nine-point scale on a continuum from "describes me best" to "describes me least." The test is completed twice to determine actual and ideal self-in-role.
    Reliability and Validity: Content validity was based on 106 ninth grade autobiographical essays on the way students see themselves now and the way they would like to be. The 50 items were pooled from these papers.

11. **Self-Concept as a Learner** (SCAL)
    Age: 10–18 years
    Obtainable from: Walter B. Waetjen
                       Office of the President
                       Cleveland State University
                       Cleveland, Ohio 44114
    Cost: 12¢ per copy.
    Description: This test is a rating scale containing 50 items. The four categories are: problem solving ability, motivation, task orientation, and class membership. The five-point scale ranges from "completely true" to "completely false."

Exhibit 10-1 continued

> *Reliability and Validity:* Test-retest reliability coefficients for total test scores are .80, .90; for motivation .61, .61; for task orientation .73, .81,; intellectual ability .80, .73; class membership .66, .75. Content validity was determined by the agreement of judges on responses of students with high and low SCAL scores.

12. **Self-Concept and Motivation Inventory**(SCAMIN)
    George A. Farrah, Norm J. Milchus & William Reitz.
    Age: Junior high and secondary school
    Obtainable from: Person-O-Metrics
    20504 Williamsburg
    Dearborn Heights, Michigan 48127
    Cost: $5 for complete specimen set, $8 per 50 response sheets, (minimum order-$10), postage added.
    Description: The theoretical constructs for this age group are role expectations and self-adequacy. Motivation is composed of academic and social goal/achievement needs and personal investment.
    Reliability and Validity: Reliability coefficients for the subparts range from .54 to .91.

13. **Self-Description, Self-Rating Scale**
    Age: 10–17 years
    Obtainable from: Edward Clifford & Miriam Clifford
    Box 3894
    Duke University Medical Center
    Durham, North Carolina 27710
    Description: The Self-Description Scale contains 20 items on a four-point scale ranging from "exactly like me" to "exactly unlike me." The Self-Rating Scale contains 15 items on a four-point scale ranging from "all of the time" to "none of the time."
    Reliability and Validity: Test-retest reliability coefficients were .54 for self-description and .57 for self rating.

14. **Self-Esteem Questionnaire** (SEQ)
    Age: 9 years and above
    Obtainable from: Test Analysis and Development Corporation
    855 Inca Parkway
    Boulder, Colorado 80303
    Cost: 75¢ and over per test and scoring service ($50 minimum) 20¢ per test alone.
    Description: The SEQ yields two scores, self-esteem and self other satisfaction, based on a total of 12 items. All items are

Exhibit 10-1 continued

> answered on a five-point scale from "not at all" to "yes, very much."
> *Reliability and Validity:* Test-retest reliability for 250 elementary
> students was about .70. Correlation of the self-esteem scale was
> .61 with the short form of the Coopersmith Self-Esteem Inventory.

15. **Self-Esteem Scale**
   Age: Adolescent
   Obtainable from: Morris Rosenberg (author)
   > Laboratory of Socioenvironmental Studies
   > National Institute on Mental Health
   > 9000 Rockville Pike
   > Building 10, Room 30–45
   > Bethesda, Maryland 20014

   Description: This instrument is designed to measure global positive or
   negative attitudes toward self. It contains ten items with a four-
   choice response format. The seven-point scale yields scores that
   reflect self-worth and self-respect.

   Reliability and Validity: Test-retest reliability was found to be .85 for 40
   college students. Construct validity was evidenced in high correlation between the Self-Esteem Scale, a scale of depressive affect,
   and a measure of psychophysiological indicators of anxiety.

16. **Self-Evaluation of Personal Action**
   Barbara J. Brandes (author)
   Age: 10–18 years
   Obtainable from: Research for Better Schools, Inc.
   > Public Information Office
   > 1700 Market Street
   > Philadelphia, Pennsylvania 19103

   Description: This 20-item scale is used to provide a quick assessment
   of self-concept in a group setting for the purpose of program
   evaluation. Emphasis is on personal actions and behaviors. This
   instrument uses a "yes"/"no" response format.

   Reliability and Validity: Based on 1,359 pupils 10 to 12 years old,
   internal consistency reliability was found to be .77. Validity was
   determined by correlating this measure with a measure of test
   anxiety. The coefficient was .49. A correlation coefficient of .35
   was found with a measure of internal locus of control.

Exhibit 10-1 continued

17. **Self-Perception Inventory** (Student Forms)
    Age: Elementary and secondary school
    Obtainable from: Anthony T. Soares and Louise M. Soares
    (authors)
    University of Bridgeport
    Bridgeport, Connecticut 06602
    Cost: $1 per specimen set, plus 25¢ postage and handling per specimen set, 10¢ each test copy
    Description: Forty traits in dichotomous pairs measure four dimensions: self-concept, ideal concept, reflected self, and student self-concept.
    Reliability and Validity: The test-retest reliability coefficient is .88. Correlation coefficient of Coopersmith's Self-Esteem Inventory was .68.

18. **Tennessee Self-Concept Scale** (TSCS)
    William H. Fitts (author)
    Age: 12 years and above
    Obtainable from: Counselor Recordings and Tests
    Box 6184 Acklen Station
    Nashville, Tennessee 37242
    Cost: 26¢ per test, 16¢ per answer sheet, 90¢ per set of scoring keys for both forms, 70¢ per manual, 90¢ per specimen set, postage extra, 50¢ scoring service per test.
    Description: The TSCS contains 100 self-descriptive statements that can be interpreted using two scoring systems, referred to as the Counseling Form and the Clinical and Research Form. The Counseling Form yields 15 profiled scores and is considered appropriate for providing feedback to an individual. The Clinical and Research Form yields 30 profiled scores and is useful for research and clinical assessment. All items use a five-choice response format ranging from "completely false" to "completely true."
    Reliability and Validity: Test-retest reliability is in the high .80s.

19. **What I Am Like**
    Cincinnati Public Schools: Psychological Services, Program Research, and Design (author)
    Age: 9–15 years
    Obtainable from: Charles B. Miller
    Psychological Services
    Cincinnati Public Schools
    230 East Ninth Street
    Cincinnati, Ohio 45202

Exhibit 10-1 continued

> *Cost:* Sample copy on request.
> *Description:* Three subtests describe the child in terms of "What I Look
>   Like," "What I Am (self-image)," and "What I Am Like When I Am
>   With My Friends." The items are written in adjective format. Each
>   adjective is rated on a five-point scale.
> *Reliability and Validity:* None reported.

hand, external control refers to the perception of a situation as being beyond
the control of the perceiver.

In contrast to self-concept, locus of control attempts to determine why
individuals succeed or fail at a task, not how they feel about either self or
about self in relationship to the task. Internalizers view their efforts as
important to the success and completion of the task. Research to measure the
effects of locus of control has been very revealing.

Fincham and Barling (1978) found that 10-year-old learning disabled
children had significantly lower perceptions of internal control than normal or
gifted children on a measure of generalized locus of control. Boersma and
Chapman (1978) reported that learning disabled children had lower internal
scores for success than others. As they grew older, both groups increasingly
attributed failure to internal causes. That is, children without learning
disabilities became greater internalizers as they grew older, while children
with such conditions became greater internalizers only after successful
experiences that displaced their fear of failure. For the most part, learning
disabled children continued to believe that success was principal to external
causes over which they had little if any control.

Hisama (1976) investigated whether or not there was a difference in the
locus of control between normal children and those with learning and
behavior problems. Specific hypotheses tested in this study were that:

1. learning disabled children would be more externally oriented than the
   nonlearning disabled
2. within the experimental group, children with internality would perform
   better than those with externality
3. there would be an interaction effect, in that the performance of children
   with externality would be reduced under the failure conditions while
   that of the internality group would not show an interaction.

His results show no differences between the handicapped and nonhandicapped groups. One interpretation would be that children with learning and

behavioral disorders are no more externally oriented than others. Moreover, Hisama notes that under experimental conditions, the internally oriented child tends to try harder even under the most adverse motivational conditions. It was true, however, that externally oriented children responded positively to success experiences, with dropoffs in performance under failure conditions.

In conclusion, learning disabled children, in contrast to others, generally perceive the locus of control for various tasks to be external to them. Younger affected children feel they are externally controlled, believing their failures are due to the difficulty of the task. Success for both groups frequently is attributed to some other person beyond the immediate scope of the task. All children become more conscious of effort with age, internalizing to a greater degree. The type of motivational condition (positive-negative-neutral) has provided inconsistent findings for learning disabled children. Generally, they do respond better in positive conditions, but then so do those without disabilities, if they are externalizers. Internalizers of both types seemingly are motivationally conscious but are more aware of pursuing a task to completion.

These data do suggest several immediate management concerns to the teacher. First and foremost, there are differences in how children perceive the task, its difficulty, and the critical factors involved in completing it. Some children are more capable of independent instruction than others. Selected learning disabled children are highly dependent upon immediate instructional feedback or they cannot proceed with a task. Achievement motivation thus is a pragmatic construct in teaching learning disabled children.

ACHIEVEMENT MOTIVATION

In 1964, Atkinson pieced together a theory of achievement motivation that was formulated on three hypotheses plus a speculative belief that the strength of the tendency to achieve success is expressed in interest and performance on a specific task. Given that assumption, the three critical variables were that:

1. the desire (drive or motive) to achieve success is a "relatively stable and relatively general disposition of personality"
2. the strength of expectancy is dependent upon the person's belief that success will follow the performance of the task
3. the relative attractiveness of success for a particular activity provides the incentive value of success.

The last two are environmental variables.

Critical to achievement motivation are several concepts beginning with *expectancy*. The concept of expectancy basically is the idea that a consequence follows an act. The concept of *incentive* places a value on the expected consequence, or goal.

In short, the strength of the tendency to achieve success is a function of the expectancy of success. This suggests that educators may influence the motivation to achieve by manipulating students' expectations concerning the consequences, or incentive value, for the goals to be attained or action to be taken. Therefore, motivation to achieve is stronger when immediate success is imminent. Tasks that are too easy fail to generate success, and those that are too difficult reduce the probability of achievement to the point where the incentive value is not worth the effort to attain the goal.

RESEARCH ON ACHIEVEMENT MOTIVATION

There has been little research on achievement motivation and learning disabled audiences. Hisama (1976), mentioned earlier, has completed the only study of which the authors are aware. The primary emphasis is on the attributions (cognitive model) of achievement motivation factors. The principal feature of the cognitive model is that success and failure experiences have important consequences for subsequent feelings, expectancies, and behavior. Within the context of loci of control and stability factors, four causal elements have appeared: ability, effort, task difficulty, and luck. The attribution model of achievement motivation postulates that it is the perceived stability of a cause that is the critical determinant of the expectancy of success.

Hisama administered the Children's Locus of Control Scale to 48 children with learning disabilities and 48 without. He then had three teams from the experimental group perform a simple task. He summarizes the major findings as: (a) there is no evidence that learning disabled children are externally oriented in terms of locus of control, (b) internally oriented children continue to put out more effort despite adverse motivational conditions, and (c) externally oriented children respond to success experiences positively but their performance is depressed under failure conditions.

Hisama believes that finding success experiences for learning disabled children is crucial in avoiding "learned" helplessness. He regards as critical the removal of any coupling of action with belief that fate, chance, or whims of another person are controlling. He calls for additional research on the effects of achievement motivation and learning disabled children.

One of the disappointments in achievement motivation research has been the mixed results obtained among pupils who display high achievement and grades in classes. The obvious problem has been that neither grades nor achievement motivation are unitary characteristics. Indeed, both are complex phenomena composed of many variables. A sampling of laboratory, experimental, and commercially available tests on achievement motivation is shown in Chapter 9, Exhibit 9-3.

LEARNED HELPLESSNESS

Self-concept, locus of control, and achievement motivation all are constructs that relate to the individual's perception of self. These factors are learned; they receive reinforcement from social cues in the environment. The motivation an individual exhibits relates to actual and perceived failure or success on a given task.

The attribution model of achievement motivation postulates that perceived stability of cause is critical to the expectancy for success. Failure, therefore, is believed to be caused by such factors as low ability levels, task difficulty, and future anticipation of failure because of lack of success earlier on a similar task. Success is caused by effort and/or luck, depending upon one's view of their attributions.

The learned helplessness theory was used originally to describe an interference with escape-avoidance behaviors of dogs prior to an inescapable shock (Seligman & Maier, 1967). Seligman (1973, 1974, 1975) broadened the work to include human behaviors such as reactive depression, stomach ulcers, voodoo deaths, and other phenomena where the person felt unable to respond positively. Seligman hypothesized that learned helplessness consists of three interrelated areas of disturbance: (1) motivational, (2) cognitive, and (3) emotional. Disruptions in these areas may contribute to (1) a reduction in the motivation to control outcomes, (2) interference with learning when individual response is necessary to control the result; (3) fear for as long as the subject is uncertain of the outcome, and then (4) depression (Seligman, 1975, p. 56).

Two studies (Klein & Seligman, 1976; Miller & Seligman, 1975) designed to isolate the factors related to Seligman's hypothesized learned helplessness theory use measures of expectancy change following success or failure. The dependent measure is the amount of expectancy change after trials of success or failure. Several studies (Phares, 1957; Rotter, Liverant & Crowne, 1961) report that reinforcement on previous trials had a greater effect on expectancies for future success when the subjects perceived reinforcement as a response contingent. However, explanations of learned helplessness are dependent upon previous research results that suggest that expectancy change is a function of response-outcome contingency. Other researchers (McMahan, 1973; Weiner, Nierenberg, & Goldstein, 1976) suggest that expectancy changes following success and failure result not from perceived response-outcome contingency but from the perceived stability of the causal attributions of performance.

Numerous Tests Involved

Researchers have used a variety of cognitive problem-solving tasks, i.e., intelligence tests (Thornton & Jacobs, 1971), block design (Dweck & Reppucci, 1973), digit-letter substitution (Dweck & Bush, 1976), discrimination learning (Eisenberger, Park, & Frank, 1976), and specially designed concept formation problems (Roth & Bootzin, 1974; Roth & Kubal, 1975). However, no work to date has adequately separated motivational and cognitive components of learned helplessness.

Five studies (Dweck, 1975; Dweck & Reppucci, 1973; Klein, Fencil-Morse, & Seligman, 1976; Tennen & Eller, 1977; Wortman, Panciera, Shusterman, & Hibscher, 1976) have investigated the role of the subject's attributions of task performance in the development of learned helplessness. The attribution theory here has been that causal factors (attributes) influence expectations for probable outcomes of future performance. The theory suggests that the subject's attribution concerning the noncontingency of reinforcement would influence both expectations and performance in future tasks. The research investigating this hypothesis generally has been supportive. Dweck and Reppucci (1973) report that following experience with noncontingent failure (unsolvable block designs), the children who showed the most performance deficits tended to attribute success or failure to ability (or inability); conversely, those who showed the fewest deficits tended to ascribe their performance to effort.

Dweck (1975) later developed a treatment program for "naturally occurring" helpless children, i.e, those who were affected more adversely by failure. In her treatment program, Dweck taught these "helpless" children to attribute failure, instead, to lack of effort. Following this "reattribution training," these children showed significant improvements in task persistence and less helplessness than did a group treated with "success-only" experiences.

Three studies (Dweck & Reppucci, 1973; Klein et al., 1976; Tennen & Eller, 1977) suggest that attribution of noncontingent failure to ability or personal competence leads to increased learned helplessness, whereas ascribing these outcomes to situational factors or task difficulty does not produce learned helplessness.

One study (Wortman & Brehm, 1975) reports findings that appear contradictory. They told their subjects that their study would deal with the effects of noise on performance and that the amount of noise would be contingent on how they achieved on several problems. The subjects then were exposed to unavoidable noise and were told they had failed to solve any of the problems. Three information conditions were used: (1) no information, (2) information that another subject could solve the problems (incompetence condition), and (3) information that another subject could not solve the problems (tasks difficulty condition).

The results indicated that the incompetence group felt more helpless and stressed but performed better than the task-difficulty group did when the same problems were presented later without the noise. It seems that the most likely conclusion in this situation is that the subjects had difficulty solving problems with accompanying noise. Thus, when problems were presented later without noise, those in the incompetence group would expect their performance to improve and would be motivated to attempt to do so. Alternatively, the task-difficult group members, who thought their failure resulted from the difficulty of the task, could not expect any change in their outcomes and thus would be less motivated to attempt solutions on later problems. The incompetence group did not produce attributions as to the general quality of competence but did to the relatively specific cause of ability to solve problems with noise present; as such, the incompetence condition was not equivalent to the ability or competence conditions of previous studies.

Role as a Performance Deficit

The literature on performance changes produced by exposure to learned helplessness supports its conceptualization as a performance deficit in cognitive problem-solving tasks. The evidence does not allow a distinction between cognitive and motivational explanations for this deficit. The performance deficits that are defined as learned helplessness may have a cognitive or motivational basis, or they may result from the impairment of both processes (Miller & Norman, 1979, p. 101).

Dweck and Bush (1976) studied the influence of sex, evaluator feedback, and attributional style of children in relation to the role of socialization on achievement. They hypothesized that evaluator feedback would provide different levels of importance for children, given their sex and age. They observed that failure feedback from adults produced problem-solving deficits in girls but facilitated performance for boys. Among boys, effort for failure was associated with the adult evaluator and ability attributions with a peer evaluator; girls showed the opposite effect. The data suggest that boys have been instructed to think independently and determine their own standards of excellence, whereas girls have been taught to depend on teacher praise and/or criticism.

Dweck, Davidson, Nelson, and Enna (1978) studied the influence of teachers' use of positive and negative feedback and its impact on children's failures. Their data showed the contingencies of teachers' feedback for girls were predicted to produce ability attributions rather than motivational beliefs. Boys received more negative evaluation and more ambiguous feedback on nonintellectual behaviors than on the quality of their intellectual work. Girls received most of their feedback on intellectual adequacy, and it was more positive and less negative than that for boys. Teachers explicitly indicated to the boys (but not to the girls) that insufficient effort would produce failures. Finally, boys received more work-related praise than girls, which the boys interpreted as a source of preferring their jobs to school.

Kennelly and Kinley (1975) explored the relationship between children's perceived contingency of teacher reinforcement, academic locus of control, and academic achievement. Sixth grade boys were administered a specially constructed "Teacher Contingency of Reinforcements Questionnaire" that categorized reinforcement into four scales: contingent punishment, noncontingent punishment, contingent reward, and noncontingent reward. Significant correlations were reported:

1. Internal subjects interpreted their teacher's actions as contingently punishing; no relation with reward was found.
2. Internal subjects demonstrated better achievement.
3. Externally oriented subjects perceived teacher punishment as occurring noncontingently.
4. External subjects exhibited significantly lower achievement than internal ones.

Research in learned helplessness has shown that the development of academic helplessness was maximized by authority figures who punished the occurrence and nonoccurrence of misbehavior with equal probability. These practices contributed to the perception of response outcome independence and the development of maladaptive attributions. Children who received only solution-specific feedback that involved no motivational component were more likely to interpret teacher criticism as suggestive of poor ability. Criticism that attributed failure exclusively to uncontrollable, invariant factors, such as ability, fostered the development of academic helplessness.

In conclusion, little attention has been directed to the study of factors that affect the cognitive, motivational, and emotional functioning of children with learning disabilities. The learned helplessness hypothesis may have merit for investigating performance difficulties in achievement situations. To date, that hypothesis has not been applied to learning disabled children. It has been evaluated with respect to other exceptional populations, namely, mentally retarded adults (Floor & Rosen, 1975), mentally retarded children (Weisz, 1978), deaf adolescents (McCrone, 1977), and emotionally disturbed children (Valle, 1978) with generally favorable results. These studies, however, were interested in determining the susceptibility of subjects to learned helplessness and did not explore attributional style as an intervening factor.

Learned helplessness theory has predicted that performance deficits caused by children's attributing them to failure are internalized as stable attributions (e.g., ability) and are impervious to response dependent success (Abramson, Seligman, & Teasdale, 1978). Research has demonstrated that when given treatment focusing on success, expectancies for future change were unaffected (Miller & Norman, 1979). The number of studies that have induced appropriate achievement-enhancing attributions in learned helpless children is increasing (Andrews & Debus, 1978; Blaess, 1977; Chapin & Dyck, 1976; Dweck, 1975, 1976; Miller, Brickman, & Bolen, 1975; Ostrove, 1977; Rhodes, 1977). Data from this work challenge the belief that achievement-enhancing attributions are clearly necessary.

INTERVENTION IN ACHIEVEMENT MOTIVATION

Social learning theory considers such factors as (1) the incentive to learn, which is related to previous success experiences, and (2) the fact that success tends also to promote the learner to view internalized factors (i.e., effort, desire). These factors are regarded as major contributors to achievement, where repeated failures frequently cause learners to look to others or to the task for an explanation as to why they did not succeed. Finally, achievement motivation declares that:

Motivation = Motive × Expectancy × Incentive

Motive is the internal drive, expectancy the goal placement or goal setting requirement for completing a task, and incentive the reinforcement that provides feedback on success or failure. Theoretically, achievement motivation theory would suggest that failure can be avoided in practically all situations if the task is sequenced in small enough steps, with proper reinforcement, and under conditions of realistic goal setting.

What may occur in school for children experiencing failure is a disruption in normal social learning. The goals become foggy or difficult to set, reinforcement is difficult to apply because of an absence of success, which generates greater dependence on external factors for an explanation of the failure.

Initially, there is a loss of social appropriateness to significant others as the capability of correctly interpreting environmental (social) cues decreases. What results is a shift in the locus of control from internal to external and a decrease in the ability to sustain achievement motivation. When such a behavioral response becomes habitual, it is referred to as learned helplessness.

A flow of activities beginning with a loss of general self-esteem is captured in this sequence:

inappropriate social response
↓
based on improperly interpreted social cues
↓
externalization of locus of control
↓
decreased achievement motivation
↓
resulting finally in learned helplessness

The critical elements are:

1. Learners always must be provided with a maximum of information about the task.
2. Learners always must be provided with "realistic" information about themselves.
3. Children are not helped in growing in their understanding of self by engaging in personal introspection (Fleming, 1971). It does help them when they discover themselves through interaction with others.
4. Self is relative to some task, person, group, situation, or environment and must be understood in that light.
5. Children need to feel they belong. Any academic task or social situation that reduces those feelings must be understood.
6. The "real reasons" and perceived reasons for failure or success should be examined periodically. One act does not make a concept of self. Instead: "The act of becoming produces a sensitivity to others and the environment, and embraces a continuous flow of experiences which result from interaction of self with all other forces." (Myers, 1971, p. 33)
7. Perceptions of task, self, others, and situation may be real or unreal, and treated as such. Perceptions, though, are but one level for understanding self-concept. The other is the feelings associated with the perception. The perception and the feelings must be understood.
8. Social judgment can be increased by studying pictures of facial expressions and environmental cues.
9. Children can explore alternative approaches to handling situations and tasks.
10. Discussion of "on-task, off-task" behaviors always is worthwhile, with explanations of the reasons for the preference of off-task behavior and their consequences for the learner.
11. Group process and role playing provide explorations of skills to enable learners to respond appropriately to many different situations. They

also promote the handling of feelings in extreme situations of learned helplessness.

12. Peer tutoring and student tutoring of others have been shown to be effective teaching techniques, instilling motivation while raising self-esteem.
13. There is no better way to assist children to feel self-competent than helping them to recognize their achievement motivation in terms of ideal and actual view of self. Two good references are *100 Ways to Enhance Self-Concept in the Classroom* (Canfield & Wells, 1976) and *Developing Understanding of Self and Others* (Dinkmeyer, 1970).

Commercially published materials available include the following:

STRENGTHEN SELF-CONCEPTS

Does the Devil Make Them Do It?

Mafex Associates, Inc.
Johnstown, Pennsylvania

A multimedia program to bring students into touch with their feelings. Grades 6–12. $82.

Focus on Self-Development Stage One, Stage Two, and Stage Three

Science Research Associates, Inc.
Chicago, Illinois

A filmstrip and cassette program designed to emphasize development of awareness of self, others, and environment. Stage One, grades K–2; Stage Two, grades 2–4; Stage Three, grades 4–6. $208 with records, $233 with cassettes.

I Like Me

Mafex Associates, Inc.
Johnstown, Pennsylvania

A group of short stories and poems helps students identify interpersonal feelings familiar to all high schoolers. Set of ten books and guide. Grades 6–12. $22.50.

Me and Others

Mafex Associates, Inc.
Johnstown, Pennsylvania

A multimedia program that enables students to develop self-awareness, awareness of others, and a sense of communication to improve peer group interaction. Grades 6–12. $109.

Meeting Yourself Halfway

Mafex Associates, Inc.
Johnstown, Pennsylvania

Easy-to-use, colorful, large format text encourages students to identify values and life styles. Grades 6–12. $18.50.

What I Like to Do

Science Research Associates, Inc.
Chicago, Illinois

An easy-to-administer and self-scoring interest inventory. Gives indication of child's interest in play, academics, arts, occupations, and reading. Grades 1–6. Inventory booklet, $15.60.

SELF-CONCEPT/SOCIAL COMPETENCY

DUSO: Developing Understanding of Self and Others

American Guidance Service, Inc.
Publishers Building
Circle Pines, Minnesota 55014

Kit consists of stories, puppets, posters, tapes, and records that deal with moral issues and situations. Two kits (K–2 and 2–4). $115 each.

The Social Learning Curriculum

The Charles E. Merrill Publishing Co., Inc.
Columbus, Ohio

A comprehensive program dealing with situations faced in life to help children adjust to the environment. Grades 1–4. $95.

Toward Affective Development

American Guidance Service, Inc.
Publishers Building
Circle Pines, Minnesota 55014

An activity-centered program dealing with motivation, feeling, understanding, and participation. Grades 3–6. $95.

THE LEARNING THEORY APPROACH

The preceding sections have described the association between behavior disorders and learning disabilities. Current research highlights the need for intensive strategies that have a high probability of shaping social and personal characteristics that will facilitate adjustment in academic, vocational, recreational, and leisure settings.

The rest of this chapter presents a detailed approach to teaching, motivating, and monitoring positive social and personal characteristics with learning disabled children and adolescents. This approach emphasizes the systematic application of learning theory principles to strengthening appropriate social behaviors and weakening disruptive conduct. The basic assumption underlying the learning theory approach is that both acceptable and deviant behaviors are acquired through individuals' interactions with historic and contemporary environment. Environments that provide children with a number of pleasant and appropriate social models and that consistently equate appropriate behavior with desirable events and/or the reduction of aversive events will maximize those individuals' repertoire of social competency behaviors. Environments that include few positive social models and do not reward appropriate behavior are not effective in developing children's social and emotional repertoires.

The present approach attempts to alter the antecedents that provoke disruptive behavior, which affects the personal characteristics that influence social development. In doing so, the emphasis is not on punishing the learner for behaving inappropriately but on restructuring the environment so that positive social conduct is likely to occur and be reinforced. It has been argued, and is emphasized throughout this chapter, that traditional approaches to the development of social competence—including the excessive use of punishments—may not be appropriate for the learning disabled student. The social development approach that follows attempts to maximize the strength of environmental influences to shape positive social behavior and internal characteristics. A glossary (Exhibit 10-2) of the vocabulary used in the learning theory literature is helpful.

Exhibit 10-2 Vocabulary of Learning Theory

GLOSSARY

Antecedent event: one that precedes a target behavior and influences the probability of its occurrence.

Associated characteristics: inferred or observed features of an individual that influence the probability a target behavior will occur.

Baseline data: a measure of the target behavior under natural conditions. Baseline data may be collected before and after intervention to assess its effects.

Consequences: events that follow a target behavior and influence the probability of its occurrence.

Contingency contract: a written agreement between a student and teacher that details specific consequences for the pupil in meeting or failing to meet predetermined performance criteria.

Contingency relationships: stable relationships between specific behaviors and consequences.

Continuous recording: an observational procedure in which naturally occurring antecedents and consequences are identified for a target behavior.

Contrived reinforcer: an artificial condition established by the teacher that increases the probability that a behavior will occur.

Exhibit 10-2 continued

Duration recording:	a measure of behavior strength that reports how long a behavior occurred.
Event recording:	a measure of behavior strength that reports the number of times a behavior occurred.
Fading antecedent conditions:	gradual removal of artificial conditions so that positive social behavior will be maintained by natural or internal factors.
Fading consequent conditions:	gradual removal of artificial consequent conditions so that positive social behavior will be maintained by natural consequences or mediational events.
Interobserver reliability:	the extent to which two independent observers agree on the occurrence or nonoccurrence of a target behavior.
Interval recording:	a measure of behavior strength that reports the number of intervals in which a behavior occurs.
Natural consequences:	events in the student's natural learning environment that influence the probability that a target behavior will occur.
Negative reinforcement:	behavior that increases in strength by removing or terminating an aversive stimulus.
Personal product:	the observable and measurable product of a student's behavior.
Positive reinforcement:	the strengthening of a behavior that produces pleasant consequences.

Exhibit 10-2 continued

Primary reinforcers:	events that have reinforcement properties because they satisfy biological or physiological needs.
Punishment:	aversive consequences that decrease the strength of a behavior.
Reponse latency:	a measure of behavior strength that indicates the amount of time that elapses from a potential cue to the initiation of the target response.
Reinforcement hierarchy:	the ranking of potential reinforcers on the basis of their strength.
Reinforcer sampling:	a procedure by which an individual is exposed to a variety of pleasant events before they are made contingent on a target behavior.
Response definition:	an objective and complete description of the target behavior.
Self-control:	the extent to which individuals are able to monitor, evaluate, and sequate their own behavior independent of external consequences.
Schedule of reinforcement:	the frequency with which reinforcers are delivered.
Secondary reinforcers:	events that have acquired their reinforcing properties by being paired with other stimuli that have reinforcing properties.

Exhibit 10-2 continued

| Target behavior: | one that an intervention program is designed to strengthen or weaken. |
| Terminal objective: | the expected result of an intervention program. |

The following information constitutes a concise guide to program development while providing flexibility in design and implementation.

DETERMINING THAT A PROBLEM EXISTS

The initial step in designing and implementing a social intervention program involves a decision on the part of the learning disabled student and significant individuals in the environment that a problem of sufficient magnitude exists to warrant intensive intercession. This decision can be reached by: (1) identifying the expectations of the student and the significant people; (2) determining the current strength of the pupil's behavior; (3) determining the discrepancy between the child's present behavior and expectations of self and others for future conduct.

The social development program will assist the learning disabled student in developing new skills or refining and strengthening existing ones. Disruptive behaviors that interfere with the acquisition of positive social behaviors also may be reduced. Positive social behaviors that are to be developed and disruptive ones that are to be weakened must be identified before an intervention program is designed. The identification of these program targets involves collecting informal assessment data from a variety of sources: student's teachers, parents, siblings, peers, guidance counselor, social worker, employment supervisor, etc.

Assessment data may include anecdotal reports, direct observations, scores on criterion referenced and norm referenced tests, observations resulting from situational performance tests, permanent products such as school assignments, self-reports, etc. Collectively, the data should provide a general idea of the strength of specific behaviors across well-defined settings. Descriptions such as overly sensitive, shy, withdrawn, disruptive, outgoing, etc., should be avoided in lieu of more specific behavioral definitions. Important conditions associated with the behavior being assessed also should be identified. For example, saying that Bill is shy does little to describe his exceptional characteristics. Saying that Bill sits alone at recess when other students are playing competitive games provides more specific and useful information from which a program can be developed.

In addition to obtaining a general idea of the current strength of problem behaviors across settings, it is important to know what significant persons in those environments expect of the student. Parents, peers, supervisors, etc., should provide information that enables the teacher to determine the optimal level of the target behavior following intervention. This level will become the terminal objective of the intervention program. For the purpose of program development, learning disabled students' exceptionalities will be defined by the discrepancy between what others expect and what they do in a number of important environments. Having identified a number of behaviors that are excessive or deficit in relation to the expectations of others, the teacher must identify specific targets of the intervention program. This is accomplished by prioritizing potential target behaviors.

PRIORITIZING TARGET BEHAVIORS

The exceptional characteristics identified in the initial phase of program development must be prioritized from least to most important to the learning disabled student's adjustment in important settings. High priority behaviors that can be programmed for without placing excessive demands on the student are selected as the intervention target. The scope of the intervention plan should be limited by the degree to which a student can respond favorably to increasing environmental demands. It is generally understood that excessive demands often result in frustration and failure for the pupil. Programs that induce high rates of failure do not succeed in teaching students to approach social situations with a high expectation of success (Gardner, 1966). The goal of social development programs is to promote a positive association between prosocial behavior and pleasant social outcomes. Therefore, an intervention program should focus only on the range of high priority behaviors that can be developed or reduced without establishing excessively frustrating conditions for the student. Behaviors excluded from the initial program may be targets in future programs.

Because deceleration programs (i.e., those designed to reduce the strength of a behavior) often involve aversive consequences, only one behavior should be targeted at a time. Since acceleration programs (those designed to strengthen a behavior) often involve positive consequences, more than one behavior may be targeted at a time. In general, the program should be designed so that the student is striving continually for positive consequences by exhibiting prosocial behavior. A fortunate side effect of a well-designed program is that while, for example, only three behaviors are targeted for intervention, a number of related ones may change: teaching and reinforcing positive social behaviors can increase positive effects and reduce disruptive verbalizations.

DEFINING THE TARGET BEHAVIORS

The target behavior(s) should be defined clearly and completely. Definitions should present all information that may be relevant to objective observation and measurement of the behavior.

The traditional test of the adequacy of a response definition is the extent to which two independent observers agree on the behavior's occurrence or nonoccurrence. This test is called interobserver reliability.

SPECIFYING POSITIVE BEHAVIORS

Alternative prosocial behaviors should be developed whenever a program involves the reduction of excessive disruptive conduct. Positive social behaviors can be targeted by determining the function of the disruptive pattern and identifying competency actions that, if developed, could produce an equal amount of satisfaction for the individual.

The overriding goal of the program is to facilitate the development of skills that allow the learning disabled student to gain satisfaction from the environment through positive social behaviors. Well-designed programs will result in prosocial behaviors being maintained following formal intervention. by natural events.

Reductive or punishment procedures alone do not have analogous educative components (Pendergrass, 1972). They rely on equating a disruptive behavior with an aversive event or the removal of a pleasant event. This association is expected to decrease the probability that the behavior will occur. When punishment is used in isolation, a suitable alternative behavior may not be developed to replace the disruptive conduct.

Punishment used in isolation has several other major negative side effects that are contrary to the goals of a social development program:

1. The person who administers the aversive consequence may become associated with unpleasant events to the extent that the ability to reinforce the child positively is decreased substantially.
2. The controlling effect of the disciplinary event may be evident only in the presence of the person who administers the punishment. As long as the teacher is in the classroom, the student will behave appropriately, but substitute teachers may not be able to control the child.
3. Punishment often results in excessive negative emotional reactions. Once punished, a student may become aggressive, fearful, withdrawn, or anxious.
4. The frequent use of mild discipline may desensitize the student to that event, thereby requiring the teacher to increase the intensity of effective punishers.

5. The excessive use of punishment may promote an avoidance of potential disciplinary situations. The learning disabled adolescent who is punished frequently in school is likely to be truant, nonresponsive, and tardy, and eventually may drop out entirely.

A more effective strategy is to instruct and reinforce the child for gaining the teacher's attention through acceptable means (e.g., raising a hand, coming forward after class, etc.). As the positive alternative behavior is being established, excessive conduct can be reduced through aversive consequences. In this way, once the punishment procedure is withdrawn, socially acceptable behavior is maintained by the affirmative relationship that the teacher has established between the positive social behavior and natural incentives (e.g., hand-raising is motivated by teacher attention).

IDENTIFYING THE SCOPE OF INTERVENTION

The setting in which skills are expected to be developed or strengthened, the important conditions under which the behavior change is likely to occur, and the individuals who will be involved in the program should be identified before intervention. These constitute the scope of the intervention plan. The way children learn and behave under one set of conditions does not always reflect the way they function under others. Therefore, it is important that intervention take place in the setting in which the behavior change is expected to occur. Numerous studies have demonstrated that behavior changes do not transfer automatically from one setting to another (Koegel & Rincover, 1974). When specifying the settings, important conditions within each one should be identified.

The final area to be considered when determining the scope of an intervention plan is the individuals who will be involved. Professionals, paraprofessionals, relatives, peers, and others all may be responsible for implementing parts of the program. The teacher must ensure that all participants are aware of their responsibilities as detailed in the plan. If the objective of a program is to develop positive self-statements while the student is at school and home, the teachers, counselor, parents, and friends may be asked to label the youth's positive social and academic behavior frequently and encourage the child to do the same.

ESTABLISHING THE PERFORMANCE CRITERIA

Sequential short-term objectives that collectively reflect the expected level of performance following intervention should be identified. Effective behavior changes that generalize to other settings and are sustained over time result from a well-designed and carefully implemented intervention program. Durable changes generally do not occur as the result of a forced exposure to new and radically different learning environments. In fact, drastic changes in educational programs or environments often result in excessive frustration and failure for the learning disabled student. Programs that introduce and expect many changes may not afford the student sufficient opportunities to succeed. The relationship between persistence and success at challenging tasks should be developed through every intervention approach. Contrary to this objective, frequent failure experiences may discourage persistence and increase a student's avoidance of challenging endeavors.

SHORT-TERM AND TERMINAL OBJECTIVES

Establishing realistic short-term objectives that encourage the learning disabled student to progress smoothly toward the major target objective facilitates a striving for success (Schuster & Gruen, 1971). Realistic short-term objectives represent small, easily attainable behavioral changes. These steps should progress in a logical sequence toward the long-term objective or the major goals of the social development program. The identification of short-term objectives must result from the teacher's understanding of the individual student's learning and behavioral characteristics. The student's entry skills, learning rate, and competing behavioral characteristics must be considered before establishing and sequencing short-term objectives.

Each short-term objective should identify the acceptable criterion level. Once the student performs consistently at that level, the intervention may be redirected to a subsequent objective. Once mastery is achieved in all of the sequential short-term steps, the terminal objective will be completed. Figure 10-1 illustrates the flow of sequential short-term objectives that comprise a terminal objective.

RECORDING BEHAVIOR CONTINUOUSLY

Once the short-term and terminal objectives are established, and before the intervention program is formalized, continuous recording is conducted to note relevant environmental influences. Continuous recording involves identifying antecedent conditions (those that precede the target behavior and influence the probability of its occurrence) and consequent conditions (those that follow the behavior and influence its occurrence). The environmental target areas and related behavioral characteristics assessed through continuous recording may become the focus of the intervention program. Antecedents and conse-

Figure 10-1 Flow of Sequential Short-Term Objectives

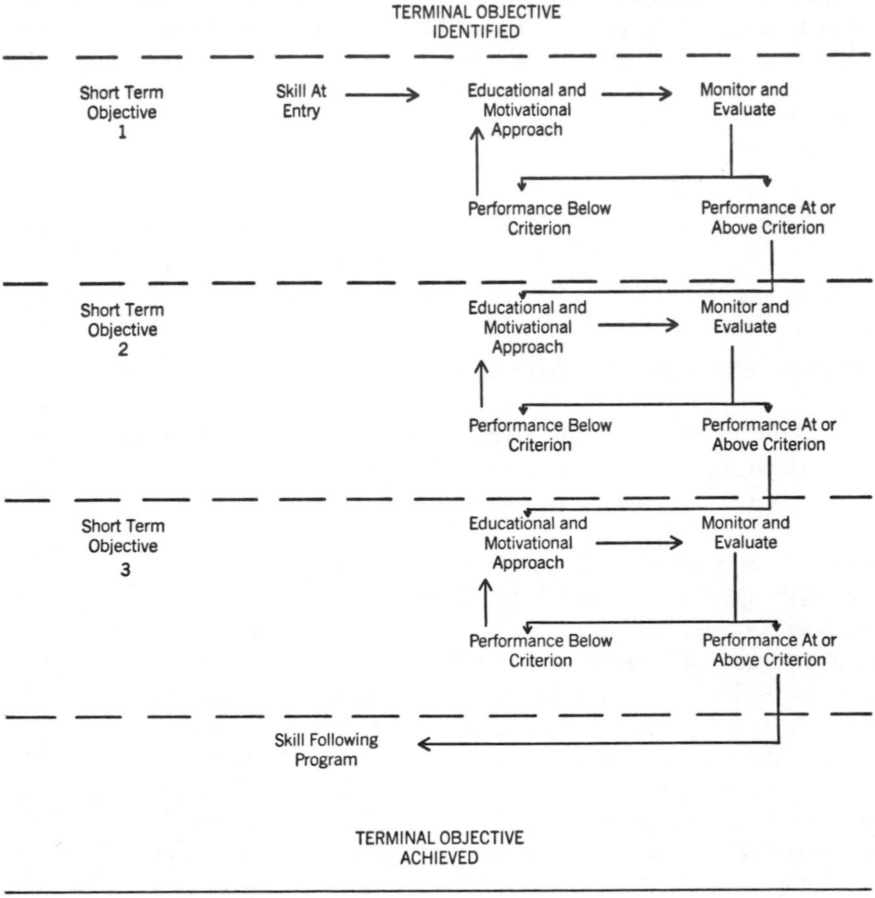

TERMINAL OBJECTIVE
IDENTIFIED

Short Term   Skill At ———→   Educational and ———→   Monitor and
Objective   Entry   Motivational   Evaluate
1   ↑ Approach

                                      Performance Below   Performance At or
                                      Criterion   Above Criterion

Short Term   Educational and   Monitor and
Objective   Motivational ———→   Evaluate
2   ↑ Approach

                                      Performance Below   Performance At or
                                      Criterion   Above Criterion

Short Term   Educational and   Monitor and
Objective   Motivational ———→   Evaluate
3   ↑ Approach

                                      Performance Below   Performance At or
                                      Criterion   Above Criterion

          Skill Following ←
          Program

TERMINAL OBJECTIVE
ACHIEVED

quences that are believed to maintain or strengthen disruptive behaviors are identified and removed while those that support positive social behaviors are intensified.

Antecedent Conditions

Antecedent conditions can cue a desirable or undesirable response, or fail to cue either type of reaction. Once it is known that a specific event triggers disruptive behavior, the cue can be altered, thereby reducing the frequency of the conduct. For example, continuous recording may reveal that when Bill is criticized by others, he becomes verbally aggressive. Intervention may involve removing the antecedent (criticism), gradually reintroducing it as he becomes more able to respond appropriately. If it is known that a natural event that should stimulate a positive social behavior does not serve this function, the event can be developed through intervention as a cue, thereby strengthening the positive conduct.

Consequent Conditions

Consequences can either strengthen, weaken, or maintain the target behavior. Continuous recording may generate hunches as to the function of specific consequences in relation to the strength of the behavior. If it is known that a specific consequence strengthens an undesirable behavior, the reinforcing factor can be removed. If it is known that positive consequences are associated with a desired social behavior, rewarding consequences can be established.

Consequences can be described as being positively or negatively reinforcing, or punishing. Positive reinforcers are events that follow a behavior and increase the probability that it will recur. Negative reinforcement involves the removal of an unpleasant event following a behavior, thereby increasing the probability of the behavior's occurrence. Punishment is defined as a reduction in the strength of a behavior resulting from the presentation of an aversive consequence.

The contingency relationships described previously occur over time as a part of the learning disabled individual's natural learning environment. The sum total of an individual's experiences determine, to a large extent, the current behavioral repertoire. Behaviors that have been positively reinforced consistently over time are strengthened and become a stable part of the individual's response hierarchy. On the other hand, behaviors that have been punished consistently are weakened and eventually drop from the functional repertoire. Continuous recording is used to identify contemporary events that reinforce or punish specific behaviors in a particular setting. These data then are translated directly into an environmentally based intervention program.

Exhibit 10-3 illustrates a form for conducting continuous observations. The student's name, the time when observations were conducted, the observer's name, and setting are reported at the top. Specific target behaviors are identified in the middle column. Antecedents and consequences are described in relationship to those behaviors.

ASSESSING THE REINFORCEMENT HIERARCHY

The assessment of an individual's reinforcement hierarchy involves identifying and ranking items or events that are considered to be enjoyable for the student. Potential reinforcers that occur as a natural consequence in the

Exhibit 10-3 Continuous Observation Form

	Student's Name _____
	Time of Observation _____
	Observer's Name _____
	Setting _____

Antecedent	Behavior	Consequence

school setting should be highlighted so that supportive consequences for social competency behaviors can be developed. Continuous recording often reveals that the consequences that normally occur in school are not effective in motivating appropriate behavior for some students.

Potential incentives can include primary or secondary reinforcers. Primary reinforcers are events that satisfy basic biological needs and are important to sustain life. They do not depend on previous learning or conditioning for the development of their reinforcing properties. Primary reinforcers including food, water, warmth, sexual stimulation, etc., seldom are used in classroom intervention programs with mildly learning disabled children and adolescents. Secondary reinforcers, on the other hand, are used frequently in the classroom. These include events that have acquired that status through frequent association with a primary reinforcer.

Primary and secondary reinforcers can be prioritized from least to most effective in motivating a behavior and least to most likely to occur naturally in the learning environment. Prioritization on the basis of reinforcer strength is important because the teacher must be certain that incentives are sufficiently powerful to influence the target behavior in the desired direction. Once the teacher has identified a range of reinforcers that are likely to be effective, it is important to specify potential reinforcers that are natural to the setting.

A number of methods can be used to assess an individual's reinforcement hierarchy. The most pragmatic is simply to ask the individual what is enjoyable. In addition to a simple interview, self-report data can be developed through a number of interesting and enjoyable activities. Small group activities can be structured in the classroom to focus on identifying and clarifying pleasant events in the student's environment. One approach may be for the instructor to ask the students to write, independently, 20 things they really enjoy, then rank them from most to least enjoyable. Each class member then discusses that pupil's top five selections and writes them on the slate board. Finally, the class may be asked to reach a consensus on the ranking. When self-report data are used, information provided by students should be substantiated through other assessment approaches. It generally is understood that students' verbal behavior (what they say they will do) is not always the same as their overt behavior (what they actually do).

An approach that may augment self-report data is to observe what the students do during free time or unstructured activities—they would be expected to engage in preferred activities when free to do so. Another method of identifying potential reinforcers is to observe what students do with their spending money. Parents may be valuable resources in identifying potential reinforcers because they can observe what students do during free time and how they spend money.

Reinforcer sampling is another effective approach to identifying and developing incentives. This involves exposing the student to a potentially enjoyable activity. Once this has been done, the teacher may make the activity contingent on a desirable behavior.

MEASURING BEHAVIOR STRENGTH

Fundamental to any intervention program is the teacher's confidence that the prescribed consequences will motivate the desired behavior. The data-keeping system provides a level of confidence in the efficacy of the intervention. Having measured the strength of the target behavior before and during intervention, the teacher can be relatively certain whether the program is or is not influencing the student's behavior. Measures of behavior strength may include event recording, measurement of personal product, interval recording, and duration recording.

Event Recording

Event recording probably is the most useful and least time consuming of all measures of behavior strength. The frequency with which a target behavior occurs is determined by counting each episode through a specified period. Frequency measures are appropriate when (1) the response has a distinct start and stop, such as words spoken, steps taken, or balls thrown, and (2) when the response lasts a relatively constant amount of time (Kazdin, 1980). Event recording should be avoided when measuring behaviors that are not discrete or of constant duration.

Frequency data often are not directly comparable from day to day, because of varying times available for observation. The frequency of response can be transformed to a rate of response that gives comparable data across observation periods. The rate of response is computed by dividing the number of occurrences (frequency) by the amount of time observed. Table 10-1 illustrates a commonly used data sheet for observations of varying length.

Table 10-1 Recording Sheet for Rate Data

Date	TIME Start	Stop	Total	Frequency	Rate
3/3	8:00	11:00	180″	36	.2
3/4	8:10	10:10	140″	14	.1
3/5	8:30	10:30	120″	18	.15

Measurement of Personal Product

Measurement of personal product is a recording procedure similar to frequency recording. This approach is particularly useful in special education classes in which academic behavior often results in some quantifiable product. When using permanent product as a dependent variable, the examiner must demonstrate that the task demands are relatively stable through the study so that the individual's performance level is not obscured by activities that vary in difficulty from session to session. When an individual is expected to do a different number of tasks from day to day, permanent product data should be expressed as the percentage of correct responses over the number of opportunities to respond.

Internal Recording

Internal recording determines the strength of behaviors that do not have discrete start or stop times and that vary in length (e.g., singing, hand waving, talking, attending, sitting). Interval data are collected by dividing a long period of time into shorter periods. For example, a 20-minute class may be divided into 40 intervals of 30 seconds each. The behavior would be scored as occurred or not occurred in each interval. The actual number of occurrences in the interval does not affect the scoring. Often, interval data may be time sampled (i.e., taken in random periods of time through the day).

Exhibit 10-4 represents a common scoring sheet used with interval recording. The numbers over each square denote the time of the interval. A + sign or − sign indicates the occurrence or nonoccurrence of the behavior. The

---

Exhibit 10-4 Scoring Sheet for Interval Recording

Student _____   − = nonoccurrence

Date _____   + = occurrence

1	2	3	4	5	6	7	8	9	10	% scored +	Time Period
+	−	+	−	−	−	+	+	−	−	40%	9:00– 9:05
−	+	−	+	+	+	−	−	+	−	50%	11:00–11:05
−	+	+	+	+	+	+	−	−	−	60%	2:35– 2:40

interval data are transformed to the percentage of intervals in which the behavior took place by dividing the number of occurrences by the number of intervals.

Duration Recording

Duration recording is useful when the intervention approach is expected to increase or decrease the amount of time an individual engages in an activity. An investigator may seek to increase the time spent on homework, or decrease the time spent in halls between classes. In these cases, the dependent measure would be duration.

SELF-CONTROL PROCEDURES

An overwhelming concern in establishing daily procedures is that the student and the stable members of the environment be as much in control of the program's operation as possible. A number of studies have demonstrated that a student's behavior can be modified through self-recording (McKenzie & Rushall, 1974), self-instruction (Thoresen, 1974), and self-reinforcement (Frederiksen & Frederiksen, 1975). Aside from being effective for some students, these procedures may make a program much less time consuming for the teacher to operate. Once baseline data are collected (the strength of the target behavior under natural program conditions), the teacher may present students with the data sheets so they can record their own behavior.

Bornstein and Querillon (1976) demonstrated an approach to self-instruction that greatly enhances the students' ability to manage their own environment. The instructional procedure encourages them to think to themselves: (a) questions about the teacher's expectations, (b) answers to the questions in the form of cognitive rehearsals, (c) self-instructions that guide them through the task, and (d) self-praise. The procedure was effective in reducing excessive classroom activity with overactive 4-year-olds.

BEHAVIORAL CONTRACTING

Behavioral contracting is an effective approach for maximizing the learning disabled student's involvement in formalizing the intervention program. A behavioral contingency contract is a written agreement, negotiated between the student and teacher, that outlines the important features of the intervention program. It includes a statement of the student's duties or responsibilities, of the positive consequences that are to follow a performance, and of special incentives for maintenance of the desirable behavior.

GROUP CONTINGENCY SYSTEMS

Group contingency systems can increase teacher efficiency in administering a number of programs at one time. In group systems, the target behaviors, incentives, methods of reinforcer delivery, and/or criteria for success may be the same. Group systems should be constructed to provide a maximum of flexibility for each student. Approaches that address the same target behaviors and use the same reinforcement procedures may be highly convenient but they are not sensitive to the individual characteristics of each student. The optimal group system provides for diversity in response requirements and reinforcement procedures across the class.

An approach to meeting these requirements is outlined in the group motivational plan format in Exhibit 10-5. This format includes five major sections: (1) participants, (2) response requirements, (3) delivery procedure, (4) schedule for exchange, and (5) the reinforcement event menu. The response requirements and procedure for delivering incentives can be varied for each participant.

It is important that students be placed in the group contingency system only after the teacher has a detailed understanding of their learning and behavior characteristics.

A social intervention program format useful in summarizing comprehensive information for formalizing an intervention program is presented in Exhibit 10-6. The program format details the major conclusions drawn from assessment data accumulated in the behavior management strategies proposed in this chapter. It also includes a procedures section, providing a working plan for the program.

FADING THE SOCIAL DEVELOPMENT PROGRAM

Once acceptable responses are attained consistently through the social development program, unnatural or intrusive elements should be faded in a gradual and systematic fashion. The haphazard and abrupt removal of a program most probably will result in rapid deterioration of targeted behaviors.

The social development program can be gradually withdrawn by: (a) fading contrived reinforcers in lieu of naturally occurring events that have developed reinforcing properties through the program, (b) reducing the frequency and predictability with which an individual is reinforced following a desirable response, (c) introducing gradually the conditions that before intervention had cued disruptive behavior, (d) fading contrived cues, and (e) developing self-control skill.

Exhibit 10-5 Group Motivational Plan Format

Participants	Response Requirement	Delivery Procedure	Aversive Consequences (if any)
1. _____	a) _____	_____	_____
	b) _____	_____	
	c) _____	_____	
2. _____	a) _____	_____	_____
	b) _____	_____	
	c) _____	_____	
3. _____	a) _____	_____	
	b) _____	_____	
	c) _____	_____	

Schedule for exchange: _____
_____
_____

Reinforcement event menu:

Consumable	Cost	Items	Cost
1. _____	_____	1. _____	_____
2. _____	_____	2. _____	_____
3. _____	_____	3. _____	_____
4. _____	_____	4. _____	_____

Activities	Cost	Privileges	Cost
1. _____	_____	1. _____	_____
2. _____	_____	2. _____	_____
3. _____	_____	3. _____	_____
4. _____	_____	4. _____	_____

Exhibit 10-6 Comprehensive Information Summary

Name: _ _____

Date: _ _____

Teacher _____

Target Behavior

1. Definition _____

2. Criteria for success _____

3. Definition _____

4. Criteria for success _____

5. Definition _____

6. Criteria for success _____

Scope of the Program

1. Setting(s) _____

2. Important conditions _____

3. Change agents _____

Potential Reinforcers

Consumables _____   Items _____

_____   _____

_____   _____

_____   _____

Activities _____   _____

_____   _____

_____   _____

_____   _____

Data Collection Procedure _____

Exhibit 10-6 continued

Program Approach

Components that focus on antecedents _____

_____

_____

Components that focus on associated characteristics _____

_____

_____

Components that focus on consequences _____

_____

_____

Maintenance Procedure _____

_____

_____

THINNING THE REINFORCEMENT SCHEDULE

A similar consideration involves thinning the reinforcement schedule. Most intensive interventions require continuous reinforcement (e.g., reinforcing each occurrence of the behavior) to establish the desired response. While this is the most powerful approach to developing a new or low probability behavior, conduct maintained by continuous reinforcement is highly susceptible to deterioration following the withdrawal of that support. Therefore, once such reinforcement has established a behavior, the support may be thinned through an intermittent fixed or variable schedule.

A fixed schedule involves reinforcing the student every two, three, four . . . number of times the behavior occurs. With the fixed schedule, both student and teacher are aware of when the reinforcement will be delivered. For example, the student may be reinforced following every fourth assignment completed, or for every three days of good behavior.

Variable schedules are different in that the student is not aware of when reinforcement will occur, such as on an average of every third day, or varying among the second, third, or fourth day. In any case, the student does not know exactly when reinforcement will be delivered.

When possible, reinforcement programs should be faded through the use of variable schedules. It has been demonstrated that fixed schedules produce a highly variable rate of behavior as the student learns to predict when reinforcement will occur and increases performance just prior to delivery. Following reinforcement, the student may be inclined to reduce performance. Variable schedules, on the other hand, produce stable response rates that are highly resistant to deterioration following the withdrawal of reinforcement.

REINTRODUCTION OF NATURAL ANTECEDENTS

Another important consideration is the gradual reintroduction of the natural antecedents that, before the program was established, cued inappropriate behavior. For example: (1) suppose failure generally preceded aggression for a learning disabled student; (2) then, once aggression control was established under failure-free conditions, reasonable amounts of failure could be reintroduced. This process challenges students to exhibit control over their conduct under conditions that before intervention resulted in observable behavior. The termination of intervention before the reintroduction of provoking cue conditions does not permit students to practice and be reinforced for positive social behaviors under adverse conditions.

CONCLUSION

Social learning theory exists that suggests that most positive behaviors have a reasonable chance for success given the aptitudes needed to learn plus reasonable reinforcement. In essence, human behaviors can be predicted or explained by examining the interaction of the learner and the environment.

The social development system described here was offered as a comprehensive approach to teaching, motivating, and monitoring positive behaviors for learning disabled children and adolescents. The system advocates the regular use of reinforcement principles as well as verbal mediation procedures in developing positive social behaviors that may replace disruptive conduct.

REFERENCES

Abramson, L.L., Seligman, M.E., & Teasdale, J.D. Learned helplessness in humans: Critique and reformulation. *Journal of Abnormal Psychology*, 1978, *87*, 49–74.

Andrews, G.R., & Debus, R.L. Persistence and the causal perception of failure: Modifying cognitive attributions. *Journal of Educational Psychology*, 1978, *70*(2), 154–166.

Archibald, W.P. Alternative explanations for self-fulfilling prophecy. *Psychological Bulletin*, 1974, *81*, 74–84.

Atkinson, J.W. *An introduction to motivation.* New York: Van Nostrand Co., Inc., 1964.

Auerbach, A.G. The social control of learning disability. *Journal of Learning Disabilities*, 1971, *4*(7), 26–34.

Berman, A., & Siegal, A.W. Adaptive and learning skills in juvenile delinquents: A neuropsychological analysis. *Journal of Learning Disabilities*, 1976, *9*(9), 51–57.

Blaess, D.A. Relative effects of attributional preference, effort verbalizations, and self-reinforcement on children's task persistence. *Dissertation Abstracts International*, 1977, *37*, 7624A.

Boersma, F.J., & Chapman, J.W. *Self-perceptions of ability, expectations and locus of control in elementary learning disabled children.* Edmonton, Alta.: University of Alberta, 1978.

Boersma, F.J., Chapman, J.W., & Maguire, T.O. *The student's perception of ability scale: An instrument for measuring academic self-concept in elementary school children.* Edmonton, Alta.: University of Alberta, 1978.

Bornstein, P.H. & Querillon, R.R. The effects of a self-instructional package on overactive preschool boys. *Journal of Applied Behavioral Analysis,* 1976, *9,* 179–188.

Brookover, W.B., & Erikson, E.L. *Sociology of education.* Homewood, Ill.: The Dorsey Press, 1975.

Bryan, T.H. Peer popularity of learning disabled children. *Journal of Learning Disabilities,* 1974, *7*(5), 261–268.

——————. Peer popularity of learning disabled children: A replication. *Journal of Learning Disabilities,* 1976, *9*(6), 49–53.

Bryan, T.H., & Bryan, J.H. *Understanding learning disabilities.* Sherman Oaks, Calif.: Alfred Publishing Co., Inc., 1975.

——————. The social-emotional side of learning disabilities. *Behavioral Disorders,* 1977, *2*(3), 141–145.

Bryan, T.H., Wheeler, R., Felcan, J., & Henek, T. Come on dummy: An observational survey of children's communications. *Journal of Learning Disabilities,* 1976, *9*(5), 661–669.

Canfield, J., & Wells, H.C. *100 ways to enhance self-concept in the classroom: A handbook for teachers and parents.* Englewood Cliffs, N.J.: Prentice-Hall, Inc., 1976.

Chapin, M., & Dyck, G. Persistence in children's reading behavior as a function of N length and attribution retraining. *Journal of Abnormal Psychology,* 1976, *85,* 511–515.

Compton, P. The learning disabled adolescent. In B. Kratoville (Ed.), *Youth in trouble.* San Rafael, Calif.: Academic Therapy, 1974.

Dinkmeyer D. *Developing understanding of self and others (DUSO).* Circle Pines, Minn.: American Guidance Service, Inc., 1970.

Dweck, C.S. The role of expectations and attributions in the alleviation of learned helplessness. *Journal of Personality and Social Psychology,* 1975, *31,* 674–685.

——————. Children's interpretation of evaluative feedback: The effect of social cues on learned helplessness. *Merrill-Palmer Quarterly,* 1976, *22,* 105–109.

Dweck, C.S., & Bush, E.S. Sex differences in learned helplessness I. Differential debilitation with peer and adult evaluators. *Developmental Psychology,* 1976, *12*(3), 147–156.

Dweck, C.S., Davidson, W., Nelson, S., & Enna, B. Sex differences in learned helplessness II. The contingencies of evaluative feedback in the classroom III. An experimental analysis. *Developmental Psychology,* 1978, *14*(3), 268–276.

Dweck, C.S., & Reppucci, N.D. Learned helplessness and reinforcement responsibility in children. *Journal of Personality and Social Psychology,* 1973, *25,* 109–116.

Eisenberger, R., Park, D.C., & Frank, M. Learned industriousness and social reinforcement. *Journal of Personality and Social Psychology,* 1976, *33,* 227–232.

Fincham, F., & Barling, J. Locus of control and generosity in learning disabled, normal achieving, and gifted children. *Child Development,* 1978, *49,* 530–533.

Fitzhugh, K.B. Some neuropsychological features of delinquent subjects. *Perceptual Motor Skills,* 1973, *36,* 494.

Fleming, R.S. Discovering self. In M.D. Cohen (Ed.), *That all children may learn we must learn.* Washington, D.C.: Association for Childhood Education International, 1971.

Floor, L., & Rosen, M. Investigating the phenomenon of helplessness in mentally retarded adults. *American Journal of Mental Deficiency,* 1975, *79,* 565–572.

Frederiksen, L.W. & Frederiksen, C.B. Teacher-determined and self-determined token reinforcement in a special education classroom. *Behavior Therapy,* 1975, *6,* 310–314.

Gardner, W.I. Effects of failure on intellectually retarded and normal boys. *American Journal of Mental Deficiency,* 1966, *70,* 899–902.

Hisama, T. Achievement motivation and the locus of control of children with learning disabilities and behavior disorders. *Journal of Learning Disabilities,* 1976, *9*(6), 58–63.

Hodgenson, D.L. Reading failure and juvenile delinquency. *Bulletin of the Orton Society,* 1974, *24,* 164–169.

Jacobson, F.N. *The juvenile court judge and learning disabilities.* Paper presented at the National Council of Juvenile Court Judges Graduate College, University of Nevada, Reno, August 12 and November 11, 1974.

Jordan, D. *Learning disabilities and predelinquent behavior of juveniles.* Report on a project sponsored by the Oklahoma Association for Children with Learning Disabilities, May 15, 1974.

Kazdin, A.E. *Behavior modification in applied settings.* Homewood, Ill.: The Dorsey Press, 1980.

Kennelly, K., & Kinley, S. Perceived contingency of teacher administered reinforcements and academic performance of boys. *Psychology in the Schools,* 1975, *12,* 449–453.

Koegel, R.L. & Rincover, A. Treatment of psychotic children in a classroom environment: Learning in a large group. *Journal of Applied Behavior Analysis,* 1974, *7,* 45–59.

Klein, D.C., Fencil-Morse, E., & Seligman, M.E.P. Learned helplessness, depression, and the attribution of failure. *Journal of Personality and Social Psychology,* 1976, *33,* 508–516.

Klein, D.C., & Seligman, M.E. Reversals of performance deficits and perceptual deficits in learned helplessness and depression. *Journal of Abnormal Psychology,* 1976, *85,* 11–26.

Larsen, S.C., Parker, R., & Jorjorian, R. Differences in self-concept of normal and learning disabled children. *Perceptual and Motor Skills,* 1973, *37,* 510.

Lerner, J.W. *Children with learning disabilities: Theories, diagnosis, and teaching strategy.* Boston: Houghton Mifflin Company, 1971.

McCrone, W.P. The effects of experimentally induced expectancies on performance in selected deaf adolescents: An investigation of learned helplessness. *Dissertation Abstracts International,* 1977, *38,* 2047A.

McKenzie, T.L. & Rushall, B.S. Effects of self-recording on attendance and performance in a competitive swimming training environment. *Journal of Applied Benavioral Analysis,* 1974, *7,* 199–206.

McMahan, I.D. Relationship between causal attributions and expectancy of success. *Journal of Personality and Social Psychology,* 1973, *28,* 108–114.

Miller, I.W., & Norman, W.H. Learned helplessness in humans: A review and attribution-theory model. *Psychological Bulletin,* 1979, *86,* 93–118.

Miller, R.L., Brickman, P., & Bolen, D. Attribution versus persuasion as a means for modifying behavior. *Journal of Personality and Social Psychology,* 1975, *31,* 430–441.

Miller, W.R., & Seligman, M.E.P. Depression and learned helplessness in man. *Journal of Abnormal Psychology,* 1975, *84,* 228–238.

Morgan, D.I. Prevalence and types of handicapping conditions found in juvenile correctional institutions: A national survey. *The Journal of Special Education,* 1979, *13*(3), 283–295.

Myers, K.E. Becoming: For child and teacher an ever-changing self-image. In M.D. Cohen (Ed.), *That all children may learn we must learn.* Washington, D.C.: Association for Childhood Education International, 1971.

Ostrove, N.M. The effects of consistency of performance feedback and incentive on expectation for future success. *Dissertation Abstracts International*, 1977, *38*, 2434B.

Pendergrass, V.E. Time-out from positive reinforcement following persistent, high-rate behavior in retardates. *Journal of Applied Behavior Analysis*, 1972, *5*, 85–91.

Phares, E.J. Expectancy change in chance and skill situations. *Journal of Abnormal and Social Psychology*, 1957, *54*, 339–342.

Poremba, C. As I was saying . . . In B. Kratoville (Ed.), *Youth in trouble*. San Rafael, Calif.: Academic Therapy, 1974.

Rhodes, W.A. Generalization of attribution retraining. *Dissertation Abstracts International*, 1977, *38*, 2882B.

Richmond, B.O., & Dalton, J.L. Teacher ratings and self-concept reports of retarded pupils. *Exceptional Children*, 1973, *40*(3), 173–183.

Rosser, G.J. A comparative analysis of the real-ideal self-concept of nondisabled and language and/or learning disabled children. *Dissertation Abstracts International*, 1974, *35*, 1-A, 270.

Roth, S., & Bootzin, R.R. The effects of experimentally induced expectancies of external control: An investigation of learned helplessness. *Journal of Personality and Social Psychology*, 1974, *29*, 253–264.

Roth, S., & Kubal, L. The effects of noncontingent reinforcement on tasks of differing importance: Facilitation and learned helplessness effects. *Journal of Personality and Social Psychology*, 1975, *32*, 680–691.

Rotter, J.B. Generalized expectancies for internal versus external control of reinforcement. *Psychological Monographs*, 1966, *80* (1, whole No. 609).

Rotter, J.B., Liverant, S., & Crowne, D.P. The growth and extinction of expectancies in chance controlled and skilled tasks. *Journal of Psychology*, 1961, *52*, 161–177.

Schuster, S.D., & Gruen, G.E. Success and failure as determinants of the performance predictions of mentally retarded and nonretarded children. *American Journal of Mental Deficiency*, 1971, *76*, 190–196.

Seligman, M.E. Fall into helplessness. *Psychology Today*, 1973, *7*(1), 43–48.

——————. Depression and learned helplessness. In R.J. Friedman and M.M. Katz (Eds.), *The psychology of depression: Contemporary theory and research*. Washington: Winston-Wiley, 1974.

——————. *Helplessness: On depression, development and death*. San Francisco: W.H. Freeman, 1975.

Seligman, M.E.P., & Maier, S.F. Failure to escape traumatic shock. *Journal of Experimental Psychology*, 1967, *74*, 1–9.

Siperstein, G.N., Bopp, M.J., & Bak, J.J. Social status of learning disabled children. *Journal of Learning Disabilities*, 1978, *11*(2), 98–102.

Tennen, H., & Eller, S.S. Attributional components of learned helplessness and facilitation. *Journal of Personality and Social Psychology*, 1977, *35*, 265–271.

Thoresen, C.E. Behavioral means and humanistic ends. In M.J. Mahoney & C.E. Thoresen (Eds.)., *Self-control: Power to the person*. Monterey, Calif.: Brooks/Cole Publishing Co., Inc., 1974.

Thornton, J.W., & Jacobs, P.D. Learned helplessness in human subjects. *Journal of Experimental Psychology*, 1971, *87*, 367–372.

Valle, J. Investigating the phenomenon of learned helplessness in emotionally disturbed children. *Dissertation Abstracts International*, 1978, *38*, 3420–3421B.

Weiner, B., Nierenberg, R., & Goldstein, M. Social learning (locus of control) versus attributional (causal stability) interpretations of expectancy of success. *Journal of Personality*, 1976, *44*, 52–68.

Weisz, J.R. Choosing problem-solving rewards and Halloween prizes: Delay of gratification and preference for symbolic reward as a function of development, motivation, and personal investment. *Developmental Psychology*, 1978, *4*, 66–78.

Wortman, C.B., & Brehm, J.W. Responses to uncontrollable outcomes: An integration of reactance theory and the learned helplessness model. In L. Berkowitz (Ed.), *Advances in experimental social psychology*. New York: Academic Press, 1975.

Wortman, C.B., Panciera, L., Shusterman, L., & Hibscher, J. Attributions of causality and reactions to uncontrollable outcomes. *Journal of Experimental Social Psychology*, 1976, *12*, 301–316.

Index